Macro-economics

Macro-economics

The Theory of Income, Employment, and the Price Level

Michael R. Darby

Associate Professor of Economics
University of California, Los Angeles

McGraw-Hill Book Company

New York / St. Louis / San Francisco / Auckland / Düsseldorf / Johannesburg
Kuala Lumpur / London / Mexico / Montreal / New Delhi / Panama / Paris
São Paulo / Singapore / Sydney / Tokyo / Toronto

Macroeconomics
The Theory of Income, Employment, and the Price Level

1234567890KPKP798765

This book was set in Times Roman.
The editors were J. S. Dietrich and Matthew Cahill;
the designer was J. Paul Kirouac, A Good Thing, Inc.;
the production supervisor was Dennis J. Conroy.
The drawings were done by Danmark & Michaels, Inc.
Kingsport Press, Inc., was printer and binder.

Library of Congress Cataloging in Publication Data

Darby, Michael R
    Macroeconomics.

    Includes bibliographies and index.
    1. Macroeconomics. I. Title.
HB171.5.D217 1976   330   75–14060
ISBN 0–07–015346–9

To Ann

Contents

Preface   xi

Part 1   Foundations for Macroeconomic Analysis

Chapter 1   **The Issues of Macroeconomic Analysis**   2
            Questions and Exercises   6
            References for Further Reading   6

Chapter 2   **The Measurement of Macroeconomic Variables I:**
            The National Income Accounts   7
            2.1   The Flows of Economic Activity   7
            2.2   The Measurement of Total Income and Output   14
            2.3   The Role of Saving in the National Income Accounting
                  Identities   25
            Summary   26
            Questions and Exercises   27
            References for Further Reading   28

Chapter 3   **The Measurement of Macroeconomic Variables II:**
            Other National Aggregates   29
            3.1   Price Indices   29
            3.2   Labor Force and Unemployment   35
            3.3   Money   37
            3.4   Business Fluctuations   44
            Summary   47
            Questions and Exercises   48
            References for Further Reading   49

Chapter 4   **Analytical Tools**   50
            4.1   Mathematical Concepts   50
            4.2   Changes over Time   56
            4.3   Interest Rates   67
            4.4   Wealth and Permanent Income   75
            Summary   78
            Questions and Exercises   79
            References for Further Reading   80

Part 2   Equilibrium Levels and Growth of Real Income and Prices

Chapter 5   The Levels of Income and Prices   82
    5.1   Introduction   82
    5.2   Determinants of Real Income   83
    5.3   Determinants of the Price Level   101
    Summary   109
    Questions and Exercises   110
    References for Further Reading   111

Chapter 6   Income and the Price Level in a Growing Economy   112
    6.1   Introduction   112
    6.2   Determinants of Real Growth   112
    6.3   Steady-State Growth of Nominal Variables   121
    Summary   135
    Questions and Exercises   135
    References for Further Reading   136

Part 3   Dynamic Adjustments to Macroeconomic Shocks

Chapter 7   Effects of a Change in the Growth Rate of the Money Supply 139
    7.1   Statement of the Problem   139
    7.2   Effects on the Growth Path of Nominal Income   140
    7.3   Effects on the Growth Paths of Real Income and the Price Level   151
    7.4   Effects on Interest Rates   166
    Summary   172
    Questions and Exercises   173
    References for Further Reading   173

Chapter 8   Effects of Fiscal and Other Domestic Shocks   175
    8.1   Government Spending and Taxation in a Growing Economy   175
    8.2   Effects of Changes in Government Spending on Nominal Income   178
    8.3   Effects of Changes in Taxation on Nominal Income   192
    8.4   Other Potential Domestic Macroeconomic Shocks   201
    Summary   207
    Questions and Exercises   208
    References for Further Reading   209

Chapter 9   International Trade and Financial Arrangements   210
    9.1   Foreign Exchange Markets   210
    9.2   Exchange Rate Systems   221

9.3   Effects of International Shocks on Aggregate Demand   **225**
9.4   Money Supply Growth and Long-Run International
        Equilibrium under Alternative Exchange Rate Systems **231**
        Summary   **234**
        Questions and Exercises   **234**
        References for Further Reading   **235**

Chapter 10   The Impact of Macroeconomic Shocks on the American Economy   237
10.1   The Historical Record: The Great Depression
        through World War II   **237**
10.2   The Historical Record: The Postwar Era   **247**
10.3   The Relative Importance of Sources of Macroeconomic
        Shocks   **259**
        Summary   **260**
        Questions and Exercises   **261**
        References for Further Reading   **262**

Part 4   The Keynesian Model

Chapter 11   The Keynesian Building Blocks   264
11.1   Underlying Assumptions   **264**
11.2   The Consumption Function   **268**
11.3   Other Expenditure Components   **273**
11.4   Keynesian Money Demand and Supply   **278**
        Summary   **282**
        Questions and Exercises   **283**
        References for Further Reading   **284**

Chapter 12   The Complete Keynesian Model   285
12.1   The IS-LM Model   **285**
12.2   Effects of Shifts in the Income-Expenditures Sector **294**
12.3   Effects of Shifts in the Monetary Sector   **298**
        Summary   **302**
        Questions and Exercises   **302**
        References for Further Reading   **304**

Chapter 13   Comparison of the Keynesian and Dynamic Models   305
13.1   Introduction   **305**
13.2   Differences concerning the Individual Keynesian
        Building Blocks   **306**
13.3   Comparison of the Complete Models   **315**
        Summary   **323**
        Questions and Exercises   **324**
        References for Further Reading   **324**

Part 5   Macroeconomic Policy

Chapter 14   Unemployment and Inflation   **328**
    14.1   Determination of the Unemployment Rate   **328**
    14.2   The Expected Rate of Inflation and the Shifting
          Phillips Curve   **335**
    14.3   The Use of Monetary Policy to Influence Employment
          and Real Income   **342**
        Summary   **349**
        Questions and Exercises   **350**
        References for Further Reading   **350**

Chapter 15   Macroeconomic Goals and Policy   **351**
    15.1   Macroeconomic Goals   **351**
    15.2   Stabilization Policy   **353**
    15.3   Macroeconomic Policy and Real Steady-State
          Variables   **364**
    15.4   Macroeconomic Policy and Nominal Steady-State
          Variables   **367**
        Summary   **375**
        Questions and Exercises   **376**
        References for Further Reading   **377**

Answers to Selected Exercises   **379**

Index   **387**

Preface

The course in macroeconomic theory has increasingly become a burden for both professor and student. Texts have presented more and more complicated models in an attempt to graft the great advances made in macroeconomics over the last 15 years onto the standard Keynesian framework developed by Sir John Hicks in 1937. The result has not been a happy one. Professors have felt compelled to assign extensive outside readings, to prepare handouts, and to fill in the remaining gaps with lectures. Little time has been left for discussing the main macroeconomic issues. The student became lost in arcane detail and wondered what the course was all about.

The time has come for a new beginning. The basic result of modern macroeconomics is that macroeconomic shocks begin processes of adjustment over time toward a new equilibrium, the process often lasting several years. But the Hicksian IS-LM framework is a static, single-period model which becomes extremely complex when one considers changing price levels, changing expectations, and the influence of real money balances on consumer spending. So it appears to me that the only way to exposit modern macroeconomics is to follow a different approach leading directly to dynamic analysis.

This book views the economy as growing along a stable path in the absence of disturbances. But from time to time disturbances do occur which alter the growth path of the economy or move the economy away from an unchanged growth path. These disturbances begin a process of adjustment over time as the economy moves to the new growth path or returns to the previous equilibrium.

By taking account of the adjustment toward a moving equilibrium, many apparent paradoxes—such as simultaneous increases in the rates of inflation and unemployment—are seen to be the natural implications of the adjustment process. The dynamic approach makes it easier for the student to understand the basic problems studied in macroeconomics: inflation, unemployment, growth, and business fluctuations. This knowledge can be used to examine the potential and limits of governmental policy.

So that the book will be widely intelligible, the mathematics has been kept to a minimum with greater emphasis placed on verbal and graphical analysis. Familiarity with high school algebra is assumed, but other required analytical tools are presented in Chap. 4. The avoidance of advanced mathematics requires the omission of a surprisingly small number of subsidiary topics.

Because of the great variation in the time devoted to the macroeconomic theory course, considerable flexibility has been built into the book. The core of macroeconomics is contained in Chaps. 1 through 8 and Chap. 10. Chapter 9 on International Trade, Part 4 on the Keynesian Model, Chap. 14 on Unemployment and Inflation, and Chap. 15 on Macroeconomic Policy can be included or omitted as time and inclination suggest. Some instructors may prefer to discuss Chaps. 11 and 12 before Part 3.

Developing a new presentation of a subject is never a one-person job and the aid of many people must be acknowledged. First comes Milton Friedman, who taught me much of my macroeconomics and engendered the desire to learn more. My undergraduate students at the University of California, Los Angeles, have been my best critics and my best reason for writing this book. Anna Schwartz and Ann Darby have both read earlier versions of the entire manuscript and made many valuable suggestions. My colleagues Robert Clower, Benjamin Klein, Axel Leijonhufvud, C. Mather Lindsay, John J. McCall, and Douglas Shetler have been most generous with comments and discussion. Good advice on some of the chapters was received from Eugene Brady, Ronald Ehrenberg, and H. Robert Heller. My research assistant Emily Spindler and secretary Dorothy Yamamoto worked far beyond the call of duty.

Michael R. Darby

Foundations for Macroeconomic Analysis

Part 1

The Issues of
Macroeconomic Analysis

Chapter
1

Why does the average price level rise or fall over time? Why do jobs seem plentiful at one time while many people are unemployed only a year later? Why does our standard of living rise over time? Why is this increase greater at some times than others? Macroeconomic analysis attempts to provide understandable answers to these questions. This understanding makes us better able as individuals to avoid some of the ill effects of inflation and the business cycle in our personal and business lives. As citizens and potential governmental representatives, knowledge of the possible alternatives enables us to evaluate proposals for government policy.

Macroeconomics: A Strategic Simplification of General Economic Theory

One approach to answering these questions would be to evaluate the price, output, and employment of each individual industry at each point in time and then to somehow add these amounts up to find out what is happening to prices, output, and employment as a whole. This approach requires the collection and manipulation of an almost infinite amount of information and is impossible as a practical matter. Instead, economists have found that it is possible to explain the behavior of the general levels of output, prices, and employment by a few basic relationships. Economic changes which cause some industries to expand and others to decline usually average out for the economy as a whole. Only a small number of economic forces change the general levels of output, prices, and employment. Macroeconomists concentrate on the latter group of forces by considering only net effects on broad economic totals or indices and not changes in individual components, such as the output of shoes.

Macroeconomic theory makes the strategic assumption that we can successfully describe the behavior of *aggregates*[1] without explicitly explaining any

---

[1] Aggregation is the economist's term for adding apples and oranges—or averaging their prices—by the use of appropriate weights. The means used to derive useful totals are described in Chap. 2.

individual components. This would not be true of just any combination of economic variables, but does appear to be true for the particular aggregates specified by the macroeconomic questions at the beginning of this chapter.

Microeconomists make use of an analogous simplification of the completely general model of economic equilibrium. In microeconomic analysis the general level of prices and income is assumed given so that a particular industry or closely related group of industries can be studied in detail. Both microeconomists and macroeconomists must neglect detail in order to obtain useful answers to the questions in which they are respectively interested.

The Dynamic Nature of Macroeconomics

The most interesting macroeconomic questions involve adjustment over time of income, employment, and the price level to changing conditions. Some of these changes proceed smoothly and the economy adjusts smoothly to them. Examples would be the relatively steady growth of the labor force and the capital stock. *Comparative dynamics* explores the effects of these changes by contrasting the development of the economy under alternative assumptions about the rates of growth of these factors. Macroeconomic shocks are sudden changes in underlying conditions. The adaptations of the economy to such unanticipated changes are analyzed as *dynamic adjustments*.

Comparative dynamics would explain steady rates of growth in the price level from year to year. A model of dynamic adjustment is used to explain the way in which this rate of growth is changed from time to time.

Mathematical simplification can be achieved by describing dynamic processes as a series of cross sections at specific points in time. By combining these cross sections, a moving path can be traced out just as many individual still pictures are combined to make a motion picture. This involves repeated solutions of *comparative statics* problems for which equilibria are defined independently of any rates of growth. Unfortunately, the comparative dynamics solutions to the macroeconomic problem are based on rates of growth. Worse, dynamic adjustments to macroeconomic shocks are characterized by disequilibrium positions adjusting toward a moving equilibrium over time. As a result the techniques of comparative statics are inadequate as a basis of macroeconomic theory. Fortunately, the great bulk of macroeconomic analysis can be understood with the use of simple graphs and high school algebra. The few exceptions are stated and explained in this book with detailed study left to more specialized courses.

Controversies in Macroeconomic Theory

Macroeconomic theory is probably the most controversial topic in economics. Through at least the mid-1930s, economists were generally agreed that the dominant variable determining the price level and the business cycle was the quantity of money existing in a country. The United States established a central bank—the *Federal Reserve System* or *Fed* for short—by the Federal Reserve Act of 1913. During the 1920s many economists argued that the Fed's ability to control the money supply eliminated the threats of depression and inflation forever.

The Great Depression of the 1930s was an immense psychological shock to these economists. It was thought that the Fed was doing all it could, and that seemed to be no help at all. Similar conditions existed in Britain. John Maynard Keynes published his *The General Theory of Employment, Interest, and Money* in 1936. This work had a huge, immediate impact. A model was presented which suggested that the quantity of money is not very important—at least during depressions—and that investment, government spending and taxation, and exports are the key variables determining the business cycle. This model, as systematized by Keynes' followers, fairly swept the economic profession. It provided economists with sensible things to say about the Depression. The Keynesian or income-expenditures model was a firmly established orthodoxy by the 1950s.

Some economists remained unconvinced of the ability of the Keynesian model to explain the phenomena observed in the real world. Milton Friedman of the University of Chicago was the acknowledged leader of the group exploring, extending, and testing the older quantity theory of money. Their research had minor effects on the thinking of the economic profession during the 1950s. The basic Keynesian model was altered in detail to meet specific objections of logical inconsistency or empirical refutation, but the basic idea remained that the quantity of money which people have does not much affect total spending.

Milton Friedman and Anna Jacobson Schwartz published their own epoch-making book *A Monetary History of the United States, 1867–1960* in 1963. This massive work of scholarship collected data on the money supply and the forces determining it, correlated money supply changes with changes in income and prices, and demonstrated that a modern quantity theory approach could explain macroeconomic events over the nearly hundred years of their study. Particularly important was the demonstration that, claims of monetary ease notwithstanding, the Federal Reserve System initiated and permitted to continue a process which reduced the United States money supply in 1933 to about 70 percent of the level in 1929. The simplest forms of the quantity theory of money would have been sufficient to explain a massive depression. This episode poses the awkward and unanswered question of why the economic profession should have accepted the Federal Reserve officials' self-serving assurances that their monetary policy was expansive and rejected the quantity theory of money which was well documented for many times and for many countries.

The publication of Friedman and Schwartz's book initiated a "monetarist revolution" which has not been much slower than the Keynesian revolution that occurred in the two decades following the publication of Keynes' book. The monetarist revolution was not without psychological assistance either: It so happened that monetary policy and government spending moved in sharply opposite directions on three occasions (1966–1967, 1968, and 1969). In each case, well-publicized predictions of monetarist economists proved right while those of Keynesian economists were wrong.[2]

Now macroeconomists are split into three main camps: the Keynesians, the monetarists, and the unconvinced. The differences—while very real—are not as great as they sometimes appear to be. This fact reflects both some movement toward synthesis of the two approaches and a substantive monetarist victory. The controversial question of the 1950s and 1960s was "Do changes in the quantity of money have a significant effect on the levels of income and employment?" This has been answered with a definite "Yes." The question of the 1970s is whether changes in government spending and taxation have significant effects on total income and employment.

The Approach of this Book

This book presents a modern quantity theory of money approach to macro-economic theory. There is no generally accepted basic model; therefore one has been created here, borrowing especially from work by Milton Friedman. The presentation is an attempt to incorporate the insights and empirical results contained in recent articles by a wide variety of economists. The resulting model bears little resemblance to the debating caricature of the "monetarist position."

It will be seen that changes in the money supply are the dominant cause of business cycles and changes in the rate of growth of the price level in the United States. This is not because changes in other variables such as government spending or exports have no effects—they do indeed. Rather the dominance of monetary changes reflects limitations in an economy like the United States on the size and persistence of changes in other variables compared to changes in the supply of money.

But we are running far ahead of our story. The remainder of Part 1 sets the stage for macroeconomic theory by introducing the measurement of macro-economic variables and developing the few special graphical and mathematical tools which greatly simplify the rest of the book. Part 2 is an examination of moving equilibrium of income, employment, and the price level. This provides the anchor about which the economy actually rides. A model of the dynamic process of adjustment to macroeconomic shocks is presented in Part 3 and used to explain U.S. macroeconomic history during the twentieth century. Part 4 expounds the traditional Keynesian model and its analysis of

---

[2] See Chap. 10 for details.

the effects of macroeconomic shocks. The dynamic and Keynesian models are compared both as to differences on specific Keynesian building blocks and on a more general level. Problems in formulating, evaluating, and predicting macroeconomic policy are examined in Part 5, especially with regard to inflation and unemployment.

☐ QUESTIONS AND EXERCISES[3]

*1 Why do macroeconomists ignore the effects of changes in the total quantity of money or of labor on individual industries?

2 How does the analysis of dynamic adjustments differ from comparative dynamics?

3 The monetarist position that changes in the rate of growth of the money supply have been the dominant cause of U.S. business cycles is not inconsistent with the view that changes in the growth rate of government spending or taxation or of exports have significant impacts on income, employment, and the price level. Explain why not.

☐ REFERENCES FOR FURTHER READING

Fisher, Irving: *The Purchasing Power of Money*, 2d ed., New York: Macmillan, 1922; reprinted New York: A. M. Kelley, Publishers, 1971. (This book presents the "equation of exchange" version of the quantity theory at its highest pre-Keynesian level.)

Friedman, Milton, and Anna Jacobson Schwartz: *A Monetary History of the United States, 1867–1960*, Princeton: Princeton for NBER, 1963, esp. Chap. 13.

Keynes, John Maynard: *The General Theory of Employment, Interest, and Money*, New York: Harcourt, Brace, 1936.

Thornton, Henry: *An Enquiry Into the Nature and Effects of the Paper Credit of Great Britain*, F. A. von Hayek (ed.), New York: Farrar & Rinehart, 1939; reprinted New York: A. M. Kelley, Publishers, 1965. (This book, first published in 1802, is one of the earliest and still one of the best expositions of the quantity theory of money approach.)

---

[3] The answers to questions preceded by an asterisk appear in the section directly following Chap. 15.

The Measurement of Macroeconomic Variables I: The National Income Accounts

Chapter 2

2.1 THE FLOWS OF ECONOMIC ACTIVITY

Introduction

The first step in understanding macroeconomics is understanding the meaning of the basic macroeconomic terms used to describe the total or average experience of the economy. Microeconomists can appeal to their students' years of experience when they discuss the price and quantity of oranges or flour. It is not so obvious how we can say that the quantity of goods and services produced in the United States was 4 percent higher last year than the year before. If the quantity of every kind of goods and service increased by exactly 4 percent, it would be obvious that any appropriate measure of their total must increase by 4 percent. But some industries expanded much more rapidly than average while others expanded less rapidly or even contracted. How can we average a 5 percent increase in automobile production with a 3 percent increase in production of beer, an 8 percent increase in telephone calls, a 2 percent decrease in production of lumber, and so forth for the hundreds of thousands of different goods and services? Answering that and similar questions is the subject of this chapter.

The Circular Flows of Economic Activity

To be understandable, definitions must fit into a broad frame of reference. This can be provided for macroeconomics by a general description of the flows of goods and services and payments in the economy. Here we are concerned only with describing the flows among the main economic sectors of the country. Analysis of why these flows are the sizes that they are comes later.

We begin our description by looking at a very simple economy which consists only of households and firms. Households own all the economic resources or *factors of production*. These resources can be aggregated into two groups: the *labor force* or human resources and the *capital stock* or nonhuman resources. Firms rent the use of these resources or *factor services* (also called *inputs*) to carry out the production of *final goods and services* (*outputs*) which are sold to the households. The owners of firms or *entrepreneurs* receive as payment for the factor services which they provide the difference between their sales revenue and their payments for factor services rented from others. This residual is termed *profits*. Competition among potential entrepreneurs assures that these profits will just equal the rental value of factor services provided by the owners. If they were greater some households would stop renting out their services and become entrepreneurs, thus lowering profits until the returns of firm owners just covered the rental otherwise available. If profits were lower than this amount, some entrepreneurs would switch to renting their factors of production until profits rose to the competitive level.

The flows of economic activity in this simple economy can be described in two equivalent ways: the flow of goods and services and the flow of payments. Payments rendered to the seller just equal the value of the goods and services rendered to the buyer. Thus flows of goods and services in one direction are always matched by flows of money in the opposite direction. Households provide the basic factor services to firms. Firms combine these inputs to the productive process to create final goods and services for sale to the households for consumption and addition to household stocks of capital. The households use their income from the sale of factor services to pay for the goods produced by the firms. The firms use their sales revenue to pay for the factor services provided by the households. Figure 2.1 illustrates this flow of goods and services and counterflow of money payments.

We would measure total income in this simple economy as the total payments for inputs. An obvious way to measure output is by the total value of final goods and services. This weights units of different kinds of goods and services by their marginal value in the marketplace—that is, their price. If one shirt sells for the same amount as five glasses, this measure of output would not be affected by an increase of one shirt and a decrease of five glasses. Firms pay out their entire revenue as rental or profit payments; so income must exactly equal output.

Economic Flows in an Economy with Financial Markets

The firms in this simple economy own no resources, but merely rent and combine the services of resources owned by the households. A more accurate description of a modern industrial economy would portray firms as owners of the capital stock of the nation and individuals as the owners of the labor force and of the securities of the firms. Capital refers to all nonhuman factors of production—machines, buildings, and the like—used in producing goods for sale. In a free society, individuals own the rights to the use of their own productive services; therefore firms can only rent labor services from households.

Most firms—as measured by the capital owned—are legally organized as corporations. Corporations have no wealth themselves. The capital owned by

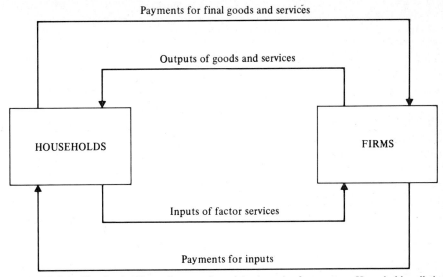

FIGURE 2.1   The circular flows of economic activity in a simple economy. Households sell the services of factors of production to firms for use as inputs to the productive process. The outputs of the productive process (final goods and services) are sold to households for consumption or addition to the stocks of capital of the households. The inner, counterclockwise flows represent the transfers of goods and services. The outer, clockwise flows represent the transfers of money payments. Income, as measured by payments for inputs, exactly equals output as measured by the value of (payments for) goods and services.

a corporation (assets) is exactly offset by claims on the firm (*securities* or liabilities) in the form of debt and residual ownership. The debt of a firm is represented by bonds or other promises to pay certain amounts of dollars at certain dates. Residual ownership or stockholders' equity is represented by stock certificates which confer on their holders a right (in proportion to each holder's fraction of the total number of shares of stock) to the amount by which assets exceed debt. The assets of a corporation frequently include the securities of other corporations. Since the liabilities of any corporation are increased by the amount of any securities of other corporations held, the holding of securities of other corporations cannot alter the equality of the capital stock and the holdings of corporate securities by households. For proprietorships and partnerships, the legal title to capital and the legal responsibility for debts belong to the individual owners. Macroeconomists find it convenient, however, to treat all firms alike, as if they were corporations owning all the capital and issuing equal securities to households.[1]

---

[1] It is quite artificial to think of an individual proprietor issuing himself an ownership certificate for the net worth of his business, but the reduction in wordiness is well worthwhile.

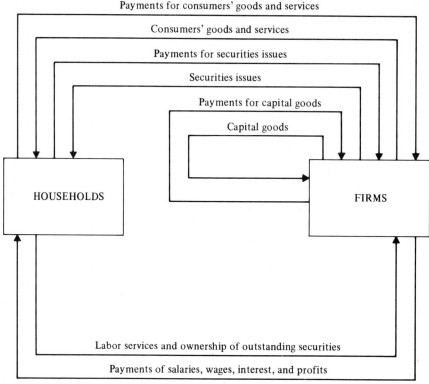

FIGURE 2.2 The circular flow of economic activity in an economy with financial markets.
In this economy, households do not directly own the capital stock or receive its rental payments.
All capital is owned by firms. Individuals own the securities of the firms and receive interest and
profits on these securities. The securities represent indirect ownership of the capital stock of the
firms. The payments of interest and profits are indirect payments of the rental earned by the
capital stock. Increases in the capital stock are financed by firms through issuance of new
securities.

Our economy can be characterized as one in which people hold their
nonhuman wealth in the form of securities issued by firms rather than in
directly owned capital goods. Firms pay wages and salaries for all labor
services provided by householders.[2] Capital services are now provided by the
capital stock owned by the firms. The rental value of the capital stock is
now received as interest and profit payments to the householders who own
the securities of the firms and who finance the capital stock. Total income
can be measured as the sum of interest and profits plus salary and wage
payments in this economy. This is indicated in the lower part of Fig. 2.2.

---

[2] This applies even to labor provided by major shareholders and, formally, to labor provided by proprietors
and partners.

The output of final goods and services is no longer sold exclusively to households. Increases in the capital stock or *investment* are now made by firms who purchase capital goods from other firms or from themselves. The firms pay out their entire sales revenue as income, and so must pay for the capital stock by an equal value of *securities issues*, the sale to households of additional securities. This can be done either by actually selling new bonds or stock certificates or by reducing the amount of profits paid out below total profits so that the value of each share of stock is increased. The latter method of "retaining earnings" is most simply thought of as a payment of total profits combined with a sale to the shareholders of securities in the value of the undistributed profits. Total output is again measured by the value of final goods and services or the sum of consumers' spending for goods and services plus the value of investment. Again output and income are identical in value.

The Flow of Goods and Services and Payments in the United States

A reasonably complete description of the flows of economic activity in the United States—or any similar industrialized country—requires the addition of two other economic sectors: government and foreign. We can add them one at a time.

The government sector purchases final goods and services from firms and labor services from households. It uses these to produce government services which are provided to households and firms. Government services are provided without charge or at arbitrary prices which only rarely cover their cost of production.[3] The bulk of funds required to pay for government purchases is raised from taxes of various kinds paid by households and firms.

Some government payments are treated as negative taxes. These are interest payments on government debt and transfer payments. Because the government capital stock is not used to produce goods sold in the market, national income accountants have so far despaired of estimating its implicit rental return. As a result government output is formally evaluated at the cost of current expenditures for labor services and final goods and services bought from firms. So government interest payments are counted as reductions in taxes instead of as part of total income. Transfer payments are payments made for other purposes than current provision of goods and services. Important examples are welfare, social security, unemployment, and veterans' benefits. They are called transfer payments because they involve taking funds from some individuals and transferring them to others who have provided no goods or services.

---

[3] Government enterprises which sell their services at market prices roughly commensurate with costs are included in the business sector as firms. Examples would be the Postal Service and municipally owned utilities and bus lines. Surpluses of government enterprise (revenue less purchases) are treated as a tax. Subsidies to government enterprises—or private firms—are treated as a negative tax.

Since no production occurs, these payments are not included in income or output. They do offset, however, part of the taxes paid by the household and business sectors.

The addition of government to the flow diagram of the economy is made in Fig. 2.3. This involves sales to the government of labor services by households and of goods and services by firms and equal-valued payments by the govern-

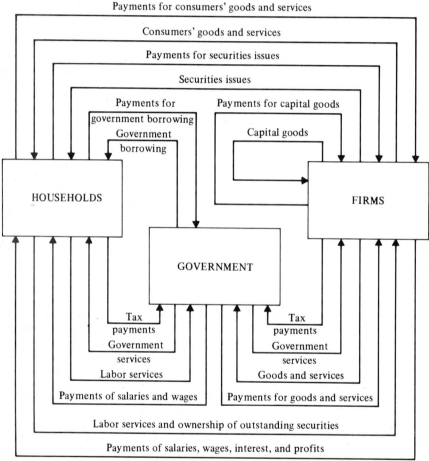

FIGURE 2.3   The flow of economic activity in an economy with financial markets and government. With the addition of government, households have an additional market for their labor services and firms have an additional market. The government provides services to and collects taxes from both households and firms, although firms may be more properly said to collect taxes from households for payment to the government. Total output is measured as the sum of consumers' spending, investment, and government spending for goods and services. Total income—or claims to output—is equal to business payments of salaries, wages, interest, profits, and taxes plus government payments of salaries and wages. Income and output are equal.

ment. In addition, the government provides government services to households and firms and is paid taxes by both.[4] Unlike firms, the government has no residual owners so net taxes do not automatically equal government purchases of goods and services from households and firms. The excess of expenditures over taxes or government deficit is financed in two ways: government borrowing and money creation. Government borrowing involves selling new issues of government debt in competition with business securities. Some government debt is held by the business sector, but this increases issues of business securities by an equal amount. So net government borrowing—though perhaps channeled through the business sector—ultimately comes from the household sector, as shown in Fig. 2.3. There is no reason for either the deficit or government borrowing to be positive. If the government pays off part of its outstanding debt the direction of flows indicated in Fig. 2.3 will be reversed. Money creation—which also can be positive or negative—is nowhere explicitly indicated in Fig. 2.3. It is implicit in the excess of the value of government purchases of goods and services over net taxes and borrowing. In the United States the government creates or destroys money through the operation of the Federal Reserve System.[5]

In the economy depicted in Fig. 2.3, total output or final goods and services would equal the sum of consumers' spending, investment, and government purchases of goods and services.[6] Total income would equal payments of salaries and wages by firms and government plus interest, profits, and taxes by firms. Again the arithmetic of the accountants' definitions keeps the value of total income—or claims to output—equal to total output. It is frequently useful to subtract all taxes paid to the government from total income to obtain *private income*. Private income is a measure of the claims to current output accruing to households.

To complete our picture of the major economic flows among sectors we must add our trade with the rest of the world. Although households and government are involved in some direct trade of goods and services with foreigners, we will confine our attention to the main activity in the business sector. All other trade will be consolidated with the trade carried out by firms. Firms both sell goods and services to households, firms, and governments in other countries (*exports*) and buy goods and services from them (*imports*). If exports exceed imports, part of output is diverted from domestic uses. If exports are less than imports, the amount of goods and services available for domestic use exceeds total output. This is so because foreigners are

---

[4] Payment of taxes and provision of government services is viewed here in a very literal sense. In a deeper sense, firms cannot bear the burden of a tax or receive the benefit of a government service. Ultimately, only people can. The incidence of government taxes and service to firms—that is, the apportionment of the burden and benefits among the customers, workers, and securities owners of firms—is a microeconomic question of public finance.

[5] See Chap. 3 for details.

[6] Including purchases of labor services.

shipping us more goods and services than we are shipping them. If imports and exports are exactly equal, the payments of importing firms for imports will be just sufficient to pay the exporting firms for their exports. The foreign exchange market is a mechanism for canceling such claims on foreigners.[7] The *balance of trade* or *net exports* is defined as the value of exports less the value of imports. If the balance of trade is positive, the difference is made up by new issues of foreign securities (including foreign government debt) bought ultimately by households or equivalent reductions in foreign holdings of American securities held by foreigners. If the balance of trade is negative, households reduce their holdings of foreign securities or foreigners equivalently increase their holdings of American securities.[8] These flows are illustrated in Fig. 2.4.

Total output is defined as the sum of consumers' spending, investment, government spending for goods and services, and net exports. Since income from foreign securities is being included in business revenue and income paid to foreigners on American securities is deducted from business revenue, net claims to output due to foreign securities will be included in business payments of interest and profits.[9] Total income is therefore still defined as payments of salaries and wages by firms and government plus payments of interest, profits, and taxes by firms. By the accounting definitions, income and output are equal.

This description of the economy has introduced many concepts in general terms. We can now examine how these and other basic concepts are measured.

2.2 THE MEASUREMENT OF TOTAL INCOME AND OUTPUT
The Problem of Double-Counting

The most obvious way to actually compute total output or income would be to add together the total sales of firms—reported on income tax returns—and government expenditures for labor services. This does not work because for nearly all firms' sales revenues are higher than the value of the goods and services which they produce. Most final goods and services[10] are produced by a series of productive processes. That is, a shirt bought by a consumer is actually a "bundle" of products: raw cotton, ginning, spinning, weaving, design, cutting, sewing, transportation, marketing.[11] In a specialized economy,

---

[7] See Chap. 9 for details.

[8] Interest received on foreign securities is accounted for as payment for an export of (capital) services and interest paid to foreigners is accounted for as an import.

[9] This is a reasonably accurate description of reality. Household holdings of foreign securities are relatively small. Foreign security issues would be largely purchased by firms which increase their own securities issues by an equal amount. Thus the flows of foreign security issues illustrated in Fig. 2.4 are in fact usually intermediated by firms.

[10] The biggest exception is labor services sold by households to government.

[11] This list is obviously incomplete! Consider the plastic buttons: soy beans, crushing, etc.

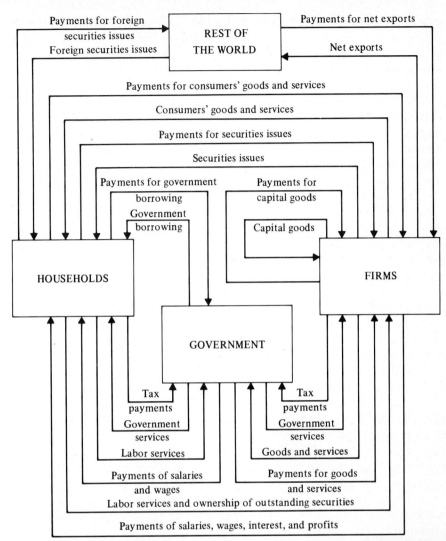

FIGURE 2.4 The flow of economic activity in an economy with financial markets, international trade, and government. Firms sell net exports to the rest of the world. The rest of the world derives funds to pay for net exports by sales (to households) of foreign securities or foreign holdings of domestic securities. Output consists of sales of goods and services to consumers, to government, to firms for investment, and (on net) to foreigners. Total income, which equals output, is the sum of business payments of salaries, wages, interest, profits, and taxes and government payments of salaries and wages.

individual processes are carried out by the firms that can do them most efficiently. The sales revenue of a firm will include both the value of its own output and the value of the raw materials it purchased from other firms. The raw materials of one firm are the finished goods of another, so we use the term intermediate goods and services for products sold by one firm to another. Final goods and services are those sold to *final users:* consumers, government, firms *if for investment*, and foreigners.

An example will help illustrate the issues involved. Let us consider a very simple final product bought by consumers: a loaf of bread. This loaf of bread is a combination of four products: wheat, milling, baking, and marketing. Ignoring other ingredients will keep the example simple, if not very tasty. If one firm carried out all of these production processes from growing the wheat to selling the bread to the consumer, the price paid by the consumer, say 50¢, is the value of the final goods and services produced. If each of these steps were instead performed at the same cost by separate firms, we have not changed in any way the goods and services produced. But the total sales of firms are considerably increased. This is illustrated in Table 2.1. The farmer—using only basic inputs for simplicity—produces the wheat required for a loaf of bread at a cost of 25¢ that includes a competitive return on the factors which he owns. He sells this wheat at a price of 25¢ to the miller. The miller converts the wheat into flour at a cost of 8¢. He then sells the flour to the baker at his production cost of 8¢ plus his raw materials cost of 25¢, or a total of 33¢. The baker turns the flour worth 33¢ into bread by using resources which cost 12¢. He sells his loaves of bread in bulk to stores at 45¢ per loaf (33¢ + 12¢). The stores display and market the bread to individual customers who are happy to pay the 5¢ resource cost of this convenience plus the 45¢ cost of bread bought in large quantities. If we look at the total resource costs of 50¢, we see that they are identical to the price of the final goods sold to the consumer. This is always true, and it enables us to see how to compute the contribution of each firm to total output. The resource cost as measured by the difference between sales revenue and the costs of raw materials used is called the *value added to gross national product* (or *GNP value added*) by each firm.

TABLE 2.1   Analysis of the value of the goods and services making up a loaf of bread

Constituent Product	Type of Firm	Product Sold	Sales Price, ¢	Resource Costs, ¢
Wheat	Farm	Wheat	25	25
Milling	Miller	Flour	33	8
Baking	Bakery	Bread in bulk	45	12
Marketing	Store	Distributed bread	50	5
		Totals	153	50

The basic difficulty with adding up total sales of all firms is the double-counting involved in counting the same constituent product each time it is included in the sales price of a composite product. Thus in our example of the loaf of bread, the total of sales prices includes the value of wheat four times, the value of milling three times, the value of baking twice, and the value of marketing once:

$$4 \times 25\mathcal{c} + 3 \times 8\mathcal{c} + 2 \times 12\mathcal{c} + 1 \times 5\mathcal{c} = 153\mathcal{c}$$

There are two alternative approaches to solving his problem of double-counting: The first is to add up the total GNP value added of all firms. The second is to add up total sales of goods and services to final users.

These two approaches come to the same thing, however. If we instruct our national income accountants to add up GNP value added for all firms, they will add up the sales minus the raw materials expenses of each firm. If instead we ask them to total only sales by firms of goods and services to final users, they will total up all sales and then subtract the sales to other than final users—that is, they will subtract the total raw materials expenses of firms since they represent the only nonfinal uses of goods and services. These two operations are of course arithmetically identical.

Gross National Product

Gross national product (GNP) is the estimate of the total value at market prices of all goods and services produced in the United States and sold to final users. This would be the sum of total GNP values added by firms plus labor services sold directly by households to the government. The Director of the Office of Business Economics in the Department of Commerce has provided a well-stated operational definition of how the national income accountants working in his office actually measure GNP:

> National output as the sum of final products can best be characterized from an operational standpoint as the sum of purchases not charged to current expense by business .... To be sure, this operational rule is not profound in expressing the ultimate goals of measurement. But it is important because it tells us in a clear, frank, and unadorned manner what we actually do when we measure the bulk of national product. Recognition of the rule helps to keep our feet on the ground.[12]

The statement of the rule is much easier than its application. It is straightforward enough for the Department of Commerce to add up total sales of firms, subtract total materials expenses, and add purchases of labor from households by all levels of government. But this would not include the value at market prices of all final goods and services produced in the United States.

---

[12] George Jaszi, An Economic Accountant's Ledger, *The Economic Accounts of the United States: Retrospect and Prospect*, supplement to *Survey of Current Business*, July 1971, p. 218.

The most important area of omission is production and consumption within the household sector. It is one thing to simplify a discussion by assuming that all production takes place in firms and quite another to actually expect all production to be listed on the tax returns of firms. Salary and wages paid by one household to another—largely for domestic service—must be added. Production within individual households—housework, child care, do-it-yourself activities—is not priced in the market, so there is no way to place a market value on it. As a result, our measure of output does not reflect all output but only output subject to market transactions. If GNP were to increase because people worked more for the market and did less at home, the value of the increase in market output would be compared with the value of the decrease in home output to compute any net gain or loss. Because of the subjective nature of evaluating home output, national income accountants have wisely chosen to produce an accurate measure of market economic activity alone. This measure can be combined with other, more subjective factors—household production, environmental quality, and the like—determining social welfare, should analysis of a particular problem require it.

One area of household production is partially included in GNP—the services of consumers' durable goods. All durable goods owned by consumers must yield a stream of services over the years sufficient to cover both the depreciation of the value of the goods as it ages and the interest or profits which could be earned were the same funds to be used instead to buy securities issued by firms. As a general rule it is argued by national income accountants that these service flows are too intimately related to individual behavior to be included in production. As a result, household purchases of consumers' durable goods such as automobiles, refrigerators, and washing machines are treated for GNP purposes as if they were consumed when purchased, like restaurant meals.[13] One major exception to this rule is made, however: owner-occupied housing. The large, well-functioning rental market suggests that housing services are easily separated from ownership and provides a solid basis for estimation of a market price for the implicit rental services provided by owner-occupied housing. On this basis, national income accountants *impute* a rental value of owner-occupied housing by estimating its equivalent GNP value added were it rented instead to someone else. In essence, individuals who buy a house are treated as if they set up a firm which invested in the house, rented it to themselves, and then paid themselves the GNP value added as profits.

National income accountants make three other major imputations for goods and services produced but not explicitly purchased in the market. The first is for salary and wages paid in kind instead of money—largely provision of

---

[13] Allowance for this accounting convention will have to be made later when we analyze in detail the determinants of the size of consumer spending.

room and board by an employer. These are treated as if they were money wages which the employee used to buy the room and board. The second imputation is for output consumed by the producer—largely home consumption of crops by farmers. This is valued as if it were sold in the market by the farmer as a firm and bought in the market by the farmer as an individual. The final imputation is for services rendered by financial institutions. Largely for legal reasons, banks and other financial institutions do not pay in full interest on deposits and then charge their depositors in full for services rendered. Instead, large parts of the interest payments and service charges are canceled out and do not show up as revenue on the books of these firms. The national income accountants include in GNP an estimate of the full value of the services actually rendered to and interest earned by depositors.

Some market transactions are not included in GNP. All illegal activity is excluded. This is occasionally justified on the moral ground that if it is illegal, it has no real value even if it does involve the production of goods and services bought by a willing buyer—as, for example, gambling and prostitution[14] as well as drugs. This argument is weak since GNP is supposed to evaluate goods and services at market prices, not some other standard of value. The more practical reason is that there are obviously no good data reported to the government on the GNP value added by illegal production.

Table 2.2 shows the components of United States GNP for 1974 from three points of view: the amounts of production, the amounts of final purchases, and the amounts of claims on output. As you would expect, the bulk of production (almost 85 percent) is carried on in firms, with smaller amounts of GNP value added by government (about 11 percent), by households (3 percent), and by income from foreign investments (0.9 percent). The bulk of purchases of final goods and services is made by households (62.7 percent), but there are substantial amounts of business purchases of capital goods (15.0 percent) and government purchases of goods and services (22.1 percent). Net exports (here 0.2 percent) are always relatively very small. The two major claims on output (or types of income) are listed as private income (69.5 percent) and net taxes (21.7 percent). The former consists of all rights of individuals to output whether paid out or accrued by firms which they own or by which they are employed. Since personal interest payments are not included in GNP, they are subtracted from interest receipts in arriving at private income. Net taxes are all tax and nontax payments to governments less transfer payments and interest paid on government debt. Transfers to foreigners (0.3 percent) are net gifts (about $\frac{1}{3}$ by households and $\frac{2}{3}$ by the federal government) to foreigners. The statistical discrepancy arises because gross national product can be computed by totaling values added by each sector of production or by adding up income.

---

[14] These activities are legal in some places, such as parts of Nevada. There the national income accountants apparently recognize a social value.

TABLE 2.2 The gross national product of the United States, 1974

Output[a]

Where Produced	Amount	% of GNP
Households	47.0	3.4%
Firms	1,177.8	84.3%
Government	160.8	11.5%
Rest of the world	11.9	0.9%
Gross national product	1,397.4	100.0%

Expenditures[b]

Final Purchases	Amount	% of GNP
Consumer expenditures	876.7	62.7%
Gross investment	209.4	15.0%
Government expenditures	309.2	22.1%
Net exports	2.1	0.2%
Gross national product	1,397.4	100.0%

Income[c]

Received as	Amount	% of GNP
Private income[d]	971.3	69.5%
Capital consumption	119.5	8.6%
Net taxes[e]	303.2	21.7%
Transfers to foreigners	3.6	0.3%
Statistical discrepancy	-0.1	-0.0%
Gross national product	1,397.4	100.0%

Amounts in billions of dollars. Totals may not add due to rounding.
Source: Calculated from data in *Survey of Current Business*, Mar. 1975.
Notes: [a] Sums of GNP value added for each sector.
[b] Purchases of final goods and services made by each sector.
[c] Claims on output.
[d] Computed as disposable personal income + undistributed corporate profits + wage accruals less disbursements + corporation inventory valuation adjustment — other personal outlays.
[e] Computed as government purchases of goods and services + government surplus (national income and product accounts basis).

Since the sources of data for each calculation are largely different, it is inevitable that a small error creeps in—sometimes positive, sometimes negative. The final claim on output is the *capital consumption allowance*. This refers to the estimated amount of capital goods used up in production both by depreciation due to use and obsolescence and to capital equipment accidentally destroyed.

The requirement for the capital consumption allowance (and the term *gross investment* listed under expenditures) is our warning that gross national product still involves considerable double-counting. Investment was defined in Sec. 2.1 as the increase in the capital stock. Gross investment must be as large as the capital consumption allowance just to maintain the capital stock at a constant level. Only to the extent that gross investment exceeds capital consumption does the capital stock increase. Thus investment is equal to gross investment less the capital consumption allowance. GNP value added is based on subtracting raw materials expense to avoid double-counting of production by other firms paid for in the sales price of a firm's product. We should also avoid double-counting of purchases of capital goods to keep the stock of capital goods in its initial condition. The using up of capital goods does not provide any *net* contribution to our ability to either consume or add to wealth, which is the most fundamental definition of income and output.[15] We conclude that gross national product is not an acceptable measure of total income or output.

Net National Product

Net national product (*NNP*) is defined as gross national product less the capital consumption allowance. This can be characterized in three equivalent ways: (1) total purchase of NNP final goods and services, (2) the total contributions of value added to net national product, and (3) total income or claims to output. These same approaches were used to analyze GNP.

The first approach applies directly the concepts of final purchases discussed in Sec. 2.1: *NNP final goods and services* are consumer expenditures, investment, government expenditures, and net exports. The approach is illustrated in Table 2.3. When Tables 2.2 and 2.3 are compared, it is clear that the only difference between the expenditures on final goods and services recorded is that GNP includes gross investment and NNP includes only investment expenditures. Since gross investment equals investment plus capital consumption, it is clear that NNP equals GNP less the capital consumption allowance.

The second approach is based on adding up NNP values added. *NNP values added* differ from GNP values added only for firms, where the definition is sales less raw materials and capital consumption expenses. Totaling

---

[15] Using up capital is how we are able—as during a war—to consume both privately and publicly a greater amount than current income. But this is done at the cost of reduction in future output because of the reduced capital stock.

TABLE 2.3 The net national product of the United States, 1974

Output[a]			Expenditures[b]			Income[c]		
Where Produced	Amount	% of NNP	Final Purchases	Amount	% of NNP	Received as	Amount	% of NNP
Households	47.0	3.7%	Consumer expenditures	876.7	68.6%	Private income[d]	971.3	76.0%
Firms	1,058.3	82.8%	Investment	89.9	7.0%	Net taxes[e]	303.2	23.7%
Government	160.8	12.6%	Government expenditures	309.2	24.2%	Transfers to foreigners and statistical discrepancy	3.5	0.3%
Rest of the world	11.9	0.9%	Net exports	2.1	0.2%			
Net national product	1,278.0	100.0%	Net national product	1,278.0	100.0%	Net national product	1,278.0	100.0%

Amounts in billions of dollars. Totals may not add due to rounding.
Source: Calculated from data in *Survey of Current Business*, Mar. 1975.
Notes: [a] Sums of NNP values added for each sector.
[b] Purchases of NNP final goods and services made by each sector.
[c] Claims on output.

[d] Computed as disposable personal income + undistributed corporate profits + wage accruals less disbursements + corporation inventory valuation adjustment − other personal outlays.
[e] Computed as government purchases of goods and services + government surplus (national income and product accounts basis).

NNP values added will give identical results to those obtained by totaling GNP values added and subtracting the capital consumption allowance from the total for firms. This is easily seen by comparing Tables 2.2 and 2.3.

The third approach is to add up all claims to output to get total income. The claims are private income, net taxes, transfers to foreigners, and statistical discrepancy. Unlike Table 2.2, Table 2.3 includes under income no entry for capital consumption allowances which in fact represent no income to anyone.

Throughout the remainder of this book we will use NNP as our empirical measure of total income. Nevertheless, it should be pointed out that the superiority of the NNP concept over the GNP concept is more one of logical consistency than of GNP telling a different story from NNP about the development and year-to-year changes in the level of economic activity. This is illustrated by the close resemblance in Fig. 2.5 of the graphs of NNP and GNP.

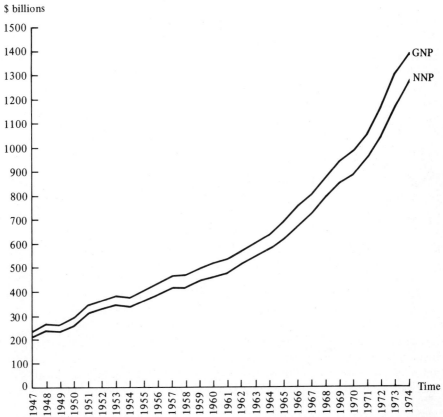

FIGURE 2.5 Net national product and gross national product in the post-World War II United States. Year-to-year movements of NNP closely mirror movements in GNP so that changes in either series can be used as an indicator of changes in economic activity.

Conceptual Problems in the Use of Net National Product

It should not be inferred that NNP is a perfect measure of the underlying concept of total income. There are three remaining areas of difficulty besides those already discussed: (1) capital consumption allowances, (2) residual double-counting of intermediate goods and services, and (3) the valuation of product at market prices. They are discussed here by way of warning that the national income accounts are nothing more—but nothing less—than the best available estimates. We will later have occasion to deal with the practical implications of some of these problems.

The difficulty with the capital consumption allowance is that the estimate is based on data reported on tax returns using an accounting concept that allocates historical costs over time. It would be preferable, though it is impossible, to have a measure of the actual reduction in the capital stock over the period evaluated at current prices. This is mainly a problem when the current prices differ markedly from purchase prices, as occurs under rapid inflations. There is a movement toward adoption of business accounting standards which reflect changes in the value of the dollar because of inflation. This should provide the needed information, otherwise the Department of Commerce soon will have to make its own estimates since rough estimates are clearly better than none at all under current conditions.

Some government services provided to business firms are essentially no different from intermediate products. An obvious—and common—example is the government taking over the maintenance of a factory driveway which was previously maintained by the firm. The firm is charged higher taxes for this service and its output and prices are unaffected. The NNP rises, however, because the cost of maintaining the road is now included both in government NNP value added and in the NNP value added of the firm (tax payments are not subtracted). It would obviously be desirable to eliminate this double-counting by subtracting the value of government intermediate services for which a tax or nontax fee is charged.[16] It is not at all obvious how to determine this amount; so it remains a problem. The same sort of problem applies to some consumer expenditures which are really costs of working. That is, recorded wages are frequently a payment for an intermediate product consisting of labor and expenses for tools and the like. Some employee expenses are deducted from salaries and wages, but there is no clear place to draw the line—other than what the tax laws happen to make deductible.

The final difficulty—the valuation of goods and services at market prices— brings us back to our original question of how we can combine different amounts of hundreds of thousands of goods and services into a meaningful index of total goods and services. The approach used was to add up their

---

[16] If the intermediate services provide an implicit subsidy, the price of the firm's output will fall and there will be no double-counting.

values according to market prices. If one thing sells for ten times what another sells for, then it is valued as equal to ten of the other. This means that the marginal valuation of willing buyers gives us our weights for adding together goods. If prices change, then so do our weights. As a practical matter there is no alternative, and it is not clear that any would be desirable for carrying out the macroeconomist's task of explaining how human behavior determines overall economic activity. For that task it is best to have a measure of economic activity that reflects the actual values placed on goods by the population rather than some alternative standard of social worth. The price which a buyer will consider paying for a product is determined by both the buyer's personal tastes and resources and the supply conditions of the product. It is assumed that these conditions do not change sufficiently rapidly—when averaged over all buyers and all products—to cause any difficulty for macroeconomic analysis. A separate difficulty, analyzed in Chap. 3, is the effect of changes in the overall level of prices or inflation on our measure of income. Special techniques are developed there to measure changes in the overall level of prices and to remove their effects from our measure of output.

2.3 THE ROLE OF SAVING IN THE NATIONAL INCOME ACCOUNTING IDENTITIES

Saving Defined

Saving is the difference between private income and consumer expenditures. Private income measures the amount available to consumers for consumption or addition to their wealth. Consumer expenditures are treated as consumption in our national income accounts, so the addition to the nonhuman wealth[17] of households, or saving, is measured by the amount of private income not consumed. It is convenient to introduce some symbols for these concepts so that the relations can be described algebraically. Private income is denoted Y^n, consumer expenditures C, and saving S. So our definition of saving is

$$S = Y^n - C \tag{2.1}$$

It will be recalled, from our description of the flows of economic activity, that household saving is used to purchase both security issues of firms and foreigners and new issues of government debt and money. Sales of outstanding securities, government debt, and government money from one household to another represent no change in the saving of the household sector but merely a transfer of assets from one household to another.

---

[17] Investments in human wealth are in part included in consumer expenditure (tuition, books, etc.) and in part excluded from our measure of income and its components altogether (wages foregone while in school or in an on-the-job training program). Consumers' durable goods are treated as if consumed immediately.

The National Income Accounting Identities

The use of saving to finance investment, net exports, and the government deficit is implicit in the national income identities for income and expenditures. Neglecting the trivial items of transfers to foreigners and statistical discrepancy,[18] total income Y is identically equal to the sum of private income and net taxes T (see Table 2.3):

$$Y = Y^n + T \qquad\qquad [2.2]$$

Total expenditures, on the other hand, are identically equal to the sum of consumer expenditures, investment I, government expenditures G, and net exports X:

$$Y = C + I + G + X \qquad\qquad [2.3]$$

Note that Y can be used interchangeably for total income and total expenditures since they are merely different names for the same concept.

Substituting [2.2] into [2.1] gives us

$$Y^n + T = C + I + G + X \qquad\qquad [2.4]$$

Since private income is the sum of consumer expenditures and saving,

$$C + S + T = C + I + G + X \qquad\qquad [2.5]$$

The left-hand side of [2.5] tells us that income is divided between paying for consumer expenditures and taxes and saving. The right-hand side shows that final purchases of goods and services consist of consumer expenditures, investment, government expenditures, and net exports. The two sides must always be equal by the very definitions of the concepts. Subtracting consumer expenditures from both sides and moving net taxes to the right,

$$S = I + G - T + X \qquad\qquad [2.6]$$

This equation says that saving is equal to investment plus the government deficit $(G - T)$ plus net exports. This is true by definition. We will frequently refer to this equation in order to check the consistency of a theory which explains the actual values of its individual components.

☐ SUMMARY

The main flows of economic activity in the United States can be described in terms of four sectors: households, firms, government, and the rest of the world. Households own the labor force which they rent out and own securities, debt,

---

[18] We can combine this with net taxes to keep the analysis simple.

and money issued by the other sectors. Firms own the capital stock which they combine with labor services to produce final goods and services purchased by consumers, government, the rest of the world, and by firms for investment in more capital. Government provides services to the other sectors, financing its activities by net taxes, borrowing, and issuing new money. Some goods and services produced in the United States are exchanged for those produced in the rest of the world. The difference in value or net exports is financed by net issues of foreign securities. Net national product (NNP) is the estimate of total output, total final purchases, and total income of the United States. Gross national product (GNP) exceeds NNP by the amount of capital consumption; the word gross warns that gross investment is included as a final purchase. Expenditures are the sum of consumer expenditures, investment, government expenditures, and net exports. Income is essentially the sum of private income and net taxes. Saving, the difference between private income and consumer expenditure, finances investment, the government deficit, and net exports.

☐ **QUESTIONS AND EXERCISES**

1 If you were asked to give a single measure representing 3 pairs of shoes, 7 movie tickets, and 328 paper clips, how would you do it? What about 2 pairs of shoes, 9 movie tickets, and 275 paper clips? What is bigger? By how much? Does it make a difference what you are going to use the measure for?

2 Why do we say that firms produce output using factor services instead of factors of production?

*3 Profits maintain the equality of output and income. Explain why.

4 Securities issues finance investment and outstanding securities finance the capital stock. What is the relation of securities issues to outstanding securities? Of investment to the capital stock? Why does the initial statement hold?

5 Why is the amount of securities issues sold to households not reduced if one firm buys the securities of another?

*6 A company had sales for the year of $2,500,000. Its expenses were:

Wages	$1,100,000
Interest	150,000
Taxes	120,000
Depreciation	300,000
Raw materials	750,000
Total expenses	$2,420,000
Net income	80,000
Sales	$2,500,000

(*a*) What was the company's GNP value added?
(*b*) What was the company's NNP value added?

7 If a steelmaker buys a coal mine from which it had been buying coal, what happens to total sales? To GNP? To NNP?

8 What happens to NNP if a man marries his housekeeper who continues to perform (almost) identical tasks?

9 Why does the inclusion of the capital consumption allowance in GNP represent double-counting?

10 In Table 2.3, what is the total value of consumer expenditures, investment, and net exports? Could this total exceed private income? Why or why not?

*11 Why is it that firms produce most of the output but do not make most of the final purchases of goods and services?

12 How much was saving in 1974?

☐ REFERENCES FOR FURTHER READING

Kendrick, John W.: "National Income and Product Accounts," in *International Encyclopedia of the Social Sciences*, London: Macmillan, 1968, **11:** 19–34. (A somewhat briefer introduction to the history and details of the United States National Income and Products Accounts.)

National Accounts Review Committee: *The National Economic Accounts of the United States: Review, Appraisal, and Recommendations*, Washington: GPO, 1958.

Rosen, Sam: *National Income and Other Social Accounts*, New York: Holt, 1972. (This book provides a thorough introduction to the detailed information included in the United States National Income and Product Accounts.)

The Economic Accounts of the United States: Retrospect and Prospect, supplement to *Survey of Current Business*, July 1971.

The Measurement of Macroeconomic Variables II: Other National Aggregates

Chapter 3

3.1 PRICE INDICES

The Average Level of Prices

The prices of individual goods and services change frequently—sometimes up, sometimes down. Historically, price changes of individual commodities primarily have reflected changes in the valuation of one commodity as compared with others. These changes in relative prices are caused by changes in the conditions of supply and demand as explained by microeconomic theory. Macroeconomists are concerned with explaining the behavior of the average level of prices. At times, there is superimposed on the shifts in supply and demand caused by such basic forces as changes in tastes or conditions of production an upward or downward bias. If this bias is upward, prices which would have risen in its absence rise more, and prices which would have otherwise fallen fall less or even rise though by less than average. If the bias is instead downward, prices which would otherwise rise, rise less or even fall while prices that would have fallen anyway fall more rapidly.

The rise and fall of the average level of prices over time creates difficulties for our measure of total income derived as the sum of the quantities times the current prices of final goods and services. The fact that net national product has increased over a particular year does not of itself tell us anything about whether more real goods and services are being produced and made available to satisfy human wants. It could instead be that income rose solely because of the bias imparted by a rising average level of prices. Our primary goal in measuring total income was to develop a weighted average of the actual apples, shirts, automobiles, television repairs, and so forth produced. Although prices provide relative weights for combining the different kinds of goods and services, they distort our measure whenever the average price level changes.

Consider for example an economy in which only three final goods and services (or three commodities) are produced. Different possible quantities and prices are given for 5 years in Table 3.1. In year 0, total income is \$4,500:

$$100 \times \$10.00 + 300 \times \$5.00 + 2000 \times \$1.00 = \$4,500$$

TABLE 3.1 Quantities and prices produced in a three-commodity economy

Year	Commodity 1 Quantity	Price	Commodity 2 Quantity	Price	Commodity 3 Quantity	Price	Income
0	100	$10.00	300	$5.00	2000	$1.00	$4,500.00
1	110	$10.00	330	$5.00	2200	$1.00	$4,950.00
2	100	$11.00	300	$5.50	2000	$1.10	$4,950.00
3	105	$11.50	315	$5.75	2100	$1.15	$5,433.75
4	95	$11.00	340	$5.00	2100	$1.05	$4,950.00
4a	95	$10.00	340	$5.00	2100	$1.00	$4,750.00
4b	100	$11.00	300	$5.00	2000	$1.05	$4,700.00

In year 1, income has increased to $4,950—an increase of 10 percent

$$\$4,950 - \$4,500 = \$450 \qquad \$450/\$4,500 = 0.10$$

This is exactly how we would want our measure of total goods and services to behave, since the quantity of each commodity increased by 10 percent. In year 2 however income is also $4,950, but the real output of goods and services is identical to that of year 0. The 10 percent rise in total income is due entirely to the 10 percent increase in each price. It would be desirable to distinguish between these two kinds of increase in the total value of final commodities.

Macroeconomists make this distinction by breaking total income Y_t into an index y_t of the total real quantity of goods and services and another index P_t of the average level of prices. These indices are defined so that—just as for an individual commodity—quantity times price equals dollar value:

$$y_t P_t = Y_t \qquad\qquad [3.1]$$

Income Y_t measured in terms of current prices times current quantities is called *nominal income*. The term nominal reminds us that this concept is measured in terms of dollars and so can change because of changes in the value of the dollar. Income as measured by an index of real goods and services is called *real income*. *Price level* is used for the average level of prices. The units in which real income and the price level are measured can be chosen in a completely arbitrary manner so long as they correspond. The most convenient unit for measuring real income is in terms of the average amount of goods and services which could be bought with $1 in a selected base year or *base-year dollars*, denoted by *R$*. The selection of a base year is completely arbitrary and only serves to provide a fixed standard for comparing the relative amounts of real income in different years. We have been using year 0 in our example as such a base for comparison. Base-year dollars are also referred to as dollars of constant purchasing power or just constant dollars. The price level for any year t is measured consistently as the number of year t dollars which it takes to buy the real goods and services which could have been bought with $1 in the base year—year t dollars per base-year dollar. The product of real income measured in base-year dollars and the price level measured in year t dollars per base-year dollar will indeed be equal to nominal income measured in year t dollars.

Returning to our example and using year 0 as our base year, it is obvious that Y_0 is \$4,500, y_0 is R\$4,500, and P_0 is \$1/R\$. This must follow from the definition of base-year dollars as the average amount of goods and services which could be bought with \$1 in the base year. In year 1, prices are unchanged so P_1 is \$1/R\$. Nominal income was computed as \$4,950. Real income is easily computed as Y_1/P_1 or R\$4,950. As noted previously, real income is thus 10 percent higher in year 1 than in year 0. In year 2, all prices are 10 percent higher so P_2 is \$1.10/R\$. Dividing nominal income by the price level gives real income y_2 of R\$4,500, the same as base-year real income. These examples are very straightforward because only prices change or only output changes. In year 3, all prices are 15 percent higher than in the base year ($P_3 = \$1.15/R\$$), and all quantities are 5 percent higher than in the base year

$$y_3 = 1.05 \times R\$4,500 = R\$4,725$$

The value of nominal income Y_3 computed in Table 3.1 (by summing the values of quantities times current prices) is \$5,433.75. This is exactly equal to $y_3 P_3$ (R\$4,725 × \$1.15/R\$).[1] So long as *all* prices or *all* quantities are proportional to those of the base year, there is no difficulty in computing the values of P_t and y_t. P_t is the proportional increase in prices and y_t is the proportional increase in quantities times base-year nominal income.

In a dynamic economy, different prices and different quantities normally change at different rates to reflect the changes in individual conditions of supply and demand. If prices and quantities did not change relative to each other, there would be no problem in measuring real income or the price level since there would be in effect just one commodity with a single price and quantity. In fact the changes from year 0 to year 4 are more representative of the sort of changes that are observed in any real economy. Some prices go up and some go down. Some quantities go up, some go down. There are two main approaches to dividing such changes into changes in real income and the price level: (1) Compute real income by applying base-year prices to the quantities actually produced. The price level is obtained by dividing nominal income by real income. (2) Compute the price level as the cost at current prices of the base-year quantities divided by the cost of those quantities in the base year. Real income is obtained by dividing nominal income by the price level.

---

[1] Nominal income increases by 20.75 percent here since (\$5,433.75 − \$4,500.00)/\$4,500.00 = 0.2075. This exceeds the sum of the percentage increases in the price level and real income because the increase in real income is valued at increased prices. Note however that 1.15 × 1.05 = 1.2075.

The first approach is actually used by U.S. national income accountants to compute real income. The procedure is illustrated by the line in Table 3.1 labeled 4a. This computes what the nominal income would have been if the same amounts were produced but sold at base-year prices for each commodity. This amount R$4,750.00 is a measure of real income in terms of the actual prices which existed in the base year. The price level is implicit in the values of nominal income and real income so P_4 is $4,950/R$4,750 or about $1.042/R$.

The second approach is used to compute many price indices such as the wholesale price index and consumer price index. Line 4b computes the amount which it would cost at year 4 prices to purchase what was actually bought in year 0 for a total cost of $4,500. The price level is the ratio of these amounts $4,700/R$4,500 or about $1.044/R$. The corresponding value of real income is nominal income divided by the price level $4,950/($1.044/R$) or about R$4,739.36. This approach computes the average level of prices relative to the base year by using base-year quantities as weights. The first approach computes the average level of output relative to the base year by using base-year prices as weights.

The two approaches normally do not give very different results. Here real income is estimated to increase from year 0 to year 4 by 5.55 percent with the first method of estimation and by 5.32 percent with the second method. The corresponding increases in the price level are 4.2 percent versus 4.4 percent. More elaborate approaches to averaging price and quantity changes are possible, but not in wide use.

The Implicit Price Deflator for Gross National Product

The most readily available estimate of the overall price level is the *implicit deflator for gross national product* or *GNP deflator*.[2] It is so named because it is implicit in Department of Commerce estimates of nominal GNP and real GNP; these are constructed as nearly as possible by the first method of using base-year prices and current quantities. Since it is impossible to actually use base-year prices for the millions of commodities which are produced, real GNP is estimated by using price indices estimated by using the second approach for very closely related commodities such as different kinds of wheat or different kinds of automobiles. The actual value of each narrow commodity group is divided by the price index for that commodity group to get a real value for the commodity group. These are then summed to obtain real GNP. Since changes in relative prices within commodity groups are very small compared to changes in relative prices among commodity groups, this closely approximates the use of base-year prices for each individual commodity. Deflator is an alternative term for price index because dividing nominal income

---

[2] The GNP deflator—like most price indices—is usually published in percentage points. The base-year GNP deflator is thus 100 percent and a price level of 1.1 is recorded as 110.

by a price index removes the effects of inflation from nominal income or *deflates* nominal income.

An NNP deflator also exists but is published only irregularly because the Department of Commerce emphasizes the larger concept of gross national product. The differences between the two deflators are normally negligible.

Consumer Price Index

The *consumer price index* (CPI) is a measure of the average level of prices for commodities purchased by a "moderate-income, urban family." The CPI is based on weighting current prices by the average quantities of goods and services purchased by a moderate-income, urban family in the base year (currently 1967) and dividing this sum by the cost of those quantities in the base year. The actual quantities used are based on extensive budget surveys carried out in the base year. The approximately 300 most important commodities are sampled monthly by employees of the Bureau of Labor Statistics which computes and publishes the CPI.

The consumer price index is a very limited price index whose application is properly restricted to evaluating the real command of moderate-income, urban families over the goods and services which they purchase. Some commodities are over-represented and others under-represented from the point of view of all consumers' command over goods and services from a given nominal income.[3] Further, the definition of "moderate income" is a rather slippery problem which must be solved each time a new base year is chosen to study changing consumption patterns.

The CPI is not of particular value in macroeconomic analysis. Its main value arises from the fact that it is available at monthly intervals while the implicit price deflators—like the national income accounts from which they are derived—are available only quarterly. The CPI can be used as an approximate indicator of what is happening to the general level of prices in intraquarter periods.

The Wholesale Price Index

The *wholesale price index* (WPI) is an index of prices charged for goods sold in primary markets. Primary markets refer to basic materials produced in manufacturing, agriculture, forestry, fishing, mining, quarrying, well operation, and gas and electric utilities. Weights are based on relative quantities in the base year.

The great advantage of this price index is that it is based on commodities for which quality changes are a minor problem. Price changes in a shirt or

---

[3] An implicit price deflator for personal consumption expenditures which can serve well for this purpose is computed by the National Income Division of the Department of Commerce, however.

television set may reflect different qualities for different models. Correcting for quality change is a challenge which many economists suspect is less than fully met. By using such basic commodities as steel and wheat and crude oil, this problem is reduced, but only at the cost of not capturing any changes in the relative prices of finished goods, marketing, and services as against basic commodities. Another advantage is that the Bureau of Labor Statistics computes and publishes this index monthly.

An important limitation is that except for goods sold on organized commodity exchanges, price data are taken from list prices reported by sellers. It has been shown[4] that these reported prices vary much less than the prices actually paid after correction for changes in discounts, shipping charges, and the like. For this reason the WPI tends to understate wholesale prices in a boom and overstate them when the economic activity is down.

Deflation of Nominal Variables

There are many macroeconomic variables which are originally measured in terms of current dollars. Any such amount is called a *nominal* amount. Important variables measured in nominal terms would be private income, saving, and the money stock held by the public.[5] To analyze the behavior of individuals and firms with respect to such variables, it is necessary to remove the effects of inflation from the data by deflating by the price level. The real amount x_t of any nominal variable X_t is obtained by dividing the nominal amount at time t by the price level at time t:

$$x_t = \frac{X_t}{P_t} \qquad\qquad [3.2]$$

Throughout this book nominal amounts will be represented by capital letters and real amounts will be represented by lowercase letters.

Deflation by the general price level P_t converts nominal amounts into base-year dollar amounts on the basis of the average price level of final goods and services. A real amount is thus measured in terms of the average real goods and services which could be purchased with or sold for $1 in the base year. This is precisely what is desired in most cases, but on occasion it will be necessary to take into account temporarily divergent movements in other important price averages such as wholesale prices and investment goods prices.

The price index P_t can also be used to find the price or value of $1 at time t. The price in dollars of $1 is not very interesting—that price is always $1. The more basic price of a dollar is the real quantity of goods and services

---

[4] See George J. Stigler and James K. Kindahl, *The Behavior of Industrial Prices*, New York: National Bureau of Economic Research, Inc., 1970.
[5] The money stock will be discussed in Sec. 3.3.

which must be sold to obtain a dollar or which can be purchased with a dollar. These goods and services are the alternative to owning a dollar. In terms of base-year dollars, this quantity is computed as $\$1/P_t$. For example, if the price level is 1.25 (that is $\$1.25/R\$1$), then the value of the dollar at time t is $R\$0.80$ since

$$\frac{\$1}{P_t} = \frac{\$1}{\$1.25/R\$1} = R\$0.80 \tag{3.3}$$

This says that goods and services which cost only 80¢ in the base year now cost $1 or, alternatively, that goods and services which could be sold for only 80¢ now bring in $1. In determining the CPI, this value is computed for the average basket of final goods and services actually sold. It would not be expected to hold exactly for each and every individual commodity since relative prices change in response to changing conditions of supply and demand in each market.

3.2 LABOR FORCE AND UNEMPLOYMENT
The Labor Force

The *age-eligible population* is the number of persons 16 years of age and over who are residents of the United States or serving in the armed forces overseas.[6] The age-eligible population is divided into three main components: the civilian labor force, members of the armed forces, and persons not in the labor force.

The *civilian labor force* is the number of civilians who have a job, are looking for a job, or are waiting to report to a job. The *total labor force* is the civilian labor force plus the number of members of the armed services. Persons who are not in the labor force include those who are engaged in housework in their own homes, in school, retired, or disabled, and seasonal workers (during the off season), as well as those who have given up looking for jobs or are not interested in working.

The civilian labor force is divided further into the employed and the unemployed. *Employed persons* are all those who are either at work or have a job but are not currently working. People are counted as "at work" if they did any work during the week for either pay or profit (self-employed) or worked without pay on a family farm or business for 15 hours or more. Persons with a job but not at work are those temporarily absent from a job because of vacation, illness, labor-management disputes, bad weather, or the like. Persons rather than jobs are counted so each person who fits any or several of the requirements is counted as one employed person even if he or she holds two jobs.

---

[6] Children 15 years and under are considered too young to be eligible for full-time work. Persons confined to institutions are similarly excluded.

Unemployed persons are those who are not employed, were available for work during the week, and either attempted to find a job within the past four weeks or are waiting to report to a job after a layoff or to a new job within 30 days. Basically, the unemployed are those available for and seeking work. This definition is based on objectively observable behavior and so is not subject to the difficulties in determining whether or not a person who is not employed "wants" to be employed. Nearly everyone would "want" to be employed at a wage of $1,000,000 per year, but the unemployed include only those who actively take steps to become employed at a wage which they think might be obtainable.

Other broader definitions of unemployment or "underemployment" can be based on the official measure of unemployment and other data if analysis of a particular problem requires it. But as in the case of the national income and product accounts, there is much to be said for the government's computing a hard, objective estimate and leaving subjective components to other analysts.

Method of Estimation

Unlike the national income and product accounts, there is no base of income tax or similar reports which can be used to estimate the total labor force and its components with the exception of membership of the armed forces. Instead a survey of about 50,000 households is conducted by the Bureau of Labor Statistics for one week each month. Well-trained interviewers ask questions designed to classify all members of the household 16 years of age and over according to the strict definitions of employed, unemployed, or not in the labor force.

The survey estimates are by no means perfect but do closely approximate the totals that would be obtained from a complete monthly census of all American households. The Bureau of Labor Statistics also uses the survey data to estimate the number employed and unemployed classified by sex, age, color, marital status, occupation, and other characteristics, and by combinations of these characteristics. The reliability of these estimates deteriorates as their proportion of the total labor force decreases however. This is true because if there are relatively few individuals with the specified characteristics in the survey sample, there is less likelihood that individual peculiarities of the households actually selected will average out.

The Unemployment Rate

The *unemployment rate* is computed by dividing the total number of unemployed by the civilian labor force. The unemployment rate estimates the fraction without jobs of all those who desired jobs at a wage that they believe obtainable in the market. This fraction—often quoted in percentage points—

is widely publicized and figures prominently in political discussions of the state of the economy.

Unemployment rates are also computed for subgroups as classified by characteristics. The unemployment rate, the white unemployment rate, and even the white male unemployment rate are well estimated by the sample in the sense that over 95 percent of the time the estimates will be within 0.3 or 0.4 percent of the actual unemployment rates that would be computed by a complete census of the population. For groups which make up a smaller fraction of the total labor force, a quite substantial margin of error must be allowed. For white females, this margin—using the 95 percent criterion—is currently about 0.4–0.6 percent. For a group as small as nonwhite teenagers, the unemployment rate computed currently has a margin of error lying between 4 and 6 percent. This means that a much smaller change in the estimated total unemployment rate provides convincing evidence of a change in the true total unemployment rate than would be required for the teenage nonwhite unemployment rate. Thus a change in an unemployment rate which would be very important if it were true must be classified as "statistically insignificant" if it can be reasonably attributed to the peculiarities of the particular samples chosen.[7]

The welfare meaning of the unemployment rate—like the total number unemployed—is quite ambiguous. There are some senses in which it is an overestimate of unused human resources and others in which it is an underestimate. These arguments are much more important—or at least selectively useful—in the political sphere than for macroeconomic analysis. For macroeconomists, the unemployment rate is a useful index with a somewhat arbitrary normal level. The relative size of (statistically significant) deviations of the unemployment rate from this normal level is all that is required.

3.3 MONEY
Money as a Particular Kind of Asset

The term "money" is used in everyday language in three different ways: income (as, "He makes a lot of money."), wealth ("They have a lot of money."), and a particular type of asset ("She has lots of money in her pocket."). In economics, the term money is used *only* in the sense of a particular type of asset. An *asset* is a form in which wealth is held, such as money, government bonds, or various corporate securities. This means that one can have constant income and wealth, yet increase one's holdings of money by selling some other assets.

---

[7] A more complete discussion of these issues is found in Geoffrey H. Moore, On the "Statistical Significance" of Changes in Employment and Unemployment, *Statistical Reporter*, no. 73–9, pp. 137–39, Mar. 1973.

Money is defined as those forms of wealth which are in fact generally used to make ultimate payment for goods, services, and debts. Not all forms of money will be acceptable for all transactions: Try to buy a package of gum with a $500 bill.[8] But each form of money must be used in making a wide variety of payments. The precise operational definition used to measure money depends on what actually is used to make payments. At different places and times, money has been gold, seashells, corn, cigarettes, stones, and many other transferrable objects.

In the United States today, everyone would agree that currency and coin issued by the federal government should be counted as money. The vast majority of payments, however, are made by transferring deposit claims against commercial banks.[9] A check is a legal order by a depositor to his bank to transfer all his rights in a certain amount of his deposit to the payee of the check. The check itself is not money but merely an instruction to make an ultimate payment by transferring deposit claims. These deposit claims against commercial banks are clearly money also. Deposit claims or *deposits* are a liability (legal obligation) of the bank to pay to the depositor a certain amount of currency and coin. It is often much easier to transfer these promises than actual currency and coin, so bank deposits have become money also.

It is not clear exactly what bank deposits should be counted as money, however. *Demand deposits* are payable on demand and transferrable by check. *Time deposits* are payable only a certain time after notice or on a fixed date and cannot be transferred by check. The actual deposits which are transferred in making payments are thus always demand deposits. On this basis, many economists argue that only demand deposits should be counted as money. Other economists raise a question of the actual as opposed to legal usage of time deposits. With certain exceptions, time deposits have been in fact generally payable on demand and until 1933 were transferrable by check. The Banking Acts of 1933 and 1935 attempted to establish a buyers' cartel price of zero by prohibiting payment of interest on demand deposits. As is the usual case with cartels, enforcement quickly breaks down because each member has an incentive to cheat on his fellows—here, by secretly paying a bit more than the cartel price and attracting more profitable deposits. The details will be discussed shortly, but one way of secretly paying interest on demand deposits is to call them time deposits. It is indeed the case that passbook savers do not need to give the required 30- to 90-day notice to obtain currency or to exchange time deposit claims for demand deposit claims. Some banks will automatically transfer claims between demand and time deposits so that only a small balance is ever classified as a demand deposit,

---

[8] This experiment provides a great excuse to write home for more money.
[9] A commercial bank is a bank which can issue deposits transferable by check.

and the remainder earns interest as a time deposit. If time deposits in commercial banks thus actually are part of the deposits used to make payments, they are money despite the legal fictions of notice for payment and the like. There are clearly some difficult issues of fact here that have not yet been satisfactorily resolved.

There are two main, competing operational measures of the money supply. The *narrow money supply* (universally known as M_1) is the sum of currency, coin, and demand deposits held by the nonbank public. The nonbank public excludes the federal government and commercial banks but includes households, firms, foreigners, states, and local governments. The federal government is excluded because its power to issue new money makes its recorded holdings an accounting artifact without any influence on its behavior. Commercial bank holdings of demand deposits, coin, and currency are excluded to prevent double-counting since these assets support their deposits. The *broad money supply* (M_2) is equal to M_1 plus time deposits at commercial banks except for negotiable certificates of deposit of $100,000 or more ("large CD's"). The exclusion of large CD's is made on the grounds that for these time deposits, the maturity date is actually enforced. There are clearly other time deposits for which legal notice or maturity is enforced by banks, but there is no way to exclude them on the basis of current data.

There are two logically acceptable operational definitions of the United States money stock—M_1 and M_2. Probably M_1 is too narrow because it excludes deposits which are in fact used for making payments. However, M_2 probably includes some deposits which are not used for making payments. Lack of data prevents a more refined intermediate concept. The evidence as to which available concept seems to work better in analyzing macroeconomic behavior is still unsettled. The issue is not very important for the purposes of this book because the two data series behave very similarly.[10] When it is necessary to give an empirical definition of money, only M_1 will normally be used for convenience.

The Money Supply Process

The United States presently is on a *fiat standard* in which money consists of pieces of paper and rights to pieces of paper. Formerly the United States was, as some other countries now are, on a *commodity standard* in which money consists of a physical commodity, such as gold, or rights to a certain number of ounces of that commodity. The Federal Reserve System, which issues nearly all money issued by the government, will, in exchange for a $5 bill, issue a

---

[10] This probably explains why the question is unsettled. The two series are so similar that there are few cases of different predictions to be analyzed statistically.

new $5 bill, five $1 bills, or some token coins,[11] but does not offer any physical commodity. American money is valuable to a person only because other people will accept it in exchange for valuable goods, and not because of any intrinsic value in and of itself. This is largely true of commodity monies also, but is less obvious because the value of the commodity in non-monetary uses—such as gold used to make jewelry—will adjust to equal the value in monetary uses. Only if monetary uses are small relative to non-monetary uses (including monetary uses in other countries) will the value of the money be little affected by the country's demand for money.

The United States money supply rests upon the *base money* issued by the federal government. Government-issued money is also called *high-powered money* for reasons which will shortly be obvious. The main issuer of base money is the U.S. central bank, the *Federal Reserve System.* The Federal Reserve System—popularly called the *Fed*—is a quasi-independent agency of the legislative branch of government which is charged with determining and carrying out monetary policy.[12] Base money is currency, coins, and deposits at the Fed. Deposits at the Fed are owned by commercial banks and are transferrable among the Fed's depositors (members) or payable in currency on demand. In this way, the Fed acts as a "banker's bank."

In a fractional reserve banking system such as exists in the United States, bankers normally hold a small fraction of the value of their deposits as reserves of base money. The remainder of the value of deposits is lent out to earn interest. Banks need hold only a small fraction of their deposits as reserves because demands for payment in base money will be approximately offset by receipts of base money. Net payments of base money are made only to the extent that total deposits decrease. When the receipts and payments of all the depositors of a bank are added together, the net change will normally be small relative to total deposits. Further, much bank lending is in the form of purchases of government and private bonds which can be easily resold to others to replenish a depleted reserve.

Banks create money to the extent that their deposits which are included in the money supply exceed their reserves which are excluded from the money supply. Since the net amount of money created by banks is used to buy debt securities, it does not affect the amount of saving available to finance investment, the government deficit, and net exports. If households increase their holdings of bank-created money instead of increasing holdings of securities, the banks will buy the securities instead. Banks are sometimes called financial

---

[11] Token coins are coins whose value as money much exceeds the value of the metal which they contain.

[12] For historical reasons, the Fed formally has commercial banks as stockholders ("members") but the usual prerequisites of ownership such as rights to residual income (profits) and selection of top management are all vested in the government. The Federal Reserve Act of 1913 established an elaborate facade to conceal the fact that it created a central bank which was an unpopular concept at the time.

intermediaries because they intermediate in this way between lenders and borrowers.[13]

The process by which the money supply is determined can be easily explained by using some algebra. The money supply will be denoted by M, the monetary base by B, bank deposits included in the money supply by BD, currency and coin held by the nonbank public by F, and bank reserves by R. The money supply is defined as the sum of currency and coin held by the nonbank public and bank deposits included in the money supply:[14]

$$M = F + BD \qquad\qquad [3.4]$$

The total amount of government-created money, B, is the sum of currency and coin held by the nonbank public and bank reserves of currency and coin ("vault cash") plus deposits at the Fed:

$$B = F + R \qquad\qquad [3.5]$$

Dividing [3.4] by [3.5] and multiplying both sides by B,

$$M = \frac{F + BD}{F + R} B \qquad\qquad [3.6]$$

Now divide the numerator and denominator of the ratio in [3.6] by BD to obtain

$$M = \frac{(F/BD) + 1}{(F/BD) + (R/BD)} B \qquad\qquad [3.7]$$

The expression

$$\frac{(F/BD) + 1}{(F/BD) + (R/BD)}$$

is called the *money multiplier* μ because the money supply is that multiple of the monetary base:

$$M = \mu B \qquad\qquad [3.8]$$

The ratio F/BD is called the cash-deposit ratio and measures the public's desired holdings of currency and coin relative to bank deposits. The ratio R/BD is called the reserve-deposit ratio and measures the banks' desired holdings of reserves as a fraction of bank deposits.

Changes in the money supply occur because of changes in base money B, in the money multiplier μ, or in both. The money multiplier can change only if the cash-deposit or reserve-deposit ratios change. The cash-deposit

---

[13] There are many other types of financial intermediaries, but claims against them are not used as money.
[14] This analysis holds for either M_1 or M_2, depending on the definition of BD used.

ratio is normally quite stable, aside from small seasonal fluctuations, and moves only with a gradual trend.[15] Nor is the reserve-deposit ratio normally the source of more than gradual changes in the money multiplier. This ratio is affected by changes in the ratio of demand to time deposits, since smaller reserves are held against the latter than the former, but these changes too occur gradually. The main source of changes in the reserve-deposit ratio is the Fed which sets the minimum required reserve ratios for various types of bank deposits. A change in required reserve ratios is a very crude policy tool and only used infrequently. Unless there are changes in the Fed's policy, the money multiplier will normally change only gradually. As a result, the control by the Fed of the monetary base is essentially the same thing as control of the money supply.

The Fed has the authority to decide how much money is created by the federal government. For a given government deficit, this determines net government borrowing.[16] New federal, state, and local bonds are in fact issued for the entire amount of the deficit (or retired if there is surplus). The Fed then buys back securities with newly created base money (or sells more securities to destroy base money). Net government borrowing is thus the deficit less base-money creation. The Fed deals primarily in U.S. Treasury securities, but some promissory notes of bankers and international reserve assets (foreign government securities and currencies and gold)[17] are bought and sold. If the Fed lends to a banker or foreign government, *net* government borrowing is decreased just as if the Fed had bought a U.S. Treasury bond.

By using its power to create and destroy the base of the money supply process, the Fed determines the amount of the U.S. money supply. Although this has not always been so—for example, the Fed did not even begin operations until 1914—it is now true.

The Real Quantity of Money

The measures of money discussed so far are all derived by totaling the value in dollars of a particular class of assets. Since these are current dollar amounts, they are measures of the nominal quantity of money. It is often useful to look instead at the quantity of money in terms of the real goods and services which could be exchanged for it. This *real quantity of money* m_t is obtained by deflating the nominal quantity of money M_t by the price level P_t

$$m_t = \frac{M_t}{P_t} \qquad\qquad\qquad [3.9]$$

---

[15] A notable exception used to occur during banking panics when people would want to reduce bank deposits because of fear that many banks would become bankrupt. This is analyzed in Chap. 8.
[16] Recall that the government deficit $G - T$ is equal to government borrowing plus government money creation.
[17] Details of transactions in international reserve assets are discussed in Chap. 9.

This measures the quantity of money at time t in terms of base-year dollars, the average amount of final goods and services which could be bought with \$1 in the base year.

Interest Payments on Bank Deposits

Bankers' associations were successful in inserting into the Banking Acts of 1933 and 1935 provisions establishing a cartel pricing scheme for bank deposits. Interest payments on demand deposits were entirely prohibited and the Fed was given authority to establish maximum interest rates on time deposits. Enforcement of the cartel was to be carried out by the Fed and other banking regulatory agencies.[18]

As microeconomists have long demonstrated, cartel agreements break down very quickly even if enforced by the government. Suppose for example that a bank can lend funds at 10 percent per annum interest and lends out 85 percent of the value of demand deposits holding 15 percent of their value as non-interest-bearing reserves. The effective interest earned by the bank on each dollar of demand deposits is 8.5 percent ($0.10 \times 0.85 = 0.085$). If zero interest is paid to depositors, that amount will all go to profit. Now a clever bank manager will see that he could get much larger deposits if he would offer say 1 percent interest on his demand deposits while other banks pay nothing. The net interest earned on deposits is reduced to 7.5 percent per annum ($0.085 - 0.01 = 0.075$), but deposits will be so much larger that profits will greatly increase. The banker cannot pay this interest in a way that the cartel enforcers (here, government bank examiners) will detect and punish. So he uses indirect payments such as free services, reduced rates on loans to depositors, and so forth.

The only problem is that other clever bank managers will have come upon the same idea and the competitive advantage of 1 percent implicit interest on demand deposits will be wiped out. The banker must pay 1 percent just to keep his original depositors. But just as it was profitable to move from 0 to 1 percent interest payments, so is it profitable to move from 1 to 2 percent. Since it is profitable for each bank individually, the competitive advantage is wiped out. This process continues until the implicit interest payments equal the net interest earned on demand deposits. Each banker bewails the fact that his fellow cartel members are such "cheats" and "chiselers" to bring this about.

This competitive process is not perfect, especially for small depositors in small, one-bank towns, but for the bulk of deposits it works out rather well. Nevertheless, there are undeniably some real costs involved in such evasions

---

[18] Needless to say, like all cartels enforced by government regulation, this scheme was sold as in the public interest to eliminate "unsound, ruinous competition."

which could be eliminated by repeal of the cartel legislation. Similar results apply for time deposits whenever the Fed sets the maximum explicit interest rate payable on time deposits below the competitive level.

As was noted previously, one of the most efficient ways to evade the prohibition on demand deposit interest is to officially maintain only a small working balance in the demand deposit and to shift in and out of time deposits as required.

As can be easily imagined, there are no official data gathered on the true interest rates paid on demand deposits nor on time deposits when the maximum rate is below the competitive rate. Some estimates are implicit in the national income and product accounts.[19] Others have been made by surveying banks,[20] or estimating the competitive equilibrium interest rate.[21] Each of these techniques has its limitations, so that none can be considered generally satisfactorily.

3.4 BUSINESS FLUCTUATIONS
Introduction

One of the main reasons for studying macroeconomics is that there are times when just about everything seems to go wrong. Real income drops quarter after quarter and so does employment. About the only thing that seems to go up is the unemployment rate. This general reversal of the normal growth of the economy is called a *contraction* or more popularly a *recession*. A particularly severe contraction is known as a *depression*. The more usual case of general growth in economic activity is called an *expansion*.

The National Bureau of Economic Research (NBER) is an independent research organization which has pioneered much of the basic collection and analysis of data on business fluctuations. The NBER found it useful to establish consistent dates for expansions and contractions so that the cyclical behavior of the economy could be consistently analyzed. These dates have been universally accepted and it is the NBER—not some government agency—that "officially" declares the beginning and end of a recession.

Business fluctuations have been traditionally called *business cycles*. This name arose because at times there appears to be a regular alternation of expansions and contractions. Nevertheless this pattern of expansion and contraction has never exhibited the regularity of timing necessary for a true

---

[19] See p. 19.
[20] Robert J. Barro and Anthony M. Santomero, Household Money Holdings and the Demand Deposit Rate, *Journal of Money, Credit, and Banking*, **4**: 397–413, May 1972.
[21] Benjamin Klein, Competitive Interest Payments on Bank Deposits and the Long-Run Demand for Money, *American Economic Review*, **64**: 931–49, Dec. 1974; and Michael R. Darby. The Allocation of Transitory Income Among Consumer Assets, *American Economic Review*, **62**: 928–41, Dec. 1972.

"cycle." For example, complete "cycles" of a contraction and expansion have been as short as $1\frac{1}{2}$ years and as long as over 8 years. Nor are business fluctuations self-generating, with each phase caused by the preceding phase. Nevertheless the use of "cycle" for "fluctuation" is well established in the macroeconomic literature and will be used similarly here.

The NBER's Classification Method

The NBER chronology of expansions and contractions consists of a list of the months and years in which an expansion ends and a contraction begins and in which a contraction ends and an expansion begins. An expansion and the successive contraction is called a *reference cycle*. The month in which an expansion ends and a contraction begins is called a *reference cycle peak*. The month in which a contraction ends and an expansion begins is called a *reference cycle trough*.

Whether the economy is in an expansion or a contraction, some specific measures of economic activity will increase and others will decrease. The NBER has chosen as reference cycle peaks those months in which the majority of measures turn from increasing to decreasing and vice versa for reference cycle troughs. It is of course true that these many individual measures will normally change direction only when real income changes direction. Using the consensus of individual measures instead of examining only real income is done for two reasons: (1) Real income is available only quarterly and the use of measures available monthly permits finer dating. (2) The use of many measures obviates the possibility that disaster in one or two industries (e.g., a crop failure) which reduces total real income will be counted as a reference cycle unless its effects spread throughout the economy. Despite this careful distinction, it is true that real income has never declined for *more* than one quarter without fulfilling this criterion for a contraction nor increased without fulfilling the criterion for the onset of an expansion.[22]

Figure 3.1 illustrates the business cycle chronology for the postwar period. This figure graphs real income, the unemployment rate, and an index of industrial production. The periods of contraction are shaded. Note that the scale of the unemployment rate is inverted since an increase in the unemployment rate indicates a decrease in economic activity. Thus expansions are characterized by increasing real income and industrial production and falling or low unemployment rates. Contractions are characterized by decreasing real income and industrial production and rising or high unemployment rates. Many other series could be illustrated with similar results,

---

[22] Excluded here are spurious falls in reported real income when the official price index rises rapidly due to the removal of price controls. The catch-up of the official index with economic reality caused a drop in reported real income of almost 13 percent from 1945 to 1947, a period classified as an expansion by the NBER. A similar aberration in the official data occurred in the first half of 1974. See Chap. 10 for details.

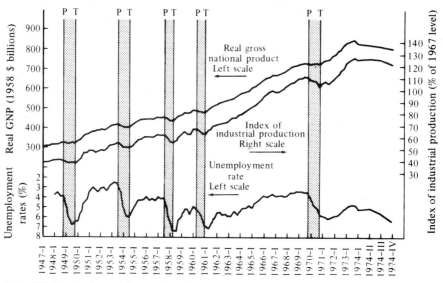

FIGURE 3.1 Business cycles as reflected in real GNP industrial production and unemployment.
NBER reference cycle peaks are indicated by a P and troughs by a T. Contractions (shaded)
are marked by falling real GNP and industrial production and by rising unemployment rates
(scale inverted). Expansions have generally rising real income and industrial production and
falling or low unemployment rates.

but these adequately suggest why macroeconomists are interested in explaining
business fluctuations.

Growth Fluctuations

The criterion that the majority of indicators of economic activity be decreasing
during a contraction conceals fluctuations which are similar in type but less
severe than the officially recognized contractions. This concealment occurs
because in the United States economic activity normally grows. Slower-than-
normal growth reduces real income and employment relative to what they
would have been and the unemployment rate rises, as for example during
the latter part of 1959 and again during 1962.

A related difficulty with the NBER's reference cycle approach is that the
economy will be characterized by slower-than-normal growth before a peak
and after a trough. So if contractions were measured by less than normal
growth, they would be somewhat longer and expansions would be somewhat
shorter than on the NBER definition.

When business fluctuations are analyzed in Part 3 of this book, it will
appear that comparison of economic activity with its normal or trend level
is the more useful approach. At the NBER, Ilse Mintz has experimented

with an alternative chronology based on growth fluctuations. Nevertheless, the standard NBER chronology doubtless still serves as a useful frame of reference for discussing both the broad and detailed features of business fluctuations.

□ **SUMMARY**

Nominal income as measured in current dollar values is an imperfect measure of economic activity because it confounds increases in the average output of real goods and services with increases in their average prices. Economists solve this problem by dividing nominal income into indices of real income and the price level. These indices are defined relative to an arbitrary base year. Real income is measured in units of the average quantities of final goods and services which could be bought with $1 in the base year (or base-year dollars $R\$$). The price index is measured in units of the cost in current dollars per base-year dollar. The age-eligible population is divided into the civilian labor force, members of the armed services, and persons not in the labor force. A monthly survey is used to allocate people between the civilian labor force and persons not in the labor force. The civilian labor force is made up of the employed (people with a job) and the unemployed (those available for and seeking work). The unemployment rate is the ratio of the number unemployed to the civilian labor force. Money is a particular type of asset or form of wealth. Money is those assets actually used to make ultimate payment for goods, services, and debts. In the United States, money is measured in two alternative ways: The narrow money supply (M_1) is currency, coin, and demand deposits held by the nonbank public. The broad money supply M_2 is M_1 plus time deposits at commercial banks, with the exception of large negotiable certificates of deposit. The money supply is a multiple of the base money issued by the federal government. Base money is equal to coin and currency plus deposits at the Federal Reserve System. Explicit interest payments are prohibited on demand deposits and limited on time deposits; so banks pay interest in indirect ways such as free services, reduced loan rates, and classifying part of demand deposits as interest-paying time deposits. The National Bureau of Economic Research (NBER) defines a contraction as a period of time during which a majority of specific indicators of economic activity are declining. An expansion is a period in which most of these indicators are rising. Expansions are characterized by rising real income and industrial production and low or declining rates of unemployment. Contractions are characterized by falling real income and industrial production and high or rising rates of unemployment. An alternative way of viewing business fluctuations compares economic activity with its normal or trend level.

☐ QUESTIONS AND EXERCISES

1 In an economy with only two final commodities, the following data are observed:

	Commodity 1		Commodity 2	
Year	Quantity	Price, $	Quantity	Price, $
1	1000	1.00	2000	2.00
2	1100	0.80	1900	2.25

Use year 1 as the base year. Compute nominal income, real income, and the price level for years 1 and 2 using base-year prices and current quantities to compute real income. Do the same for base-year quantities and current prices to compute the price level.

*2 (a) Complete the following table:

Year	Y_t	y_t	P_t
1	1000.00		1.000
2	1102.50		1.050
3	1212.75	1050.00	
4	1210.00		1.100

(b) Which year has the highest nominal income? Which year has the highest real income? Which year has the highest price level?

(c) The data listed for Y_t are measured in billions of dollars. In what units are the y_t data measured? The P_t data?

3 The wholesale price index is estimated from data on many more commodities than is the consumer price index, yet the CPI is a broader index than is the WPI. In what sense is "broader" used in this statement?

4 If the age-eligible population of 150,000,000 can be divided into 3,000,000 in the armed forces, 85,000,000 employed, 5,000,000 unemployed, and 57,000,000 not in the labor force, what is the unemployment rate?

5 Suggested adjustments to the number unemployed include subtraction of job vacancies, addition of "unemployed equivalents" for people working part-time or in different jobs than desired, inclusion of "discouraged workers" who do not seek work only because they do not believe there are any jobs at an acceptable wage, and exclusion of those who have refused a job offer. Can you see problems of interpretation and data collection in any of these suggestions?

*6 Can a person with a $10,000 per year income have more money than a person with a $100,000 per year income? Why or why not?

7 Some economists have argued that in some sense credit card accounts (in the amount of the credit limit) are money because they are used to purchase goods and services. A credit card purchase is an exchange of goods and services for a debt (promise to pay) of the cardholder. In what sense is a credit card line of credit not general purchasing power? Does signing a credit card slip make or order an ultimate payment?

8 If a particular bank has deposits included in the money supply of $100 million and holds $14 million in reserves (deposits at the Fed plus vault cash), how much money can this bank be said to have created? What is the meaning of "created" here?

9 (*a*) The cash-deposit ratio is 0.3, the reserve-deposit ratio is 0.2, and base money is $100 billion. How much is the money multiplier? The money supply?

(*b*) Assume that the Fed increases reserve requirements and the reserve-deposit ratio rises to 0.25, other things staying the same. How much is the money multiplier? The money supply?

□ **REFERENCES FOR FURTHER READING**

The references to Chap. 2 also deal with the concepts discussed in Sec. 3.1.

Burger, Albert E.: *The Money Supply Process*, Belmont, Calif.: Wadsworth, 1971.

Jordan, Jerry L.: Elements of Money Stock Determination, *Federal Reserve Bank of St. Louis Review*, **51** (10):10–19, Oct. 1969.

Mintz, Ilse: *Dating Postwar Business Cycles*, New York: NBER, 1969.

Mitchell, Wesley C.: *What Happens During Business Cycles: A Progress Report*, New York: NBER, 1951.

Moore, Geoffrey H.: *How Full is Full Employment? And Other Essays on Interpreting the Unemployment Statistics*, Washington: American Enterprise Institute for Public Policy Research, 1973.

(The money supply process is analyzed at greater length in any recent textbook designed for a course in money and banking. More elaborate models are found in the first two references.)

Analytical Tools

4.1 MATHEMATICAL CONCEPTS

Many quantitative variables were introduced in Chaps. 2 and 3. In order to understand their interrelationships considerable care and rigor in thought is required. At times, mathematical expressions are necessary to maintain the required clarity. Fortunately all the main points of macroeconomics as discussed in this book can be understood with the use of only high school algebra and a few special techniques or "tricks of the trade" explained in this chapter. These techniques are essentially ways of describing or illustrating macroeconomic variables so that their interrelationships are easier to see and understand.

Sections 4.1 and 4.2 explain most of the mathematical and graphical tools used in the rest of this book. Some of these are applied in the discussions in Secs. 4.3 and 4.4, but others will not be used until Parts 2 and 3. Students with a very good mathematical background will only need to review this section for notational definitions. But most students will find it useful to work through the examples now and refer back to this material when a concept is used in the later analysis of macroeconomic problems.

Stocks and Flows

Most basic macroeconomic variables are classified as either stocks or flows. A *stock* variable is an amount measured without time dimensions. A *flow* variable is an amount measured per unit of time. The value of a stock variable at a particular time of a particular day could be calculated by actually totaling the amounts of things measured by that variable which exist at that time and date. Examples would be the age-eligible population and the money stock. Flows occur over time and can only be observed by measurements made over a period of time. Real and nominal income and saving are examples of flows being total amounts per period.

National income accountants measure income over quarterly intervals, but report income and its components at annual rates. This is equivalent to observing that someone drove 10 miles in 15 minutes or drove at a speed of

40 miles *per hour*. Income is reported in per annum terms by dividing the total purchases of final goods and services made in 3 months by $\frac{1}{4}$ ($\frac{3}{12} = \frac{1}{4}$). This converts the quarterly totals into amounts easily comparable with annual totals or any other periods converted into annual rates.

In this book, the year will be used as the standard unit of time. Flows are computed by dividing periodic totals by the period expressed in years. Shorter observations reduce both numerator and denominator proportionally; so shorter periods neither increase or decrease flows expressed at annual rates. It simplifies many problems to be able to discuss flow variables at a specific point in time rather than over a period of time. This would be roughly the same thing as the current reading on the speedometer in the automobile example. This is done formally by assuming that the period of observation is an arbitrarily small period of time h beginning at the particular instant in question. The income actually measured over a quarter is simply the average of all these instantaneous measures of incomes. In the same way, if you drive 30 minutes with the speedometer reading 10 miles per hour and 30 minutes with the speedometer reading 20 miles per hour, you will actually cover the average number of miles, 15 ($10 \times \frac{1}{2} + 20 \times \frac{1}{2} = 15$), in 1 hour.

Comparing Values of Macroeconomic Variables

Macroeconomic problems often involve measuring differences between values of a particular variable, such as the stock of money or nominal income. These comparisons may be of the value at one time to a value at a later time or of the value which would occur under one hypothetical set of conditions to the value which would occur under alternative conditions. Comparisons of values which would occur at the same instant under alternative conditions are the easiest, because no allowance need be made for the passage of time. These comparisons will be discussed first.

The simplest way of describing differences between two alternative values of variables is simply to subtract one from the other, such as $M_t^2 - M_t^1$. This *algebraic difference* is measured in the same units as the variable being considered. This can be awkward when the variable is an index and the units are arbitrary and difficult to interpret. The algebraic difference does not provide information about whether the difference between the two values is large or small.

An alternative technique which eliminates units and measures the relative size of the difference is to take the ratio of one variable to the other, such as M_t^2/M_t^1. One or the other set of conditions can be chosen as the base for such comparisons. The ratios of values under alternate conditions (denoted by "2" here) to values under base conditions ("1") for many variables often can be usefully related.

For variables which are always positive, a third measure is widely used. The *proportionate difference* of any variable a_t^2 from a_t^1 is their ratio minus 1.

When the proportionate difference is quoted in percentage points, it is also called the *percentage difference*. Note that the proportionate difference can also be defined as the algebraic difference divided by the base value used for comparison:

$$\frac{a_t^2 - a_t^1}{a_t^1} = \frac{a_t^2}{a_t^1} - 1 \qquad\qquad [4.1]$$

A specific example may help to distinguish these concepts. Suppose $M_t^1 = \$200$ billion and $M_t^2 = \$220$ billion. The algebraic difference is $220 billion $- \$200$ billion $= \$20$ billion. Their ratio is $220 billion/$200 billion $= 1.1$. The proportionate difference between M_t^2 and M_t^1 is $1.1 - 1 = 0.1$ (or $20 billion/$200 billion $= 0.1$). This is a percentage difference of 10 percent ($0.1 = 10$ percent).

Functional Relationships

Much of the content of any science is contained in functional relationships which detail how one variable is dependent on (determined by) one or more other variables. In economics, the functional relationships are generalizations about aggregate human behavior. If any variable a_t is a function of the variables b_t, c_t, and d_t, say, this is written as

$$a_t = f(b_t, c_t, d_t) \qquad\qquad [4.2]$$

The *value* of the function $f(\ )$ is a_t, and b_t, c_t, and d_t are its *arguments*. Often the function is denoted by the same letter as the variable which it determines:

$$a_t = a(b_t, c_t, d_t) \qquad\qquad [4.3]$$

A comparison often made by economists concerns the difference in a_t when one of the arguments, say b_t, of the function $a(\ )$ differs by a small amount from original base conditions and all other arguments are constant. This comparison is often made in terms of the algebraic differences $a_t^2 - a_t^1$ and $b_t^2 - b_t^1$. The comparison is usually expressed by the ratio of the algebraic differences $(a_t^2 - a_t^1)/(b_t^2 - b_t^1)$. For the sort of functions which are met in macroeconomics, the value of this ratio will normally be of the same sign and magnitude regardless of whether b_t^2 is slightly smaller or slightly larger than b_t^1. This is true because if a small increase in b_t, $b_t^2 - b_t^1$, increases a_t by a certain amount, $a_t^2 - a_t^1$, then an equal decrease in b_t, $-(b_t^2 - b_t^1)$, will cause a decrease in a_t of about $-(a_t^2 - a_t^1)$. Since ratios are being compared, the signs cancel out.

$$\frac{-(a_t^2 - a_t^1)}{-(b_t^2 - b_t^1)} = \frac{a_t^2 - a_t^1}{b_t^2 - b_t^1} \qquad\qquad [4.4]$$

In this case, $a_t^2 - a_t^1$ and $b_t^2 - b_t^1$ are both positive; so the ratio is positive.

This is expressed by saying a_t is an *increasing function* of b_t, which means higher values of b_t, other arguments being held constant, will cause higher values of a_t and lower values of b_t will cause lower values of a_t. If increases in b_t, other arguments held constant, cause decreases in a_t and decreases in b_t cause increases in a_t [$(a_t^2 - a_t^1)/(b_t^2 - b_t^1)$ is negative], a_t is a *decreasing function* of b_t.

The simplest numerical example of a function is a linear equation such as

$$a_t = 2b_t + 7c_t - d_t \qquad [4.5]$$

Assume in case 1, $b_t^1 = 5$, $c_t^1 = 2$, $d_t^1 = 1$. Then

$$a_t^1 = 2 \times 5 + 7 \times 2 - 1 = 23$$

In case 2, let $b_t^2 = 5.1$. This comparison is made for other arguments constant, so $c_t^2 = c_t^1 = 2$ and $d_t^2 = d_t^1 = 1$. Therefore

$$a_t^2 = 2 \times 5.1 + 7 \times 2 - 1 = 23.2$$

The ratio of the algebraic differences is

$$\frac{a_t^2 - a_t^1}{b_t^2 - b_t^1} = \frac{23.2 - 23}{5.1 - 5.0} = \frac{.2}{.1} = 2 \qquad [4.6]$$

If instead, $b_t^2 = 4.9$, then $a_t^2 = 2 \times 4.9 + 7 \times 2 - 1 = 22.8$, and

$$\frac{a_t^2 - a_t^1}{b_t^2 - b_t^1} = \frac{22.8 - 23}{4.9 - 5.0} = \frac{-.2}{-.1} = 2 \qquad [4.7]$$

For linear equations, this ratio of algebraic differences is always exactly equal to the coefficient of the argument under consideration (in this case, 2). Other functional forms are more difficult computationally and the exact equality of the ratio of algebraic differences regardless of whether the argument increases or decreases holds only for arbitrarily small changes in the argument. These computations are straightforward for those familiar with calculus, but are not required for understanding the material in this book.

Frequently the arguments of a function are of much different magnitude or even different units than is the value of the function. Suppose for example that b_t was measured in base-year dollars and a_t was measured in current dollars. In this case, the coefficient of b_t in the linear equation [4.5] will have units and would be written in full as \$2/R\$. The ratio of the algebraic differences will also be \$2/R\$. Note that an increase in b_t from 5 to 5.1 is a percentage increase of 2 percent while the resulting increase in a_t from 23 to 23.2 is only 0.87 percent. In some cases, it is desirable to have an alternative measure of the effect of an argument on the value of a function—a measure which is both free of units and assesses the relative changes in value and argument: The *elasticity of a_t with respect to b_t* is the proportionate difference in a_t divided by the proportionate difference in b_t for very small changes in b_t and with all other arguments constant:

$$\eta_{a, b} = \frac{(a_t{}^2 - a_t{}^1)/a_t{}^1}{(b_t{}^2 - b_t{}^1)/b_t{}^1} \qquad b_t{}^2 - b_t{}^1 \text{ very small} \qquad [4.8]$$

The symbol $\eta_{a, b}$ is used to denote the elasticity of the value a_t with respect to the argument b_t. Since $\eta_{a, b}$ need not be constant for all values of the arguments of $a(\quad)$,[1] the values of the arguments at which the elasticity is computed are sometimes noted as $\eta_{a, b}(b_t, c_t, d_t)$. For the numerical example

$$\eta_{a, b}(5, 2, 1) \approx \frac{0.0087}{0.0200} = 0.435 \qquad [4.9]$$

The approximately equals sign ($\approx$) is used because a change of 0.1 is only approximately "very small."

The Use of Logarithms

Logarithms are used for two distinct purposes: computation and scaling. Most students will recall having been exposed to a confusing mass of eminently forgettable detail on the use of logarithms in performing calculations. These details may remain forgotten so far as this book is concerned. The use of logarithms for scaling data avoids a great deal of mathematical complexity, however, so that technique will be explained here.

If a_t is positive, it can be written as another number greater than 1 raised to some power. That is, if e is greater than 1, it is possible to find a number z_t such that

$$a_t = e^{z_t} \qquad [4.10]$$

This is also written as

$$\log_e a_t = z_t \qquad [4.11]$$

Any number greater than 1 would do, but there is one that arises naturally in many important applications, and so it will be used exclusively in this book. This number is in fact called e; it is the base of natural logarithms and has a value of $2.71828\ldots$[2] The notation will be simplified by dropping the indication of the base e:[3]

$$\log a_t = \log_e a_t \qquad [4.12]$$

The value of $\log a_t$ increases as a_t increases so that one and only one value

---

[1] Indeed it is not constant for linear functions, as in [4.5].
[2] Like the number $\pi = 3.14159\ldots$, e is found in the solutions to many different kinds of real-world problems.
[3] Natural logarithms are indicated by some authors as ln a_t. Since no other bases are used, the notation "log a_t" is generally used in economics.

of log a_t corresponds to every (positive) value of a_t. The definition of logarithms implies that log $1 = 0$, and that numbers smaller than 1 have negative logarithms and numbers greater than 1 have positive logarithms.[4]

Three very useful properties of logarithms are

1 If $a_t = b_t c_t$, then log $a_t =$ log $b_t +$ log c_t.

2 If $a_t = b_t/c_t$, then log $a_t =$ log $b_t -$ log c_t.

3 If $a_t = b_t{}^{c_t}$, then log $a_t = c_t$ log b_t.

A great many macroeconomic relationships are multiplicative or involve ratios. Converting these relationships by taking logarithms permits a discussion of a simple linear relationship. This especially simplifies graphical illustrations. Graphing log a_t instead of a_t is simply a rescaling to different units similar to converting data collected in $ billion to units of $ trillion. The major difference is that the logarithmic transformation of the units converts the data so that if the ratio of two values, say $a_t{}^2/a_t{}^1$, is a certain number, say λ, the algebraic difference of their logarithms (the *logarithmic difference*) will be a constant log λ whatever the value of $a_t{}^1$. This occurs because

$$\log a_t{}^2 - \log a_t{}^1 = \log \frac{a_t{}^2}{a_t{}^1} = \log \lambda \qquad [4.13]$$

Graphs of the logarithms of values are said to have *ratio scales* because of this fact.

It so happens that if λ is close to 1 (say $0.8 \leq \lambda \leq 1.2$), then

$$\log \lambda \approx \lambda - 1 \qquad [4.14]$$

This convenient approximation is illustrated in Table 4.1 which gives the values of log λ corresponding to selected values of λ. Substitution of [4.14] into [4.13], shows that

$$\log a_t{}^2 - \log a_t{}^1 \approx \frac{a_t{}^2}{a_t{}^1} - 1 \qquad [4.15]$$

for $a_t{}^2/a_t{}^1$ close to 1. The right-hand sides of [4.15] and [4.1] are identical, so that logarithmic differences are an alternative measure of proportionate differences between plus and minus 0.20 (or 20 percent).

This result can be applied immediately to the elasticity of a_t with respect to b_t. Since $b_t{}^2 - b_t{}^1$ is very small (relative to $b_t{}^1$), so $a_t{}^2 - a_t{}^1$ will be very small relative to $a_t{}^1$. Since the elasticity is a ratio of small proportionate differences

$$\eta_{a, b} = \frac{(a_t{}^2 - a_t{}^1)/a_t{}^1}{(b_t{}^2 - b_t{}^1)/b_t{}^1} = \frac{\log a_t{}^2 - \log a_t{}^1}{\log b_t{}^2 - \log b_t{}^1} \qquad b_t{}^2 - b_t{}^1 \text{ very small} \qquad [4.16]$$

---

[4] This is based on the facts that $e^0 = 1$ and $e^{-a_t} = 1/e^{a_t}$.

TABLE 4.1   Values of log λ

λ	log λ	$\lambda - 1$	λ	log λ	$\lambda - 1$
0.10	−2.3026	−0.90	1.01	0.0099	0.01
0.50	−0.6932	−0.50	1.02	0.0198	0.02
0.80	−0.2231	−0.20	1.03	0.0296	0.03
0.85	−0.1625	−0.15	1.04	0.0392	0.04
0.90	−0.1054	−0.10	1.05	0.0488	0.05
0.91	−0.0954	−0.09	1.06	0.0583	0.06
0.92	−0.0845	−0.08	1.07	0.0677	0.07
0.93	−0.0726	−0.07	1.08	0.0770	0.08
0.94	−0.0619	−0.06	1.09	0.0862	0.09
0.95	−0.0513	−0.05	1.10	0.0953	0.10
0.96	−0.0408	−0.04	1.15	0.1398	0.15
0.97	−0.0305	−0.03	1.20	0.1823	0.20
0.98	−0.0202	−0.02	2.00	0.6932	1.00
0.99	−0.0101	−0.01	10.00	2.3026	9.00
1.00	0.0000	0.00			

This is convenient if the function relating a_t to b_t and other variables is linear in the logarithms. An example would be

$$a_t = \frac{(b_t)^3 (c_t)^2}{d_t} \tag{4.17}$$

Taking logarithms, this becomes

$$\log a_t = 3 \log b_t + 2 \log c_t - \log d_t \tag{4.18}$$

Since this is a linear equation the ratio of the algebraic difference in $\log a_t$ to the algebraic difference in $\log b_t$ is equal to the coefficient of $\log b_t$:

$$\frac{\log a_t^2 - \log a_t^1}{\log b_t^2 - \log b_t^1} = 3$$

Only if $\log a_t$ is a linear function of $\log b_t$, is the elasticity of a with respect to b a constant regardless of the values of the arguments of the function determining a_t.

4.2   CHANGES OVER TIME
Description of Variables Over Time

Most macroeconomic analysis is concerned with comparative dynamic or dynamic adjustment problems. That is, macroeconomic problems usually analyze the behavior of key aggregates *over time*. Extensions of the techniques discussed so far are essential to the analysis of these problems.

The values of economic variables over time can be illustrated either in graphical or tabular form. Figure 4.1 shows an example of how any variable, say a_t, can be represented by a graph. The horizontal scale or axis measures time in years. The beginning of each year is indicated by the date. The vertical scale measures the value of a_t. At the beginning of 1970, the value of a_t (a_{1970}) is 2.00. By the beginning of 1975, the value of a_t (a_{1975}) has increased to about 2.88. The great advantage of the graphical presentation is that important features of the behavior of the variable, such as the decline during 1971 are immediately obvious.

Data are not available on a continuous basis, however. Instead, observations of a_t are available only at particular intervals, such as quarterly. These observations may be either the actual value at particular dates a fixed interval apart, or average values over periods of a fixed length. So graphs constructed from periodically gathered data can only approximately represent the true value of the variable between observations. Of course, more frequent observations increase both the accuracy with which a_t is represented and the annual cost of gathering data.

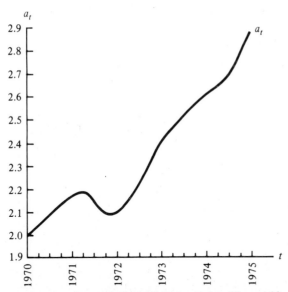

FIGURE 4.1 **Example of graphical presentation of the variable** a_t **over the period 1970–1975.** The horizontal scale or axis measures time. The beginning of each year is noted below this scale. The vertical scale or axis measures the value of a_t. The value of a_t at any instant of time t^* is found by finding t^* on the horizontal axis, locating the point on the graph of a_t directly above t^* and then reading its value from the vertical scale. If, for example, t^* were 1973, this procedure would indicate that a_{t^*} is about 2.41.

The values of a_t at a particular interval can be presented as in Table 4.2. This form of presentation of actual observations allows more exact numerical calculations, but it is harder to keep particular values in perspective with a table than with a graph.

A third way to present the variable a_t is by graphing log a_t as in Fig. 4.2. The vertical scale at the left is divided numerically in the usual manner—equal distances represent equal algebraic differences. The vertical scale on the right is marked according to equal algebraic differences in the value of a_t. The distances decrease as the value of a_t increases because 0.1 is a smaller proportionate increase the higher is the value of a_t. The graphs in this book will usually have only the left-hand vertical scale. Some authors present the right-hand vertical scale instead, sometimes omitting entirely the word "log" and heading the scale "ratio scale."

Measures of Change Over Time

As with measuring differences between alternative values at the same time, it is valuable to have standardized techniques for describing changes in values over time. The simplest measure of change in any variable a_t from time t to time $t + h$ is the *algebraic change* $a_{t+h} - a_t$. The algebraic change in a variable from t to $t + h$ will be measured in the same units as the variable itself.

Algebraic changes in a variable at different times and in different variables are comparable only if identical periods between beginning and ending dates are used. This is not always convenient, especially when observations are collected with different frequencies. *Algebraic changes at annual rates* are computed by dividing the algebraic change by the period in years over which the change is computed

$$\frac{a_{t+h} - a_t}{h} \qquad\qquad [4.19]$$

The algebraic change at annual rates of a variable is measured in the units of the variable per annum.

Consider for example the data in Table 4.2. Assume for this example that the data are measured in $ billion. The algebraic change a_t from 1970.00 (the beginning of 1970) to 1970.25 (the beginning of the second quarter of 1970) is

$$a_{1970.25} - a_{1970.00} = \$2.04 \text{ billion} - \$2.00 \text{ billion} = \$0.04 \text{ billion}$$

The algebraic change at annual rates is

$$(a_{1970.25} - a_{1970.00})/0.25 \text{ year} = \$0.04 \text{ billion}/.25 \text{ year} = \$0.16 \text{ billion/year}$$

So the algebraic change over the first quarter of 1970 is at an annual rate of $0.16 billion/year.

Proportionate changes are computed to obtain the relative size of the change

TABLE 4.2   Example of tabular presentation of the variable a_t over the period 1970–1974

t	a_t	t	a_t
1970.00	2.0000	1972.75	2.3169
1970.25	2.0400	1973.00	2.4096
1970.50	2.0808	1973.25	2.4578
1970.75	2.1224	1973.50	2.5069
1971.00	2.1649	1973.75	2.5571
1971.25	2.1865	1974.00	2.6082
1971.50	2.1428	1974.25	2.6343
1971.75	2.0999	1974.50	2.6870
1972.00	2.0999	1974.75	2.7676
1972.25	2.1629	1975.00	2.8783
1972.50	2.2278		

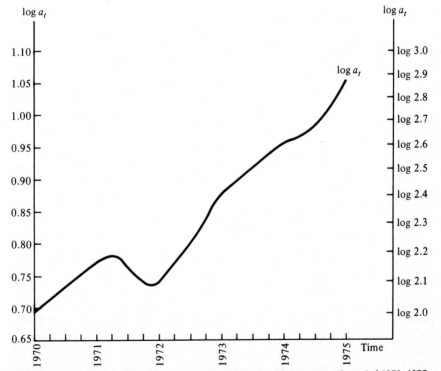

FIGURE 4.2   Example of graphical presentation of the variable log a_t over the period 1970–1975.
The left-hand vertical scale measures the numerical value of log a_t in the usual manner: equal
distances are equal quantities. The right-hand scale is marked according to equal algebraic
differences in a_t. Since logarithmic difference is approximately the algebraic difference divided
by the level of a_t, these markings come closer together as one reads up the scale. Normally,
only one of the two vertical scales will be presented. If the word *log* is omitted before the
values of a_t in the right-hand type of scale, this is noted by the heading *Ratio Scale*.

independent of the units of the particular variable. The *proportionate change* in any variable a_t from t to $t + h$ is algebraic change divided by the initial value:

$$\frac{a_{t+h} - a_t}{a_t} \qquad\qquad [4.20]$$

Proportionate changes are measured as pure numbers (no units). A proportionate change quoted in percentage points is also known as a percentage change.

In order to ease comparability and interpretation, proportionate changes are converted to annual rates. The *proportionate change at annual rates* in any variable a_t is computed by dividing the proportionate change by the period in years over which the change is computed:

$$\frac{a_{t+h} - a_t}{a_t \times h} \qquad\qquad [4.21]$$

Proportionate changes at annual rates are measured in per annum units. They are sometimes quoted in percentage points as *percentage changes at annual rates*.

Refer again to the data in Table 4.2. The proportionate change in a_t from 1970.00 to 1970.25 is

$$\frac{\$2.04 \text{ billion} - \$2.00 \text{ billion}}{\$2.00 \text{ billion}} = \frac{\$0.04 \text{ billion}}{\$2.00 \text{ billion}} = 0.02$$

The percentage change at annual rates from 1970.00 to 1970.25 is 0.02/0.25 year = 0.08/year = 8 percent per annum. Note that the expression [4.21] implies that the proportionate change at annual rates can also be computed as the algebraic change at annual rates divided by the initial value. For this example, that would be ($0.16 billion/year)/$2.00 billion = 0.08/year.

Carrying the example forward to the next quarter's algebraic change

$$a_{1970.50} - a_{1970.25} = \$2.0808 \text{ billion} - \$2.04 \text{ billion} = \$0.0408 \text{ billion}$$

The algebraic change at annual rates is $0.0408 billion/0.25 year = $0.1632 billion/year. Both exceed the corresponding values for the previous quarter of $0.04 billion and $0.16 billion/year. The proportionate change is $0.0408 billion/$2.04 billion = 0.02. The proportionate change at annual rates is 0.02/0.25 year = 0.08 per year. The proportionate changes and proportionate changes at annual rates are identical for the two quarters, but not the corresponding algebraic changes. This is because the increase in a_t during the first quarter means that the algebraic change must be larger during the second quarter to equal the same fraction of a_t at the beginning of the second quarter.

If a_t and a_{t+h} are close in value, the proportionate change in a_t can be measured approximately as the logarithmic change:

$$\frac{a_{t+h} - a_t}{a_t} \approx \log a_{t+h} - \log a_t \qquad [4.22]$$

The reason this approximation works was explained for [4.15]. Similarly, the proportionate change at annual rates can be approximated by the logarithmic change divided by the period in years over which the change is computed:

$$\frac{a_{t+h} - a_t}{a_t \times h} \approx \frac{\log a_{t+h} - \log a_t}{h} \qquad [4.23]$$

The quality of these approximations can be illustrated easily. The proportionate change from 1970.00 to 1970.25 is approximately $\log 2.04 - \log 2.00 = \log (2.04/2.00) = \log 1.02 = 0.0198$ (from Table 4.1). The proportionate change at annual rates is therefore approximately $0.0198/0.25$ year $= 0.0792$. These values are quite close to the exact values of 0.02 and 0.08. The approximation improves as the ratio a_{t+h}/a_t nears the value of 1.

The two concepts of change most commonly used are the algebraic change at annual rates and the proportionate change at annual rates. They have simple geometric interpretations. The algebraic change at annual rates is the slope of the triangle with h as the base and $a_{t+h} - a_t$ as the height. This is illustrated in Fig. 4.3, which is an enlargement of Fig. 4.1 for the period 1970.00 through 1972.00. The slope of the graph of a_t between 1970.25 and 1970.50, for example, is the height divided by the base of the right triangle constructed at those points ($0.0408 billion/0.25 year = $0.1632 billion/year). The corresponding triangle between 1971.50 and 1971.75 is inverted because a_t decreases. The slope is negative whenever a_t decreases, in this case $-$0.0429 billion/0.25 year $= -$0.1716 billion/year. The proportionate change at annual rates is (approximately) the slope of the graph of $\log a_t$ between t and $t + h$. This is illustrated in Fig. 4.4. The slope of $\log a_t$ between 1970.25 and 1970.50 is $0.0198/0.25$ year $= 0.0792/$year ≈ 8 percent per annum. The slope of $\log a_t$ between 1971.50 and 1971.75 is $-0.0202/0.25$ year $= -0.0808/$year ≈ -8 percent per annum.

Instantaneous Measures of Changes

It often simplifies problems to analyze algebraic and proportionate changes at annual rates for a specific point in time rather than over a period of time. This is done in the same way that instantaneous rates are defined for flow variables: The time period h is chosen to be arbitrarily small. These instantaneous measures of changes are given special names.

The *rate of change* in any variable a_t at time t is the algebraic change at

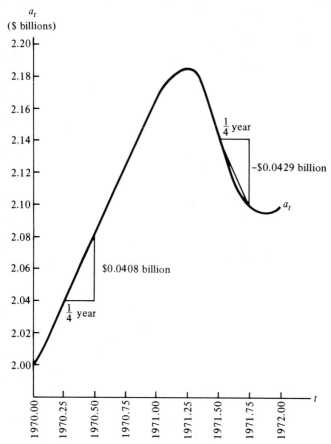

FIGURE 4.3   Enlarged detail of Fig. 4.1 illustrating graphical interpretation of algebraic change at annual rates. The algebraic change at annual rates between t and $t + h$ is the slope of the graph of a_t between t and $t + h$. For 1970.25 to 1970.50 ($h = 0.25$ year), this is $\$0.0408/0.25$ year = $\$0.1632$/year. For 1971.50 to 1971.75, this is $-\$0.0429/0.25$ year = $-\$0.1716$/year. This slope is an average over the specified interval as can be seen over the interval from 1971.50 to 1971.75, where the actual values of a_t depart significantly for a while from the straight line connecting $a_{1971.50}$ and $a_{1971.75}$.

annual rates from t to $t + h$ where h is arbitrarily small. The rate of change in any variable a_t is denoted by Δa_t;[5] so

$$\Delta a_t = \frac{a_{t+h} - a_t}{h} \qquad h \text{ arbitrarily small} \qquad [4.24]$$

---

[5] Those familiar with calculus will observe that $\Delta a_t = da_t/dt$.

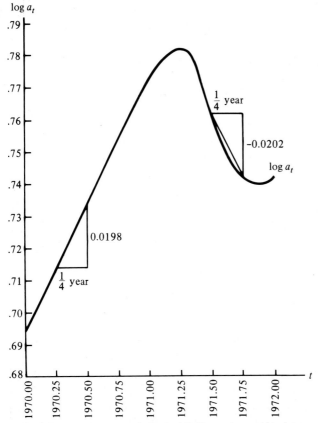

**FIGURE 4.4   Enlarged detail of Fig. 4.2 illustrating graphical inter-
pretation of proportionate change at annual rate.** The graphical
interpretation of proportionate changes at annual rates is based on
the fact that logarithmic differences approximately equal proportionate differences. Therefore, the algebraic change at annual rates in
$\log a_t$ will approximately equal the proportionate change at annual
rates in a_t. For example, from 1970.25 to 1970.50, the proportionate
change at annual rates is $0.0198/0.25$ year $= 0.0792$/year and from
1971.50 to 1971.75 is $-0.0202/0.25$ year $= -0.0808$/year.

The difference between the rate of change in a_t and the algebraic change at
annual rates can be best illustrated by example. The algebraic change at annual
rates from 1970.00 to 1971.00 is

($2.1649 billion − $2.00 billion)/year = $0.1649 billion/year

The algebraic change at annual rates from 1970.00 to 1970.50 is

($2.0808 billion − $2.00 billion)/0.50 year = $0.1616 billion/year

TABLE 4.3 Algebraic changes at annual rates from a_{1970} to a_{1970+h}

h, year	$\dfrac{a_{1970+h} - a_{1970}\dagger}{h}$
1.0000	0.1649
0.5000	0.1616
0.2500	0.1600
0.1250	0.1592
0.0625	0.1588
0.0100	0.1584
0.0010	0.1584
0.0001	0.1584
0.0000	0.1584‡

† In \$ billion/year.
‡ Limiting value for arbitrarily small h = rate of change in a_{1970}.

The algebraic change at annual rates from 1970.00 to 1970.25 is

(\$2.04 billion − \$2.00 billion)/0.25 year = \$0.16 billion/year

These results and others for finer divisions are recorded in Table 4.3. The rate of change in $a_{1970.00}$ is seen to converge to \$0.1584 billion/year. The algebraic change at annual rates over any period is an average of the rate of change in the variable over the period.

The *growth rate* of any variable a_t at time t is the proportionate change at annual rates from t to $t + h$ where h is arbitrarily small. The growth rate of any variable a_t is denoted by g_{at}; so

$$g_{at} = \frac{a_{t+h} - a_t}{a_t h} = \frac{\log a_{t+h} - \log a_t}{h} \qquad h \text{ arbitrarily small} \qquad [4.25]$$

Note that for h arbitrarily small a_{t+h} is arbitrarily close to a_t, thus the second equality is exact rather than an approximation as in [4.23]. Comparing [4.24] and [4.25] provides an equivalent definition of the growth rate g_{at}:[6]

$$g_{at} = \frac{\Delta a_t}{a_t} = \Delta \log a_t \qquad [4.26]$$

The geometric interpretation of the rate of change Δa_t is the slope of the

---

[6] Those familiar with calculus will observe that

$$g_{at} = \frac{1}{a_t}\frac{da_t}{dt} = \frac{d \log a_t}{dt}$$

graph of a_t exactly at time t. The growth rate g_{at} is interpreted as the slope of the graph of log a_t exactly at time t. Six rules relate any line a_t to its slope Δa_t.[7]

1 Whenever a_t is increasing Δa_t is positive.
2 Whenever a_t is decreasing Δa_t is negative.
3 Whenever a_t is neither increasing nor decreasing, Δa_t is zero.
4 If a_t rises more rapidly or falls less rapidly over time, Δa_t rises.
5 If a_t rises less rapidly or falls more rapidly over time, Δa_t falls.
6 If a_t follows a straight line over time, Δa_t is a constant.

These rules are illustrated by Fig. 4.5. From year 0 to year 2 and from year 5 to year 7, a_t is increasing and Δa_t is positive (Rule 1). From year 3 to year 5 and from year 7 to year 9, a_t is decreasing and Δa_t is negative (Rule 2). From year 2 to year 3, and exactly at years 5 and 7, a_t is neither increasing nor decreasing and Δa_t is zero (Rule 3). From year 4 to year 6 and from year 8 to year 9, a_t rises more rapidly or falls less rapidly as time goes on, so Δa_t rises (Rule 4). From year 0 to year 1, from year 3 to year 4, and from year 6 to year 8, a_t rises less rapidly or falls more rapidly as time goes on, so Δa_t falls (Rule 5). From year 1 to year 2, and from year 2 to year 3, a_t follows a straight line and Δa_t is constant (Rule 6). Note that the sudden change in the slope at exactly year 2 is represented by a drop in Δa_t.

The Equation of Constant Growth

Many economic processes are characterized by a constant growth rate. Over any period t_0 to t_1 for which a variable a_t has a constant growth rate $\bar{g}_a$, the value of a_t can be calculated as

$$a_t = a_{t_0} e^{\bar{g}_a(t - t_0)} \qquad [4.27]$$

This is true because taking logarithms yields

$$\log a_t = (\log a_{t_0} - \bar{g}_a t_0) + \bar{g}_a t \qquad [4.28]$$

which is the equation for a straight line with slope ($\Delta \log a_t = g_{at}$) equal to $\bar{g}_a$.

The Growth Rate of a Product

If a variable a_t is the sum of two other variables b_t and c_t ($a_t = b_t + c_t$), then

$$a_{t+h} - a_t = b_{t+h} - b_t + c_{t+h} - c_t \qquad [4.29]$$

---

[7] Note that this a_t may be log b_t.

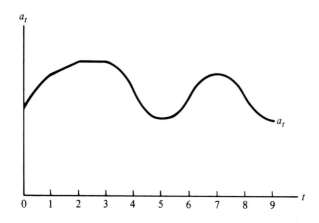

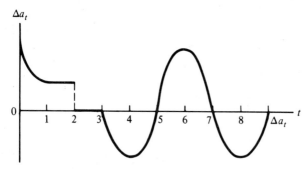

FIGURE 4.5 Illustration of relationship between a_t and Δa_t. The upper panel illustrates the hypothetical behavior of some macroeconomic variable a_t between years 0 and 9. The lower panel illustrates the behavior of the rate of change of a_t, Δa_t, as found by computing the slope of the graph of a_t. The sign of Δa_t indicates whether a_t is rising ($+$), neither rising nor falling ($\Delta a_t = 0$), or falling ($-$). The slope of Δa_t indicates whether the slope of a_t is becoming more positive ($+$), neither more nor less positive [$\Delta(\Delta a_t) = 0$], or less positive ($-$). Note that the abrupt change in the slope of a_t at year 2 causes a corresponding abrupt change in the graph of Δa_t.

Dividing both sides of [4.29] by an arbitrarily small h yields:

$$\Delta a_t = \Delta b_t + \Delta c_t \qquad\qquad [4.30]$$

where $a_t = b_t + c_t$. That is, the rate of change of the sum equals the sum of the rates of change.

Assume instead that a_t is the product of two other variables b_t and c_t ($a_t = b_t c_t$), so that

$$\log a_t = \log b_t + \log c_t \qquad\qquad [4.31]$$

Equation [4.30] applies in this case, therefore

$$\Delta \log a_t = \Delta \log b + \Delta \log c_t \qquad [4.32]$$

By the definition of growth rates

$$g_{at} = g_{bt} + g_{ct} \qquad [4.33]$$

where $a_t = b_t c_t$. That is, *the growth rate of a product is the sum of the growth rates of its factors.* This result makes sense because a 1 percent increase in either b_t or c_t will cause a 1 percent increase in a_t.

4.3 INTEREST RATES
The Interest Rate

The basic concept of the *interest rate r* is the growth rate of an amount of money lent at interest where no payment of principal or interest is made until the end of the loan. That is, the dollar value of a loan and accumulated interest (an asset to a lender and a liability to a borrower) grows at a constant rate r. In interest problems it is customary to date time from 0 at the time of the loan. The dollar value A_t of the loan at time t can be computed (see [4.27]) as

$$A_t = A_0 e^{rt} \qquad [4.34]$$

The interest rate r is also called the force of interest or the continuously compounded interest rate. In later chapters, it will be seen that the continuous growth in the amount of a loan reflects the continuous flow of services from the capital stock which can be financed with a loan.

The fundamental interest equation [4.34] is actually used to compute the amounts due on a variety of loans, the most familiar of which is the continuously compounded savings account. Before the advent of electronic calculators and computers, the explicit use of a formula requiring raising e to a decimal fraction was a formidable chore. Instead, various approximations arose to permit easier calculations of the amounts due. Since these approximations are still in widespread use and require less mathematical background, they will be discussed here in considerable detail. It is important to keep in mind the basic concept of the interest rate as the growth rate of A_t, so that the approximations can be compared against a common standard.

Like all variables with a constant, positive growth rate, the value A_t of a loan grows exponentially as in Fig. 4.6. The figure is drawn from a rate of interest of 10 percent per annum with all interest accumulated and itself earning interest up to time t. Note that the slope ΔA_t steadily increases. This must be the case if $\Delta A_t / A_t$ equals 10 percent, since this implies that

$$\Delta A_t = 0.10 A_t \qquad [4.35]$$

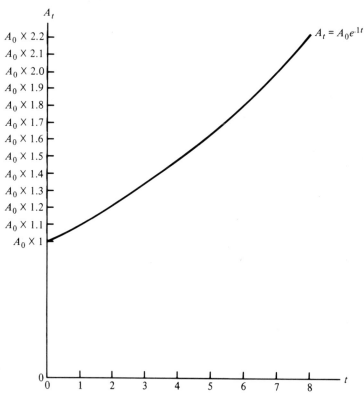

FIGURE 4.6 **Exponential growth of amount** A_t **of an original loan of** A_0 **at interest.**
An amount A_0, lent at interest rate $r = 0.10$/year (10 percent per annum), will grow
as illustrated if interest is accumulated as earned. Note that $(A_1 - A_0) = 0.105A_0$,
that $(A_8 - A_7) = 0.212A_0$, that $(A_1 - A_0)/A_0 = 0.105$, and $(A_8 - A_7)/A_7 = 0.212/$
$2.014 = 0.105$. Thus, the algebraic change at annual rates increases over time as
A_t increases, while the proportionate change at annual rates over 1-year periods
is constant at 0.105/year.

The graph of $\log A_t$ on the other hand is a straight line with slope 0.10
passing through $\log A_0$ (see Fig. 4.7).

The Annually Compounded Interest Rate

Many students feel more familiar with the *annually compounded interest rate*
denoted by r^1. On a loan of A_0 for one year, the amount of principal and
interest repaid at the end of the year is

$$A_1 = (1 + r^1)A_0 \qquad\qquad [4.36]$$

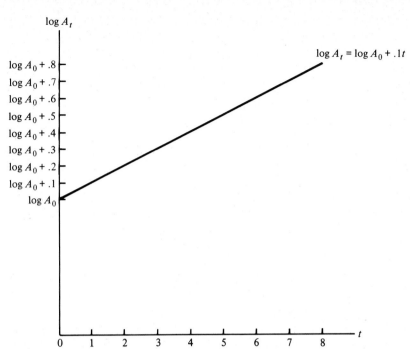

FIGURE 4.7 **Straight-line growth of log A_t for an original loan of A_0 at interest.** An amount A_0, lent at a rate of interest $r = 0.10$/year (10 percent per annum), has a value at time t, whose logarithm will grow at the constant rate r as illustrated.

It can be seen by substituting $t = 1$ into [4.34], that

$$A_0 e^r = (1 + r^1)A_0$$
$$r^1 = e^r - 1$$

[4.37]

So knowledge of the interest rate is sufficient to compute the annually compounded interest rate, and vice versa. For example, if r was known to equal 9.53 percent per annum, Table 4.1 and the fact that $\lambda = e^{\log \lambda}$ can be used to find $r^1 = e^{0.0953} - 1 = 1.10 - 1 = 0.10 = 10$ percent per annum. So a loan of \$100 would require a repayment of $1.10 \times \$100 = \$110$ at the end of a year whether formula [4.34] or [4.36] is used.

Often a loan may extend over a period of several years. The amount of principal and interest due at the end of the first year A_1 is, in effect, lent for a second year. So the amount due at the end of the second year A_2 is equal to $1 + r^1$ times the amount lent at the beginning of the second year A_1:

$$A_2 = (1 + r^1)A_1$$
$$= (1 + r^1)(1 + r^1)A_0$$
$$= (1 + r^1)^2 A_0$$

[4.38]

An example may help. Suppose that the loan considered in the last paragraph could be and was extended for another year at the same interest rate. Although no actual payments would be made, the extension of the loan is equivalent to a repayment of $110 ($100 of *principal* A_0 and $10 of *interest* $A_t - A_0$) and a new one-year loan of $110. This new loan would require a repayment of $1.10 \times \$110 = \$121$. Solving directly by formula [4.38] gives the same answer:

$$(1.1)^2 \times \$100 = 1.21 \times \$100 = \$121$$

The final payment of $121 consists of $100 principal, $20 for two years' interest at 10 percent per annum on the $100, and $1 for one year's interest on the first year's interest of $10. The accumulating or relending of interest is called *compounding* interest.

Just as the loan can be extended for a second year, so can a loan be made for t years with interest compounded annually at the rate r^1. Repeating the derivation of [4.38] $t - 2$ times more yields

$$A_t = (1 + r^1)^t A_0 \qquad\qquad [4.39]$$

For example a 4-year loan of $100 at 10 percent per annum compounded annually requires a payment of $(1.1)^4 \times \$100 = 1.4641 \times \$100 = \$146.41$ at the end of 4 years. Note that since $(1 + r^1) = e^r$, [4.39] is consistent with the basic interest equation [4.34].

Other Periodic Interest Rates

Loans are often for shorter periods than a year. A great deal of borrowing is done for 3-month periods, and some for periods as short as a day. Although [4.34] or [4.39] could be used with fractional exponents, for computational convenience *periodic interest rates compounded j times annually* (denoted r^j) are often quoted. These interest rates are the proportionate change at annual rates in A_t from time 0 to h, where $h = 1/j$:

$$r^j = \frac{(A_h/A_0) - 1}{h} = \left(\frac{A_h}{A_0} - 1\right)j \qquad\qquad [4.40]$$

Using [4.34],

$$hr^j = e^{hr} - 1 \qquad\qquad [4.41]$$

The amount A_h due at the end of h year is

$$A_h = (1 + hr^j)A_0 \qquad\qquad [4.42]$$

If, for example, h is $\frac{1}{4}$ so that interest is compounded four times a year, and r^4 is 9.645 percent per annum, a $100 loan would return at the end of a quarter $(1 + 0.25 \times 0.09654) \times \$100 = 1.02411 \times \$100 = \$102.41$.

If the loan is renewed for a second period of h,

$$A_{2h} = (1 + hr^j)^2 A_0 \qquad [4.43]$$

Following the lines used to derive [4.39], it can be shown that

$$A_t = (1 + hr^j)^{tj} A_0 \qquad [4.44]$$

If the previously considered 1-quarter loan were extended to 4 quarters $(t = 1)$ at the same quarterly compounded interest rate $r^4 = 9.645$ percent per annum, the amount due would be $A_1 = (1.02411)^4 \times \$100 = 1.09998 \times \$100 = \$110.00$. Obviously a quarterly compounded interest rate of 9.645 percent per annum is equivalent to an annually compounded interest rate of 10 percent per annum for loans of even numbers of years. Note that $(e^{0.25 \times 0.0953} - 1) \times 4 = (e^{0.023825} - 1) \times 4 = (1.024113 - 1) \times 4 = 0.09645$. Since $r^1 = 10$ percent and $r^4 = 9.645$ percent per annum are both derived from an interest rate of $r = 9.53$ percent per annum, they must be equivalent.

In the examples used, the quarterly compounded interest rate exceeds the continuously compounded interest rate, and the annually compounded interest rate exceeds the quarterly compounded interest rate. This happens because the annually compounded interest rate includes implicitly all the interest earned on interest compounded quarterly. In turn, the quarterly compounded interest rate includes all the interest earned on interest compounded even more frequently. If the frequency of compounding is increased from quarterly to monthly to weekly to daily to by the hour, minute, second, and so forth, compounding becomes continuous and occurs an infinite number of times per year. This continuously compounded interest rate r^∞ is in fact our basic concept of the interest rate $(r^\infty = r)$. Table 4.4 shows how the periodic interest rates do indeed converge to the basic interest rate for a wide variety of values of r. Note that the difference between r^j and r increases as r increases but decreases as j increases.

Present Values

The basic equation [4.34] can be usefully inverted to

$$A_0 = \frac{A_t}{e^{rt}} = e^{-rt} A_t \qquad [4.45]$$

In this formulation A_0 is said to be the value now $(t = 0)$ or the *present value* of an amount A_t to be paid t years in the future. A_0 is the amount that must be lent now at the interest rate r in order to have A_t at the end of t years. A_0 is also the amount which could be borrowed and consumed now and paid back with interest by an amount A_t to be received at the end of t years. Thus, in both senses, A_0 is the present value of A_t. If, for example, r is 9.53 percent per annum, the present value of $110 to be paid in one

TABLE 4.4 Interest rates and corresponding periodic interest rates

Interest Rate Concept	Frequency of Compounding Per Year	Rate of Interest					
		.01	.05	.10	.20	.50	1.00
r^1	1	.01005	.05127	.10517	.22140	.64872	1.71828
r^2	2	.01002	.05063	.10254	.21034	.56805	1.29744
r^4	4	.01001	.05031	.10126	.20508	.53259	1.13610
r^{12}	12	.01000	.05010	.10042	.20168	.51056	1.04285
r^{52}	52	.01000	.05002	.10010	.20039	.50241	1.00968
r^{365}	365	.01000	.05000	.10001	.20005	.50034	1.00137
r^{1000}	1,000	.01000	.05000	.10000	.20002	.50012	1.00050
r^{10000}	10,000	.01000	.05000	.10000	.20000	.50000	1.00005
r^∞	∞†	.01000	.05000	.10000	.20000	.50000	1.00000

† Continuous compounding, $r^\infty = r$.

year is $\$110/e^{0.0953} = \$110/1.1 = \$100$. Dividing an amount t years in the future by e^{rt} is called *discounting* the amount.

Many contracts, such as bonds and mortgages, specify a number of annual payments for n years. The present value of the series of payments equals the sum of the present values of each payment:

$$A_0 = \frac{A_1}{e^r} + \frac{A_2}{e^{r2}} + \cdots + \frac{A_n}{e^{rn}}$$ [4.46]

$$= \sum_{t=1}^{n} \frac{A_t}{e^{rt}} = \sum_{t=1}^{n} e^{-rt} A_t$$

Since these are annual payments, an equivalent present value formula is

$$A_0 = \sum_{t=1}^{n} \frac{A_t}{(1 + r^1)^t}$$ [4.47]

The simplest example would be a bond that pays $\$10$ after one year, $\$10$ after the second year, and $\$110$ after the third year. If r^1 was 10 percent per annum, the present value of the bond would be $\$10/1.1 + \$10/1.1^2 + \$110/1.1^3 = \$9.091 + \$8.264 + \$82.644 = \$100.00$. Competition among borrowers and lenders will assure that the amount lent just equals the present value of the bond at the competitive interest rate r^1.

The Present Value of a Perpetuity

Some bonds and other forms of wealth yield a constant stream of income A every period. A favorite example are the consols of the British government which pay a certain number of pounds each year. The present value of a perpetuity yielding A at the end of this and each succeeding year is computed as

$$A_0 = \sum_{t=1}^{\infty} \frac{A}{(1 + r^1)^t} = A \sum_{t=1}^{\infty} \frac{1}{(1 + r^1)^t}$$ [4.48]

It can be shown[8] that the infinite sum equals $1/r^1$ so that the present value

---

[8] If $0 < \gamma < 1$, then a well-known result from algebra (see any book of math tables) is that

$$\sum_{t=0}^{\infty} \gamma^t = \frac{1}{1 - \gamma} \quad \text{or} \quad \sum_{t=1}^{\infty} \gamma^t = \frac{1}{1 - \gamma} - 1$$

Substituting $\frac{1}{1 + r^1}$ for γ and simplifying yields

$$\sum_{t=1}^{\infty} \frac{1}{(1 + r^1)^t} = \frac{1}{r^1}$$

If a perpetuity yields a *continuous flow* of income at the rate A per annum, advanced techniques can be used to show that its present value is $A_0 = A/r$.

of a perpetuity is

$$A_0 = \frac{A}{r^1} \tag{4.49}$$

If the annually compounded interest rate is 5 percent per annum, a perpetuity paying $100 per year would sell for $100/0.05 = $2000.

The Nominal and Real Interest Rates

The interest rate discussed so far is the growth rate of the dollar value A_t. Since it is in terms of dollar amounts—or their growth rate—it is called the nominal interest rate. An alternative concept is the growth rate of the real value of the loan a_t as measured in base-year dollars:

$$a_t = \frac{A_t}{P_t} \tag{4.50}$$

Assume that the growth rate of the price level is a constant amount g_P^*. Then the growth rate of the real value of the loan is

$$g_{at} = g_{At} - g_{Pt} \qquad \bar{g}_a = r - g_P^* \tag{4.51}$$

This amount $\bar{g}_a$ is therefore a possible measure of the rate of interest, corrected for inflation.

The simple formula [4.51] is an appropriate measure of the real interest rate only in an economy in which interest payments are not taxable to their recipient nor tax deductible to their borrower. In the United States the whole nominal interest payment increases the taxable income of the lender and reduces the taxable income of the borrower. If τ^r is the marginal income tax rate of borrowers and lenders, the nominal interest rate r^* relevant to lenders and borrowers is the nominal interest rate reduced by the tax savings of the borrowers and the tax liabilities of the lenders:

$$r^* = r - r\tau^r = (1 - \tau^r)r \tag{4.52}$$

The after-tax dollar value of the loan A_t^* grows at the rate r^*, and the real, after-tax value of the loan $a_t^* = A_t^*/P_t$ grows at the rate

$$r^{r*} = r^* - g_P^*$$
$$= (1 - \tau^r)r - g_P^* \tag{4.53}$$
$$r = \frac{r^{r*} + g_P^*}{1 - \tau^r}$$

The nominal interest rate paid in the market can be analyzed as equal to the *real after-tax interest rate* r^{r*} plus the rate of inflation g_P^* divided by 1 minus the tax rate τ^r. In the United States, τ^r lies somewhere between $\frac{1}{4}$ and $\frac{2}{5}$.

This means that if the real after-tax interest rate is constant, a 1 percentage point rise in the rate of inflation will increase the observed nominal interest rate by $1\frac{1}{4}$ to $1\frac{2}{3}$ percentage points. This larger increase in the nominal interest rate than in the rate of inflation is necessary because the lender is in effect paying part of the borrower's taxes.

The *real interest rate* is defined as the interest rate which would exist in the absence of inflation. This is measured by subtracting from the nominal interest rate the increase in the interest rate to correct for inflation $g_P^*/(1 - \tau^r)$:

$$r^r = r - \frac{g_P^*}{1 - \tau^r} \qquad r = r^r + \frac{g_P^*}{1 - \tau^r} \qquad\qquad [4.54]$$

As an example, suppose the conditions of the economy imply a real after-tax interest rate of 2 percent and a rate of inflation of 4 percent. Also suppose that the marginal tax rate on interest payments is $\frac{2}{5}$. The nominal interest rate will be $(0.02 + 0.04)/(1 - 0.4) = 0.06/0.6 = 0.10 = 10$ percent per annum. The real interest rate is $0.02/0.6 = 0.0333 = 3\frac{1}{3}$ percent per annum. It should be noted that these formulas hold exactly only for continuously compounded interest rates and tax payments. If annually compounded interest rates and tax payments are substituted, a very small error will arise.

It often happens that the average rate of inflation occurring over the life of a loan is different from the expected rate of inflation at the time the loan is made. If the rate of inflation is higher than expected, borrowers who pay back less valuable dollars than expected are winners and lenders who are paid back the less valuable dollars are losers. If the rate of inflation is less than expected, lenders win and borrowers lose. If the actual rate of inflation equals the expected rate of inflation, the nominal interest rate will just compensate for inflation and neither borrower nor lender will win or lose from inflation.

4.4 WEALTH AND PERMANENT INCOME
The Wealth Constraint

Individuals make decisions on the basis of the resources available and opportunities open to achieve their basic goals. The opportunities are alternative uses of the total available resources—purchases of clothes substitute at market prices for purchases of food or movie tickets; more total consumption now can be exchanged for less consumption next year. An increase in the total resources available to all individuals will have predictable effects on the quantities of goods and services purchased and on many other aspects of aggregate consumer behavior.

The total resources available to support current and future spending by consumers is called *wealth*. It is desirable to measure nominal wealth in terms of total current dollar value or real wealth in base-year dollars (command over real goods and services). Whether for the economy as a whole or a single individual, it is very difficult to measure wealth. Only a fraction of the nonhuman wealth is traded on well-organized markets such as the New York Stock Exchange from which the current value can be computed. Worse, human wealth (the present value of an individual's rights in his expected future income) cannot be traded at all,[9] and human wealth is about three-quarters of total wealth. As a result, direct estimates of wealth are insufficiently precise for general use in macroeconomic analysis.

Permanent Income

An alternative concept of the total resources available for present and future consumption is the stream of real income available in perpetuity from the current level of real wealth. This concept is called *permanent income* y_{Pt}. If $r_P{}^r$ is the rate[10] which converts the perpetuity stream of private income into real wealth v_t, then

$$v_t = \frac{y_{Pt}}{r_P{}^r} \qquad [4.55]$$

$$y_{Pt} = r_P{}^r v_t \qquad [4.56]$$

Permanent income is the highest real rate at which consumption could be maintained forever, since wealth is neither increased or decreased if the income of a perpetuity is exactly consumed. If some income is instead used to add to wealth, this maximum consumption level will increase over time. The standard terminology is undoubtedly unfortunate, since "permanent" income in fact normally increases over time because people consume a smaller amount than they could, if they so desired, in perpetuity. Indeed, private income excludes part and consumption includes the rest of investments in human wealth,[11] so that wealth would in fact increase even if all private income was consumed were these investments to be continued

If private income and permanent income were always equal, there would be a constant growth rate of real wealth due to saving and investment in human capital, say $\bar{g}_v$. The growth rate would be a constant because, under these conditions, saving and investment in human capital are a constant fraction of wealth or permanent income, or so the hundred-odd years of

---

[9] It is possible to borrow against human wealth, but this provides much too low an estimate of the value to an individual of his own productive powers.

[10] This is one of the many broader applications of the concept of an interest rate as a number to convert future receipts into present values beyond the strict application to the valuation of explicit loans to be repaid in dollar-denominated amounts. In order to correspond to real private income, the rate $r_P{}^r$ must be real, after taxes, and exclusive of the average returns from wealth received in nonmarket forms (and so excluded from private income). On the basis of empirical evidence, this rate is assumed to be roughly constant for long periods of time.

[11] See Sec. 2.3.

available U.S. data indicate.[12] This simply states that $\Delta v_t / v_t \ (g_{vt})$ is a constant. Since $r_P{}^r$ is an approximately constant, long-run average yield on wealth, the growth rate of permanent income $(g_{y_{Pt}})$ equals the growth rate of real wealth.[13] That is, permanent income would grow according to

$$y_{Pt} = y_{P0} \, e^{\bar{g}_v t} \tag{4.57}$$

It is not the case, however, that private income and permanent income are always equal. Around cyclical peaks, income is higher than could be expected on a long-run average; the opposite is true for cyclical troughs. Private income is therefore divided between permanent income and these windfall gains or losses called *transitory income* y_{Tt}:

$$y_t{}^n = y_{Pt} + y_{Tt} \tag{4.58}$$

Since consumption is based on wealth, or permanent income, the flow of transitory income increases or decreases the rate of change in wealth by its full amount, whether positive or negative, respectively. The *flow* of transitory income will change the *stock* of wealth from what it would have otherwise been only over time.

Estimating Permanent Income

These considerations can be combined to obtain a usable estimator of permanent income in terms of quarterly observations comparable to the national income accounts data. Permanent income for period t is equal to planned permanent income y_{Pt}^{*} in period t plus the rate $r_P{}^r$ times the change in wealth due to the windfall:

$$y_{Pt} = y_{Pt}^{*} + r_P{}^r \, \tfrac{1}{4} \left(y_t{}^n - y_{Pt}^{*} \right) \tag{4.59}$$

Planned permanent income is the previous quarter's permanent income adjusted for one quarter's growth, $e^{0.25 \, \bar{g}_v} y_{Pt-1/4}$ or $(1 + \alpha) y_{Pt-1/4}$. Because private income and planned permanent income are measured at annual rates, their difference must be multiplied by 0.25 year to get the actual amount of the windfall change in wealth in base-year dollars. By [4.56], the associated change in permanent income is $r_P{}^r$ times this change in wealth. Substituting for

---

[12] The issues involved here are of course complex. A more detailed introduction to consumption-saving behavior is given in Sec. 8.3.

[13] Taking growth rates of [4.56]

$$g_{y_{Pt}} = g_{r_{Pt}{}^r} + g_{vt}$$

Since $r_P{}^r$ is a constant, $g_{r_{Pt}{}^r}$ is 0, thus

$$g_{y_{Pt}} = g_{vt}$$

planned permanent income and simplifying, permanent income is estimated on a quarterly basis as

$$y_{Pt} = \tfrac{1}{4}r_P^r y_t^n + (1 - \tfrac{1}{4}r_P^r)(1 + \alpha)y_{Pt-1/4} \qquad [4.60]$$

This equation can be used in connection with a model of consumer spending based on permanent income to derive an estimator of permanent income.[14] The real yield on wealth r_P^r is estimated as approximately 10 percent per annum.

Implications for Macroeconomic Analysis

A wealth or permanent income constraint is an argument in several behavioral functions to be discussed. Thus it is appropriate to have seen that an empirical estimator of the constraint can be constructed from the relatively good national income accounts data for use in confronting and testing these theories against the real world.

It is of special interest that differences in actual and expected permanent income change wealth dollar for dollar over a year, but that the resulting percentage change in wealth is only about 10 percent (r_P^r) of the percentage difference between actual and expected income. This permits a useful analysis of differential effects of planned changes in wealth and changes in wealth due to windfall or transitory income.

☐ SUMMARY

Stock variables are measured in units without time dimensions. Flow variables are measured as rates per annum. Comparisons of alternative values of variables at the same time can be made in terms of the algebraic difference, the ratio, and the proportionate difference. Behavioral functions are used to explain how the value of one variable is determined by other variables. The elasticity of the value of a function with respect to one of its arguments is the proportionate difference in the value of the function divided by the (very small) proportionate difference in the argument, all other arguments constant. Logarithms are useful for scaling variables to highlight proportionate differences. The rate of change of a variable is its algebraic change at annual rates measured over an arbitrarily short period of time. The growth rate of a variable is the proportionate or logarithmic change at annual rates measured over an arbitrarily short period of time. The growth rate of a variable is also equal to the rate of change divided by the level of a variable and to

[14] The remaining statistical problems are difficult but are not important for the analysis required in this book. Details are found in Michael R. Darby, The Permanent Income Theory of Consumption—A Restatement, *Quarterly Journal of Economics,* **88:**228–50, May 1974.

the rate of change in the logarithm of the variable. The rate of change of a variable which is the sum of other variables is the sum of their rates of change. The growth rate of product is the sum of the growth rates of its factors. The interest rate r (also known as the continuously compounded interest rate) is the growth rate of an amount of money lent at interest where no payment of principal or interest is made until the end of the loan. The periodic interest rate compounded j times annually, r^j, is the proportionate change at annual rates in such a loan over a period of time equal to $1/j$ years. This equals $e^{r/j} - 1$. The most important periodic interest rates are the annually and quarterly compounded interest rates, r^1 and r^4, respectively. The present value of a stream of future payments is the sum of their values discounted to the present. The nominal interest rate observed in the market equals the sum of the real after-tax interest rate and the expected rate of inflation divided by one minus the income tax rate on interest payments. The real interest rate, which is the nominal interest rate if the expected rate of inflation is zero, equals the real after-tax interest rate divided by one minus the tax rate. Permanent income is the stream of real income available in perpetuity from the current level of real wealth. It can be estimated from the national income accounts data. Differences in actual private income and permanent income change wealth dollar for dollar and permanent income by about 10 percent of the difference over a year's time.

□ **QUESTIONS AND EXERCISES**

*1 (a) Many flows can be identified with rates of change in stocks. What flow equals the rate of change in capital?

(b) In what units is the rate of change in nominal income measured?

2 (a) Use the given information to complete the following table, where t is the time index, Y_t is nominal income, y_t is real income, and P_t is the price index.

t	Y_t	$\dfrac{Y_t - Y_{t-1}}{Y_{t-1}}$	P_t	$\dfrac{P_t - P_{t-1}}{P_{t-1}}$	y_t	$\dfrac{y_t - y_{t-1}}{y_{t-1}}$	$\dfrac{P_t - P_{t-1}}{P_{t-1}} + \dfrac{y_t - y_{t-1}}{y_{t-1}}$
0	1000.00	———	1.000	———	1000.00	———	———
1	1102.50		1.050		1050.00		
2	1212.75		1.155		1050.00		
3	1271.80		1.132		1123.50		

(b) What year had the greatest proportionate change in prices over the previous year? The greatest proportionate change in real income? The smallest proportionate change in nominal income?

(c) Note that $Y_t = y_t P_t$. What condition holds for the growth rates g_{Yt}, g_{yt}, and g_{Pt}? How is this approximately illustrated by the tabulated values of proportionate changes? Why can these proportionate changes be interpreted as at annual rates?

*3 A specific functional form of $a_t = a(b_t, c_t, d_t)$ is $a_t = (b_t d_t)/(c_t)$. In this case is $a(\ \ )$ an increasing or decreasing function of b_t? c_t? d_t? What is the value of $\eta_{a,b}$? $\eta_{a,c}$? $\eta_{a,d}$?

4 Between t_0 and t_1, real income is given by the equation $y_t = y_{t_0} e^{0.04(t-t_0)}$.
 (a) What is the growth rate of real income?
 (b) At a certain time t^* in this period $y_t = R\$100$ billion/year. What is the value of Δy_{t^*}?

5 Use the information in Table 4.3 and the fact that $a_{1970} = \$2$ billion to compute g_{a1970}. What is the proportionate change at annual rates in this a_t between 1970 and 1971?

6 (a) A certain consol of the British government pays £15 every half-year. If the next interest payment is $\frac{1}{2}$ year away (interest was just paid) and the semiannually compounded interest rate on consols is 6 percent per annum, what is the price in pounds of this consol?
 (b) What would be the price if the semiannually compounded interest rate were to rise to 9 percent per annum?

*7 Many bonds, such as U.S. Treasury bills, are promises to pay a certain amount on a certain date. The interest rate is not explicitly stated, but is implicit in the price for which they are sold. Because this price discounts the amount to be paid in the future to its present value, they are called *discount bonds*.
 (a) A discount bond which pays $1000 in one year sells for $892.86. This yields an annually compounded interest rate of _____ per annum.
 (b) If the buyer of the bond pays a marginal tax rate of $\frac{1}{3}$, he receives an after-tax nominal interest payment of $_____, or _____ per annum, compounded annually.
 (c) The price level is expected to rise over the life of the bond from 2.00 to 2.08. The anticipated annually compounded real after-tax interest rate is _____ per annum.
 (d) Use formula [4.53] to compute the real after-tax interest rate with the nominal interest rate computed in part (a), a tax rate of $\frac{1}{3}$, and an expected inflation rate of 0.04 per annum. This answer is only approximately equal to the rate computed in part (c). Can you suggest why?

☐ **REFERENCES FOR FURTHER READING**
No special readings are suggested for this material. Some readings discussing this material in part will be listed as it is applied in future chapters.

Equilibrium Levels and Growth of Real Income and Prices

Part 2

Macroeconomic theory explains and predicts the behavior of the levels of real income and prices. This understanding of real income and the price level is used to study special problems such as employment and the international balance of payments.

The theory is expressed by a framework or model which focuses on the main forces by leaving out much unessential detail. A useful approach to learning how this model works is to concentrate first on determining the equilibrium levels and growth paths of real income and prices around which the actual levels and growth paths fluctuate. Once the general area in which the economy will be operating is known, it is easier to see how macroeconomic shocks will cause the actual values of real income and prices in the economy to diverge from their equilibrium values.

The chapters in Part 2 concern the first problem—the general macroeconomic trends in an economy. In Part 3, economic fluctuations caused by changes in the underlying conditions are discussed. Part 2 provides the basic tools for studying the rate of increase in the standard of living and the rate of inflation. Part 3 deals with the causes and effects of the business cycle or changes in the rates of growth of real income, employment, and the price level.

Chapter 5 shows how the levels of real income and prices are determined by the resources, technology, institutions, and tastes of the economy. Chapter 6 considers how changes in these basic factors over time will cause growth in real income and the price level.

The Levels of Income and Prices

Chapter 5

5.1 INTRODUCTION

Macroeconomics is essentially an explanation of the behavior of the level of real income and of prices. This chapter discusses the main forces determining these levels. In the next chapter, we will see how gradual changes in the underlying factors cause growth in income and prices. In both chapters the analysis is framed in terms of an economy in full-employment equilibrium. *Full-employment equilibrium* cannot be completely defined at this point, but the underlying idea is simple enough. *Equilibrium* refers to the position towards which an economy tends at a particular point in time. *Full employment* refers to the idea that in equilibrium all resources will be fully employed in their highest valued uses—though for some resources the highest valued use may be search for paid employment.[1]

The factors underlying macroeconomic equilibrium can be divided into two essentially separate groups: the real and the monetary. Although this division—like that between supply and demand in microeconomics—is not perfect, the exceptions are minor enough that the framework captures all the main points.

The main outline can be described simply before a more detailed study is begun. Real income—the total final goods and services produced—is determined by (1) the resources of labor and capital which actually exist, (2) the technology and institutions which govern the possible ways these resources can be combined to produce final output, and (3) tastes which influence both the composition of goods actually produced and the amount of labor services made available. Market output will be the largest amount that can be produced, given the knowledge and institutions of the society and the resources made available. Total demand will just equal the total amount produced since people must either consume or save and the interest rate on savings will equate business demand for increased capital to the amount of output

---

[1] In an economy undergoing frequent changes in the exact structure of output and receiving continuously new entrants in the labor market, some unemployment will always be present. So long as unemployment is at the normal rate implied by the nature of the economy this is considered full employment. Actual employment can be greater or less than full employment.

not consumed. Monetary factors are negligible in the determination of real income. But one of the institutions underlying the real equilibrium of modern economies is the widespread use of money as a medium of exchange. Prices are quoted in terms of money. The ratios of the prices of individual goods are determined by the real factors, but their general level is determined by monetary factors. The price level adjusts to equate the demand for money with the amount in existence.

In this chapter and the next, government expenditure and taxation will be combined with consumer spending and income. This discussion views the government as essentially a consumer cooperative providing jointly consumed goods and apportioning the costs. Similarly, international trade is ignored as if the United States were a closed economy. These simplifications will be abandoned later to discuss the effects of changes in government spending and taxation and in international trade.

5.2 DETERMINANTS OF REAL INCOME

The Meaning of Real Income

Recall from Sec. 3.1 that nominal income Y_t can be decomposed into an index of real income y_t and the price level P_t such that

$$Y_t = y_t P_t \qquad \text{or} \qquad y_t = \frac{Y_t}{P_t} \qquad\qquad [5.1]$$

Real income is expressed in base-year dollars ($R\$$): the average amount of real goods and services which could be bought with $1 in the base year. Real income is an aggregate measure in terms of physical units of all final goods and services produced. It also measures the command over real commodities of all income received.

Real income is a basic measure of output available for satisfying human wants devoid of the veil of a changing price level. With rapid inflation nominal incomes and prices can double every year, but no one need be any better off for it. When the rate of inflation is negative, both nominal incomes and prices may fall year after year while real incomes steadily rise.

Analysis of the determinants of real income must be the first task of a macroeconomist. In this chapter, a detailed, cross-section analysis of a particular instant of time is presented. This permits a simplification of notation by omitting the time subscript t from all variables, since they are all measured at the same instant.

The Aggregate Production Function

Real income in an economy is determined by the amounts of labor and capital used in production and by the technology and institutions of the economy. All human inputs to the productive process are summed as labor and all produced means of production are called capital. Labor and capital are used here to refer to the flows of labor and capital services (or inputs). The term labor force and capital stock will be used in full for the corresponding stock concepts.[2] Labor and capital—like real income—are idealized aggregate indices of the diverse types and qualities of workers on the one hand and machines, buildings, roads, inventories, and the like on the other. The technology and institutions of the society will determine how the labor and capital are combined to produce output. The relationship between the factors of production labor l and capital k and the output y produced in an economy at a particular time is summarized by the aggregate production function $f(\ )$:

$$y = f(k, l) \tag{5.2}$$

Output is an increasing function of capital and labor. Increases in either or both factors of production will increase output by the amount indicated by the aggregate production function.

The production functions for individual firms which we study in microeconomics are strictly technological statements of the greatest possible amount that could be produced on the basis of the current state of knowledge. The aggregate production function of macroeconomics reflects both these technological possibilities and the further constraints on production due to government laws and regulations, monopoly powers, and other institutional restrictions. Also underlying the aggregate production function is the general composition of output as determined by the individual supply and demand relations for the various goods and services. These underlying conditions are assumed to be constant—or, later, changing over time in carefully specified ways—for our analysis.

Labor is the quality-adjusted number of man hours employed for production. This takes into account both the number of people actually employed and the fraction of time available worked by each. The adjustment for the quality of workers is extremely important since the average level of training has been rising steadily over time in the United States. The increase in productivity due to training is said to reflect investment in the stock of human capital. *Human capital stock* is a term for our own total productive capacity. Economists use the term as a reminder that labor, like machine services, flows from a stock which has been built up by past investment. In the United States, the major portion of labor income—and total national income as well—can be attributed to training as opposed to the return to raw labor. The main forms of investment in human capital are education and, even more important, on-the-job training. An hour of an operating engineer's time may be ten times as productive and ten times as well paid as an hour of raw labor; so each

---

[2] Note below, however, that capital input is in fact estimated as proportional to the capital stock.

hour of the engineer's time counts ten times as much in our index of labor input as does an hour of raw labor.

Capital, or more precisely *nonhuman capital*, is a quality-adjusted index of the machines, buildings, inventories, and other nonhuman inputs used in production. It would be desirable to have a measure of machine hours similar to the labor index so as to account for the intensity of use. However, since the intensity of capital use does not seem to have any long-run trend— in contrast to the average numbers of hours worked—economists rarely attempt such an intensity adjustment. The capital stock measures only the stock of capital goods used in market production and not those goods, such as private cars, used in direct household production which is not included in income. The capital stock as defined here does not include government-owned capital such as army bases. The value of the services of government-owned capital goods is generally not included in market income aside from its effects on the amount produced by other factors of production. The governmentally provided capital is a factor underlying the position of the aggregate production function, but is not included among the purchased factors of production. Some advanced treatments explicitly include governmentally provided factors of production in the production function. Like labor or real income, capital is an index of widely divergent sorts of things weighted by relative values.

Real income is determined, given the production function, by the amounts of capital and labor used. Therefore, to understand the determination of real income we must examine the demands for and supplies of the factors of production.

The Demand for Labor

The demand for labor is derived from the production function. For a given amount of capital, say k_0, we can graph the amount of output which will be produced using various amounts of labor, as shown in Fig. 5.1. In the relevant range of values for labor, output increases as labor is increased but at a decreasing rate. This is summarized by the *Law of Diminishing Returns*: For fixed values of other inputs, unit increases in the variable factor of production will, at least beyond some point, cause decreasing increases in output. The increase in output per unit increase in labor is given by the slope, $(y_1 - y_0)/(l_1 - l_0)$, of the $y = f(k_0, l)$ line. Diminishing returns are illustrated in Fig. 5.1 by the decreasing slope of this line.

The increase in total output due to one more unit of labor for each amount of labor is called the marginal product of that amount of labor. Employers will desire to employ more labor whenever the marginal product of labor is greater than its cost in wages and less when its marginal product is less than the wage rate. Thus the quantity of labor demanded at each wage is that for which the marginal product of labor equals the wage. The demand curve

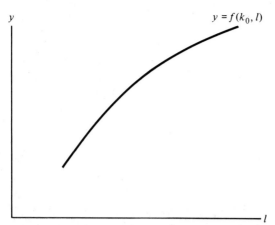

FIGURE 5.1 Graph of the aggregate production function for a given capital stock k_0. Output y increases with increased labor inputs l, but at a decreasing rate. The increase in output per unit increase in labor is given by the slope of the $y = f(k_0, l)$ line for each level of labor input.

relating wages and the quantity of labor is drawn in Fig. 5.2 by plotting the slope of $y = f(k_0, l)$ in Fig. 5.1 against the corresponding amounts of labor. The general form of the demand function is

$$l^d = l^d(w, k) \tag{5.3}$$

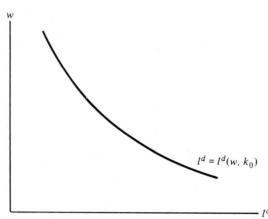

FIGURE 5.2 The demand for labor for a given capital stock k_0. Lower real wage rates w increase the demand for labor l^d. For larger capital stocks than k_0, the demand curve would be located above and to the right of the $l^d = l^d(w, k_0)$ line.

Demand for labor is a decreasing function of the real wage rate w since the greater the real wage, the smaller is the labor input that can be profitably employed. Conversely, a lower real wage encourages employers to hire more laborers until the increase in output due to an additional worker ceases to exceed the cost in output terms of the additional worker. Given the real wage, the demand for labor will generally increase with the amount of capital used in combination with labor. The greater capital available per unit of labor allows an additional worker to produce more than if he were less well equipped. This is roughly the other side of the law of diminishing returns which stated that in the relevant range the marginal product of labor falls as the quantity of labor increases relative to the fixed quantity of capital. Here the marginal product of labor rises as capital is increased relative to a fixed quantity of labor. The law of diminishing returns implies this last statement exactly only for certain types of production functions, but it will generally hold in the range in which economies actually operate.

The Demand for Capital

The arguments used to derive the demand for labor can be repeated for the demand for capital. Thus Fig. 5.3 illustrates the output associated with different stocks of capital for a given amount of labor l_0. The *marginal product of capital*, the increase in output due to a unit increase in capital, is equal to the slope of the $y = f(k, l_0)$ line. The demand for capital for the given

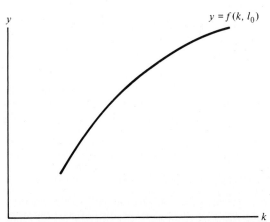

FIGURE 5.3 **Graph of the aggregate production function for a given labor supply** l_0. Output y increases with increased capital k, but at a decreasing rate. The increase in output per unit increase in capital is given by the slope of the $y = f(k, l_0)$ line for each level of capital input.

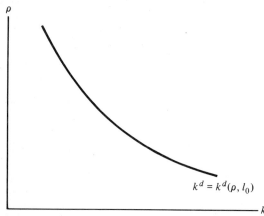

FIGURE 5.4 The demand for capital for a given amount of labor l_0. Lower real rental rates ρ increase the demand for capital k^d. For larger amounts of labor than l_0, the demand curve would be located above and to the right of the $k^d = k^d(\rho, l_0)$ line.

amount of labor l_0 is graphed in Fig. 5.4 by plotting the slope of the $y = f(k, l_0)$ line and the corresponding capital amounts shown in Fig. 5.3. More generally, the demand for capital is a decreasing function of the real rental rate ρ and an increasing function of the amount of labor used:

$$k^d = k^d(\rho, l) \qquad\qquad [5.4]$$

The real rental rate of capital corresponds to the real wage rate of labor. The purchase price of a unit of capital is analogous to the capital value of a unit of labor. The price of capital appears unique at first because there is essentially no market for the sale of people. People do borrow against their future earnings, however, and do invest in training so that this difference between nonhuman capital and human capital is more one of degree than of kind. The fact that firms usually purchase their machines but rent their labor inputs is an unnecessary complication for economies in long-run equilibrium such as we are discussing here.

The Supply of Labor

The supply of labor depends upon the total, quality-adjusted, units of labor available in the age-eligible population and their average rate of participation in the labor force. At any point in time the quality and size of the age-eligible population is fixed, so the supply of labor reflects changes in the fraction of units of labor working at the time. Despite our use of continuous time, we will adjust the fraction working for regular fluctuations over the course of a week, due to holidays, and seasons of the year. These fluctuations and similar ones in income and prices are not of interest to macroeconomists and are removed from the various data series by averaging and seasonal adjustment.

The key determinants of the labor participation rate π are the real wage rate, the average quality of labor q, and the per capita income from capital:

$$\pi = \pi(w, q, \rho k/n) \qquad [5.5]$$

where n is the age-eligible population. The effect of the real wage rate on the participation rate is ambiguous. The participation rate measures the average fraction of time actually working,[3] the alternative being leisure—including nonmarket production and educational investment in human capital. A high wage rate increases income and therefore the attractiveness of leisure. In addition high wages relative to the costs of education increase the desirability of staying in school, but wages and costs of education normally move in proportion. Thus, although an increase in the real wages increases the attractiveness of working, it also increases the attractiveness of alternatives to work, and the net effect of an increase in real wages may increase or decrease the participation rate.[4] The effect of the average quality of labor is ambiguous for similar reasons. If we measure q in units of raw labor, the average wage received per hour worked—as opposed to unit of labor provided—is wq. So an increase in quality, for a given wage per unit of labor, will also increase the attractiveness of work and at the same time increase per capita income and therefore the attractiveness of leisure. An increase in per capita income from capital increases the attractiveness of leisure, but not of labor, and so reduces the participation rate, given the real wage rate and average quality of the population.

The labor supply is equal to the participation rate times the average quality times the size of the population

$$l^s = \pi(w, q, \rho k/n) \cdot qn \qquad [5.6]$$

An increase in real wages, other things equal, may either increase or decrease the labor supply, depending upon the exact nature of the underlying tastes. Empirical evidence on the effect of the real wage on the labor supply is very tenuous. Some studies suggest a *backward-bending supply curve of labor*, as shown in Fig. 5.5(a), while others suggest a positively sloped labor supply curve, as shown in Fig. 5.5(b). Whatever the sign of the net effect, it appears to be small relative to the effect of the real wage on the demand for labor. The total effect on labor supply of an increase in quality, other things equal,

---

[3] This use of the term "participation rate" should not be confused with the data collected by the U.S. Department of Labor on the fraction of the population which is in the labor force.

[4] The source of the difficulty is that both leisure and commodities purchased with real income enter into individuals' utility functions. An increase in the wage rate raises the amount of market goods obtained for each hour of leisure foregone. Microeconomists analyze the situation in terms of opposing income and substitution effects.

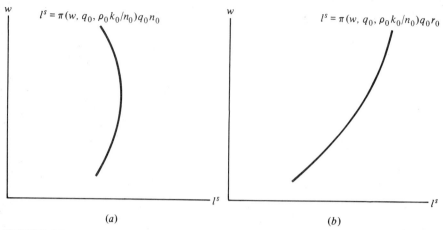

$$l^s = \pi(w, q_0, p_0 k_0/n_0)q_0 n_0$$

$$l^s = \pi(w, q_0, p_0 k_0/n_0)q_0 r_0$$

(a)   (b)

FIGURE 5.5 **Possible labor supply functions.** In the case of a backward-bending labor supply curve, increases in the real wage above some point reduce the quantity of labor supplied as more leisure is consumed. The supply curve in (b) shows a supply curve which slopes upward for all wages.

is almost surely positive with the direct proportional effect of increased quality swamping any possible effect on the participation rate. Similarly, an increase in population, other things equal, will increase the labor supply both directly and by increasing the participation rate. Increases in either the rental rate or stock of capital or both, other things equal, will decrease the labor supply.

The Supply of Capital

Capital is measured as only those capital goods used in production and its amount can be changed over time only by the processes of investment and depreciation. Much the same argument could in fact be made about the supply of labor were it not for the relatively easy substitution of leisure for work. The capital stock will be seen to have a very definite desired level at any point in time, and the difference between actual and desired level of capital is an important determinant of the rate of investment. But discussion of changes in the capital stock, like that of changes in the size or quality of the population, is left to the analysis of economic growth and dynamic adjustments in later chapters.

For analysis of the level of income, the supply curve of capital is vertical at the existing amount as illustrated in Fig. 5.6, or algebraically

$$k^s = k_0 \tag{5.7}$$

The current rental rate on capital serves to allocate the fixed amount of capital and does not affect the amount available now, but only in the future.

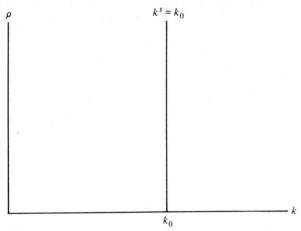

FIGURE 5.6 The supply curve of capital. The capital stock k is fixed at any point in time. The rental rate, ρ, allocates the available capital among alternative uses but does not affect the amount of capital currently available.

Determination of Equilibrium Real Income

The equilibrium level of real income, the inputs of capital and labor, the real rental rate on capital, and the real wage can be determined from the aggregate production function, the demand and supply functions for labor and capital, and the existing level of the capital stock and size and quality of the age-eligible population. Substituting the existing values and noting that the quantities of capital and labor demanded and supplied equal the quantities used in equilibrium, we have a formal system of five equations and the five unknowns y, k, l, ρ, and w:

$$y = f(k, l) \tag{5.8}$$

$$l = l^d(w, k) \tag{5.9}$$

$$l = \pi(w, q_0, \rho k/n_0) \cdot q_0 n_0 \tag{5.10}$$

$$k = k^d(\rho, l) \tag{5.11}$$

$$k = k_0 \tag{5.12}$$

These equations are a way of summarizing the millions of individual demand curves, supply curves, and production functions which describe the various markets in the economy. The mathematical solution of this system can be illustrated graphically.

First the labor market equations [5.9] and [5.10] are graphed in Fig. 5.7, given $k = k_0$. The labor demand curve can be graphed quite simply, since it relates labor only to the real wage w and the given capital stock k_0. The

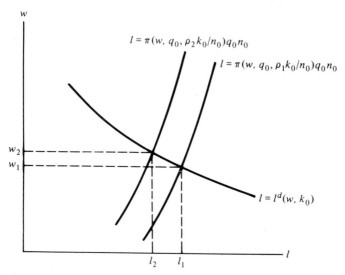

FIGURE 5.7 Derivation of labor market equilibrium curve. The quantity of labor demanded is a function of the real wage w and the given stock of capital k_0. The quantity of labor supplied is a function, aside from given values, of both the real wage and the real rental rate on capital, ρ. A supply curve for labor can be drawn for each possible value of ρ. Examples are drawn for the values ρ_1 and ρ_2, where ρ_2 is greater than ρ_1 so that the labor supply curve associated with ρ_2 is above and to the left of the curve for ρ_1. Equilibrium values of labor and the real wage associated with ρ_1 and ρ_2 are l_1, w_1 and l_2, w_2, respectively. A value of l can thus be associated with every value of ρ. Each combination (ρ, l) for which the labor market is in equilibrium is plotted in Fig. 5.8 as the negatively sloped LE curve.

labor supply function, however, explains the quantity of labor supplied by the real wage and the real rental rate on capital ρ, as well as variables given at the time of analysis. The labor supply function can be plotted on the basis of a given value of ρ such as ρ_1 however. If ρ was ρ_1, then the labor market would be in equilibrium at l_1 and w_1. If ρ was instead ρ_2, which is larger than ρ_1, the labor supply function would lie above and to the left of the one for ρ_1. Equilibrium in the labor market if ρ equaled ρ_2 would occur for l_2 and w_2. For every value of ρ, there will be an associated value of l and w. The labor market equilibrium (LE) curve in Fig. 5.8 plots every possible combination of ρ and l for which the labor market is in equilibrium. The LE curve has a negative slope because higher values of ρ are associated with smaller values of l as was shown for ρ_1 and ρ_2. The LE curve also can be derived for backward-bending labor supply curves for which the effect of real wages on the quantity of labor supplied is less than the effect on the quantity of labor demanded.

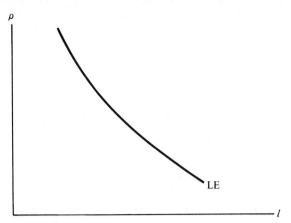

FIGURE 5.8   The labor market equilibrium or LE curve. The LE curve shows all combinations of ρ and l for which the labor market is in equilibrium.

The capital market equations are graphed in Fig. 5.9. The capital supply curve is a vertical line through the existing amount k_0. The capital demand function explains the quantity of capital demanded as determined by both the real rental rate ρ and the labor used l. This function can be plotted for given values of l such as l_1. If the quantity of labor used is l_1, then the rental rate on capital must be ρ_1 for the demand for capital to equal the existing supply. If l was instead l_2, which is larger than l_1, the capital demand function would lie above and to the right of the one for l_1. Equilibrium in the capital market if l equaled l_2 would occur if ρ was ρ_2. For every value of l, there will be an associated value of ρ. The capital market equilibrium (KE) curve in Fig. 5.10 plots every combination of ρ and l for which the capital market is in equilibrium. The KE curve has a positive slope because higher values of l are associated with higher values of ρ as was shown for l_1 and l_2.

The LE curve shows all combinations of ρ and l for which the labor market is in equilibrium. The KE curve shows all possible values for which the capital market is in equilibrium. By plotting the LE and KE curves on one graph as shown in Fig. 5.11, we find the only combination of ρ and l for which both the labor and capital markets are in equilibrium at the same time. These values, ρ^e and l^e, are not determined in the capital market or in the labor market separately, but by the interaction of the two markets. The equilibrium value of capital is the existing stock k_0. The equilibrium real wage rate and real income are found by substitution of the other values in the labor demand function and aggregate production function. This is shown graphically in Figs. 5.12 and 5.13. Figure 5.12 reproduces the labor demand

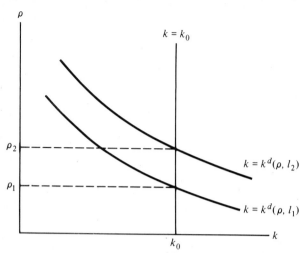

FIGURE 5.9 Derivation of the capital market equilibrium curve.
The capital supply is fixed at the existing amount k_0. The
quantity of capital demanded is a function of both the real rental
rate ρ and the quantity of labor l. A demand curve for capital can
be drawn for each possible value of l. Examples are drawn for l_1
and l_2, where l_2 is greater than l_1, so that the capital demand
curve associated with l_2 lies above and to the right of the one for l_1.
Equilibrium values of the rental rate associated with l_1 and l_2 are
ρ_1 and ρ_2, respectively. A value of ρ can thus be associated with
every value of l. Each combination (ρ, l) for which the capital
market is in equilibrium is plotted in Fig. 5.10 as the positively
sloped KE curve.

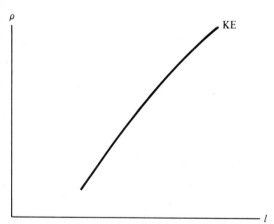

**FIGURE 5.10 The capital market equilibrium curve, or KE
curve.** The KE curve shows all combinations of ρ and l
for which the capital market is in equilibrium.

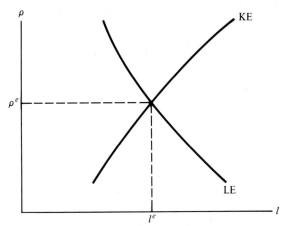

FIGURE 5.11   Use of the KE and LE curves to find the equilibrium values of ρ and l. The point where the positively sloped KE curve intersects with the negatively sloped LE curve shows the only combination of ρ and l for which the capital and labor markets are in simultaneous equilibrium. These values, ρ^e and l^e, are those which will be achieved by the interaction of the supply and demand functions for capital and labor.

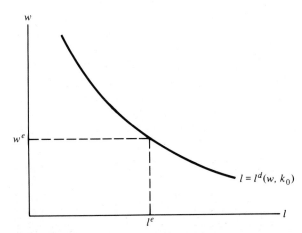

FIGURE 5.12   Determination of the equilibrium real wage w^e. The equilibrium real wage w^e is the one for which the quantity of labor demanded is equal to the equilibrium amount l^e.

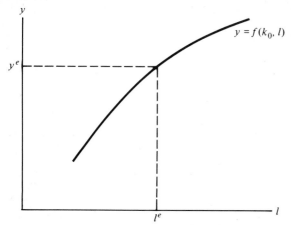

FIGURE 5.13   Determination of equilibrium real income y^e.
The equilibrium real income is the amount produced using
k_0 and l^e.

function for k_0 which was graphed in Fig. 5.7. The equilibrium real wage w^e
is the one corresponding to l^e. Figure 5.13 graphs the production function
for the existing capital stock k_0. Equilibrium real income y^e is the amount
which is produced by the existing capital stock k_0 and the equilibrium
quantity of labor l^e.

The Demand for Output

The demand for output did not explicitly enter into the determination of
real income. This is because the labor supply function implicitly reflects the
choice between market goods and leisure. Income exactly equals output; so
that the means of making purchases is just equal to the purchases to be made.

A possible difficulty arises because consumers use their income not only
to consume but also to save. The only way that society as a whole can save,
in the sense of nonconsumption of income, is to use part of output to add
to the capital stock so as to increase future output. That is, society can save
only by investing. This point is easy to see by dividing output into its two
possible uses, consumption c and investment i:

$$y = c + i \qquad\qquad [5.13]$$

However, saving s is the portion of income which is not consumed

$$y = c + s \qquad\qquad [5.14]$$

Combining [5.13] and [5.14], we have

$$c + s = c + i \qquad\qquad [5.15]$$

Subtracting consumption from both sides, we obtain the equality of saving and investment:[5]

$$s = i \qquad\qquad [5.16]$$

This condition is not always true by the nature of individual plans, except in a simple economy in which the only way to save is by investing in capital goods. In modern market economies, individual saving plans—net of any government deficit in the current consolidated accounts—are not automatically identical to the investment plans of firms. Yet, after the fact, net purchases of securities by individuals must exactly equal net issuance of securities by firms to finance investment.[6]

It is easy to see that the amount of real output that is not consumed must equal the amount added to the capital stock, but this does not show how the desired amount of saving is equated to the desired amount of investment. The difference is analogous to the market for corn, the amount supplied must exactly equal the amount demanded in equilibrium, but the desired sales and purchases are equated by the movement of the price of corn. Investment is simply the amount of additional capital demanded and saving the amount of additional capital supplied. We call the demand function and supply function for additional capital the investment function and saving function, respectively.

The desired level of investment depends upon the interest rate[7] r that must be paid or foregone to finance new capital, the cost of capital goods, and the expected rental stream to be generated by the new capital. If the rental stream is more than sufficient to cover payments on a loan which covers the cost of the investment, the investment will be made. The number of investments which can cover the loan payments decreases as the rate of interest increases. The cost of capital goods relative to other goods rises or falls when the rate of investment is high or low relative to capacity in the capital goods industry, but these variations are discussed with other disequilibrium behavior in Parts 3 and 4. Similarly the state of expectations about the future rental rate on capital is largely predetermined for the equilibrium discussed in this chapter. It will be seen later that a considerable controversy exists over whether expected future rentals are based essentially on observed past and present rental rates and growth in income or whether independent moods of optimism and pessimism play an important part in determining investment. For the current discussion of long-run equilibrium,

[5] This is a simplified version of [2.6] corresponding to consolidation of government into the consumer accounts and to neglect of international trade so that net exports are zero.

[6] See Secs. 2.1 and 2.3 for details.

[7] Strictly speaking, the real interest rate r is applicable to investment and saving decisions. At a particular instant of time, the expected rate of inflation is constant and the distinction is unnecessary. The distinction will be introduced in later chapters.

only the effects on expectations from current income and rental rate on capital are included in the investment function:

$$i = i(r, y, \rho) \tag{5.17}$$

Investment is a decreasing function of the interest rate r, and an increasing function of income y and rental rate ρ, to the extent that they create expectations of high future rental rates. The values of y and ρ for which the labor and capital markets are in equilibrium were previously determined to be y^e and ρ^e. The investment function for those equilibrium values of y and ρ is graphed in Fig. 5.14.

The saving function, like the investment function, is complicated by expectational factors in disequilibrium. For long-run analysis, we can concentrate on the effects of income and the interest rate. Individuals choose to save because a positive real interest rate permits exchange of a dollar's worth of real goods and services now for a larger amount of real goods and services in the future. This exchange of present for future goods is accomplished by saving. Individuals do not choose to save all their income, however, because the more that is saved the less is present consumption relative to future consumption. Saving proceeds only to the point that the marginal utility of a dollar's worth of consumption now is equated to the marginal utility of the future consumption that could be obtained by saving

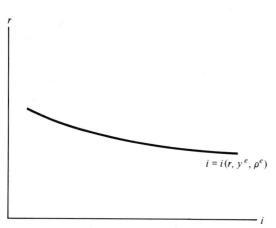

FIGURE 5.14   The investment function at equilibrium levels of income and the rental rate on capital. At lower interest rates, investment projects yielding lower expected future rental streams become attractive, so that investment increases. The position of the curve is determined by the investments actually available and the expected returns on those investments.

a dollar. The marginal utility of consumption declines with its level, so this implies that future levels of consumption will exceed current levels in equilibrium. The lower marginal utility associated with higher levels of future consumption just offsets the lower current price, given the interest rate, of future consumption relative to the marginal utility of current consumption. It may be that the utility of the same consumption level in the future is valued less than it is in the present, but saving to increase future consumption relative to more expensive present consumption generally also occurs. The data indicate that for over a century U.S. saving has been a constant fraction of income in long-run equilibrium. This constant, long-run saving ratio is consistent with, but not required by, the economic theory of optimal consumption over time.[8]

The effect of the interest rate on saving is very little understood. In part this reflects the differing impact of different changes that could alter the interest rate. The main reason for our lack of knowledge is that the long-run interest rate, when adjusted for the influence of expected inflation, has changed so very little over time. The effect of an increase in the interest rate is generally thought to be a small increase in the saving rate but others argue that the effect would be a small decrease analogous to the backward-bending supply curve for labor. It will be assumed that the effect of an increase in the interest rate is a slight increase in the saving rate, but none of the arguments will be based on this precise shape. The saving function

$$s = s(y, r) \qquad\qquad [5.18]$$

is illustrated for the equilibrium value of income y^e in Fig. 5.15.

Investment is equated to saving, as required by the equilibrium condition [5.16] by movements in the interest rate. This is illustrated in Fig. 5.16. In full moving equilibrium, as discussed in Chap. 6, the interest rate will be equated to the rental rate of capital by the cumulative effects over time of investment on the capital stock.

Movements in the interest rate assure that the total amount demanded will be just equal to total output in equilibrium. In the complete model, decisions of firms and households are made consistent by the operation of three prices: the wage rate w, the rental rate ρ, and the interest rate r. Households will have plans for working, consuming, and saving so that the income earned and its disposition between current and future consumption will be as determined by utility maximization. Net investment will be equated to net saving by adjustment of the rate of interest paid on financial assets.

---

[8] See, for example, Milton Friedman, *A Theory of the Consumption Function*, Princeton: Princeton University Press for NBER, 1957; and Paul A. David and John J. Scadding, Private Savings: Ultrarationality, Aggregation, and "Denison's Law," *Journal of Political Economy*, **82**: 225–49, Mar./Apr. 1974.

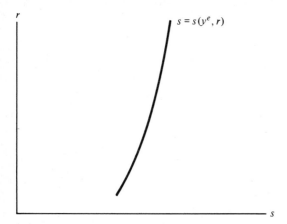

FIGURE 5.15   The saving function at the equilibrium level of income. An increase in the interest rate slightly increases the saving associated with each level of income in long-run equilibrium.

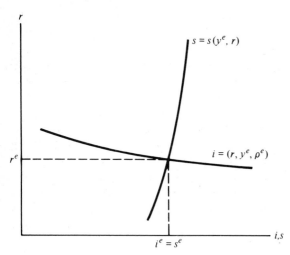

FIGURE 5.16   Equilibrium of the demand and supply of additional capital goods. The interest rate moves to r^e to equate investment to saving at $i^e = s^e$.

Summary of the Determination of Real Income

Real income is determined by the amount of labor employed with the existing capital stock as the largest amount which can be produced from those factors given the technological know-how, institutional framework, and composition of output as determined by tastes and relative costs of production. The amount of labor supplied and demanded is such that total income just equals the amount of market goods desired for current consumption and for addition to the capital stock so as to increase future income, given the relative value of the output produced by labor at the margin and the leisure which can be substituted for work. Investment is equated to saving, or nonconsumption of income, by changes in the interest rate which firms pay savers who finance the investments of the firms.

5.3   DETERMINANTS OF THE PRICE LEVEL
Nominal Income and the Price Level

One of the most productive institutions in modern market economies is the widespread use of money to avoid barter. *Barter*, direct trade of one commodity for another without the use of money, imposes two special constraints on market exchange: (1) one party must want to buy what the other wants to sell and to sell what the other wants to buy; and (2) purchases must coincide in time with an equal-valued sale. Barter requires the investment of much time used in searching for the best combination of offers; it also restricts the size and timing of transactions. The costs of these transactions are greatly reduced by the expression of all prices in terms of units of a single commodity and using that commodity as the second item in each transaction. This commodity, money, serves as an information, guarantee, or rationing device to assure that one cannot buy things worth more than the goods one sells where a running total is kept over time by the level of one's money balance. As a result of the ability to trade with general rights to present or future goods, people are willing to sell when and to whom their output is most valued and buy when and from whom their purchases are cheapest.

The value of money relative to goods can change substantially with changes in supply or demand conditions for money. The value in terms of money of the goods and services produced will vary inversely with the value of a unit of money in terms of the goods which it can purchase. That is, the price of money in terms of goods is $1/P$, or the amount of goods that it would cost now to buy \$1, the goods being measured in base-year dollars.[9] Nominal

---

[9] See the end of Sec. 3.1.

income, measured in current dollars, is simply the product of real income and the price index,

$$Y = yP \tag{5.19}$$

which varies, as previously stated, inversely with the value of money.

The value of money—and thus nominal income—is determined just as that of any other commodity by its supply and demand.

The Supply of Money

The American money supply consists of currency and coin which are directly controlled by the Federal Reserve System plus deposits at commercial banks[10] which are indirectly controlled by the Fed. The quantity of money supplied is determined by government monetary policy as explained in Sec. 3.3. The Fed has not always exercised that control in a conscious effort to achieve a particular level of the money supply. Under other monetary systems, the nominal supply of money may be dependent not on governmental policy but on such factors as the amount of gold in the country if gold is the monetary base instead of fiat money issued by the government.

For the analysis of the determination of the price level, it will be assumed that the nominal supply of money is fixed at some value M_0 by the government's monetary policy:

$$M^s = M_0 \tag{5.20}$$

Similar results can be obtained from more complex money supply models appropriate to other institutional frameworks. The price level is determined for a given value of the nominal money supply. Of considerable interest are the implications of alternative choices of the nominal money supply for the price level.

The supply of money in real terms varies inversely with the price level:

$$m^s = \frac{M_0}{P} \tag{5.21}$$

The real and nominal supply of money are graphed in panels (a) and (b), respectively, of Fig. 5.17.

---

[10] Whether only demand (checking) deposits or all deposits are included depends on whether one is using the narrow (M_1) or broad (M_2) definition of money. This distinction, which is treated in courses in money and banking, will not be made in the general presentation here.

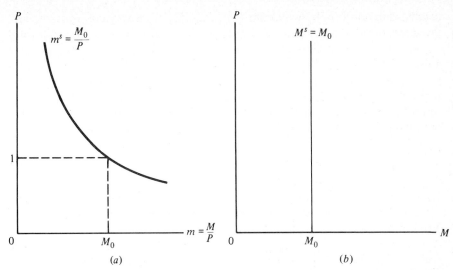

FIGURE 5.17 Money supply as a function of the price level. The Federal Reserve System determines the nominal amount of money existing as M_0, as shown by a vertical line in (b). The real value of the nominal stock of money is dependent upon the price level, as shown by the rectangular hyperbola in (a).

The Demand for Money

Money is used to avoid the costs associated with barter. The demand to hold money is derived from a comparison of the expected gains of holding an additional dollar over some period with the alternatives to holding the dollar. The foregone gains or alternative costs of increasing or decreasing money holdings can be divided into two types: (1) the marginal cost of changing money balances and (2) the marginal cost of holding money balances. In order to increase (decrease) money balances, one must sell (buy) something else. When it is attractive to buy or sell some commodity or service, fluctuations in money balances obviate the costs of simultaneously selling or buying another commodity or service, respectively. These costs are avoided so long as money is allowed to vary with the partially random pattern of receipts and expenditures. There will however be an optimal amount of money to hold, and individuals will arrange their normal patterns of receipts and expenditures so that their money balances usually fluctuate around this amount. Unusually large deviations from this average amount will be met by adjustments of the size and timing of investments in other assets; in this way, the cost of adjusting cash balances is reduced. Here we are interested only in the determinants of the average desired level of cash holdings or the long-run demand for money—not the way in which the cash balances of a particular individual or firm vary between paydays (and the like) nor in the details of the process by which the total quantity of money currently desired, given the costs of moving to the long-run desired amount, is adjusted toward the long-run desired amount. The latter process is the key to the timing of adjustments to disequilibrium and is discussed in Part 3. The long-run demand for money is based upon a comparison of the marginal gains and costs of holding money aside from any costs of moving from the current money holdings to the desired money holdings.

In the following chapters, it will be useful to express the demand for money in terms of a particular identity called the "Cambridge equation":

$$M \equiv \phi y P \qquad [5.22]$$

This identity defines *fluidity* ϕ as the ratio of money to income.[11] The long-run demand for money is expressed in this format as:

$$M^D = \phi^* y P \qquad [5.23]$$

The identity [5.22] must always hold. The behavioral equation [5.23] provides the desired value ϕ^* toward which the actual value adjusts.

The key determinant of the long-run demand for money is total real (human and nonhuman) wealth v. In long-run equilibrium, the actual yield from wealth must equal its long-run expected yield r_v, so that

$$y = r_v v \qquad [5.24]$$

This implies that desired fluidity ϕ^* is $1/r_v$ times the desired ratio $(m/v)^*$ of money to wealth. Since the average yield on wealth does not change much, the long-run demand for money is determined by the factors which determine the relative attractiveness of money as a way of holding wealth: the level of wealth or income, the yield on money r_M, the yields on alternative assets—such as those on short-term bonds r_S and long-term bonds r_L—and a term u to take into account changes in technology, institutions, tastes, and other factors economists are not yet able to measure:

$$m^d \equiv \frac{M^d}{P} = \phi^*(y, r_M, r_S, r_L, u)y \qquad [5.25]$$

Desired fluidity is determined by the function $\phi^* = \phi^*(y, r_M, r_S, r_L \, u)$.[12]

Income (as a proxy for total wealth) appears both as an argument of the function ϕ^* and as a factor by which ϕ^* is multiplied to obtain the real demand for money. The potential amount of exchange to be accomplished by

[11] The ratio is the same whether real money and income $(M/P)/y$ or nominal money and income $M/(yP)$ is used. Fluidity is more widely known as the "Cambridge k" because the symbol k was used instead of ϕ in the original versions at Cambridge University in England.
[12] See, for example, Milton Friedman, The Quantity Theory of Money—A Restatement, in Milton Friedman (ed.), *Studies in the Quantity Theory of Money*, Chicago: University of Chicago Press, 1956; also Milton Friedman, Money: Quantity Theory, in *International Encyclopedia of the Social Sciences*, New York: The Macmillan Company and the Free Press, **10**: 432–447, 1968.

money rises in close proportion to income and wealth, so that the effect of income on ϕ^* measures whether people use more or less money in proportion to the exchange to be accomplished as income rises. The effect of income on money demand is most easily seen by examining the elasticity of money demand with respect to income $\eta_{m^d, y}$. Elasticity was introduced in Chap. 4 as the percentage change in one variable divided by the small percentage change in the other (causal) variable. By applying the rule that the elasticity of a product is the sum of the elasticities of the factors, we have

$$\eta_{m^d, y} = \eta_{\phi^*, y} + \eta_{y, y} \qquad [5.26]$$

The elasticity of income with respect to income is of course 1 (one), so the elasticity of money demand with respect to income is one plus the elasticity of desired fluidity with respect to income:

$$\eta_{m^d, y} = 1 + \eta_{\phi^*, y} \qquad [5.27]$$

Some economists emphasize the possible economies of scale in holding inventories of money as income increases and expect that the increase in money demand would be proportionately less than the increases in income, so that $\eta_{\phi^*, y}$ would be a negative fraction. Other economists emphasize the increased value of time as income rises and note that higher average money balances allow less time to be spent planning receipts and expenditures and making adjustments in cash balances. These economists expect that the rise in cash balances would be proportionately greater than the rise in income; thus, $\eta_{\phi^*, y}$ would be positive. Economists have been unable to discover which force is more important because expected real income rises very smoothly over time. Since the technological, institutional, and taste factors summarized by u also change smoothly over time, we have no real evidence on the separate, *ceteris paribus* effect of changes in real income; there is only evidence on the combined effects as measured over time of both income and the other factors u. Fortunately for macroeconomists, we are usually only interested in this combined effect, which can be estimated from the data.

The total yields, at the margin, of all forms of wealth when both the direct —or pecuniary—yields and the indirect, nonpecuniary yields in the form of services are considered must be equal in equilibrium. Pecuniary yields refer to the rate per dollar of asset of direct payments and price appreciation. Also included for money are indirect payments in the form of reduced prices for other services, such as loans, by which banks evade the limitation on interest payments on deposits. Nonpecuniary yields refer to the services of an asset directly consumed, such as driving an automobile. For money, the main nonpecuniary services are in the value of reduced transaction costs. Other assets can be used to bridge the period between receipt and expenditure, but will only be used to the extent that the time and extra yield above the yield on money are sufficient to compensate for the extra transaction costs of buying and selling the asset. For this reason, an increase in the pecuniary yield of money, other things being equal, will increase the demand for money and decrease the demand for other assets; the reverse is true for a decrease. The nonpecuniary yield of money, as for other assets, falls as the fraction of wealth held as money increases. Thus an increase in the pecuniary yield of money will cause an equilibrating fall in the nonpecuniary yield of money and a rise in the nonpecuniary yield of the assets reduced relative to money. The opposite shift occurs when an increase in the pecuniary yield on a substitute for money decreases the demand for money. The impact of the same change in the pecuniary yield of another asset on the demand for money will depend on whether the other asset is a good or poor substitute for money. Good substitutes for money are found in the various short-term assets such as savings and loan deposits, commercial paper, and Treasury bills. Long-term bonds as well as corporate stocks are subject to large price fluctuations and are poor substitutes for money. The yields on some substitutes for money, particularly durable consumer goods, are all nonpecuniary and not explicitly included in the demand for money function. A general increase in market interest rates as measured by r_t has a positive impact by increasing r_M, a negative impact by increasing r_S, and a zero or small negative impact by increasing r_L. The net effect of increases in interest rates appears to be zero or slightly negative in the post–World War II United States, though there would be some shifting from currency to bank deposits.

Increases in the general level of market interest rates have had small effects on money demand in the postwar United States because the elasticity of money demand with respect to the pecuniary yield on money $\eta_{m^d,\,r_M}$ (which is equal to $\eta_{\phi^*,\,r_M}$) is of about the same magnitude and opposite sign as the elasticity of money demand with respect to the pecuniary yield on short-term bonds, $\eta_{m^d,\,r_S}$, while the elasticity of money demand with respect to the pecuniary yield on long-term bonds is about zero. If all three yields change in proportion, or at least the first two, as is often the case, the net impact on the demand for money is about zero. Increases in reserve requirements increase the costs to banks of providing deposits, and so decrease the pecuniary yield on money and the demand for money.[13]

The three yields in the demand for money function will normally vary in a predictable, approximately proportionate manner with the index of market interest rates. Also, the technology, institutions, and tastes reflected in u are fixed at the time of our analysis. These observations allow us to write the demand for money more compactly as

$$m^d \equiv \frac{M^d}{P} = \phi(y, r)y \tag{5.28}$$

[13] This is a continuing controversy which will be met again in later chapters. The position taken here is presented in Benjamin Klein, Competitive Interest Payments on Bank Deposits and the Long-Run Demand for Money, *American Economic Review*, **64:** 931–49, Dec. 1974; and Michael R. Darby, The Allocation of Transitory Income Among Consumers' Assets, *American Economic Review*, **62:** 928–41, Dec. 1972.

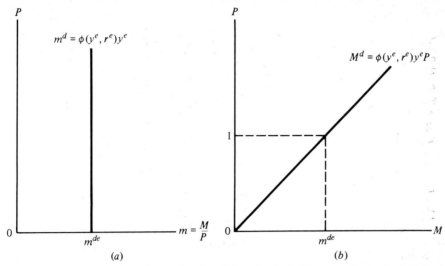

FIGURE 5.18 Money demand as a function of the price level. The general price level P does not affect the real demand for money graphed in (a). The nominal demand for money increases in proportion to the price level in (b). At $P = 1$, the nominal demand for money is equal in magnitude to the real demand for money m^{de}.

If we were to analyze a policy change that would alter the relationship of r_M, r_S, and r_L to r or changes in the basic technology and institutions, it would be necessary to use the more detailed money demand function [5.25] and information about the changed relationships. To obtain a general understanding of the determination of the price level, this detail is not necessary.

Examination of the real demand for money function given in [5.28] shows that the real amount of money demanded is determined by the values of real income and the interest rate determined in achieving real equilibrium. This can be graphed either in terms of the demand for real money balances or, multiplying both sides of [5.28] by P, in terms of the demand for nominal money balances. This is illustrated in panels (a) and (b), respectively, of Fig. 5.18. The real demand for money is completely determined as m^{de} by the real equilibrium of the economy, but the nominal money demand varies directly as the price level.

The Equilibrium Price Level

The equilibrium price level is determined by the condition that money supply must equal money demand:

$$M^S = M^D \tag{5.29}$$

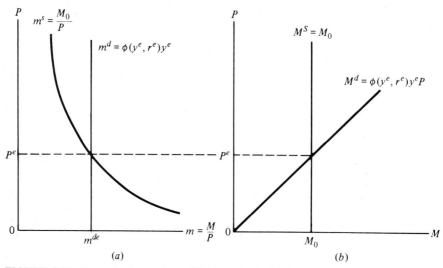

FIGURE 5.19 **Determination of the equilibrium price level.** The real conditions underlying the demand for money fix the real amount of money demanded at m^{de}. Governmental monetary policy fixes the nominal amount of money supplied. In real terms (a), the quantity of money supplied is equated to the fixed amount demanded at the equilibrium price level P^e. In nominal terms (b), the quantity of money demanded is equated to the fixed amount supplied at the equilibrium price level P^e.

This can also be written in real terms by dividing both sides of [5.29] by the price level P:

$$m^s = m^d \tag{5.30}$$

Using the equilibrium values for income y^e and the interest rate r^e determined by the real sector, [5.20], [5.28], and [5.29], or equivalently [5.21], [5.28], and [5.30], are consistent sets of three equations in three unknowns which can be solved for equilibrium money supply, money demand, and the price level.

The graphical solution of these equations is presented in Fig. 5.19. Panel (a) depicts the price level changing so that the real supply of money is equated to the real demand for money as determined by real conditions. Panel (b) shows the other side of the coin in nominal terms. Price-level changes adjust the nominal amount of money demanded to the fixed nominal amount supplied. The geometric construction of the graphs assures that the equilibrium price level P^e will be the same for both approaches.

Conditions of demand determine the real quantity of money, conditions of supply determine the nominal quantity of money, and the price level conforms so that the two amounts are equivalent when adjusted by the price level into the same units. Were the price level below the equilibrium level so that the quantity of money supplied exceeded the quantity of money demanded, whether measured in real or nominal terms, there would be increased bids for the fixed amount of goods produced as people attempt to reduce the excess money balances. This would drive the price level upward toward its equilibrium level. Conversely, if the price level were too high so that the quantity of money demanded exceeded the quantity of money supplied, people would reduce their bids and the price level would fall toward its equilibrium level.

An important implication of this model is that the equilibrium price level is proportional to the nominal quantity of money supplied. This can be seen most easily by noting that the nominal quantity of money is equal to the real quantity of money times the price level.

$$M = mP \qquad\qquad [5.31]$$

In equilibrium, the nominal quantity of money is equal to the amount supplied and the real quantity of money equals the fixed real amount demanded. So [5.31] can only hold if a 5 percent increase in the amount of money supplied causes a 5 percent increase in the price level.

Equilibrium nominal income is the product of the equilibrium real income and the equilibrium price level,

$$Y^e = y^e P^e \qquad\qquad [5.32]$$

Since real income is fixed by the real conditions of technology, institutions, and tastes, nominal income—like the price level—is proportionate to the nominal quantity of money supplied.

□ **SUMMARY**

Real income is determined by the interaction of the real possibilities summarized by the aggregate production function, the amount of capital available, and the amount of labor used according to its relative values in work and leisure. The saving and investment functions determine the rate of interest and the division of production between current consumption and additions to capital stock. The nominal quantity of money supplied is determined by the monetary policy of the Federal Reserve System. The real quantity of money demanded is determined by the conditions of the real equilibrium. The equilibrium price level equates the quantity of money demanded and supplied when measured in the same units, either base-year dollars or current dollars. The price level and nominal income are proportionate to the nominal quantity of money supplied.

☐ QUESTIONS AND EXERCISES

1 If there were an age-eligible population of 120 million people who had an average quality equivalent to six units of raw labor, what would be the rate of labor input if the population actually worked an average of $\frac{1}{4}$ of the time?

2 It is difficult to add different kinds of machines and buildings to obtain a measure of capital. Is this problem conceptually any different from estimating real income or real labor input? Explain why or why not.

3 Part of the rental value of the capital stock accrues to individuals who do not work in any case, such as retired people. Does this eliminate or merely reduce the change in the quantity of labor supplied, other things being equal, if the rental rate on capital somehow increases? Would these people really not work even if the rental rate on capital fell to zero?

4 What is the difference between the labor market equilibrium (LE) curve and the demand curve for labor? What is the difference between the capital market equilibrium (KE) curve and the demand curve for capital?

*5 Use graphical analysis to compare two alternative states with the same amount of capital, average quality of labor, and behavioral functions, but with different age-eligible populations, n_1 and n_2 where n_1 is less than n_2. What will be the effects on the equilibrium values of y, ρ, w, l, and k? Can you make any general statements as to the ratio l_1/n_1 compared to l_2/n_2?

6 An investment project is expected to yield returns of $10, $10, and $110 at the end of 1, 2, and 3 years, respectively, and nothing thereafter. If the investment costs $100 now, would it be profitable at a market interest rate of 8 percent per annum, compounded annually? 10 percent? 12 percent?

7 Explain why $s = i$ is a condition of equilibrium and does not imply identical saving and investment functions?

8 If individuals were free to use money however they wanted except that they had to hold exactly $100 at noon each Sunday, the economy would be a sort of barter economy. Explain why?

*9 Why is $1/P$ called the price of money instead of r_M?

10 (a) Explain why this formula is a useful approximation:

$$\frac{\phi_1^* - \phi_0^*}{\phi_0^*} = \eta_{\phi^*, y} \frac{y_1 - y_0}{y_0} + \eta_{\phi^*, r_M} \frac{r_{M1} - r_{M0}}{r_{M0}} + \eta_{\phi^*, r_S} \frac{r_{S1} - r_{S0}}{r_{S0}} + \eta_{\phi^*, r_L} \frac{r_{L1} - r_{L0}}{r_{L0}}$$

(b) Consider these empirical estimates of the elasticity of desired fluidity with respect to interest rates:

$$\eta_{\phi^*, r_M} \approx \frac{r_{M0}}{\phi_0^*} \frac{\phi_1^* - \phi_0^*}{r_{M1} - r_{M0}} = 0.6$$

similarly

$$\eta_{\phi^*, r_S} \approx -0.6, \ \eta_{\phi^*, r_L} \approx 0$$

(Source: Michael R. Darby, The Allocation of Transitory Income Among Consumers' Assets, American Economic Review, **62**: 933, Dec. 1972.) If $\phi_0^* = 0.25$ where $y = 1000$, $r_{M0} = 0.04$, $r_{S0} = 0.05$, $r_{L0} = 0.06$, what value would ϕ^* have if $y = 1000$,

$r_{M1} = 0.04$, $r_{S0} = 0.06$, $r_{L0} = 0.06$? Approximately what value would ϕ^* have if $y = 1000$, $r_{M1} = 0.048$, $r_{S0} = 0.06$, $r_{L0} = 0.072$?

11 Why do we discuss the real money supply adjusting to equal the fixed real money demand, but talk about the nominal money demand adjusting to equal the fixed nominal money supply? Why are these statements not contradictory?

*12 Consider two alternative states which differ only in the nominal supply of money. In state 1, $M_1^s = 200$, $P_1^e = 1.25$, $y_1^e = 800$. What is Y_1^e? ϕ_1^e? In state 2, $M_2^s = 300$. What are P_2^e, y_2^e, Y_2^e, ϕ_2^e? What are M_2^s/M_1^s, P_2^e/P_1^e, y_2^e/y_1^e, Y_2^e/Y_1^e, ϕ_2^e/ϕ_1^e?

□ **REFERENCES FOR FURTHER READING**

The material in Sec. 2.2 aggregates and generalizes the material found in standard microeconomics texts.

Friedman, Milton: The Quantity Theory of Money—A Restatement, in Milton Friedman (ed): *Studies in the Quantity Theory of Money*, Chicago: The University of Chicago Press, 1956.

Income and the Price Level in a Growing Economy

Chapter 6

6.1 INTRODUCTION

Rising standards of living, income, and often prices characterize the world's economies. Growth in the equilibrium levels of income and prices occurs because of changes in their underlying determinants. In this chapter, the emphasis is on the steady, gradual changes in these factors that determine the trend or *secular* rates of growth of income and prices over long periods of time. In Part 3, we will study the fluctuations—the booms and busts of the business cycle—which result from fluctuations in the rate of change of the underlying determinants.

A moving equilibrium or *steady state* refers to an economy in which all economic aggregates—such as income, price level, population, and money supply—are growing at constant rates. If all these growth rates are zero so that all these aggregates have the same value year after year, the steady state is called a *stationary state*. The steady-state growth path of an economy is a useful standard against which the actual current economic performance can be measured.

The underlying factors in a growing economy can be divided into the same two broadly separate classes of real and monetary factors that were useful for analyzing the determination of the levels of income and prices. The separation is usually less clear-cut, however, in an economy characterized by steady-state growth, because current rates of growth will continue into the future and expectations of the future have a pervasive influence.

6.2 DETERMINANTS OF REAL GROWTH
The Proximate Determinants of Real Income Growth

Growth in real income occurs only through growth in the inputs to the productive process, labor and capital, through changes in the aggregate production function, or both. Although one normally thinks of an upward secular growth in real income, continuing adverse changes—such as those due to the introduction of a fatal disease to an isolated country—may cause negative rates of growth over a period of some time.

In analyzing steady-state growth, basic determinants are separated into two groups: (1) those affected in a predictable way by economic factors and (2) those which are not. The determinants in the first group are said to be *endogenous*, or determined within the economic model based on the given values of the second group of *exogenous* determinants which define the outside conditions to which the economic system adjusts. Much recent history of economic thought is based on reclassifying exogenous determinants as endogenous variables while economists expand their understanding of economic influences on such traditionally "noneconomic variables" as population growth, education, marriage, crime, and legal structures. This expansion of the class of endogenous variables also reflects an expanded technical ability to deal with many factors at the same time, so that previously neglected minor influences no longer need be ignored. Modern models of economic growth have become very complex and mathematically elegant explanations of the reasons behind some generally observed empirical regularities. Only the most basic results are presented here, leaving more detailed discussions to specialized courses.

In most simple growth models the growth rate of labor is assumed to be fixed by noneconomic factors at the constant rate $\bar{g}_l$. A constant growth rate of labor and the amount of labor at any point in time make it possible to compute the amount of labor at every instant. More elaborate models have been developed in which the growth rate of labor is influenced by economic factors. Because essentially the same results are obtained by more complicated methods, it will be assumed in the current presentation that the growth of labor is an exogenously fixed factor to which the economy adjusts. The effects on the economy of alternative growth rates of labor would be a problem in comparative dynamics.[1]

The growth rate of capital g_{kt} at any time t is the rate of change in the capital stock Δk_t divided by the capital stock:[2]

$$g_{kt} = \frac{\Delta k_t}{k_t} \qquad [6.1]$$

If the capital stock is measured in base-year dollars, the rate of change in the capital stock will be equal to the rate of real investment i_t. Thus,

$$g_{kt} = \frac{i_t}{k_t} \qquad [6.2]$$

---

[1] See problem 3 in the Questions and Exercises.
[2] Recall or review the discussion of rates of change and growth rates in Sec. 4.2.

That is, the growth rate of capital equals the proportionate rate per annum at which capital is increased by investment.

The simplified national accounting system used in this and the preceding chapter was shown in [5.16] to imply that real saving s_t and real investment will be equal:

$$s_t = i_t \tag{6.3}$$

It was also noted in Chap. 5 that real saving can be approximated very well as a constant, say σ, times real income y_t:

$$s_t = \sigma y_t \tag{6.4}$$

Combining [6.2], [6.3], and [6.4],

$$g_{kt} = \sigma \frac{y_t}{k_t} \tag{6.5}$$

That is, the growth rate of capital equals the saving-income ratio times the ratio of income to capital. The equation is used to endogenously determine the growth rate of capital.

The analysis is greatly simplified by assuming that the aggregate production function $y_t = f(k_t, l_t)$ is homogeneous of the first degree and does not change over the period being studied. The first requirement means that output changes in proportion to changes in capital and labor (constant returns to scale). So if both capital and labor were doubled, income would also be doubled. If the aggregate production function is of this form, it can also be written as

$$y_t = k_t f(1, l_t/k_t) \tag{6.6}$$

since total output will equal output per unit of capital times the total capital stock. The ratio of output to capital can be found by dividing both sides of [6.6] by k_t

$$\frac{y_t}{k_t} = f(1, l_t/k_t) \tag{6.7}$$

This ratio is graphed in Fig. 6.1 as a function of the labor-capital ratio. As when the production function was graphed for a given quantity of capital in Chap. 5 (Fig. 5.1), the decreasing slope of the curve reflects the smaller increase in output from a given increase in labor as the ratio of labor to capital increases.

The requirement that the aggregate production function not change over time is not as strong as would first appear. Changes in technology are possible so long as they are embodied in our measures of capital and labor as quality changes. The government-supplied factors of production, implicit in the aggregate production function, will normally increase in proportion with capital and labor; thus, one can act as if the production function was an unchanging homogeneous-of-degree-one function of capital and labor alone.

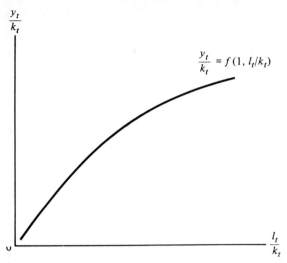

FIGURE 6.1 **The output-capital ratio as a function of the labor-capital ratio.** For an aggregate production function that is homogeneous of the first degree, the entire production function can be summarized by the production function for a unit of capital and its share of labor l_t/k_t. The decreasing slope of the curve reflects the Law of Diminishing Returns.

Steady-State Real Equilibrium

The growth rate of capital was shown in [6.5] to equal the saving-income ratio σ times the output capital ratio. Combining this result with [6.7] expresses the growth rate of capital as an increasing function of the labor-capital ratio:

$$g_{kt} = \sigma f(1, l_t/k_t) \qquad [6.8]$$

The graphical interpretation is presented in Fig. 6.2. Note that output is measured in units of base-year dollars per year and capital in units of base-year dollars, consequently the output-capital ratio is measured in per annum units as is the growth rate of capital.

The constant growth rate of labor can be illustrated on the same diagram as a horizontal line intersecting the vertical axis at $\bar{g}_l$ which is measured in per annum units. This is done in Fig. 6.3.

The fact that $l_t = k_t(l_t/k_t)$ and the rule on the growth rate of a product implies that

$$g_{(l/k)t} = g_{lt} - g_{kt} \qquad [6.9]$$

The growth rate of the labor-capital ratio is positive whenever the growth rate of labor exceeds the growth rate of capital; its growth is negative whenever the growth rate of labor is less than the growth rate of capital. Figure 6.3 shows that should any labor-capital ratio be smaller than l_t^e/k_t^e, the growth

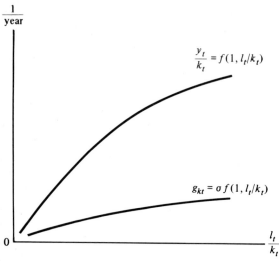

FIGURE 6.2 Relation of the growth rate of capital to the output-capital ratio. The growth rate of capital is obtained by multiplying the output-capital ratio by the constant fraction σ. Since the output-capital ratio increases, at a diminishing rate, with increases in the labor-capital ratio, so does the growth rate of capital.

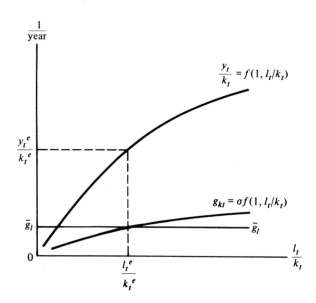

FIGURE 6.3 Determination of real sector growth equilibrium. For any l_t/k_t greater than l_t^e/k_t^e, g_{kt} exceeds $\bar{g}_l$ and l_t/k_t will be falling toward l_t^e/k_t^e. Similarly, for any l_t/k_t less than l_t^e/k_t^e, $\bar{g}_l$ exceeds g_{kt} and l_t/k_t will be rising toward l_t^e/k_t^e. Thus, the economy tends toward l_t^e/k_t^e and $g_{kt} = \bar{g}_l$. Output per unit of capital will therefore tend to y_t^e/k_t^e with $g_{yt} = g_{kt}$.

rate of the labor-capital ratio would be positive so that the labor-capital ratio would approach l_t^e/k_t^e over time. If there were, instead, any labor-capital ratio greater than l_t^e/k_t^e, the growth rate of the labor-capital ratio would be negative so that the labor-capital ratio would approach l_t^e/k_t^e over time. At l_t^e/k_t^e, the growth rate of capital g_{kt} just equals the growth rate of labor, $\bar{g}_l$, consequently the labor-capital ratio remains constant $(g_{(l/k)t} = 0)$.

Thus, a stable-equilibrium labor-capital ratio (l_t^e/k_t^e) exists. It is maintained when saving is just sufficient to finance capital for use with new units of labor in the same proportion as exists for the previous amounts of labor. Should a macroeconomic shock such as that discussed in Part 3 move the economy away from this equilibrium, it will return over time.

Since there is a constant-equilibrium labor-capital ratio, output per unit of capital will also be constant at

$$\frac{y_t^e}{k_t^e} = f(1, l_t^e/k_t^e) \tag{6.10}$$

as shown in Fig. 6.3. This ratio can be constant only if the growth rate of real income is equal to the growth rate of capital, which is the constant growth rate of labor. Thus, in full, steady-state equilibrium, it follows that

$$\bar{g}_y = \bar{g}_k = \bar{g}_l \tag{6.11}$$

The endogenous growth rates of real income and capital thus adjust to the exogenous constant growth rate of labor.

Implications of Steady-State Growth for the Standard of Living

The *standard of living* is measured by per capita real income, or y_t/n_t in terms of the age-eligible population. The growth rate of per capita real income is the difference between the growth rates of real income and population:

$$g_{(y/n)t} = g_{yt} - g_{nt} \tag{6.12}$$

Assuming a constant growth rate of population $\bar{g}_n$ and recalling that the steady-state growth rate of real income equals the constant growth rate of labor $\bar{g}_l$,

$$\bar{g}_{y/n} = \bar{g}_l - \bar{g}_n \tag{6.13}$$

Consequently, per capita real income grows at the rate by which the growth of labor exceeds the growth of population.

The quantity of labor is the product of the participation rate π_t, the quality index q_t, and the age-eligible population n_t; so the growth rate of labor is the sum of the growth rates of these three factors:

$$g_{lt} = g_{\pi t} + g_{qt} + g_{nt} \tag{6.14}$$

If it is assumed that each of these growth rates is a constant—$\bar{g}_\pi$, $\bar{g}_q$, and $\bar{g}_n$, respectively—substitution in [6.13] shows that

$$\bar{g}_{y/n} = \bar{g}_\pi + \bar{g}_q \qquad\qquad [6.15]$$

Thus growth in the standard of living ultimately reflects growth in the labor participation rate and in the average quality of labor.

The participation growth rate reflects trends in the average work week and work life as well as in sex and race participation. The growth rate of average quality reflects the impact of steadily increased education and on-the-job training. In the United States, the distinctly positive trend in the growth rate of the quality of the labor force has been the major determinant of growth in per capita real income. The fact that the growth rate of the standard of living can be increased if the growth rate of participation is increased reminds us that the data of the national income accounts are only one factor which must be combined with evaluations of leisure and social institutions to make a comparison of different economies across time or space.

The distribution of income between labor and capital is also implied by the growth model. A constant labor-capital ratio implies that the steady-state growth of the economy occurs at a single point on the per unit of capital version of the aggregate production function:

$$\frac{y_t^e}{k_t^e} = f\left(1, l_t/k_t\right)$$

As a result, the marginal products of capital and labor—and thus the real rental rate on capital and the real wage of labor—are constants.

The average real interest rate paid on all securities will equal this constant real rental rate per unit of capital.[3] In steady-state equilibrium, firms cannot pay out more than the rental earned on their capital, while competition among firms for financing prevents them from paying less. The real wage as measured per unit of raw labor is also constant, but the average hourly wage of individual workers will rise with their growing average quality.

Since a constant amount is earned per unit of capital and per unit of labor and since capital and labor grow in constant proportion, the ratio of peoples' total earnings from capital to their total earnings from labor will be constant in steady-state equilibrium. This, in fact, is found to hold fairly well over long periods of time. In the United States, personal income is derived on average about one-quarter from capital and three-quarters from labor.[4]

---

[3] Some securities with below-average risk or inconvenience of trading will pay less than average so that those accepting correspondingly less attractive securities can be paid more.
[4] Irving B. Kravis, Relative Income Shares in Fact and Theory, *American Economic Review*, **49**: 917–949, Dec. 1959.

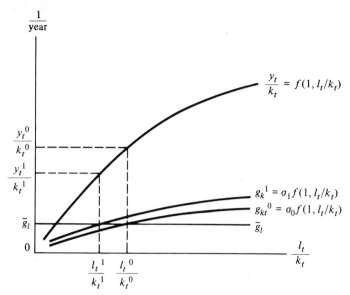

FIGURE 6.4 **The effects of alternative saving-income ratios on steady-state equilibrium.** State 0 is characterized by σ_0 and state 1 by σ_1. All other conditions are the same, but σ_1 is greater than σ_0. The resulting equilibria are $l_t^0/k_t^0 > l_t^1/k_t^1$ and $y_t^0/k_t^0 > y_t^1/k_t^1$. Although the real income per unit of capital is lower in state 1 than in state 0, the higher total amount of capital and equal amounts of labor imply that real income will be higher in state 1 than in state 0. In each state the growth rate of capital and real income will equal the growth rate of labor $\bar{g}_l$.

The Effects of the Saving-Income Ratio on Steady-State Equilibrium

A surprising result of the analysis of steady-state equilibrium is that the saving-income ratio σ does not affect the growth rate of real income. The growth rate of real income adjusts to equal the growth rate of labor. The saving-income ratio does, however, generally affect the level of real income at any particular point in time.[5]

The effects of alternative values of the saving-income ratio are analyzed by comparative dynamics. Suppose that two alternatives are compared, σ_0 and σ_1, and that σ_1 is greater than σ_0. All other conditions are assumed equal. This means that in each instance there is the same growth rate of labor $\bar{g}_l$ and aggregate production function $f(\ )$. Figure 6.4 repeats Fig. 6.3 but with two alternative curves for the growth rate of capital: $g_{kt}^0 = \sigma_0 f(1, l_t/k_t)$ and $g_{kt}^1 = \sigma_1 f(1, l_t, k_t)$. Equilibrium exists in each case where the growth rate of capital equals the growth rate of labor $\bar{g}_l$. The equilibrium labor-capital

---

[5] It is therefore possible to build neo-Malthusian growth models in which the growth rate of labor depends on the *level* of per capita income so that the saving-income ratio will affect the growth rate of real income. The empirical relevance of such models is far from clear, particularly for developed nations.

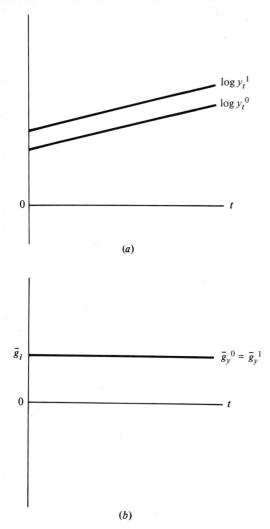

(a)

(b)

FIGURE 6.5 **Growth paths of real income for alternative saving-income ratios.** The growth paths of y_t^0 and y_t^1 where $\sigma_t^0 < \sigma_t^1$ are illustrated in (a). At any instant t, $y_t^1 > y_t^0$, but the growth rates are identical and equal to $\bar{g}_t$ [see (b)]. So the growth paths are parallel straight lines with slope $\bar{g}_t$. Note that the quantity $\log (y_t^1/y_t^0) = \log y_t^1 - \log y_t^0$ is a positive constant, so that y_t^1/y_t^0 is a constant ratio with a value greater than 1.

ratios are denoted l_t^0/k_t^0 and l_t^1/k_t^1. The corresponding equilibrium income-capital ratios are y_t^0/k_t^0 and y_t^1/k_t^1. Thus, a higher saving-income ratio implies a lower labor-capital ratio.

Since the quantity of labor is exogenously given at any point in time, a lower labor-capital ratio implies that there is more capital with σ_1 than with

σ_0. Consequently, a higher saving-income ratio implies a higher, constant capital-labor ratio. Since k_t^1 exceeds k_t^0, and l_t^1 is equal to l_t^0 for any time t,

$$y_t^1 = f(k_t^1, l_t^1) > f(k_t^0, l_t^0) = y_t^0 \qquad [6.16]$$

and the levels of real income, real income per unit of labor, and per capita real income are all higher in an economy with a higher saving-income ratio, all other things equal.[6]

A useful graphical device for summarizing this result is to graph $\log y_t^0$ and $\log y_t^1$ over time. The path over time of the logarithm of a variable is called that variable's *growth path*. The growth paths of y_t^0 and y_t^1 are shown in panel (*a*) of Fig. 6.5. Panel (*b*) shows the paths over time of their growth rates. The growth path of y_t^1 is parallel to but above the growth path of y_t^0.

Summary of the Real Steady-State Equilibrium

Real income grows at a constant rate equal to the growth rate of labor. Capital grows at the same rate. Per capita income grows at the sum of the growth rates of the labor participation rate and the labor quality index. The real rental rate on capital, the real wage rate, and the real interest rate are also constant. Alternative saving-income ratios affect the steady-state level, but not the growth rate, of real income.

6.3 STEADY-STATE GROWTH OF NOMINAL VARIABLES
The Dynamic Version of the Cambridge Equation

The growth of nominal variables is most easily analyzed in terms of the Cambridge equation [5.22] which is rewritten here:

$$M_t = \phi_t y_t P_t \qquad [6.17]$$

The nominal money supply equals the product of fluidity, real income, and

---

[6] For those who recall their trigonometry, a more elegant demonstration is possible. The equilibrium real income per unit of labor is

$$\frac{y_t^e}{l_t^e} \equiv \frac{y_t^e/k_t^e}{l_t^e/k_t^e}$$

The right-hand expression is the tangent of the angle formed by the horizontal axis of Fig. 6.3 and a line through the origin and the point $(l_t^e/k_t^e, y_t^e/k_t^e)$. Because $y_t/k_t = f(1, l_t/k_t)$ is concave from below, higher values of l_t^e/k_t^e are associated with smaller angles and hence tangents. Therefore, the higher equilibrium labor-capital ratio associated with a lower saving-income ratio implies a lower equilibrium real income per unit of labor. Since $l_t^0 \equiv l_t^1$ and $n_t^0 \equiv n_t^1$, the statements for real income and per capita real income follow directly.

the price level. Applying the rule on the growth rate of a product yields the *dynamic Cambridge equation*:

$$g_{Mt} = g_{\phi t} + g_{yt} + g_{Pt} \qquad [6.18]$$

The growth rate of the nominal money supply equals the sum of the growth rates of fluidity, real income, and the price level. In a discussion of steady-state equilibrium, it is unnecessary to distinguish between actual and desired fluidity because they are equal in equilibrium.

The growth rate of desired fluidity is imperfectly understood since it reflects the combined effects of the growth of real income and the growth of that measure u_t of technical and institutional conditions—such as the ratio of all transactions to income transactions. It is observed, however, that there are long periods, measured in decades, over which the trend growth rate of fluidity seems nearly constant. The desired fluidity may also be affected by the interest rates of money, short-term bonds, and long-term bonds. The effect of the level of interest rates is confined to the level of fluidity and not its growth rate, however. So long as interest rates are constant, as it will be seen they are, they have effects on the level, but not the growth rate of fluidity.

Determination of the Rate of Inflation

The constant growth rates of fluidity and real income are determined by conditions of the real economy and denoted as $\bar{g}_\phi$ and $\bar{g}_y$, respectively. The growth rate of the nominal money supply is itself a policy variable which, for purposes of analysis, one assumes has been determined to be some constant $\bar{g}_M$. A rearrangement of [6.18] shows that the *rate of inflation* or the rate of growth in the price level is equal to the difference between the growth rate of the money supply and the sum of the growth rates of fluidity and real income:

$$g_{Pt} = g_{Mt} - g_{\phi t} - g_{yt} \qquad [6.19]$$

But the real demand for money is equal to the product of fluidity and real income and therefore grows at the rate of $g_{\phi t} + g_{yt}$. This equation shows that the rate of inflation equals the amount by which the rate of nominal money creation by the government exceeds the rate of growth in the real demand for money. For steady-state equilibrium, substitution of the three constant values for the growth rates on the right hand gives the constant rate of inflation which will result:

$$\bar{g}_P = \bar{g}_M - \bar{g}_\phi - \bar{g}_y \qquad [6.20]$$

This rate of inflation will maintain continuous equality—once it is in a position of equilibrium—of the supply and demand for money.

An alternative, and frequently more useful, way of looking at these relationships is in terms of the growth rate of nominal income. Since nominal income is equal by definition to the product of real income and the price level, the growth rate of nominal income is the sum of the growth rates of real income and the price level:

$$g_{Yt} \equiv g_{yt} + g_{Pt} \tag{6.21}$$

Substituting [6.21] in [6.18],

$$g_{Mt} = g_{\phi t} + g_{Yt} \tag{6.22}$$

Growth in the money supply will be absorbed by growth in fluidity or by growth in nominal income. For the given growth rates of money and fluidity, the constant growth rate of nominal income is

$$\bar{g}_Y = \bar{g}_M - \bar{g}_\phi \tag{6.23}$$

the amount by which the growth rate of the nominal money supply exceeds the growth rate of fluidity, which may be positive, zero, or negative. The constant rate of inflation is then found by use of [6.21] to be

$$\bar{g}_P = \bar{g}_Y - \bar{g}_y \tag{6.24}$$

which is the same as the rate found directly in [6.20]. The two-step approach of finding the effect of the growth rate of money on the growth rate of nominal income and spending and then finding the effect of the growth rate of nominal income on the rate of inflation is basic to the analysis of shocks to moving equilibrium in Part 3.

The relationships among the levels and growth rates of money, fluidity, nominal income, real income, and prices are summarized graphically in Fig. 6.6. The general features of the equilibrium are similar to the conditions in the United States in the era between the Korean and Vietnamese wars: fluidity is less than unity and falling, while the trend rate of monetary growth leads to an only slightly positive rate of inflation. The level variables are all measured in logarithms so that a straight line indicates a constant growth rate. Also, recall from Chap. 4 that the logarithm of a product equals the sum of the logarithms of the factors; thus $\log M_t = \log Y_t + \log \phi_t$ and $\log Y_t = \log y_t + \log P_t$. Panel (a) shows that the logarithm of nominal income plus the logarithm of fluidity[7] equals the logarithm of the money supply over the whole period. The growth paths of money and fluidity are given by government policy and the real economy, respectively, with nominal income determined by their interaction. Panel (b) contains graphs of the growth rates of these three variables, which are the slopes of the respective graphs of the logarithms of the levels in panel (a). Panel (c) depicts a reproduction of the growth path of the logarithm of nominal income and shows the division between real income and the price level. Here the growth path of the logarithm of

---

[7] Fluidity is less than unity and has a negative logarithm.

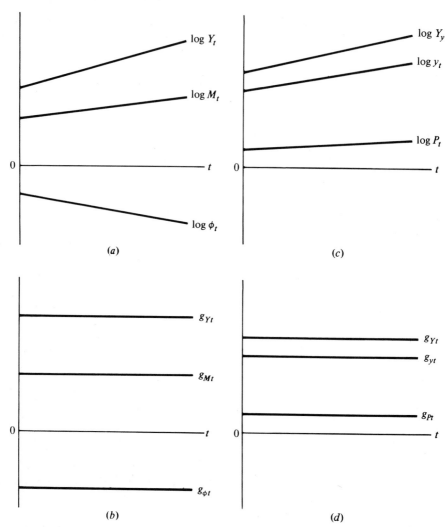

FIGURE 6.6   Graphical presentation of steady-state equilibrium.

real income is fixed by the conditions of the real economy; the growth path of the logarithm of nominal income was determined in panel (a); and the growth path of the logarithm of the price level is determined as the difference between the other two. Panel (d) illustrates the growth rates which are the slopes of the growth paths in panel (c). Note that [6.22] and [6.21] hold for panels (b) and (d), respectively.

The concepts of inflation and the price level lend themselves to easy confusion which should be carefully avoided. *Inflation* properly refers to a condition of *rising* prices or a positive rate of inflation. This should not be confused with prices which are *high* relative to past levels. Prices must have risen at some time in the past in order to be high in the present, but ending inflation would simply require a zero growth rate or constant price level, not a return of prices from their high level to some—which?—"normal" level. *Deflation* is a condition of *falling* prices—not low prices—or a negative rate of inflation. The term *rate of deflation* is sometimes used for minus the rate of inflation.

In the discussion in Chap. 5 of the effect of a 10 percent increase in the money supply on the price level, it was shown that the price level would also increase by 10 percent. That result was for a hypothetical comparison of two alternative money supplies at the same point in time. In this chapter we have been considering the actual effects expected to result from changes in the money supply that occur over a time during which the conditions of the real economy will be changing in predictable ways. If the money supply grows by 10 percent *over a year* in an economy in steady-state equilibrium, one must subtract the rate of growth in real income and fluidity to derive the rate of increase in prices over time. For example, if these rates were 3 percent and 1 percent, respectively, the price level would increase by 6 percent.[8] Nevertheless, were the money supply to be 10 percent lower at each point in time—though growing by 10 percent over the year—then the price level at each point in time would be 10 percent lower than in the first case. This latter comparison is made for given points in time for which the conditions of the real economy are the same—a problem in comparative statics.

The rate of inflation, though dependent on the growth rates of real income and fluidity, is essentially a monetary phenomenon in this sense: Changes in the rate of growth in money are matched percentage point for percentage point by changes in the rate of inflation, and changes in the growth rate of the money supply, being subject to government policy, can change widely as compared to the growth rates of the real variables. More generally, inflation results from a more rapid increase in the nominal money supply than the real money demand.

Special Theories of Inflation

The theory of inflation just discussed has been—with the possible exception of the downward sloping demand curve—the most thoroughly tested and documented of economic propositions. Despite the universal conformity of economic experience in different times and different countries to the theory, there is an almost equally universal tendency in each case to attempt to explain inflations at the time they occur by special circumstances rather than

---

[8] This ignores the trivial error terms involved in discrete time approximations to the continuous time growth rates for which the theory was derived.

the general rule. Such rationalizations are particularly valued by politicians wishing to bear neither the blame for the costs of reducing the rate of inflation—discussed in Parts 3 and 5—nor the blame for the continuation of high rates of monetary growth and inflation.

The special circumstances most widely offered as explanation for the inflation of the 1960s and 1970s are the powers possessed by monopolistic businessmen and unionists to set prices and wages. These powers have been used greedily, thereby causing inflation. Like any popular fallacy, this rationalization is based upon a kernel of truth: Monopoly power due to market closure reduces real income and raises the price level for a given quantity of money relative to the values they would have were markets open to entry. But this is an argument for high, not rising prices. A monopolist may be able to change his price from the profit maximizing one, but only if he is willing to suffer a reduction in income. Only if monopoly power due to market closure is increasing will the rate of growth of income fall and prices rise. So any effect of monopoly on the rate of inflation is associated only with periods of changing degrees of market closure. If market closure increases, the aggregate production function is affected adversely; the reverse is true for a decrease in market closure. There is no evidence of any change in the degree of market closure in the 1960s and 1970s or of monopolists doing anything other than adjusting their nominal price to reflect inflation.[9]

Inflation and Interest Rates

The nominal interest rate r_t observed in the market was shown in Chap. 4 to be determined by the real interest rate r_t', the expected rate of inflation g_{Pt}^*, and the marginal tax rate τ_t' as

$$r_t = r_t' + \frac{g_{Pt}^*}{1 - \tau_t'} \qquad [6.25]$$

In full steady-state equilibrium the expected rate of inflation must equal the actual rate $\bar{g}_P$. The real interest rate is constant due to the constant marginal product of capital. If the marginal tax rate is also held constant at $\bar{\tau}^r$, the nominal interest rate will be constant at

$$\bar{r} = \bar{r}^r + \frac{\bar{g}_P}{1 - \bar{\tau}^r} \qquad [6.26]$$

---

[9] Curiously, the only case in modern American history, aside from wars, of an apparent major shift in the aggregate production function was associated with the passage (June 1933) of the National Industrial Recovery Act and the declaration two years later by the Supreme Court that the act was unconstitutional. The act raised prices and wages by closing markets to competition, but the high real income associated by the politicians with high prices did not appear. Instead, industrial production was below that achieved in 1933 before the NIRA until several months after the Supreme Court declaration.

The equilibrium nominal rate of interest can be characterized as a monetary phenomenon much as is the rate of inflation. The influence, however, runs from money-supply growth to the rate of inflation to the expected rate of inflation and finally to the nominal interest rate.

Effects of Monetary Growth on Real Money Balances

The nominal level of interest rates was expected to have little effect on the trend growth rate of fluidity, at least over a rather broad range. The level of interest rates may well affect the level of the real demand for money at each point in time, however. This is illustrated in Fig. 6.7 in terms of alternate growth paths of fluidity. If the interest elasticity of desired fluidity is less than zero, as many economists believe to be the case, higher rates of interest will cause downward parallel shifts in the growth path of the logarithm of fluidity.

A further complicating factor arises because the level of monetary exchange as against barter is one of the factors underlying the aggregate production function. If high interest rates cause people to resort to more barter to economize on money holdings, real income net of the costs of making transactions will be reduced for any level of capital and labor. As a result there will also be a small downward parallel shift in the growth path of the

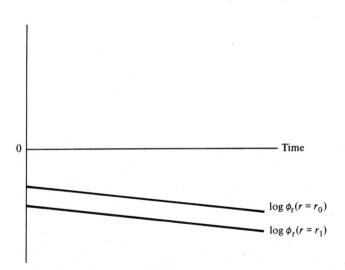

FIGURE 6.7 **Effects of the nominal interest rate on the growth path of fluidity.** A high rate of interest r_1 will cause desired fluidity to be below that associated with a low rate of interest r_0. The growth rate of desired fluidity is the same in both cases, and so the lines have identical slopes.

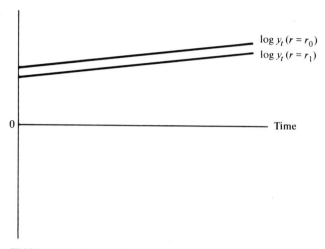

FIGURE 6.8 Effects of the nominal interest rate on the growth path of real income.
A high nominal interest rate r_1 will reduce real income below that associated with a
low nominal interest r_0, if real resources are substituted for real money balances.
The growth paths are parallel because the growth rates (slopes) are the same.

logarithm of real income, as shown in Fig. 6.8.[10] The lower level of income
at each point in time reflects the substitution of real resources—to compute
payrolls more often, make more trips to the bank, make more detailed plans
of cash flow and the like—for the services of real money balances which
are free to society at the margin. There may also be a small change up or
down in the real rental rate on capital and the real interest rate, but this
effect is negligible.

The empirical issues of the existence of net negative impacts of increases
in interest rates on the desired level of fluidity and on real income are still
unsettled.[11] To the extent that banks successfully evade restrictions on interest
payments on deposits and so pay competitive interest rates (see Sec. 3.3), the
effect of the nominal interest rate may well be very small on the demand for
money as a whole. Higher interest rates would tend to decrease the desired
ratio of currency to deposits, however. In European hyperinflations, defined
by price increases of at least 50 percent per *month*, the reduction in fluidity

[10] There may be an offsetting increase in the saving-income ratio, but the effect on the aggregate production
function would appear to dominate. This is, however, an open empirical question. See the "References for
Further Reading" for literature surveys by Harry Johnson and Allan H. Meltzer.
[11] The difficulty in evaluating the empirical data occurs because actual fluidity is expected for other reasons
(discussed in Part 3) to vary over the business cycle in much the same way as it would because of cyclical
variations in interest rates. Economists who include some or all of these other reasons in their analyses
report a much smaller—or no—influence of interest rates on the long-run desired level of fluidity than those
who leave the alternative forces out of their statistical analyses.

and real income is very obviously related to the rate of inflation but this may be due to the breakdown of competitive interest on deposits as part of the general breakdown of debt financing during these periods. For the range of interest rates observed in the 1950s and 1960s in the United States, effects on both fluidity and real income appear quite small and are neglected entirely in some analyses.

These possible indirect effects of the rate of growth of the nominal money supply on fluidity and real income break down the strict separation of the real economy from the nominal money supply even in long-run equilibrium. The simple separation of Chap. 5 was based on an implicitly given value of the expected rate of inflation, which is determined in a steady state. The level of the money supply, given its rate of growth, affects only the price level and not the real economy; but the rate of growth of the money supply, for a given money supply, can affect both the price level and the real economy.

A Problem in Comparative Dynamics

The best way to master these theoretical results is by working through an actual problem. The problem will be to compare and contrast the growth paths of the major macroeconomic variables for two alternative constant rates of monetary growth $\bar{g}_M{}^0 = 0.03$ and $\bar{g}_M{}^1 = 0.07$. The hypothetical economy with the 3 percent growth rate of the money supply is called state 0 and the alternative economy with the 7 percent growth rate is state 1. The economies are alike with respect to basic resources, tastes, technology, and institutions.

The best way to start answering the problem is to prepare a table of known results as in Table 6.1. The actual values for the problem can then be substituted to get the corresponding numerical answers which are entered in Table 6.2. Some values are given as the basis of the problem. Others are either assumed or observed to reflect the real resources, tastes, technology, and institutions of the economy. The remaining values in the table are derived on the basis of these given values. Figure 6.9 represents the results graphically.

For this problem there are given values for the growth rate of the money supply $\bar{g}_M{}^0 = 0.03$ and $\bar{g}_M{}^1 = 0.07$ and these are entered into the tables. The growth rates of fluidity, real income, and the real interest rate will be the same for all growth rates of the money supply—at least over some broad range—and these are observed to be $\bar{g}_\phi = -0.02$, $\bar{g}_y = 0.04$, and $\bar{r} = 0.03$.[12] The growth rate of nominal income was found in [6.23] to be the difference between the growth rates of the money supply and of fluidity; so $\bar{g}_Y{}^0 = \bar{g}_M{}^0 - \bar{g}_\phi = 0.03 - (-0.02) = 0.05$ and $\bar{g}_Y{}^1 = g_M{}^1 - \bar{g}_\phi = 0.07 - (-0.02) = 0.09$. The rate of growth of nominal income in state 1 is higher than that

---

[12] These values approximate the values observed in the United States during the 1960s.

TABLE 6.1   General comparative dynamics results

Variable	State 0	State 1
Growth rate of money supply[a]	$\bar{g}_M{}^0$	$\bar{g}_M{}^1$
Growth rate of fluidity[b]	$\bar{g}_\phi$	$\bar{g}_\phi$
Growth rate of nominal income	$\bar{g}_Y{}^0 = \bar{g}_M{}^0 - \bar{g}_\phi$	$\bar{g}_Y{}^1 = \bar{g}_M{}^1 - \bar{g}_\phi$
Growth rate of real income[b]	$\bar{g}_y$	$\bar{g}_y$
Growth rate of prices = rate of inflation	$\bar{g}_P{}^0 = \bar{g}_Y{}^0 - \bar{g}_y$	$\bar{g}_P{}^1 = \bar{g}_Y{}^1 - \bar{g}_y$
Real interest rate[b]	$\bar{r}^r$	$\bar{r}^r$
Nominal interest rate (tax rate $= \tau$)	$\bar{r}^0 = \bar{r}^r + \dfrac{\bar{g}_P{}^0}{1-\tau}$	$\bar{r}^1 = \bar{r}^r + \dfrac{\bar{g}_P{}^1}{1-\tau}$
Case (a) (negligible $\eta_{\phi,r}$):		
Money supply[a]	$M_t{}^0$	$M_t{}^1$
Level of fluidity[b]	$\phi_t{}^0$	$\phi_t{}^1 = \phi_t{}^0$
Nominal income	$Y_t{}^0 = M_t{}^0 \vert \phi_t{}^0$	$Y_t{}^1 = Y_t{}^0 \dfrac{M_t{}^1}{M_t{}^0}$
Real income[b]	$y_t{}^0$	$y_t{}^1 = y_t{}^0$
Price level	$P_t{}^0 = \dfrac{Y_t{}^0}{y_t{}^0}$	$P_t{}^1 = P_t{}^0 \dfrac{M_t{}^1}{M_t{}^0}$
Case (b) (significant $\eta_{\phi,r} < 0$):		
Money supply[a]	$M_t{}^0$	$M_t{}^1$
Fluidity[b,c]	$\phi_t{}^0$	$\phi_t{}^1 = \gamma_1 \phi_t{}^0$
Nominal income	$Y_t{}^0 = M_t{}^0 \vert \phi_t{}^0$	$Y_t{}^1 = Y_t{}^0 \dfrac{M_t{}^1}{\gamma_1 M_t{}^0}$
Real income[b,c]	$y_t{}^0$	$y_t{}^1 = \gamma_2 y_t{}^0$
Price level	$P_t{}^0 = \dfrac{Y_t{}^0}{y^0}$	$P_t{}^1 = P_t{}^0 \dfrac{M_t{}^1}{\gamma_1 \gamma_2 M_t{}^0}$

[a] Assumed for purposes of comparative analysis.
[b] Determined by the real resources, tastes, technology, and institutions of the economy.
[c] The constants γ_1 and γ_2 (see text for determination) lie between zero and one.

in state 0 by the difference in the growth rates of money, $\bar{g}_M{}^1 - \bar{g}_M{}^0 = 0.07 - 0.03 = 0.04$. The rate of inflation in state 1 is higher than that in state 0 by the same amount, since, from [6.24],

$$\bar{g}_P{}^0 = \bar{g}_Y{}^0 - \bar{g}_y = 0.05 - 0.04 = 0.01$$

and

$$\bar{g}_P{}^1 = \bar{g}_Y{}^1 - \bar{g}_y = 0.09 - 0.04 = 0.05$$

TABLE 6.2   Solution to example

Variable	State 0	State 1
Growth rate of money supply	3%†	7%†
Growth rate of fluidity	−2%†	−2%
Growth rate of nominal income	5%	9%
Growth rate of real income	4%†	4%
Rate of inflation	1%	5%
Real interest rate	3%†	3%
Nominal interest rate (tax rate = $\frac{1}{3}$†)	4.5%	10.5%
Case (a) (negligible $\eta_{\phi,r}$):		
Money supply	200†	200†
Fluidity	0.2†	0.2
Nominal income	1000	1000
Real income	800†	800
Price level	1.25	1.25
Case (b) (significant $\eta_{\phi,r} < 0$):		
Money supply	200†	200†
Fluidity ($\gamma_1 = 0.75$†)	0.2†	0.15
Nominal income	1000	1333
Real income ($\gamma_2 = 0.98$†)	800†	784
Price level	1.25	1.70

† Given data for solution.

The nominal rates of interest are given by [6.26] if the marginal tax rate is assumed to be $\frac{1}{3}$, as

$$\bar{r}^0 = \bar{r}^r + \frac{\bar{g}_P{}^0}{1 - \bar{\tau}^r} = 0.03 + \frac{0.01}{1 - \frac{1}{3}} = 0.045$$

and

$$\bar{r}^1 = \bar{r}^r + \frac{\bar{g}_P{}^1}{1 - \bar{\tau}^r} = 0.03 + \frac{0.05}{1 - \frac{1}{3}} = 0.105$$

Since

$$\bar{r}^1 - \bar{r}^0 = \frac{\bar{g}_P{}^1 - \bar{g}_P{}^0}{1 - \bar{\tau}^r}$$

the growth rate part of the results can be summarized as: *Different growth rates of the money supply do not affect the rates of growth of fluidity and real income or the real interest rate, but cause identical differences in the rates of growth of nominal income and prices and differences in nominal interest rates $1/(1 - \bar{\tau}^r)$ times as large as the difference in money-supply growth rates.*

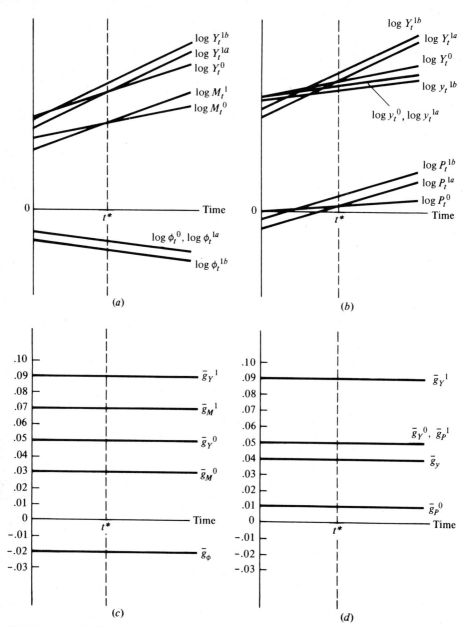

FIGURE 6.9   Graphical solution to comparative statics problem. The numerical values in Table 6.2 correspond to time t^* in the graphs.

The results for relative levels of aggregate magnitudes—if the differences in monetary growth rate are known—are complicated by the potential effects of the higher nominal interest rate in state 1 on fluidity and real income. Some economists argue that these effects are trivial and can be neglected, while others read the evidence differently and expect significant effects. These differences can be contrasted by solving the problem for two cases: Case (a) assumes that nominal interest rates affect neither desired fluidity nor real income; Case (b) assumes that there is a significant negative elasticity $\eta_{\phi, r}$ of fluidity with respect to the nominal interest rate.

To solve Case (a) for specific numerical values, it is necessary to examine a specific point in time t^*, although the general solution holds for any point of time at which the steady states were to hypothetically exist. The easiest arbitrary point in time to examine is the instant when the money supply in state 1 has just caught up with and not yet passed the money supply in state 0. A specific value of the money supply is assumed to exist at time t^* for purposes of the numerical example; so $M_{t^*}{}^0 = M_{t^*}{}^1 = 200$. The values of fluidity and real income are set by the real conditions of the economy at $\phi_{t^*}{}^0 = 0.2$ and $y_{t^*}{}^0 = 800$. The real growth paths are assumed to be unaffected by the higher nominal interest rate in state 1; so $\phi_t{}^1 = \phi_t{}^0 = 0.2$ (at t^*) and $y_t{}^1 = y_t{}^0 = 800$ (at t^*). The nominal income version of the Cambridge equation is

$$M_t = \phi_t \, Y_t \qquad\qquad [6.27]$$

The nominal incomes are thus $Y_t{}^0 = M_t{}^0/\phi_t$ and $Y_t{}^1 = M_t{}^1/\phi_t$. To compare relative values it is useful to substitute $M_t{}^0/Y_t{}^0$ for ϕ_t in the $Y_t{}^1$ equation:

$$Y_t{}^1 = \frac{M_t{}^1}{M_t{}^0/Y_t{}^0}$$

$$= Y_t{}^0 \frac{M_t{}^1}{M_t{}^0} \qquad\qquad [6.28]$$

Substituting the numerical values, $Y_{t^*}{}^0 = 200/0.2 = 1000$ and $Y_{t^*}{}^1 = 1000$ $(200/200) = 1000$. The price level can be determined by using the definition of real income $y_t = Y_t/P_t$. So

$$P_t{}^0 = \frac{Y_t{}^0}{y_t{}^0} = \frac{1000}{800} = 1.25 \text{ (at } t^*)$$

and

$$P_t{}^1 = \frac{Y_t{}^1}{y_t{}^1} = \frac{1000}{800} = 1.25 \text{ (at } t^*)$$

For more general comparisons the fact that $y_t{}^1 = y_t{}^0$ can be used to derive $P_t{}^1 = P_t{}^0(Y_t{}^1/Y_t{}^0) = P_t{}^0(M_t{}^1/M_t{}^0)$. In the absence of any real effects of the level of nominal interest rates, fluidity and real income have the same values in state 1 as in state 0, while nominal income and the price level in state 1 are a multiple M_t^1/M_t^0 of their values in state 0. The growth rate of the multiple M_t^1/M_t^0 is $\bar{g}_M{}^1 - \bar{g}_M{}^0$.

The solution to Case (b) is different because of the effects of the nominal interest rate on fluidity and real income. The numerical solution will assume the same values of money supply at the instant for which Table 6.2 is compiled. The levels of fluidity and real income recorded for state 0 in Case (a) will also be used; so state 0 is identical for Case (a) and Case (b). But for state 1, the higher nominal rate of interest causes a lower level of fluidity and real income. It is not possible to specify this effect precisely without going into more detail about the demand for money and aggregate income than currently is known. In more general terms, fluidity in state 1 will be some fraction γ_1 of fluidity in state 0. If, for example, $\gamma_1 = 0.75$, $\phi_t^1 = \gamma_1 \phi_t^0 = 0.75\,(0.2) = 0.15$ (at t^*). Real income will also be smaller in state 1 than state 0 by some fraction γ_2, but the impact of the reduced fluidity on real income should be much less in percentage terms. That is, γ_1 will be positive and less than γ_2 which is less than 1. For example, if $\gamma_2 = 0.98$, $y_t^1 = \gamma_2 y_t^0 = 0.98\,(800) = 784$ (at t^*). Using [6.27] and $\phi_t^1 = \gamma_1 \phi_t^0$, nominal income is

$$Y_t^1 = \frac{M_t^1}{\gamma_1 M_t^0 / Y_t^0}$$

$$= Y_t^0 \frac{M_t^1}{\gamma_1 M_t^0} \qquad\qquad [6.29]$$

$$Y_{t^*}^1 = 1000 \frac{200}{(0.75)(200)} = 1333$$

The price level is found to be

$$P_t^1 = \frac{Y_t^1}{y_t^1}$$

$$= \frac{Y_t^0 (M_t^1 / \gamma_1 M_t^0)}{\gamma_2 (Y_t^0 / P_t^0)}$$

$$= P_t^0 \frac{M_t^1}{\gamma_1 \gamma_2 M_t^0}$$

$$P_{t^*}^1 = 1.25 \frac{200}{(0.75)(0.98)(200)} = 1.70 \qquad\qquad [6.30]$$

In this case, there are real effects of the higher rate of inflation which reduce fluidity and real income in state 1 to multiples γ_1 and γ_2, respectively, of their values in state 0 at any point in time. The values of nominal income and the price level in state 1 are multiples $M_t^1/\gamma_1 M_t^0$ and $M_t^1/\gamma_1\gamma_2 M_t^0$, respectively, of their values in state 0. The growth rate of both multiples is $\bar{g}_M^1 - \bar{g}_M^0$.

Fluidity, real income, and the real interest rate are classed as the real variables; the nominal money supply, nominal income, price level, and the nominal interest rate are classed as nominal variables. Different levels of the nominal money supply affect only the nominal variables and not the real variables. The growth rate of money may influence the levels of both fluidity and real income, however, at least at high rates of growth.

☐ SUMMARY

In the steady state the growth rates of real income and capital are equal to the growth rate of labor. The constant ratio of capital to labor leads to a constant real rental rate on capital, real interest rate, and real wages. Per capita income grows by the sum of the growth rates of labor-force quality and participation of the population. The saving-income ratio affects the level but not the growth rate of real income. The growth rate of fluidity is also observed to be constant over long periods of time. Nominal income grows at the rate by which the growth rate of the money supply exceeds the growth rate of fluidity. The rate of inflation is the difference between the rates of growth of nominal and real income. The nominal interest rate exceeds the real interest rate by the rate of inflation divided by the marginal fraction of income left after income taxes. Nominal variables, but generally not real variables, are influenced in steady-state equilibrium by the rate of growth which the government chooses for the nominal money supply. This choice may, however, affect the *levels* of fluidity and real income by shifting their growth paths. Higher growth paths of fluidity and real income are associated with lower rates of money-supply growth and the resulting lower nominal interest rates.

☐ QUESTIONS AND EXERCISES

*1 Can you think of any economies, present or past, which would approximate a stationary state? Does a constant population imply a stationary state of no growth?

2 (a) The hypothetical aggregate production function $y = 3k^{1/2}l^{1/2} = 3\sqrt{kl}$ is homogeneous of the first degree. Illustrate this by computing y_0 for $k_0 = 40{,}000$ and $l_0 = 160{,}000$ and y_1 for $k_1 = 1$ and $l_0 = 4$ and the ratios y_1/y_0, k_1/k_0, l_1/l_0.

(b) Divide the production function in part (a) by k and show that output per unit of capital is dependent on the ratio of labor to capital but not their levels.

*3 Two economies are alike in their aggregate production function and saving-income ratio, but differ in their growth rates of labor which are $\bar{g}_l^0$ in country 0 and $\bar{g}_l^1$ in country 1. Assume $\bar{g}_l^0$ is less than $\bar{g}_l^1$. Use a graph to derive and compare the equilibrium labor-capital ratios in the two countries. Can you tell which country will have the highest income per unit of labor? The highest per capita income? Explain.

4 Does a high level of education imply a higher growth rate of per capita income? Does a rising level of education imply a higher growth rate of per capita income?

5 "Inflation results to the extent that growth in the money supply exceeds growth in real goods and services." Evaluate critically.

6 During the post-World War I German hyperinflation, German central bankers claimed that the inflation could not be blamed on them because they were just meeting the increased demand for money due to increased income. Indeed they claimed, monetary policy was tight because interest rates were high and money was a smaller fraction of income. What is wrong with this argument?

7 A comparative dynamics problem: Compare the effects of alternative rates of monetary growth by filling in the blanks in the following table.

Variable	State 0	State 1
Growth rate of the money supply	6%	11%
Growth rate of fluidity		
Growth rate of nominal income	5%	
Growth rate of real income		
Growth rate of the price level	2%	
Real interest rate		
Nominal interest rate (tax rate $= \frac{1}{2}$)	8%	

*8 In the comparative dynamics problem of Table 6.2, a 7 percent increase in the money supply over a year would be required for a 5 percent increase in prices. At the end of Chap. 4, the comparative statics analysis demonstrated that "a 5 percent increase in the amount of money supplied causes a 5 percent increase in the price level." Can both statements be correct? Explain.

☐ **REFERENCES FOR FURTHER READING**

Johnson, Harry G.:   Money in a Neo-Classical One-Sector Growth Model, in *Essays in Monetary Economics*, London: G. Allen, 1967.

Meltzer, Allan H.:   Money, Intermediation, and Growth, *Journal of Economic Literature*, 7: 27–56, Mar. 1969.

Solow, Robert M.:   *Growth Theory: An Exposition*, New York: Oxford University Press, 1970.

Dynamic Adjustments to Macroeconomic Shocks

Part 3

The economy does not continuously maintain the smooth steady-state equilibrium discussed in Part 2. Instead changes in the underlying conditions of the economy occur from time to time which cause the actual values of at least some macroeconomic variables to deviate from their equilibrium values. These disturbances to underlying conditions are called *macroeconomic shocks.*

Macroeconomic shocks can cause deviations of actual values from long-run equilibrium values—or *disequilibrium*—either by altering the steady-state equilibrium itself or by displacing real income, the price level, or both from unchanged steady-state growth paths. The economy then converges over time to the existing steady-state growth path in the absence of further shocks.

The actual behavior of the economy reflects the interaction of two types of forces: The first continually moves the economy over time toward equilibrium if it is not there and maintains steady-state equilibrium if it exists. The second kind of force, when it is present, may reinforce or overwhelm the tendency toward equilibrium by altering either the actual or equilibrium growth paths of real income and the price level.

The analogy is often made to a hanging pendulum which has a vertical equilibrium position. A blow from a hammer may move the pendulum away from this equilibrium but it will eventually return there in the absence of further blows. If the pendulum is swinging out of equilibrium, a blow can either give further impetus or absorb the motion of the pendulum. Though the oscillatory adjustment of the pendulum to equilibrium may not be noticeable in the economy, the principle is much the same.

Macroeconomic shocks are discussed in three general groups: Chapter 7 analyzes the effects of a change in the growth rate of the nominal money supply. This shock receives separate treatment because of its importance in the real world and because it is a simple case that introduces the forces involved in the dynamic adjustment of the economy to macroeconomic shocks. Chapter 8 studies all other potential macroeconomic shocks which occur within the domestic economy. Chapter 9 relates the American economy to the rest of the world and considers possible shocks affecting the United States from the outside. Chapter 10 then discusses the interaction of these shocks within the context of the last half-century of American experience. The empirical importance of different sources of macroeconomic shocks is also assessed there.

Effects of a Change in the Growth Rate of the Money Supply

7.1 STATEMENT OF THE PROBLEM

This chapter is concerned with only one question: Starting from a steady state with a money-supply growth rate of $\bar{g}_M{}^0$, what would be the effects of a change at time t^* to a new, different growth rate $\bar{g}_M{}^1$ which is maintained indefinitely thereafter. The final solution when the economy has achieved steady-state growth was contrasted with the initial steady state in the comparative dynamics problem at the end of Chap. 6. Here the concern is with what happens between t^* and the time when the economy ultimately converges to the new moving equilibrium.

Interest focuses on the interim period of disequilibrium because the economy is rarely in full steady-state equilibrium and because the period of disequilibrium explains many of the phenomena of the business cycle. The problem as stated is somewhat artificial, since a change in the money-supply growth rate usually occurs long before the economy has adjusted to the preceding growth rate change, but in an intermediate textbook all possible initial conditions cannot be considered separately. The influence of initial conditions in reinforcing or offsetting the effects explained here is discussed in Chap. 10 in connection with the actual record of twentieth-century U.S. macroeconomic history.

The stated problem suggests that the Federal Reserve System increases the rate of growth of the money supply and all other macroeconomic shocks are excluded. This, however, is impossible because government transactions (with the accounts of the Federal Reserve System and Treasury consolidated) are subject to the budget identity

$$G_t \equiv T_t + \Delta B_t + \Delta D_t \tag{7.1}$$

That is, the rate of government spending G_t at time t is equal to the total of the rate of taxes T_t and the rates of change in base money ΔB_t and in the national debt held by the public ΔD_t, each of the variables being measured in nominal terms. Changes in base money and the national debt, if positive, are the possible ways to finance an excess of government spending over taxation; if they are negative, these changes are the alternative possible uses of an excess of taxes over government spending. Assuming that the money multiplier grows at a constant rate, the change in the growth rate of the money supply will require an equal change in the growth rate of base money. The growth rate of base money is the rate of change in base money divided by its level to convert the absolute change into proportionate terms:

$$g_{Bt} = \frac{\Delta B_t}{B_t} \qquad\qquad [7.2]$$

The required change in ΔB_t must be offset by changes in G_t, T_t, or ΔD_t. In this chapter it is assumed that changes in the rate of base-money creation are offset by an opposite change in the rate of increase in the national debt. In the next chapter, effects of changes in the rate of government spending and taxation offset by changes in the rate of increase in the national debt will be discussed. The results of the two chapters can be combined to analyze the effects of an increased growth rate of money which finances an increased rate of government spending or decreased rate of taxation.

7.2 EFFECTS ON THE GROWTH PATH OF NOMINAL INCOME
Changes in Steady-State Growth Paths

The effects of the monetary shock described in Sec. 7.1 are most readily understood by examining, first, the effects on fluidity and nominal income and, then, how fluctuations in nominal income are divided between real income and the price level. Consider first the case in which the new rate of growth in the money supply $\bar{g}_M{}^1$ is greater than the old growth rate $\bar{g}_M{}^0$.

The actual growth path of the money supply is illustrated in panel (a) of Fig. 7.1. The increased trend rate of growth of the money supply is indicated by the increased slope of the logarithm of the money supply at t^*. Panel (b) shows this directly as a sudden jump at t^* in the growth rate of the money supply which is the slope of the log M_t line in panel (a).

The steady-state growth paths that fluidity and nominal income would follow if the economy were somehow to immediately and completely adjust to the new, higher rate of money-supply growth are useful standards for comparison. At the end of Sec. 6.3, this very problem was solved in a slightly different setting. Up to t^*, the growth paths desired are the ones which were derived for state 0 defined by a monetary growth rate $\bar{g}_M{}^0$. After t^*, the growth paths for state 1 defined by $\bar{g}_M{}^1$ are those sought. These growth paths and growth rates are illustrated in panels (a) and (b), respectively, of Fig. 7.2. The growth path and growth rates of the money supply are reproduced from Fig. 7.1. Consider initially the case in which the elasticity of the demand for money with respect to the general level of market interest rates is zero because of the payment of competitive interest rates on money. The complication of effects of the level of interest rates on the desired level of fluidity will be added later.

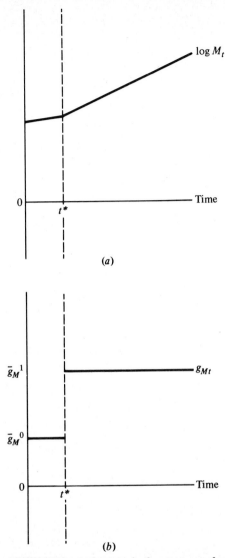

FIGURE 7.1 An increase in the money-supply growth rate at t^*. At t^*, monetary policy changes and the growth rate of the money supply is increased from $\bar{g}_M{}^0$ to $\bar{g}_M{}^1$. This change is shown in (a) by an increase in the slope of the log M_t line at t^*; (b) shows a discontinuous jump at t^* in the money-supply growth rate from $\bar{g}_M{}^0$ to the higher rate $\bar{g}_M{}^1$, which is maintained thereafter.

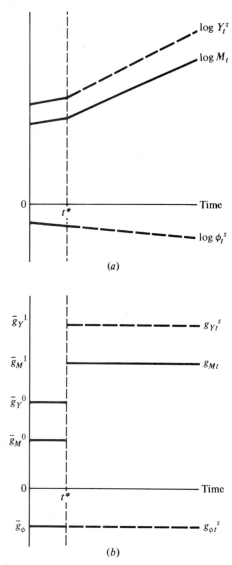

FIGURE 7.2 Steady-state growth paths for fluidity and nominal income. The steady-state growth path of fluidity is fixed by the conditions of the real economy and not affected by the growth rate of the money supply. The entire increase in the growth rate of the money supply (slope of the log M_t line) after t^* is reflected in an equal increase in the steady-state growth rate of nominal income (slope of the log Y_t^s line).

The increase in the growth rate of the money supply does not affect the growth path of fluidity at all, but merely causes an equal increase in the slope of the growth path of nominal income at t^*. These changes maintain consistency with the basic identities that must hold for the actual values of money, nominal income, and fluidity:

$$\log M_t \equiv \log \phi_t + \log Y_t \qquad\qquad [7.3]$$

$$g_{Mt} \equiv g_{\phi t} + g_{Yt} \qquad\qquad [7.4]$$

If a superscript s is used to denote the steady-state values associated with the *given actual level and growth rate of the money supply at time t*, then these identities also hold:

$$\log M_t \equiv \log \phi_t^s + \log Y_t^s \qquad\qquad [7.5]$$

$$g_{Mt} \equiv g_{\phi t}^s + g_{Yt}^s \qquad\qquad [7.6]$$

Subtracting [7.5] from [7.3] and [7.6] from [7.4], and rearranging terms,

$$\log \phi_t - \log \phi_t^s \equiv -(\log Y_t - \log Y_t^s) \qquad\qquad [7.7]$$

$$g_{\phi t} - g_{\phi t}^s \equiv -(g_{Yt} - g_{Yt}^s) \qquad\qquad [7.8]$$

So if there should be any disequilibrium between the actual and steady-state values for fluidity, it is always of the same magnitude and opposite sign as the disequilibrium of nominal income where the level disequilibria are measured in logarithmic (or proportionate) terms and the growth rate disequilibria are measured in absolute terms.

Adjustment of Actual Growth Paths to the Steady-State Growth Paths

The simple steady-state growth paths of fluidity and nominal income must be drawn in broken lines, because the real world adjusts only slowly toward the new growth paths. There is a substantial period of disequilibrium for fluidity and nominal income.

Although the steady-state growth path of fluidity is characterized by stability while the steady-state growth path of nominal income adjusts passively to the growth path of the money supply, these roles are practically reversed at the beginning of a new monetary policy. In the short run, the growth path of nominal income shows relatively great inertia while the growth path of fluidity adjusts passively to the change in money-supply growth. This difference arises because the government, by changing the rate at which it creates money, causes a net unplanned increase in money holdings by individuals. When the government borrows less than anticipated because of increased money creation, planned loans of money are frustrated. Some of the money will be lent out for other uses immediately but this displaces funds normally lent there.

Alternative uses of money are not generally found instantly, so money holdings will exceed the desired level. Total money balances cannot be reduced by spending them in any case, since one person's expenditure of money is another person's receipt of money, the total being fixed at any moment by the government's monetary policy. The effect of the eventual attempts by individuals to reduce their excess cash balances by spending money is to increase the rate of expenditures on final goods and services. This increase in nominal income increases the nominal demand for money and so removes the disequilibrium. It appears that any individual can reduce his money balances to a desired level, but this is impossible for all individuals taken together. Nevertheless their attempts to accomplish the impossible, which must be frustrated, are essential to reestablishing equilibrium by increasing the demand for money in nominal terms. The faster individuals attempt to reduce their excess cash balances by spending, the faster will nominal income rise to reestablish equilibrium between the actual and desired values of fluidity. Exactly how do individuals attempt to manage their money holdings?

Money balances serve much as do the shock absorbers on an automobile: They absorb immediately most of any shock and spread out its impact as they slowly return to their equilibrium value. The increase in the rate of growth of the money supply, over that built into the plans for receipts and expenditures, will be a continuing shock tending to increase actual money balances (and, therefore, observed fluidity) above their long-run desired levels, which can be measured by $\log \phi_t - \log \phi_t^s$. This force will continue until planned patterns of expenditures and receipts have adjusted to the new equilibrium. But individuals who hold the excess-money balances which result increase their rate of spending above what it would otherwise be in an attempt to draw down the excess balances. They can only transfer the fixed nominal amount of money from hand to hand, but the increased spending will lead to increases in nominal income which will, through its effects on the price level and real income, increase the nominal demand for money toward the actual amounts supplied and held. As plans are adjusted, the shock weakens and the disequilibrium in fluidity begins to be reduced.

This process can be summarized in terms of a single equation:

$$g_{\phi t} = \bar{g}_\phi + (g_{Mt} - g_{Mt}^*) - \lambda(\log \phi_t - \log \phi_t^s) \qquad [7.9]$$

This equation says that the growth rate of fluidity will exceed its steady-state rate by the excess of the actual growth rate of the money supply over the growth rate g_{Mt}^* built into planned receipts and expenditures less a positive multiple λ of the logarithmic difference between actual fluidity and its steady-state desired value.[1] At the beginning of the new policy there is no fluidity

---

[1] This equation omits the effects on the growth rate of fluidity of other shocks discussed in Chap. 8.

disequilibrium ($\log \phi_t = \log \phi_t{}^s$) and the implicitly planned growth rate of the money supply would be $\bar{g}_M{}^0$. So the growth rate of fluidity is at first

$$g_{\phi t} = \bar{g}_\phi + (\bar{g}_M{}^1 - \bar{g}_M{}^0) \qquad\qquad [7.10]$$

But since actual fluidity is growing faster than desired fluidity, fluidity disequilibrium will arise and increase over time, which reduces the observed growth rate by λ times the increasing disequilibrium. As the implicitly planned money-supply growth rate increases towards the new actual value $\bar{g}_M{}^1$ this will also decrease the observed rate of growth of fluidity. Eventually these latter two forces will dominate the effect of the increase in the growth rate of money, and the actual growth rate of fluidity will be less than the steady-state rate $\bar{g}_\phi$ until the fluidity excess is worked off. Then planned money growth will equal actual money growth ($g_{Mt}^* = \bar{g}_M{}^1$) and actual fluidity will equal desired steady-state fluidity ($\log \phi_t = \log \phi_t{}^s$), so that once again the actual growth rate of fluidity will equal the steady-state growth rate of fluidity ($g_{\phi t} = \bar{g}_\phi$). This pattern is graphed in Fig. 7.3. Note that the disequilibria between actual and steady-state logarithms of levels and growth rates are drawn so that the disequilibria for fluidity and nominal income are always exactly offsetting, consistent with [7.7] and [7.8]. The slow adjustment of nominal income toward its new growth path due to the initial absorption of part of the monetary shock by changes in fluidity has the important implication that there must be a cyclic adjustment of the growth rate of nominal income. Since the growth rate of nominal income is at first slower than its new, increased steady-state rate, it must later rise for a while above the new steady-state rate until the average actual growth rate since t^* equals the steady-state growth rate and the actual level equals the steady-state level.

The key step in this process is the statement that increased spending of money balances will increase spending for final goods and services and so increase nominal income. Exactly how this occurs is one of the main substantive issues in modern macroeconomics. It is clear that excess money balances are spent almost exclusively on the purchase of other assets and not on consumption in the sense used in price theory—the consumption of the services of goods. Keynesian economists[2] believe that excess money balances are spent only on financial assets. The modern quantity theorists point out that individuals have a much wider range of stores of value as alternatives to money, most significantly consumers' durable goods such as automobiles, washing machines, and clothes. Individuals can vary their rate of purchase and replacement of these goods according to whether they have a current excess or shortage of money balances relative to their desired level. The aggregate influence of many individuals buying new cars, new suits, and so forth a few

[2] See Part 4 for the Keynesian model.

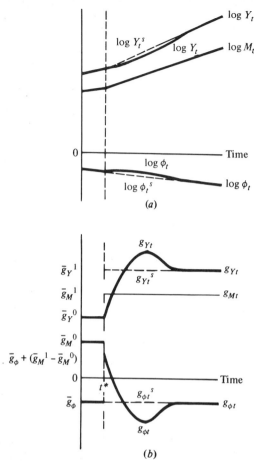

FIGURE 7.3 Growth paths of fluidity and nominal income implied by gradual adjustment of fluidity. The increased rate of growth of the money supply at t^* causes an unplanned excess of money receipts over money expenditures. Initially, this all goes to increase the actual rate of growth of fluidity. Over time, however, people increase their planned rate of money expenditures both because their expected money receipts adjust toward their higher actual money receipts and because planned money expenditures are temporarily increased above expected money receipts to draw down the accumulated money balances in excess of desired money balances. This increased spending leads both directly and indirectly to higher rates of growth in spending on final goods and services (nominal income). This change, in turn, increases the nominal demand for money; eventually it is sufficiently increased to make the supply and demand of money equal again. Although the public as a whole cannot reduce the excess nominal money balances by spending them (since one person's expenditure is another's receipt), the attempt to do so increases the nominal money demand, thus eliminating the excess money balances.

weeks earlier than planned can be enormous. The empirical evidence suggests that excess money balances increase the rates of purchases of both financial assets and consumers' durable goods.

Purchases of consumers' durable goods, though not pure consumption, are included in the demand for final goods and services as part of consumer expenditures. Increased demand for financial assets—and the decreased supply of government bonds—will lower the interest rate[3] and thus increase the rate of investment which is also included in the demand for final goods and services. An additional effect occurs because individuals also increase their rate of purchases of assets, including consumers' durable goods, when they receive such unexpected increases in income as will occur because of the other increases in the demand for final goods and services.[4] Increased real income will also increase the desirability of investment to firms, as discussed in Chap. 5, by increasing the current rental rate on capital (reflected in increased profits) and by possibly increasing the rental rates on capital expected in the future. So the excess-money balances do indeed increase spending for final goods and services by both directly and indirectly increasing consumers' expenditures and by indirectly increasing investment.

These changes in nominal income will affect desired fluidity differently depending on whether they are made up of changes in real income or changes in the price level. The real income in the demand for money functions [5.25] and [5.28] represents an index of both the wealth to be allocated among various assets and of the number of transactions to be made with money. A temporary or transitory increase in income does not represent a proportionate change in wealth or even transactions. As a result a transitory real income receipt 1 percent higher than the steady-state level will raise the real demand for money above the steady-state level by much less than 1 percent, and the desired fluidity ϕ_t^* will fall. Changes in the price level affect the nominal demand for money and nominal income proportionately so that their ratio, desired fluidity, is unchanged. Since the logic behind [7.9] suggests that the growth rate of fluidity—and hence nominal income—will be affected by the disequilibrium between actual and currently desired levels, the equation as written is based on the incorrect assumption that desired fluidity will always equal its steady-state value. When real income is temporarily above its steady-state value, desired fluidity will be temporarily below its steady-state value.

The pattern of adjustment of the level of actual fluidity to desired fluidity can be combined with the pattern of adjustment of desired fluidity around the steady-state growth path as shown in Fig. 7.4. Until the increased

---

[3] The effects on interest rates are discussed in detail in Sec. 7.4 below.
[4] This "multiplier" effect of the original increases in spending will be discussed further in connection with the Keynesian model, early versions of which placed great emphasis on this effect.

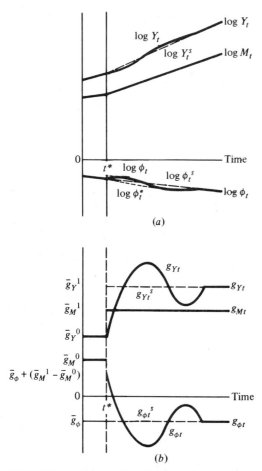

(a)

(b)

FIGURE 7.4   Growth paths of fluidity and nominal income showing effects of gradual adjustment of fluidity and changes in desired fluidity. The increased rate of growth of the money supply at t^* causes the rate of growth of fluidity to increase as excess money balances are built up. As the rate of growth in nominal income increases, real income is increased temporarily above its steady-state growth path. This increase causes desired fluidity to fall (as indicated by the dotted line) below its steady-state growth path because nominal money demand increases proportionately less than nominal income. As actual fluidity is adjusted to desired fluidity by increased growth in nominal income, the level of nominal income rises above its steady-state growth path. The effect on real income is only temporary, however, and, as the price level adjusts upward, desired and actual fluidity return to their steady-state growth path. The initial rate of growth of fluidity is faster than the steady-state rate, and this is more than offset by the later growth that is slower than steady state; the difference is made up by another period of growth that is faster than steady state. For nominal income, the initally too-slow rate of growth is more than made up by the later, more rapid rate of growth; consequently the difference is offset by another period of slower growth. The criterion for fast or slow is the steady-state growth rate.

spending causes increases in real income, desired fluidity is equal to its steady-state value and the graph is the same as in Fig. 7.3. As increased spending begins to increase real income, the desired fluidity falls below the steady-state path. Actual fluidity gradually adjusts to the artificially low desired fluidity and falls for a while *below* the steady-state growth path so that the level of nominal income rises for a while above its new steady-state path. This cyclical fluctuation of the *levels* of fluidity and nominal income around their growth paths occurs because increases in real income absorb less of the new money balances through increases in the nominal demand for money than do equal percentage increases in the price level. We are getting ahead of our story, however, because we have not yet discussed how changes in spending are divided between changes in real income and in the price level. Figure 7.4 is drawn based on the effects actually observed in the United States. The interaction of changes in spending with changes in real income is discussed later. The cyclical fluctuations of fluidity and nominal income around their growth paths imply even more pronounced cyclical fluctuations in their growth rates. Again the average growth rates over the whole period of adjustment equal the corresponding steady-state growth rates. The actual rate of growth of nominal income is first below its (increased) steady-state rate, then above for a while, again below that rate, and finally equal to the steady-state rate. The same statement holds for the growth rate of fluidity with "above" and "below" just reversed.

This presentation has inferred the behavior of the growth rate of nominal income from the growth rate of fluidity. This emphasizes the importance of the cyclical adjustments in money demand to changes in the growth rate of the nominal money supply. A more direct approach to the determination of the growth rate of nominal income may clarify the process further. Recall from the nominal income version of the dynamic Cambridge equation that the growth rate of nominal income equals the growth rate of the nominal money supply less the growth rate of fluidity:

$$g_{Yt} = g_{Mt} - g_{\phi t} \tag{7.11}$$

The growth rate of fluidity is given by [7.9] emended by substitution of the desired level of fluidity ϕ_t^* for the steady-state level ϕ_t^s. Substituting into [7.11] and simplifying:

$$g_{Yt} = g_{Mt}^* - \bar{g}_\phi + \lambda(\log \phi_t - \log \phi_t^*) \tag{7.12}$$

This equation states that the growth rate of nominal income equals the difference between the growth rate of money reflected in expenditure and receipt plans and the steady-state growth rate of fluidity plus a term to reflect any increased (or reduced) growth in spending in an attempt to reduce excess (or build up short) money balances.

It is clear that immediately after a change in the growth rate of the nominal money supply there is no change in the growth rate of nominal income.

Only as g_{Mt}^* exceeds $\bar{g}_M{}^0$ and $\log \phi_t - \log \phi_t^*$ becomes positive through the passage of time does the growth rate of nominal income increase and eventually overshoot the steady-state rate $\bar{g}_M{}^1 - \bar{g}_\phi$. Full equilibrium is finally achieved when the planned and actual growth rates of the nominal money supply are equal and the actual, desired, and steady-state levels of fluidity are equal.

Precise estimates of the timing of this pattern of adjustment are not available, but it is known that the cumulative effects of the monetary policy change on the growth of nominal income become quite apparent about three-quarters of a year after the policy change. It appears to take a period of perhaps 4 years at the new monetary growth rate before the whole pattern of adjustment is completed.[5] These times are influenced by the initial conditions and by the absolute size of the change in monetary growth rate. Large changes in the growth rate of the money supply are reflected in large changes in the actual growth path of nominal income which are much more quickly noticeable than are small changes.

Summary of the Effects on Fluidity and Nominal Income of an Increase in Money Supply Growth

An increase in the rate of growth of the money supply will at first cause increased holdings of real money balances because, on the average, individuals have an unplanned excess of money receipts over money expenditures. These excess money balances are measured as a rise in actual fluidity above its desired level. Increased purchases of other assets increase nominal income noticeably in about three quarters. When the growth rate of nominal income equals and then exceeds the amount of the increase in the money-supply growth rate, actual nominal income stops falling proportionately below its new steeper steady-state growth path and begins to close—at yet higher rates of growth— the gap that was opened by the lag in response of nominal income to monetary policy. The unexpected increase in spending causes real income to temporarily rise above its steady-state path. This causes a temporary reduction in desired fluidity so that as actual money holdings approach their desired level, the level of nominal income temporarily rises above the level indicated even by the increased steady-state growth path of nominal income. The divergences of real income and desired fluidity from their steady-state growth paths are eliminated about four or five years after the change in monetary policy, assuming no other policy change intervenes. So a change in monetary policy begins a cyclical process of adjustment of nominal income toward a new steady-state equilibrium.

---

[5] Empirical estimates generally involve simultaneous consideration of the effects of changes in real government spending. Citations are therefore delayed until that discussion in Sec. 8.2.

Effects on Fluidity and Nominal Income of a Decrease in Money Supply Growth

The effects of an increase in the money-supply growth rate (or stimulative monetary policy) are just reversed for a decrease in the money-supply growth rate (or restrictive monetary policy). The decrease in the rate of growth of the money supply is absorbed at first by reductions in actual money holdings relative to desired money holdings. This is reflected in Fig. 7.5 by a lower growth rate of fluidity (that is, a faster rate of decrease). As the rate of purchases of assets other than money is reduced, spending on final goods and services or nominal income is also reduced. In about three-quarters of a year, the proportionate gap between actual nominal income and the lowered growth path of equilibrium nominal income stops increasing and starts to decline. This process involves growth of nominal income for a while at a rate slower than even the decreased steady-state rate of growth of nominal income. The decrease in the rate of growth of nominal income may be large enough that the growth rate of nominal income is negative, though this is not the case for the example graphed. The cyclical adjustment will be intensified by the temporary declines in real income which cause a less than proportional decline in desired money balances so that desired fluidity rises and the *level* of nominal spending falls for a while below even its decreased steady-state growth path. The divergences of real income and desired fluidity from their steady-state growth paths are eliminated about four or five years after the initial change in monetary policy, assuming no other policy change intervenes. A decrease in the growth rate of the money supply thus causes cyclical adjustments of the level and growth rate of nominal income around the new lower steady-state growth path.

7.3 EFFECTS ON THE GROWTH PATHS OF REAL INCOME AND THE PRICE LEVEL

Effects on the Steady-State Growth Paths

Since growth in real income is valued and inflation is disliked, interest focuses on how the growth rate of nominal income is divided between the growth rates of real income and the price level. The observed effects of monetary policy on nominal income are reflections of the effects on the growth paths of real income and the price level. Let us recall that nominal income Y_t is equal by definition to the product of real income y_t and the price level P_t. Therefore, the logarithm of nominal income equals the sum of the logarithms of real income and the price level:

$$\log Y_t \equiv \log y_t + \log P_t \qquad [7.13]$$

Also the growth rate of nominal income is equal to the sum of the growth rates of real income and the price level:

$$g_{Yt} \equiv g_{yt} + g_{Pt} \qquad [7.14]$$

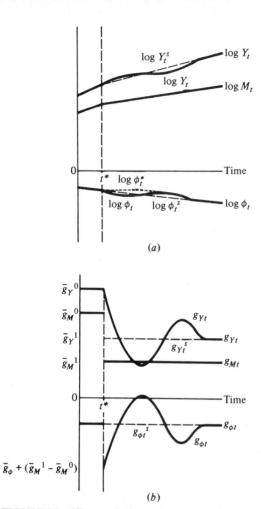

(a)

(b)

FIGURE 7.5   Effects on fluidity and nominal income of a decrease in money supply growth. A decrease in the growth rate of the money supply causes an equal reduction in the slope of the steady-state path of nominal income. At first, the decrease is met by reductions of actual cash balances below desired levels, but over time the rate of spending on final goods and services is decreased. As the rate of growth of nominal income decreases, real income is temporarily reduced below its steady-state growth path. This causes desired fluidity to rise (as indicated by the dotted line) above its steady-state growth path because nominal money demand decreases proportionately less than nominal income. As actual fluidity is adjusted to desired fluidity by decreased growth in nominal income, the level of nominal income falls below its steady-state growth path. The effect on real income is only temporary, however, and, as the price level adjusts downward, desired and actual fluidity return to their steady-state growth path. The initial slower growth of fluidity is more than offset by the later faster growth; the difference is made up by another period of slower growth. The criterion for slow or fast is again the steady-state rate. For nominal income, the initially too-rapid growth is more than made up by the later slower growth; so the difference is offset by another period of faster growth.

The effects of an increased growth rate of the money supply on the steady-state growth paths of real income and the price level were previously derived at the end of Chap. 6. Figure 7.6 presents the relevant portions of the graphical solution (Fig. 6.9) for the case in which there are no net interest rate effects on the demand for money. The complications of an interest-elastic demand for money are added in Sec. 7.4. The slope of the steady-state growth path of nominal income is increased at time t^* by the amount $(\bar{g}_M{}^1 - \bar{g}_M{}^0)$ of the increase in the growth rate of the money supply. Increased money supply growth does not alter the steady-state growth path of real income, but increases the steady-state growth rate of the price level by the full amount of the increase in the growth rate of the money supply. In this case, a change in the growth path of the nominal money supply affects the growth paths of nominal variables but not of real variables.

Effects of Monetary Policy on the Output and Prices of Individual Industries

A stimulative monetary policy leads to increased demand for final goods and services. This increased demand is at first met in large part by sales of increased real quantities of goods and services as production is increased and inventories are reduced. These effects on real variables occur because most supply curves are not vertical and do not immediately adjust to the changed steady-state growth path.

Consider an industry with standard upward-sloping, short-run supply and downward-sloping demand curves. These curves will be shifting to the right over time as part of the general growth of the economy, but for illustrative purposes it is desirable to look at the curves at a particular instant of time as shown in Fig. 7.7. If monetary policy increases the demand for the commodity x to D^1 from D^0 (which it would have been were it not for the effects of the stimulative policy), then the quantity of x sold increases from $q_0{}^x$ to $q_1{}^x$ and the price of x from $P_0{}^x$ to $P_1{}^x$. The final equilibrium is achieved when rising nominal costs of factors of production shift the supply curves up to where they intersect the higher demand curves at the same point as the intersection of the supply and demand curves which would have existed at the same instant of time under the original monetary policy. This is illustrated in Fig. 7.8. It takes some time for the prices of factors of production to adjust to the new equilibrium and during this period a very distinct pattern of adjustment occurs: Relative to equilibrium output, the real quantities produced and sold first increase above and then return to equilibrium while the price paid moves gradually upward over time from the old to the new equilibrium.

This pattern occurs over time as demand curves first shift out more rapidly than supply curves, causing increasing divergence of real output from equilibrium. Then, as supply curves begin to catch up in response to rising prices of factors of production, real output moves back toward equilibrium, while

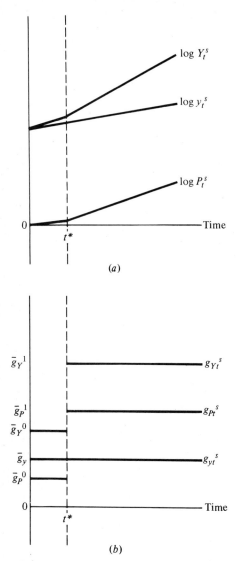

FIGURE 7.6 Steady-state growth paths of real income, the price level, and nominal income. The steady-state growth path of real income is fixed by the conditions of the real economy and not affected by the growth rate of the money supply. The increase in the growth rate of the money supply at t^* causes an equal increase in the steady-state rate of inflation (slope of the log P_t line). The increase in the steady-state rate of inflation is reflected by the equal increase in the steady-state growth rate of nominal income (slope of the log Y_t line).

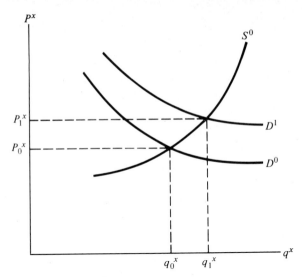

FIGURE 7.7 **Effect on increase in demand on the output and price of an individual industry.** If the supply curve S^0 is not affected by the causes of the outward shift of the demand curve from D^0 to D^1, the equilibrium price will increase from P_0^x to P_1^x, and the equilibrium quantity will increase from q_0^x to q_1^x. The supply and demand curves are drawn for a particular instant of time. In addition to the shifts illustrated here, the supply and demand curves of a growing industry shift to the right *over time*.

prices continue to move upward toward their new equilibrium. Since equilibrium real output increases over time, actual real output may either decrease or increase at less than the equilibrium rate as the gap between actual and equilibrium real output is closed.

Similar patterns of adjustment occur for monopolized industries as the demand curve first shifts out relative to the marginal cost curve, causing profit-maximizing output and price to increase. As the marginal cost curve catches up with the shifts in demand, prices rise further and quantities adjust *back* toward the steady-state equilibrium quantities.

Search Unemployment and the Short-Run Supply Curve of Labor

Firms can increase output only by increasing their employment of factors of production. It is the relative stability of the supply curves of factors of production in terms of their nominal prices that prevents industry supply curves from immediately shifting up to the new equilibrium at higher output prices and no increase in output. The key stability is in terms of the supply curve of labor. Nominal wages are often said to be *sticky*. This means that the *rate of growth* in nominal wages changes relatively slowly. As a result, firms wishing

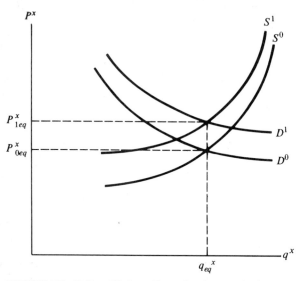

FIGURE 7.8 Full equilibrium effects of an increase in the money supply on supply and demand curves of an individual industry. As was shown in Chaps. 5 and 6, an increase in the money supply affects only prices and not real output in final equilibrium. Viewed for a particular industry, the process can be described by a series of shifts in supply and demand curves. The increased spending for final goods and services increases the demand for the output of the industry, as was shown in Fig. 7.7. Firms adjust output and prices by moving along their short-run supply curve S^0. This curve takes into account only the effects of increases in the output of the industry on its costs of production. However, the demand for nearly all industries is increased simultaneously. This is unlike the standard examples of microeconomics. The effect of all industries increasing their demand for labor at once is to increase wages of labor and so shift the supply curves upward. This shift makes the increase in prices appear to be due to increases in costs, but the increases in costs and ability of firms to pass on cost increases is due to the increase in demand for goods and services that is caused by the increased rate of growth in the money supply. If costs increased immediately, the industry supply curve would shift up from S^0 to S^1 as soon as the demand curve shifted from D^0 to D^1, with no effect on output and only an increase in prices. This full equilibrium is not achieved immediately because—as explained later in the text—the rate of growth in wages is slow to change or *sticky*. Instead, the demand curves shift out first, and then the supply curves start shifting over time up from S^0 to S^1. As the supply curves shift from S^0 to S^1, output is reduced toward equilibrium and prices are increased toward equilibrium.

to increase their output to meet increased demand can at first hire more workers at almost the same nominal wage as they would have had to pay in the absence of the increased growth rate of the money supply. Labor is the only variable factor of production in the short run;[6] hence, short-run

---

[6] Strictly speaking, this holds at the microeconomic level only for integrated industries. A similar result will hold for industries which are not integrated if supply curves of the final goods and services are drawn to reflect increased prices of intermediate goods and services as a result of increased demand for the final product.

supply curves will shift only if there are wage rate changes. Therefore, slow adjustments in nominal wages are the main reason for initially sticky supply curves for final goods and service (as seen in Fig. 7.7). These sticky supply curves in turn imply effects on real income when the growth rate of the money supply is changed. The eventual adjustment of nominal wages to their new equilibrium growth path returns the individual industry supply curves to equilibrium (as seen in Fig. 7.8) so that steady-state growth is again achieved. Consequently, sticky wages are the key to the short-run effects of changes in the growth rate of the money supply on real income.

The main reason that wages are sticky lies in the behavior of unemployed workers searching for new jobs. In steady-state growth equilibrium there will normally be a certain percentage of the labor force unemployed and searching for new or first jobs. Normally, over 50 percent of unemployed people have been unemployed 5 weeks or less and most find an acceptable job within a month and a half. So there is a very considerable turnover among the unemployed.[7]

In addition to true *search unemployment*, the unemployment data also include some individuals who are essentially unemployable in the sense that their marginal product as a worker is less than either applicable minimum wages or total welfare benefits or both. There are, of course, borderline cases of workers who are occasionally hired at an acceptable wage only to be soon fired when the employer is better able to evaluate the worker's low marginal product. Also some new entrants to the labor force might easily earn above minimum wage with training but cannot accept a below-minimum wage to compensate a potential employer during their period of training. Since minimum wages and welfare benefits are adjusted fairly rapidly for inflation, variations in unemployment can be studied as due to variations in search unemployment with the small percentage of legislatively determined unemployables taken as constant or moving similarly.

An unemployed worker must search for a new job because information about the opportunities available to him is costly. He must actually go from firm to firm until he receives an offer of a nominal wage which seems acceptable when compared to the expected costs and benefits of further search. If he begins his search believing that the range of wages being offered is lower than it really is, the worker will believe himself lucky to have found a good wage offer after less than usual search. If the job search were to start with a belief that the range of wages being offered is higher than it really is, the worker will spend a longer than average time searching for a new job. So the difference between the actual and expected nominal wage[8] is an important determinant of the amount of time each worker who becomes

---

[7] See Chap. 14 for detailed data and computations.
[8] The difference between the actual and expected distributions is measured here by the difference in their average values.

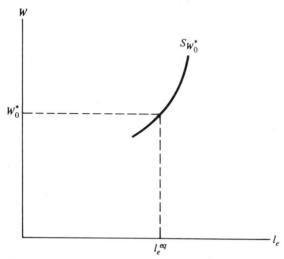

FIGURE 7.9   Short-run supply curve of labor to firms. The nominal wage affects the supply of labor to firms, given the expected nominal wage rate W_0^*, by making actual job offers appear relatively attractive or unattractive compared to the expected results of further search for a job. If the actual wage W exceeds the expected wage, the labor actually employed by firms exceeds the equilibrium amount l_e^{eq}; therefore, the unemployment rate is below normal. Conversely, when the actual wage rate is less than the expected wage rate, actual employment is below equilibrium and the unemployment rate is above normal. Higher expected nominal wage rates shift the short-run labor supply curve upward.

unemployed will spend in search and thus of the total number of people who will be unemployed at one time. When actual wages exceed their expected level, time spent searching and hence total unemployment will fall. Since expectations of nominal wages available adjust slowly to changes in their trend rate of growth, a small increase in wages above their trend will cause a large temporary increase in the number of workers employed. Expectations will eventually catch up with actuality of course, but meanwhile nominal wages are sticky in the sense that the short-run supply of employed labor[9] is relatively elastic with respect to the nominal wage rate, as shown in Fig. 7.9.

Other factors make for sticky nominal wages as well, the most important being explicit and implicit contracts which have terms quoted in nominal wages. Explicit contracts, usually negotiated through labor unions, cover a bit less than a quarter of the labor force. But many nonunionized employers implicitly offer terms of employment which keep nominal wages relatively stable in good times and bad as much as union contracts do explicitly.

---

[9] Though not nearly so much for the labor force consisting of employed plus unemployed workers. There is also some variation in the participation rate because of variation in the average hours worked per week.

In some industries, firms quote prices for considerable periods of time at the expected market clearing price, with random fluctuations in demand from day to day or month to month being met from inventories. This behavior—closely analogous to the search behavior of unemployed workers—means that sales will rise when the actual market clearing price is above the expected market clearing price set by firms. Demand for labor will then increase to replace the depleted inventories as well as to meet the increase in product demand. Similar effects can occur where firms are engaged in long-term contracts to sell unspecified quantities at fixed prices.

Thus nominal wages and prices do not adjust immediately to their new steady-state growth paths because of the pervasive influence of the slowly adjusting expectations of wages and prices. This was seen to cause real income and employment to rise for a while above their equilibrium levels and then return to their moving equilibrium values when stimulative monetary policy was initiated. Prices and wages, on the other hand, adjust steadily, if slowly, from their old to their new steady-state growth paths.

Effects of Monetary Policy on Aggregate Real Income and the Price Level

The effects of a stimulative monetary policy on aggregate real income and prices are of the same nature as the effects on the individual industries. In Fig. 7.10 this is illustrated by the temporary rise in real income above its steady-state growth path. Prices at first grow only slightly more than they would have in the absence of the stimulative monetary policy and only slowly adjust towards their new, steeper, steady-state growth path. Since real income rises for a while above its equilibrium level by growing at a rate faster than the steady-state equilibrium rate, the growth rate of real income must later be at a less than equilibrium rate so that the gap between actual and equilibrium real income is eliminated. In the graphical example, real income actually falls for a while (when the growth rate is negative), but less extreme policy changes could involve a period of slow increase in real income without any period of actual decline. The rate of inflation, on the other hand, is at first below the increased steady-state rate; therefore, it must rise later above the steady-state rate for a while to close the gap between the actual and steady-state equilibrium price level. Note that in the latter part of the adjustment period prices rise faster than the steady-state equilibrium while real income growth slows and unemployment rises toward the equilibrium rate.

The earlier part of the adjustment to stimulative monetary policy is politically attractive to government policymakers because people are able to find apparently attractive jobs quickly, real income rises rapidly, and the increase in the rate of inflation is still moderate. The latter part of the adjustment with much increased rates of inflation, slow or negative growth in real income, and rising unemployment is politically very costly. This makes *further increases in the rate of growth* of the money supply politically attractive in

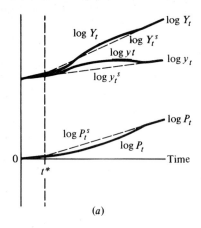

(a)

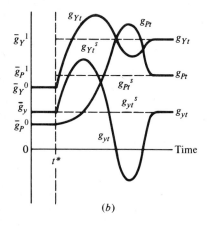

(b)

FIGURE 7.10   Effects of an increase in the money-supply growth rate on the growth paths of real income and the price level. The more rapid increases in the demand for final goods and services increase both real income and the price level, as compared to the values on their steady-state paths if the previous rates of monetary growth had been continued. The new steady-state growth path of the price level is steeper by the amount of increase in the money-supply growth rate, but the steady-state growth path of real income is unchanged. As the rate of spending continues to accelerate, for a while real income rises further above its steady-state growth path. The rate of inflation also accelerates, however, as sticky nominal wages adjust to the increases in the derived demand for labor. As the adjustments in wages and supply curves overtake the shifts in demand curves, the excess of actual real income above the steady-state equilibrium begins to be eliminated. Since real income at first grows more rapidly than the steady-state rate because of the stimulative monetary policy, it must later grow less rapidly than the steady-state rate to re-establish equilibrium. In the example illustrated, the rate of growth of real income even becomes negative for a while. The rate of inflation on the other hand is initially slower than the increased steady-state rate; consequently there must be a period of rates of inflation above the steady-state rate before equilibrium is reestablished. The actual growth path and growth rate of nominal income are equal to the sums of the growth paths and growth rates, respectively, of real income and the price level.

order to delay the completion of the adjustment process, at least until after the next election. Chapter 14 will discuss the cumulative nature of monetary policy as a means of pushing unemployment below its equilibrium rate.

These patterns of adjustment of real income and the price level underlie the actual growth path of nominal income discussed in Sec. 7.2 and repeated in Fig. 7.10. The unexpected or transitory increase in real income, it will be recalled, increases the nominal demand for money less than proportionately so that the growth path of nominal income rises for a while even above its increased steady-state growth path.

As with nominal income, precise estimates of the timing of these adjustments do not yet exist. The cumulative effects of monetary policy changes on the growth rate of real income are normally quite evident in two to four quarters however. Effects on the rate of inflation are not usually noticeable for six to eight quarters after the monetary policy change.[10] Most of the adjustment process appears complete in 4 to 5 years.

The interrelationship of the division of nominal income between the price level and real income and the level of nominal income can be illustrated by short-run supply and demand curves for a particular point in time. The aggregate supply curve gives the total amount of real output which will be produced at each general price level given not only the available resources, technology, and institutions, but also the expectations about wages and prices underlying the search and inventory behavior and the contracts which are present in the economy. Figure 7.11 presents the short-run aggregate supply curve for a particular point in time. In long-run equilibrium, real income is not influenced by the price level, but in the short run increases in the price level are associated with increases in real income because of the effects of wage and price expectations on the individual short-run supply curves.

The aggregate demand curve is elastic with respect to the price level since lower price levels are associated with higher nominal incomes for a given money supply. An elastic demand curve is one for which revenue, the product of price and quantity, increases as price is decreased. For the aggregate demand curve (illustrated in Fig. 7.12) revenue (Py) is nominal income. Aggregate supply and demand curves are combined in Fig. 7.13. Their intersection determines the equilibrium levels of real income y^e and prices P^e for that point in time. The nominal income is computed as

$$Y^e = P^e y^e \qquad\qquad [7.15]$$

Since nominal income varies according to precisely where the aggregate supply

---

[10] Curiously almost exactly the same timing relationships appear to have been present in nineteenth-century Britain. See W. Stanley Jevons, *Investigations in Currency and Finance*, 2d ed., London: Macmillan and Co., Ltd., 1909, Note B, pp. 100–101, where it is remarked that "*an expansion of the currency occurs one or two years previous to a rise of prices* [Jevons' italics]." Milton Friedman used modern correlation techniques to confirm Jevons' observation.

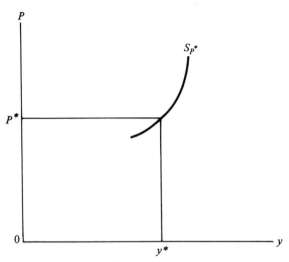

FIGURE 7.11   The short-run aggregate supply curve for a particular point in time.
The short-run aggregate supply curve S_{P*} shows the level of real output which
would be produced at each price level. This curve is drawn not only on the
basis of the basic resources, institutions, tastes, and technology of the economy, but
also on the basis of the expected levels of prices and wages, summarized as P^*,
implicit in the search for jobs, inventory behavior of firms, and contracts for labor,
goods, and services. The level of real income if the actual price level P equals the
expected price level is y^*. This y^* is the long-run equilibrium income of Chap. 5,
and is shown for the time the aggregate supply curve is drawn as the steady-state
growth path level of real income. If the actual price level is higher than expected,
higher levels of real income would be produced. Price levels lower than expected lead
to a lower real income than y^*. The aggregate supply curve becomes very steep at
price levels much higher than expected because of the very limited amount of further
reduction in search unemployment that can occur. It can be said that the further
real income is above the long-run equilibrium associated with normal levels of
unemployment, the smaller will be the increase in real income associated with a
given increase in nominal income and the greater will be the increase in the price
level.

curve crosses the aggregate demand curve, it is seen that the determination of
nominal income, real income, and the price level is indeed mutual despite the
necessarily sequential presentation above. The growth paths of nominal income,
real income, and the price level illustrated in Fig. 7.10 show the values
indicated by the intersections of aggregate supply and demand curves shifting
over time in reflection of both the basic determinants of steady-state growth
and adjustments of expectations about wages and prices and of actual money
balances toward desired money balances.

**Summary of the Effects on Real Income and the Price Level of an Increase in Money
Supply Growth**

As the stimulative monetary policy begins to increase spending on final goods
and services, firms are faced with an increased demand. Because of sticky

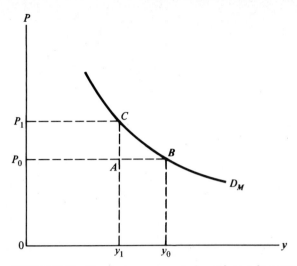

FIGURE 7.12 **The short-run aggregate demand curve for a particular point in time.** The short-run aggregate demand curve D_M shows the real amount of final goods and services which would be purchased at each price level, given actual nominal money supply and expected rate of money receipts at the time for which the curve is drawn. For a given nominal income Py, the greater P is (and therefore the lower y is) the higher is the demand for money, since short-run fluctuations in real income cause fluctuations in the demand for money that are less than proportional. The greater is the nominal demand for money, given the supply, the lower the rate of spending will be. Since total revenue (Py) of each point on the aggregate demand curve is nominal income, and lower price levels are associated with higher nominal incomes, the aggregate demand curve drawn for a particular point in time is elastic ($\eta_{y,P} < -1$). The nominal income, for example, associated with (y_0, P_0) is greater than that for (y_1, P_1) since the area $y_1 ABy_0$ is larger than $P_0 ACP_1$.

expectations about the rate of change of nominal wages and prices, short-run supply curves are not shifted upward much by the increased outward shift of aggregate demand. As a result, increased growth in spending reflects in part an increased growth in real output and in part increased growth in prices. Over time, expectations adjust toward actuality and decreasing fractions of increased growth in spending are for increased growth in real output and increasing fractions are for increased growth in the price level. Since real income at first rises above its steady-state growth path by growing at a faster than steady-state rate of growth, it must later return to its steady-state growth path by growing at lower rates—perhaps even negative—than the steady-state growth rate. The steady-state growth path of prices becomes steeper by the full amount of the increase in the growth rate of the money supply. At first the growth rate of prices is little increased from the old growth rate so that the price level falls below its now steeper steady-state growth path. In order to reestablish equilibrium, early rates of inflation below the steady-state rate must be made up by rates of inflation higher than the

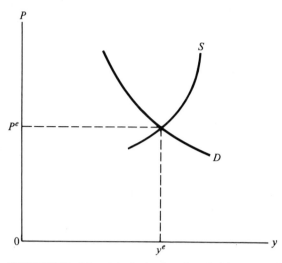

FIGURE 7.13 Mutual determination of nominal income, real income, and the price level. Short-run equilibrium real income y^e and price level P^e are determined by the intersection of the aggregate supply and demand curves existing at each point in time. Equilibrium nominal income is $Y^e = P^e y^e$. The level of nominal income varies along both the aggregate supply curve and the aggregate demand curve; hence equilibrium nominal income must be determined simultaneously with the determination of real income and the price level and not by reference to conditions determining aggregate demand or supply alone.

steady-state equilibrium rate. The paths of nominal income, real income, and the price level are simultaneously mutually determined.

Effects on Real Income and the Price Level of a Decrease in Money Supply Growth

The effects of a decrease in the money-supply growth rate are just the reverse of the effects of an increase in the money-supply growth rate. As the restrictive monetary policy begins to decrease spending on final goods and services, firms are faced with a decreased demand. Because of sticky expectations about the rate of change of nominal wages and prices, short-run supply curves are not shifted downward much by the smaller outward shift (or possibly even inward shift) of aggregate demand. As a result, decreased growth in spending reflects in part a decreased (perhaps negative) growth in real output and in part decreased growth in prices. This is illustrated in Fig. 7.14. Over time, expectations adjust toward actuality and decreasing fractions of decreased growth in spending are for decreased growth in real output and increasing fractions are for decreased growth in the price level. Since real income at first falls below its steady-state growth path by growing at a less than steady-state rate of growth, it must later return to its steady-state growth path by growing at rates higher than the steady-state growth

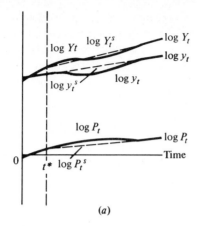

(a)

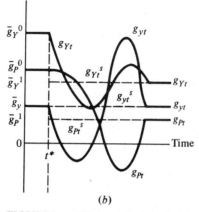

(b)

FIGURE 7.14   Effects on the growth paths of real income and price level of a decrease in the money-supply growth rate. A decrease in the rate of growth of the money supply does not affect the steady-state growth path of real income, which is determined by conditions of the real economy. The steady-state rates of growth of the price level and nominal income are both decreased by the amount of the decrease in the rate of growth of the money supply. The restrictive monetary policy leads to less rapid increases—or possibly even decreases—in the demand for final goods and services. This decrease in aggregate demand, compared to what it would have been under the previous monetary policy, decreases the rates of growth of both real income and price level. These decreases cause real income to fall below its steady-state growth path. The rate of inflation also slows as sticky nominal wages adjust to the decreases in the derived demand for labor. As the adjustments in wages and supply curves overtake the shifts in the demand curves, the gap between actual real income and steady-state real income is gradually eliminated. Since real income at first grows less rapidly than the steady-state rate (even falling for a while in this example) because of the restrictive monetary policy, it must later grow more rapidly than the steady-state rate to reestablish equilibrium. Conversely, the rate of inflation is initially faster than the decreased steady-state rate; hence there must be a period of rates of inflation below steady-state rates before equilibrium is reestablished. The actual growth path and the growth rate of nominal income are equal to the sums of the growth paths and growth rates, respectively, of real income and the price level.

rate. The steady-state growth path of prices becomes less steep by the full amount of the decrease in the growth rate of the money supply. At first the growth rate of prices is little decreased from the old growth rate so that the price level rises above its now less steep, steady-state growth path. In order to reestablish equilibrium, early rates of inflation above the steady-state equilibrium rate must be made up by rates of inflation lower than the steady-state equilibrium rate. This pattern of adjustment suggests the political difficulty involved in a policy change to reduce the rate of inflation: The initial effect is to reduce growth in real income and increase unemployment with relatively little effect on the rate of inflation. Only later—perhaps after the next election —does the unemployment rate return to normal levels and the inflation rate show sharp reductions.

7.4 EFFECTS ON INTEREST RATES

Cyclical Adjustments of Interest Rates to an Increased Growth Rate of the Money Supply

The steady-state equilibrium value of the nominal interest rate r was shown in Chap. 6 to increase by $1/(1 - \bar{\tau}^r)$ times the increase in the rate of growth in the money supply, where $\bar{\tau}^r$ is the marginal income tax rate. The steady-state value of the real interest rate r' is unchanged. This is illustrated in Fig. 7.15. Interest rates display a cyclical pattern of adjustment to an increased growth rate of the money supply which can be discussed as due to the net effect of four forces: the liquidity effect, the income effect, the financial effect, and the expectations effect. The liquidity effect refers to the tendency of the price of bonds to be driven up by the reduced rate of issuance of new government bonds to the public[11] and the increased demand for nonmoney forms of wealth as a use for excess cash balances. An increase in the price of existing bonds is the same thing as a decrease in the nominal market interest rate. The income effect refers to the tendency of increases in real income and ultimately the price level to absorb excess cash balances and offset part of the reduction in interest rates due to the liquidity effect. The financial effect refers to a temporary increase in bank demand for short-term negotiable bonds until loans to private customers are expanded in proportion to the multiple expansion of bank deposits. In steady-state equilibrium, the net effect of the first three forces is zero. Nominal interest rates will be increased however by the expectations effect. The expectations effect refers to the increase in the nominal interest rate to compensate the lender for the loss in value of future money receipts because of the inflation expected to occur

---

[11] Recall that the increased growth rate of the money supply is brought about by a reduced rate of issuance of government bonds.

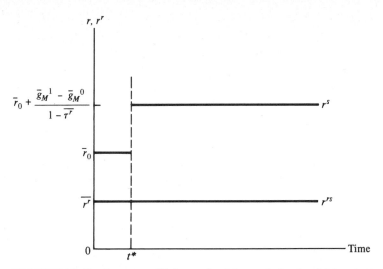

FIGURE 7.15 Steady-state equilibrium paths of the nominal and real interest rates.
An increase in the rate of growth of the money supply from $\bar{g}_M{}^0$ to $\bar{g}_M{}^1$ at time t^*
increases the steady-state level of the nominal interest rate r^s from $\bar{r}_0$ to
$\bar{r}_0 + (\bar{g}_M{}^1 - \bar{g}_M{}^0)/(1 - \bar{\tau}^r)$, where $\bar{\tau}^r$ is the constant marginal income tax rate. The
steady-state level of the real interest rate is unchanged at $\bar{r}^r$.

over the life of the bond. It was shown in Chap. 4, that under the U.S.
income-tax laws, the nominal interest rate will also reflect the amount of tax
liability transferred from borrower to lender. At first, the liquidity effect is
dominant and increasing so that both nominal and real interest rates fall
for about the first 6 months after the policy is changed—as shown in Fig. 7.16.
Because of the financial effect reflecting sticky interest rates on bank loans, this
fall will for a while be disproportionately reflected in the interest rates on
short-term negotiable bonds. The income effect then becomes increasingly
important relative to further increases in the liquidity effect and interest rates
begin to rise, the nominal interest rate returning to its original level in about
15 months on average.[12]

It is not clear how soon the expectations effect develops. The timing may
well vary with the size and frequency of fluctuations in the rate of inflation
which influence the expected value to participants in the bond market of
following closely developments of such early indicators of the future rate of
inflation as the rate of growth in the money supply. Some economists, for
example, believe that the expectations effect operates more quickly in the 1970s
because of the wide fluctuations in the rate of inflation experienced in the

---

[12] See Michael R. Darby, The Financial and Tax Effects of Monetary Policy on Interest Rates, *Economic Inquiry*, **13:** 266–276, June 1975, for further discussion of the theoretical and empirical literature.

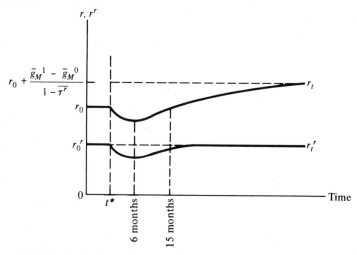

FIGURE 7.16 Cyclical adjustment of interest rates to an increase in the rate of growth of the money supply. An increase in the rate of growth of the money supply at first causes the nominal and real interest rates to fall because of the liquidity effect. At approximately 6 months, the income effect becomes dominant and the interest rates begin to rise. After about 15 months, the nominal interest rate reaches its initial level. The real interest rate takes a bit longer to reach its equilibrium level because the expectations effect widens the gap between nominal and real interest rates as expected rates of inflation rise.

1960s. The expected rate of inflation over the life of a short-term bond will also respond more rapidly to the current rate of inflation than will the expected rate of inflation for a long-term bond. The expected rate of inflation implicit in the nominal interest rate on a long-term bond is a weighted geometric average of the rates of inflation expected over each year that the bond is outstanding; this period may encompass many changes of government. Thus the buyer and seller of a long-term bond will take account of a longer span of history in predicting the expected rate of inflation than the record of the current administration. In fact monetary policy has not remained stable enough in recent history to yield any real evidence on just how long it takes to achieve full steady-state equilibrium with respect to all interest rates, but there are some suggestive analyses which indicate years for the short-term interest rates and decades for the longest-term interest rates. During the period of adjustment in which actual rates of inflation are greater than expected, net debtors win a capital gain and net creditors lose because the creditors are paid back dollars less valuable in terms of the goods and services which they can buy than was expected when the loans were made. Expected rates of inflation appear to adjust more rapidly in economies with large frequent changes in the growth rate of the money supply.

Cyclical Adjustments of Interest Rates to a Decreased Rate of Growth of the Money Supply

The effects of a decreased rate of growth of the money supply—and increased rate of issuance of bonds—are just the opposite of the effects for a stimulative monetary policy. As illustrated in Fig. 7.17 interest rates first rise for about 6 months, then begin to decline. The nominal interest rate falls back to its original level in about 15 months historically, and then continues to decline toward the steady-state rate which is lower by $1/(1 - \bar{\tau}^r)$ times the decrease in the growth rate of the money supply.

Interest Rate Effects on Fluidity, Nominal Income, Real Income, and the Price Level

So far the discussion of this chapter has been simplified by considering only the case in which the level of interest rates does not affect the demand for money, due to competitive interest payments on money. Many economists believe that an increase in the level of interest rates will decrease the levels of the demand for money and fluidity. As a statistical matter, given the cyclical behavior of the level of interest rates, it is not easy to distinguish whether changes in fluidity reflect the level of interest rates or gradual

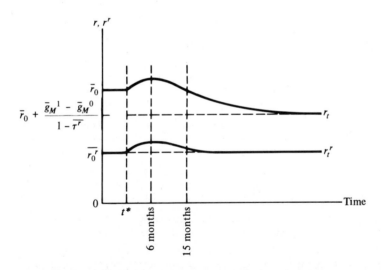

FIGURE 7.17 Cyclical adjustments of interest rates to a decrease in the rate of growth of the money supply. A decrease in the rate of growth of the money supply at first causes the nominal and real interest rates to rise because of the liquidity effect. At approximately 6 months, the income effect becomes dominant and the interest rates begin to fall. After about 15 months, the nominal interest rate reaches its initial level $\bar{r}_0$. The real interest rate takes a bit longer to reach its constant equilibrium level $\bar{r}^r$ because the expectations effect decreases the gap between nominal and real interest rates as expected rates of inflation fall.

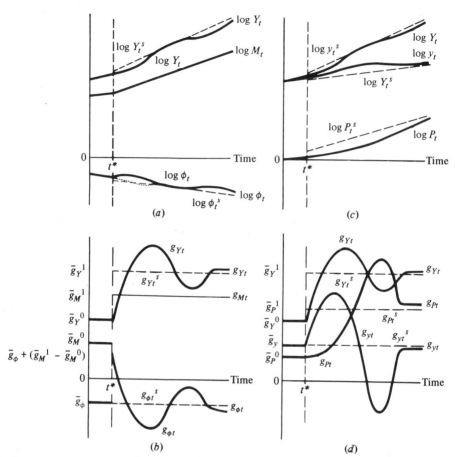

FIGURE 7.18 Differences in the adjustment process to an increase in the growth rate of the money supply if the demand for money is affected by the level of nominal interest rates. The cyclical adjustments of fluidity, nominal income, real income, and the price level seem to be nearly the same in the presence of effects of the level of interest rates on the demand for money. There is an extended period of time, however, during which the actual rates of growth of these variables differ slightly from the steady-state growth rates to accomplish the downward shifts in the equilibrium levels of fluidity and real income implied by gradually increasing interest rates. In an economy experiencing frequent, large changes in the money-supply growth rate, the expected rate of inflation and nominal interest rates will adjust much more rapidly than has been usual for the United States, and the shifts may significantly affect the cyclical adjustment process.

adjustment to monetary shocks and less than proportional effects of temporary fluctuations in income on the demand for money. Much the same pattern is implied for fluidity in either case. As a result, though the causation of the fluctuations in fluidity is a bit different, interest effects on the demand for money do not alter the general nature of the effects of an increase or decrease in the growth rate of the money supply on nominal income, real

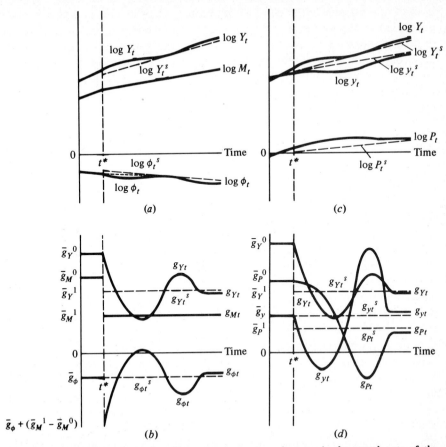

FIGURE 7.19 Differences in the adjustment process to a decrease in the growth rate of the money supply if the demand for money is affected by the level of nominal interest rates. As with a stimulative monetary policy (see Fig. 7.18), if the demand for money is affected by the level of nominal interest rates, a restrictive monetary policy causes a similar adjustment process to that observed under no interest rate effects.

income, and the price level. The only changes indicated in Figs. 7.18 and 7.19, respectively, are to show the extended period of time over which the expected rate of inflation—and therefore interest rates—adjust and change the equilibrium levels of fluidity and real income. For an increased rate of growth of the money supply, the growth rates of fluidity and real income are slightly below full steady-state equilibrium (and their reflections in the growth rates of nominal income and the price level slightly above) for the extended period of adjustment. The reverse is true for a decrease in the growth rate of the money supply.

The main difference between the results implied by the case in which the level of interest affects the demand for money and the case in which it does not is that in the former case the process of adjustment of the growth paths of fluidity, nominal income, real income, and the price level is extended for a period of some time. During this extension of the period of adjustment, however, there are no cyclical fluctuations in the growth rates of these variables and the economy has much the same appearance as if it were in full steady-state equilibrium.

☐ SUMMARY

Adjustments to macroeconomic shocks in the form of changes in the rate of growth of the money supply are complicated by short-run effects on fluidity and real income which are not present when the new steady-state growth of the economy is achieved. An increased growth rate of the money supply at first causes increased holdings of real money balances as individuals have an unplanned excess of money receipts over money expenditures. These excess money balances raise actual fluidity above desired fluidity. As individuals increase their demand for assets other than money, aggregate demand for final goods and services is increased relative to what it would otherwise have been. A compensating shift in aggregate supply does not occur because of the effects of sticky expectations about the growth rates of nominal wages and prices. As a result both real income and prices are increased relative to what they would have been had the prior rate of monetary growth been continued. This is reflected as an increase in the rate of growth of nominal income, the total value of final goods and services. The actual growth path of real income is above the steady-state growth path for a while and then returns. The actual growth path of the price level adjusts from the old growth path to the new, steeper growth path. The actual growth path of nominal income fluctuates cyclically about the new, steeper, steady-state growth path—first below and then above for a while. These patterns of adjustment, if allowed to run to completion, imply first a boom with low unemployment rates and then a recession of sorts with low but rising unemployment, slow if any growth in real income, and sharply increased rates of inflation. In final equilibrium, the net effect is to increase the rates of growth of nominal income and of prices by the amount of the increase in the growth rate of the money supply. Precisely reverse effects occur for decreases in the growth rate of the money supply. Increased growth rates in the money supply cause nominal interest rates to fall at first and then rise above their original levels. The opposite occurs for decreases in the growth rate of the money supply. To the extent that the level of nominal interest rates affects the demand for money, there is a further period of adjustment in which the growth rates of fluidity, nominal income, real income, and the price level differ slightly from their full steady-state equilibrium values.

☐ **QUESTIONS AND EXERCISES**

*1 (a) Why is the initial impact of a change in the growth rate of the money supply on the growth rate of fluidity instead of nominal income?

(b) Why is the long-run impact on the growth rate of nominal income instead of fluidity?

(c) Under what conditions is the steady-state growth path of fluidity affected by such a change?

2 If a transitory increase of real income of 2 percent causes a 1 percent increase in real money demand, what would be the effect on desired fluidity?

3 In Fig. 7.4, why must the areas between the actual and steady-state values of g_{Yt} which are below $\bar{g}_Y{}^1$ exactly equal the areas which are above $\bar{g}_Y{}^1$? Why is this not also true for Fig. 7.18?

4 Explain the effects of a decrease in the growth rate of the money supply on the growth rate of nominal income in terms of [7.12].

5 Unemployment is temporarily reduced by stimulative monetary policy because firms and individuals take actions that they would not if they were aware of true conditions. Evaluate.

*6 Significant changes are observed to occur in the growth rate of prices charged by producers and wholesalers before they occur in the growth rate of prices of final goods and services (that is, the price level). Can you explain how this difference might be caused by inventory behavior on the part of processors, wholesalers, and retailers?

7 Why do adjustment lags imply a cyclical adjustment process for the growth rates of real income and the price level?

*8 (a) In countries which undergo frequent, large changes in the rate of monetary growth, it is too costly to base one's behavior on extrapolations of the past. Explain why this means that "stimulative" monetary policy in such a country will have relatively little temporary effect on real income.

(b) Part (a) implies that a country with very stable or very unstable monetary growth will closely approximate steady-state growth equilibrium at each point in time. Is there any reason to suppose that the growth path of real income will be lower with highly variable monetary policy than with highly stable monetary policy? (*Hint:* How do people make decisions if they cannot extrapolate the past?)

9 Explain why the initial effect on the nominal interest rate of a change in the growth rate of the money supply is opposite from the long-run effect.

☐ **REFERENCES FOR FURTHER READING**

Darby, Michael R.: The Allocation of Transitory Income Among Consumers' Assets, *American Economic Review,* **62:** 928–941, Dec. 1972.

Friedman, Milton: *A Theoretical Framework for Monetary Analysis,* New York: NBER, 1971.

——— **and Anna J. Schwartz:** Money and Business Cycles, *Review of Economics and Statistics,* **45:** 32–64, Feb. 1963 (Supp.).

————: The Demand for Money: Some Theoretical and Empirical Results, *Journal of Political Economy*, **67**: 327–351, Aug. 1959.

————: The Lag in the Effect of Monetary Policy, *Journal of Political Economy*, **69**: 447–466, Oct. 1961.

Trends and Fluctuations in Monetary Growth, *Federal Reserve Bank of St. Louis Review*, **54**(9): 6–10, Sept. 1972. Highly recommended for illustrating the application of the theory to the real world.

Effects of Fiscal and Other Domestic Shocks

8.1 GOVERNMENT SPENDING AND TAXATION IN A GROWING ECONOMY

Nonmonetary Shocks

In contrast to Chap. 7, this chapter is primarily concerned with macroeconomic shocks that do not alter the growth path of the nominal money supply—that is, with *nonmonetary shocks*.[1] Particularly important are changes in the growth rates of government spending and taxation (*fiscal shocks*). Other domestic shocks are considered in Sec. 8.4 and shocks arising in foreign trade in Chap. 9.

As with monetary shocks, nonmonetary shocks are analyzed within the framework of the Cambridge equation:

$$g_{Mt} = g_{\phi t} + g_{Yt} \qquad [8.1]$$

Since the growth path of the nominal money supply is unaltered, non-monetary shocks can affect the growth rate of nominal income only if the growth rate of fluidity is changed. So the analysis of these shocks must explain how the desired growth path of fluidity is changed or how the actual growth path of fluidity comes to diverge from the desired growth path, or both. If a macroeconomic shock changes neither the growth path of the nominal money supply nor the growth path of fluidity, it has no effect whatsoever on nominal income.

The Government Budget Identity

The government budget identity relates total government expenditures G_t to their means of finance. Rewriting [7.1] here:

$$G_t \equiv T_t + \Delta D_t + \Delta B_t \qquad [8.2]$$

That is, nominal government expenditures are identically equal to the sum of nominal taxes T_t, the rate of change in nominal government debt ΔD_t, and

---

[1] The sole exception is the analysis of banking panics in Sec. 8.4.

the rate of change in nominal base money ΔB_t. The difference between expenditures and taxes—the amount financed by money creation and debt issuance—is the government *deficit*. Expenditures, revenues, and borrowings of state and local governments are consolidated with the federal government.

Fiscal shocks which change the growth paths of government spending or taxation must also change the deficit. Since only the effects of fiscal shocks are discussed here, it is assumed that this change in the deficit is entirely reflected in changes in the issuance of government debt with no change in money creation. Combined effects of monetary and fiscal shocks are discussed in Chap. 10. But for the present, an increase in government spending is assumed to be financed by an increase in government borrowing. Similarly, an increase in taxes is offset by an equal decrease in borrowing.

Describing Fiscal Shocks

Simple but realistic descriptions of fiscal shocks are a rare commodity. The difficulty arises because the relevant concepts of real government spending and taxation are constrained by the tastes, institutions, and resources of the society.

These constraints make it impossible simply to assume that the growth rate of real government spending is increased, say, by 2 percent per annum. If γ_t is the fraction of income spent by the government $(\gamma_t \equiv G_t/Y_t \equiv g_t/y_t)$,[2] then the growth rate of this fraction is equal to the difference in the growth rates of real government spending and real income:

$$g_{yt} = g_{gt} - g_{yt} \tag{8.3}$$

But real government spending could not possibly exceed real income; so the maximum conceivable value of the fraction γ_t is 1. Once the government spends all real income, the growth rate of real government spending is absolutely limited by the growth rate of real income. But the fraction of income spent by the government will surely never reach this absolute limit.[3]

The fraction of income that people want the government to spend for them, rather than spend it themselves is determined by individual preferences and opportunities as expressed through political institutions. Except for cases of war (which may be interpreted as a temporary shift in tastes) or revolution (which alters the weighting of individuals' tastes), the desired level of γ_t will be affected primarily by such basic economic variables as wealth and the relative prices of government and private goods.

---

[2] Care must be taken here to avoid confusion of the notation for real government expenditures g_t with the notation for the growth rate of X_t, g_{xt}. Similarly for real taxes t_t and the time subscript t.
[3] Even in feudal, socialistic, communistic, and other command economies, the fraction of income spent by the government has never reached 1.

TABLE 8.1 Ratio of government expenditures for goods and services to net national product— United States: 1869–1974

Years	γ_t
1869 & 1879	0.044
1879 & 1889	0.049
1889 & 1899	0.060
1899–1908	0.056
1909–1918	0.063
1919–1928	0.086
1929	0.089
1930	0.112
1935	0.153
1940	0.152
1945	0.410
1950	0.142
1955	0.202
1960	0.216
1965	0.219
1970	0.247
1974	0.242

Earlier data are averages for estimates of indicated years.

Sources: 1869–1928: *Historical Statistics of the United States, Colonial Times to 1957;* 1929–1974: computed from data in *The National Income Accounts of the United States, 1929–1965,* and *Survey of Current Business,* July 1973 and March 1975.

The peacetime values of the government spending-income ratio γ_t have changed only gradually, as illustrated in Table 8.1. While there is surely room for year-to-year adjustments in the rate of growth of government spending, it is somewhat unrealistic to suppose that government spending can be moved far from the value determined by the trend of public desires.[4] Nearly identical statements could be made about the fraction of income paid to the government in taxes net of transfers. For both taxes and spending, real conditions limit the range of variation that actually occurs.

In a growing society, one might observe almost any pattern of gradual change in the government spending-income and taxation-income ratios. The problems considered in this book are based on the assumption that the

---

[4] This is not meant to suggest that the trend is absolutely fixed. In fact, the average rate of growth of γ_t over the whole period 1869 through 1974 was about 0.017. This can be broken into three rather distinct subperiods, however: from 1869 through 1929, the average growth rate was 0.013, from 1929 through 1955, 0.032, and from 1955 through 1974, 0.010.

long-run desired *levels* of these ratios are constant. Any given pattern of equilibrium growth in these ratios is in fact sufficient to obtain results qualitatively identical to those presented here. The assumption that the normal growth rates of these ratios are zero simplifies the description and mathematics by allowing shocks to be described completely as changes in the levels of these ratios rather than describing in detail the precise changes in their equilibrium growth paths.

Macroeconomists are primarily interested in the effects of short-term variations in government spending or taxation which leave the government spending-income and taxation-income ratios the same at the end as at the beginning of the process. These temporary variations can be and are used as a conscious government policy and are therefore called *fiscal policy*. Fiscal policy is often used as a component of a more general stabilization policy aimed at offsetting the effects of other macroeconomic shocks on real income, employment, and the price level. This sort of fiscal policy is also known as compensatory finance. The formulation of stabilization policy is discussed in Part 5 of this book. Fiscal policy has also been used at times in an attempt to move the economy from a steady-state growth equilibrium to a boom, particularly shortly before a national election. For the present, the concern is solely with the effects and limitations of particular fiscal policies. The interaction of fiscal policy with other macroeconomic shocks is considered in the historical context of Chap. 10.

As in the case of monetary policy, the analysis of fiscal policy generally assumes that offsetting changes in the rate of government borrowing occur so that the government budget identity always holds. The exception is the analysis of a fiscal policy in which fluctuations in government spending are exactly offset by equal fluctuations in taxes. These are called *balanced budget shocks* because there is no change in the rate of deficit finance.

Macroeconomists have little to say about the long-run effects of a permanent change in the growth path of government spending or taxation. This mainly reflects the rarity and uniqueness of substantial, sudden changes in the relative scale of government. It is very hazardous to attempt scientific generalization on the basis of very special cases that typically involve changes in economic structure as well as scale of government. The attempt will certainly not be made here.

8.2 EFFECTS OF CHANGES IN GOVERNMENT SPENDING ON NOMINAL INCOME
A Stimulative Fiscal Policy

Suppose that the federal government decided to increase its real expenditures unusually rapidly over a short period of time. For simplicity, it is also assumed that monetary policy (the growth paths of the nominal monetary base and the nominal money supply) and the growth path of real taxes are unchanged. So the entire increase in government spending is financed by an equal increase in the rate of government borrowing.[5]

A thorough analysis of the effects of an increase in the rate of government spending paid for by increased borrowing is extremely tedious since the effects will depend on the actual programs in which government spending is increased. For example, an increase in government spending and borrowing for hydro-electric dams may exactly replace private investment and financing. Similarly, if the government institutes a housing program by buying houses for people and issuing them transferrable leases, then government bonds would just replace private mortgages. In neither of these cases would one expect to detect any effect on total income, but only on how national income accountants divide it. If government hires more people to serve as social workers, however, there is no obvious automatic, equal decline in the private demand for social workers. Instead of examining the effects of each possible sort of increase in government expenditures, fiscal policy is assumed to raise or lower spending in a mixture of programs as might actually occur. Thus a temporary increase in real government spending involves some programs which directly replace private investment and financing, others for which there is no competing private provision, and many intermediate projects.

This fiscal policy may be illustrated (as shown in Fig. 8.1) by a very rapid rate of growth of government spending as the programs get started until the full increase is achieved and government spending grows along a growth path ($\log g_t$) parallel to the original growth path. The corresponding increase in government borrowing is shown by a steeper growth path of government debt ($\log d_t$).

A Comparative Statics Approach

The traditional approach to the study of increased government expenditures is a comparative statics analysis. This analysis highlights forces which might cause a change in the desired growth path of fluidity and consequently in the growth path of nominal income. Thus it will serve as a useful prelude to a more complete analysis of dynamic adjustments.

The comparative statics problem is to compare the effects on nominal income of two alternative rates of government spending g^0 and g^1. It is assumed that g^1 exceeds g^0 and that the difference is entirely reflected in an equal difference in government borrowing.

Consider first the equilibrium of state 0. There would be some equilibrium

---

[5] In principle, the match between the increase in real government spending and in real government borrowing need not be exact. This is true because induced fluctuations in the growth path of the price level could alter the *real* revenue from money creation. In practice, this qualification can be neglected as the plausible amounts involved are trivial.

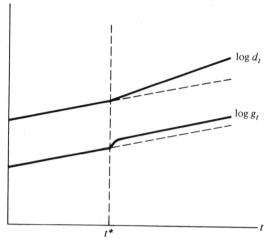

FIGURE 8.1 An increase in government expenditures financed by an increased rate of government borrowing. The increase in government spending, g_t, is illustrated by a brief period of very rapid growth in government spending until a higher growth path is reached that is parallel to the original growth path (indicated by the dotted line). Government spending then grows at the same rate as previously. The increase in the size of government borrowing is illustrated by a steeper slope of the growth path of the real government debt d_t. Recall that real government borrowing Δd_t is the flow corresponding to the stock of real government debt. The increased flow increases the growth rate of government debt $(g_{dt} = \Delta d_t/d_t)$ and the growth rate is the slope of the growth path.

combination of real income y^0, price level P^0, interest rate r^0, nominal money supply M^0, real saving s^0, real investment i^0, and a real deficit of $\Delta b^0 + \Delta d^0$. This combination is illustrated in Fig. 8.2. The saving available for private investment is found by subtracting the given government deficit from saving.[6] This amount must equal the desired level of investment at a combination of real income, price level, and the interest rate at which money demand equals money supply.

Now suppose that real government spending was increased from g^0 to g^1 and real government borrowing was increased by an equal amount from Δd^0 to Δd^1. This increase in government spending requires a reallocation of resources from the production of goods and services for the private sector—especially investment—to production for the government. The reduction of private investment is achieved both by direct government replacement of private investment and by a rise in the interest rate as the increased government borrowing drives down the price of bonds. Recall from Chap. 5 that higher

---

[6] Net exports are assumed to be zero in the present chapter as their inclusion only clutters the analysis without altering the conclusions.

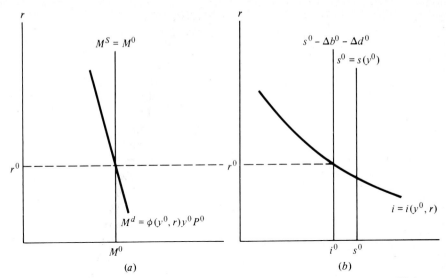

FIGURE 8.2 Equilibrium conditions in state 0. The graphs show the economy in equilibrium at real income y^0, price level P^0, interest rate r^0, nominal money supply M^0, real savings s^0, real investment i^0, and a real deficit of $\Delta b^0 + \Delta d^0$. The levels of real income, the price level, and the interest rate are such that nominal money demand is equated to the given nominal money supply (*a*) at the same time that saving minus the government deficit equals investment (*b*). Remember that investment and the government deficit are the alternative uses (besides net exports) of saving.

interest rates reduce private investment because the present value of the stream of future benefits from an investment project becomes 'lower as the interest rate by which they are discounted increases. Thus, fewer investment projects can justify their initial costs at higher interest rates. These higher interest rates may, however, decrease the demand for money, thus creating excess cash balances and an increase in aggregate demand. That is, people and firms will attempt to run down their cash balances by purchasing a larger total of government and private bonds and consumers' durable goods. This reduces the required decrease in investment as total income rises.

The nominal demand for money function can summarize the discussion:

$$M_t^d = \phi(y_t, r_t)y_t P_t \qquad [8.4]$$

Assume that just before the policy change the economy was in equilibrium with money supply M^0 equal to money demand $M^d = \phi(y^0, r^0)y^0 P^0$ as shown in Fig. 8.3 (panel *a*). If there were no change in real income or the price level in response to the policy change and the interest rate rose to r^1 to reduce investment by the amount which government spending increased (panel *b*), excess money balances of $M^0 - M^1$ would be created. This is the source of the increase in aggregate demand. To the extent that government expenditures

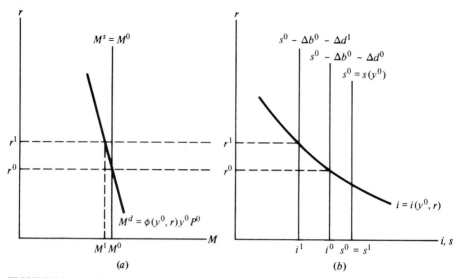

FIGURE 8.3 Creation of excess money balances by increased government spending financed by borrowing. Initially, the economy is at equilibrium at real income y^0, price level P^0, interest rate r^0, nominal money supply M^0, real saving s^0, real investment i^0, and a real deficit of $\Delta b^0 + \Delta d^0$. The increased government spending increases the real deficit to $\Delta b^0 + \Delta d^1$ ($\Delta d^1 - \Delta d^0 = g^1 - g^0$). If there is at first no change in income and price level, investment must fall to i^1 ($i^0 - i^1 = \Delta d^1 - \Delta d^0 = g^1 - g^0$), and the interest rate must rise to r^1 to induce investors to reduce investment by so much. This rise in the interest rate reduces the demand for money—creating excess money balances of $M^0 - M^1$ which will increase aggregate demand.

replace private investment, the investment demand curve will at the same time shift to the left and so reduce the amount of excess money balances created. Unless the increased expenditures replace private investment dollar for dollar, there will be some remaining pressure for the interest rate to rise, however.

As the increase in aggregate demand is translated into an increase in real income, desired fluidity will fall even further since a $1 increase in real transitory income increases money demand by considerably less than indicated by the average level of fluidity. This strengthens the effect on aggregate demand of the initial decline in desired fluidity due to increased interest rates.

Different economists like to describe this initial increase in aggregate demand and its effects on nominal income in different, though equivalent words. The modern quantity theorist would say that an increase in government spending financed by borrowing initially increases aggregate demand by driving interest rates up so that the demand for money falls and excess money balances are created. These excess money balances—as in the case of a monetary shock— reduce the decline in investment (required to offset the increased government spending) and even increase consumer spending. Economists in the Keynesian tradition, who are primarily concerned with the new short-run equilibrium as will be seen in Part 4, put this another way. For them, government spending directly increases income which in turn increases spending by consumers and even investors until the increased income provides enough additional saving to finance the increased government deficit. The increased income, however, increases the demand for money which drives up interest rates which reduces investment and income. Essentially, the quantity theory approach considers why a decrease in investment to the full extent of the increase in government spending would lead to a reduction of money demand below the quantity supplied so that income must rise. The Keynesian approach shows that the increase in income which would result if the interest rate were constant would increase the demand for money above the quantity supplied, so that nominal income must rise by less than this amount. Each, because of the limitations of language, sequentially discusses simultaneous interactions.

A Dynamic Version of the Comparative Statics Analysis

The key idea from the comparative statics analysis is that a rise in the interest rate caused by increased government spending will reduce desired fluidity and so permit or encourage an increase in nominal income. Put this way, the increase in government spending—not desirable for itself—appears to be a rather inefficient way to achieve about the same effects as a brief interlude of very rapid money creation. The actual effects are even less impressive.

The comparative statics analysis does reasonably well in the first few quarters after the policy starts. Aggregate demand increases are translated into increased employment and (perhaps slightly at this stage) prices; so nominal income rises above its previous growth path. If the comparative statics analysis captured the essential points, nominal income should converge on a new growth path higher than and parallel to the old growth path, as in Fig. 8.4. Since the rise in nominal income will be reflected by a temporary rise in real income at first, desired fluidity will fall even below the new equilibrium growth path. This is illustrated by a cyclical convergence of fluidity and nominal income to their new growth paths.

The parallel upward shift in the steady-state growth path of nominal income would be reflected in an equal, parallel, upward shift in the steady-state growth path of the price level. Similarly any downward parallel shift in the steady-state growth path of real income due to the lower ratio of capital accumulation to income would also cause an upward parallel shift in the steady-state growth path of the price level. A careful specification of the implied process of cyclical adjustment of real income and the price level will not be attempted at this point.

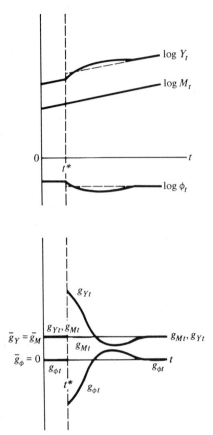

FIGURE 8.4 Dynamic representation of comparative static results on effects of increased government spending on nominal income. If the increased rate of government spending and borrowing raises the rate of interest and thereby lowers desired fluidity, fluidity will fall (and nominal income rise) to a growth path below (above)—but parallel to—the prior growth path. Fluidity is illustrated as undershooting its new growth path (and hence nominal income overshooting) because of the reduction in desired fluidity associated with transitory increases in real income. Note that the assumed zero steady-state growth rate of fluidity implies that the steady-state growth rates of nominal income and the money supply are identical.

Adjustment of the Interest Paid on Money

Recalling the discussion of Chaps. 5 and 7, it is not clear that an increase in the level of interest rates will much affect the desired level of fluidity. This is because the interest rate paid by banks on their deposits adjusts to compete with the higher rates available in the market and earned on the assets of banks. That is, a more complete statement of the demand for money is (see [5.25]):

$$M_t^d = \phi^*(y_t, r_{Mt}, r_{St}, r_{Lt})y_t P_t \qquad [8.5]$$

where r_{Mt}, r_{St}, and r_{Lt} are the interest rates on money, short-term bonds, and long-term bonds, respectively. Particularly in the United States where interest cannot legally be explicitly paid on demand deposits, banks slowly adjust the rate at which they pay this interest implicitly through "free" services, fee reductions, favorable loan interest rates for depositors, and so forth. Thus when interest rates—particularly interest rates on short-term bonds—begin to rise in response to the fiscal policy change, there will be little if any corresponding rise in the interest which banks pay on money. This causes the fall in the demand for money emphasized in the comparative statics analysis. That is, the rise in the yield on short-term bonds relative to demand deposits gives individuals and firms an incentive to draw down their money balances by buying the bonds with higher yields or reducing their own borrowing. As the higher interest rates persist, banks find it profitable to compete by raising the interest rates which they pay on their deposits. This rise in the interest rate on money increases the desired fluidity (demand for money). That is, it no longer pays to expend so much time and effort making do with reduced cash balances relative to income when the yield advantage of short-term bonds is reduced or eliminated. This rise in the interest rate paid on money would eliminate much or all of the initial effect of the higher level of interest rates on desired fluidity and therefore nominal income.

Shock Absorber Behavior of Money Balances

The comparative statics analysis assumes that the economy is continuously in equilibrium. Firms faced with the choice of sharply cutting back investment or reducing money balances below their desired level may well choose to let money balances serve as a shock absorber. The resulting increase in total spending or reduction in fluidity could be viewed in two alternative ways: The sudden increase in government borrowing temporarily reduces money demand below the level that would be predicted by the money demand function, and consequently income rises. Alternatively, the rise in income due to government spending is not choked off as quickly as might be supposed since money demand does not react immediately to the changes in income.

In operation, shock absorber responses of fluidity to sudden changes in government spending and borrowing have the same effects as slow adjustments in the interest rate paid by banks on their deposits. Each implies a larger decrease in fluidity in the short run than will ultimately occur.

Changes in the Relation of the Short-Term Interest Rate to Investment Demand

Yet another set of forces operates to reduce the initial impact of increased government borrowing and spending on the demand for money. These forces operate to reduce the increase in the short-term interest rate required to achieve any given reduction from the original growth path of the desired quantity of investment.

First, the increased short-term interest rate causes a larger increase in the level of the long-term interest rate as time progresses. This occurs because high past and current short-term interest rates lead people to expect future short-term interest rates to be high. Since long-term interest rates are a geometric average of expected future short-term interest rates, adjusted for the risk of being wrong, rising expectations of future short-term interest rates will increase the long-term interest rate.[7] These increases in longer-term interest rates will reduce investment at a less elevated level of the short-term interest rate. Since the long-term interest rate has practically no effect on the demand for money, a reduced short-term interest rate and higher longer-term interest rate will increase the desired level of fluidity associated with any given reduction in investment.

Investment projects are normally planned and produced over a substantial length of time. It takes a much more substantial rise in the level of interest rates to convince investors to abandon or postpone completion of a project that has been partially completed than to abandon one which has not been started. Losses due to the unexpected rise in interest rates may be much smaller if the project, say a factory building, is completed than if it is abandoned. At the beginning of the change in fiscal policy, interest rates must rise much higher, since nearly all the reduction of investment must come in new projects, not those underway. As time passes, projects underway are completed, and all investment must be profitable at the going interest rate. This reduction in projects underway permits more new projects to be started—though still fewer than before the change in fiscal policy—and interest rates to fall. This situation will also increase the desired level of fluidity associated with any given reduction in investment.[8]

Summary of Effects of Adjustments Working through the Demand for Money and Investment Demand

An increased rate of government spending and borrowing reduces the desired and actual level of fluidity by increasing interest rates on short-term bonds relative to the interest rate paid on money. Further, shock absorber behavior

---

[7] The economic literature on this problem, known as the term structure of interest rates, is immense. Key references are to David Meiselman, *The Term Structure of Interest Rates*, Englewood Cliffs, N.J.: Prentice-Hall, Inc., 1962; Reuben A. Kessel, *The Cyclical Behavior of the Term Structure of Interest Rates*, NBER Occasional Paper No. 91, New York: Columbia University Press, 1965; and Burton G. Malkiel, *The Term Structure of Interest Rates; Expectations and Behavior Patterns*, Princeton: Princeton University Press, 1966.

[8] It will be seen in Sec. 8.3 that the behavior of saving partially offsets these effects by increasing the required reduction in investment the longer any increase in income is maintained. For example, a transitory increase of income by $1 billion would increase saving by about $500 to $600 million. The long-run increase in saving due to a permanent $1 billion increase in income would be only about $100 million. The period of transition is very long so that this effect can be safely neglected in this case.

of money balances may temporarily reduce the actual level of fluidity below the desired level indicated by the money demand function. This initial fall in desired fluidity is reduced or eliminated over time because of (1) adjustments in the interest rates which banks pay on their deposits and (2) reduction of the level of the short-term interest rate associated with each rate of investment. Both of these forces act to move nominal income back toward its original growth path, but have opposite effects on the level of the short-term interest rate. The increased rates paid on bank deposits tend to increase short-term interest rates by requiring a larger reduction in investment to accommodate the increase in government spending. The reduction in the short-term interest required for any given level of investment tends to reduce this interest rate. Whether the short-term interest rate tends to rise or fall during this latter part of the process of adjustment is an unsettled empirical issue.

The Issues in the Fiscal Policy Controversy

A very lively debate—which was called "the question of the 1970s" in Chap. 1—is in progress in macroeconomics over the size of the initial increase in nominal income and whether the whole initial increase is eliminated in equilibrium. A related question is how such changes in nominal income as do occur are divided between changes in real income and the price level. The same questions are debated with regard to the effects of tax reduction, as will be seen in the next section (8.3).

There is no way to deduce whether the adjustment process is carried to the point where any effect on nominal income is eliminated or whether this adjustment process is so fast that there is not even a temporary increase in nominal income. To answer such a question about the facts one must turn to the data.

There are serious statistical problems in interpreting what the data tell us, although these are not so serious as those who dislike the results would claim. The basic difficulty lies in the question of whether measures of fiscal and monetary policy are influenced by other factors which also influence nominal income. If they are, statistical procedures will mistakenly attribute the influence of the neglected other factors to the fiscal or monetary policy measures which they influence. The same sort of difficulty would arise if one's shoe size was used as a predictor of one's ability to do long division, neglecting the common causal factor of age. These problems would not arise if economists were free to experiment by choosing different combinations of monetary and fiscal policy, but the obvious costs imposed on society by such a program makes the very idea bizarre. Since we must make do with the "experiments" which policymakers and events have provided us, our answers are subject to these questions. To date, the basic empirical relationships have held up well under three approaches to checking for other neglected variables: (1) a historical analysis of the exact causality of particular changes in monetary and fiscal policy, (2) tests of relationships for long periods and different countries so that widely different institutions determine monetary and fiscal policy, and (3) statistical analysis of timing relationships between policy changes and nominal income changes.[9]

Empirical Results on Effects of Increased Government Spending and Borrowing

The general—though not unanimous—conclusion of these recent empirical studies is that an increase in the scale of government spending financed by borrowing increases nominal income temporarily, but that this effect on nominal income is eliminated within a year to a year and a quarter. Nominal income rises relative to its steady-state growth path for 6 to 9 months and then begins to move back toward the steady-state growth path.[10] The maximum increase in nominal income above the level that would otherwise occur (at 6 to 9 months) appears to be a bit less than the increase in government spending in dollar amounts but of the same order of magnitude. The peak percentage or logarithmic increase in nominal income is much less than the percentage or logarithmic increase in government spending. This pattern is illustrated in Fig. 8.5. A series of increases in government expenditures above trend growth are required if the increase in nominal income above the steady-state growth path is to be prolonged.

A coordinated fiscal policy in the United States can be attempted only by the federal government. Currently expenditures by the federal government for goods and services are about 9 percent of net national product (for 1974, $116.9 billion/$1,278.0 billion = 0.091). Were nominal income to be increased at the peak by the full dollar amount of a 10 percent increase in the federal government spending-income ratio, the maximum increase in nominal income would be 0.9 percent above trend $(0.1 \times 0.09 = 0.009)$. Thus, even a very substantial change in the scale of federal government spending relative to the

---

[9] The empirical work has been going on for some time. Principal references are to Milton Friedman and Anna Jacobson Schwartz, *A Monetary History of the United States, 1867–1960,* Princeton: Princeton University Press for NBER, 1963; Milton Friedman and David Meiselman, The Relative Stability of Monetary Velocity and the Investment Multiplier in the United States, 1897–1958, in E. Cary Brown, et al., *Stabilization Policies,* Research Studies prepared for the Commission on Money and Credit, Englewood Cliffs, N.J.: Prentice-Hall, Inc., 1963; see also comments and reply on this paper in the *American Economic Review,* **55**: 693–792, Sept. 1965; Leonall C. Andersen and Jerry L. Jordan, Monetary and Fiscal Actions: A Test of Their Relative Importance in Economic Stabilization, *Federal Reserve Bank of St. Louis Review,* **50**(11): 11–24, Nov. 1968, see also comment and reply on this paper in the same *Review,* **51**(4): 6–16, Apr. 1969; Michael W. Keran, Monetary and Fiscal Influences on Economic Activity—The Historical Evidence, *Federal Reserve Bank of St. Louis Review,* **51**(11): 5–24, Nov. 1969; Michael W. Keran, Monetary and Fiscal Influences on Economic Activity: The Foreign Experience, *Federal Reserve Bank of St. Louis Review,* **52**(2): 16–28, Feb. 1970; E. Gerald Corrigan, The Measurement and Importance of Fiscal Policy Changes, *Federal Reserve Bank of New York Monthly Review,* **52**(6): 133–145, June 1970; Christopher A. Sims, Money, Income, and Causality, *American Economic Review,* **62**: 540–552, Sept. 1972; and Peter Schmidt and Roger N. Waud, The Almon Lag Technique and the Monetary Versus Fiscal Policy Debate, *Journal of the American Statistical Association,* **68**: 11–19, Mar. 1973.

[10] Some Keynesian econometric models (e.g., the MPS model) imply a longer period until the peak—say five to six quarters—and a permanent residual effect on nominal income and the price level. In that case, the pattern of Fig. 8.4 would hold. The question, of more theoretical than practical importance, remains an open one.

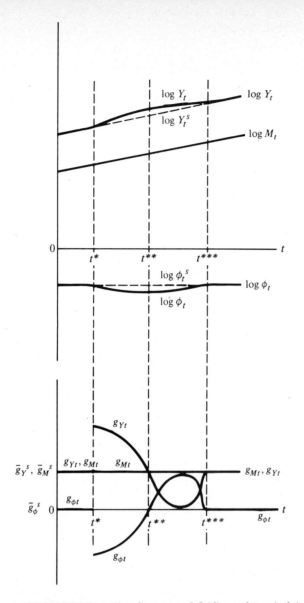

FIGURE 8.5 Dynamic adjustment of fluidity and nominal income to a sudden increase in the rate of government spending and borrowing at t^*. The increased rate of government spending and borrowing increases short-term interest rates and decreases fluidity ($g_{\phi t}$ less than $\bar{g}_\phi^s = 0$ here). In 6 to 9 months at t^{**} fluidity is at its lowest level relative to its steady-state growth path. Since monetary growth is held constant for purposes of analysis and $\log Y_t \equiv \log M_t - \log \phi_t$, nominal income is farthest above its steady-state growth path at t^{**}. As the interest rate paid on bank deposits is increased and investment demand as a function of the short-term interest rate is reduced, fluidity begins to rise toward its steady-state growth path ($g_{\phi t}$ greater than $\bar{g}_\phi^s$). Similarly, the difference between the actual and steady-state growth paths of nominal income is reduced (g_{Yt} less than $\bar{g}_Y^s$). After a year to a year and a quarter at t^{***}, fluidity and nominal income return to their steady-state growth paths.

desired level would have at the peak only a relatively trivial impact on nominal income.

Little empirical research has been done on the division of the change in nominal income between changes in real income and the price level. Extension of the results for monetary shocks suggests that the temporary increase in nominal income will almost entirely reflect increases in real income.

Analysis of the Effects of a Decrease in Government Spending and Borrowing

A restrictive policy of a temporary decrease in government spending and borrowing has entirely symmetric effects on nominal income. Initially, short-term interest rates fall sharply to induce an increase in investment to replace the reduced government spending. At lower short-term interest rates, desired fluidity is increased and nominal income falls, the low point relative to the steady-state growth path coming in 6 to 9 months. Banks gradually lower the interest rates which they pay on money, long-term interest rates decline over time, and investment projects underway increase. All of these forces tend to move desired fluidity and nominal income back to their steady-state growth paths, but the net effect on the level of the short-term interest rate is uncertain. Nominal income and fluidity revert to their steady-state growth paths in about a year to a year and a quarter. This process is summarized in Fig. 8.6.

Return of Government Expenditures and Borrowing to Desired Levels

The original problem was made both simpler and more realistic by the assumption that government spending was only temporarily increased relative to the growth path implied by the resources and tastes of the society. Were this not the case we would have had to consider the cumulative effects on real income of a permanently decreased ratio of investment to real income. If one is to neglect this effect as being small during the relevant time span, then it must be that government spending is soon reduced to its desired growth path. Further, extra government debt on which interest must be paid will have accumulated (recall Fig. 8.1). The additional government interest payments would require permanently higher taxes or lower (other) transfer payments. Instead the accumulated government debt normally would be worked off either by a further temporary decrease in government spending below the desired growth path or by a temporary increase in taxes.

A temporary increase in government spending followed by a temporary decrease in government spending is a policy of lumping growth in government expenditures in time. A complete policy round would involve a stimulative fiscal shock (the original increase in government spending), a larger restrictive fiscal shock (the movement below the desired level), and finally another stimulative shock (as government spending returns to normal). It would be

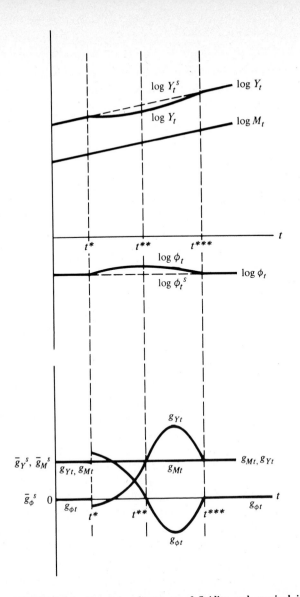

FIGURE 8.6 Dynamic adjustment of fluidity and nominal income to a sudden decrease in the rate of government spending and borrowing at t^***.** The decreased rate of government spending and borrowing decreases short-term interest rates and increases fluidity ($g_{\phi t}$ greater than $\bar{g}_\phi{}^s = 0$ here). In 6 to 9 months at t^{**}, fluidity is at its highest level relative to its steady-state growth path. Since monetary growth is held constant for purposes of analysis and $\log Y_t \equiv \log M_t - \log \phi_t$, nominal income is farthest below its steady-state growth path at t^{**}. As the interest rate paid on bank deposits is decreased and investment demand as a function of the short-term interest rate rises, fluidity begins to fall toward its steady-state growth path ($g_{\phi t}$ less than $\bar{g}_\phi{}^s$). Similarly, the difference between the actual and steady-state growth paths of nominal income is reduced ($g_{Y t}$ greater than $\bar{g}_Y{}^s$). After a year to a year and a quarter at t^{***}, fluidity and nominal income return to their steady-state growth paths.

lucky indeed were there any other offsetting macroeconomic shocks which might make this a desirable pattern, but more on this subject in the discussion of macroeconomic policy (Chap. 15).

8.3 EFFECTS OF CHANGES IN TAXATION ON NOMINAL INCOME

The Similarity Between a Tax Reduction and a Government Spending Increase

A temporary tax reduction financed by borrowing replaces some tax receipts with an equal amount of additional government bonds.[11] If there were no changes in consumer spending, there would be equal increases in private income y_t'' and saving s_t in view of the definitions:

$$y_t'' \equiv y_t - t_t \tag{8.6}$$

$$s_t \equiv y_t'' - c_t \tag{8.7}$$

If people just replaced "purchases" of tax receipts with purchases of government bonds, there would be no effects on consumer expenditures for goods and services or on investment—and government spending is held constant for analysis of the current problem. Consequently the interest rate, the demand for money, and aggregate demand would be unchanged.

It is traditionally argued, however, that decreases in taxes will increase consumer expenditures. Thus, saving increases by less than the reduction in taxes and the corresponding increase in government borrowing. To the extent that consumer expenditures are increased by a tax reduction, resources must be shifted from production of investment goods to production of consumption goods. The increase in consumer expenditures which is induced by the tax reduction is exactly comparable to an equal increase in government spending financed by borrowing. The increase in spending—in the one case by consumers and the other by the government—is matched by an equal decrease in savings available for private investment. The required reduction in investment in each case drives up short-term interest rates; this increase, by reducing desired fluidity at least temporarily, increases aggregate demand. There would be differences in the detail of the adjustment process since the government spending case involves adjustment by firms and consumers to an accomplished fact while the taxation case requires an adjustment of consumer spending to initiate the process. But generally the increase in consumer spending due to reduced taxation has the same effect as increased government spending which does not directly replace private investment.

---

[11] An alternative analysis of the effects of tax reductions would involve a reduction of tax rates. The actual real taxes collected and government borrowing then varies with real income. It is analytically and statistically simpler to consider reductions in the growth path of real taxes analogous to the increase in the growth path of real government spending illustrated in Fig. 8.1.

The impact on aggregate demand of a reduction in taxes is highly dependent on the ratio of the induced increase in consumer spending to the decrease in taxes. If this ratio is close to zero, as initially supposed, the effects on aggregate demand will be negligible. If this ratio is close to the historically observed value of $1 - \sigma^*$, 0.9, the impact would be of similar magnitude to that of a temporary increase in government spending. The observed ratio of induced increase in consumer spending to decrease in taxes is intermediate between these two values of 0.9 and 0. To understand why, one must examine the determination of consumer spending in somewhat more detail than has been previously necessary.

An Introduction to Consumer Expenditure Theory[12]

The key concept in consumer expenditure theory is the distinction between the pure consumption of service flows $c_t{}^f$ and consumer expenditures c_t. *Consumption of service flows* (or *consumption*) is the idealized concept of price theory which measures the use of goods and services. *Consumer expenditures* refer to all market purchases of goods and services. The difference arises because of semidurable and durable goods such as clothing, automobiles, and dishwashers. Consumer expenditures include automobiles, for example, when they are purchased by consumers. Consumption, in contrast, includes the automobile services which flow over time from the consumers' stock of automobiles. That is, consumption excludes purchases of durable and semidurable goods but includes their implicit rental value.

Consumer expenditures differ from consumption by the amount that increases in the stock cd_t of consumer durable and semidurable goods exceed the imputed (interest) yield on the stock:

$$c_t = c_t{}^f + \Delta cd_t - r_c{}^r cd_t \qquad [8.8]$$

This equation reflects the fact that consumer expenditures include increases in the stock of consumer durable and semidurable goods—analogous to net investment by firms—which are excluded from consumption. Consumption on the other hand includes an imputed return at the rate $r_c{}^r$ on the stock of durable and semidurable goods which is excluded from consumer expenditures. Consumer expenditure theory focuses on the explanation of consumption $c_t{}^f$ and the rate of change in the stock of consumer durable and semidurable goods (for short, the rate of change in durables) Δcd_t. The level of the stock

[12] The discussion of this subsection draws heavily on the ideas and estimates presented in Michael R. Darby, Postwar U.S. Consumption, Consumer Expenditures, and Saving, *American Economic Review*, **65**: 217–222, May 1975; More advanced treatments of some of the issues discussed in the text are found in Michael R. Darby, The Permanent Income Theory of Consumption—A Restatement, *Quarterly Journal of Economics*, **88**: 228–250, May 1974; and Michael R. Darby, The Allocation of Transitory Income Among Consumers' Assets, *American Economic Review*, **62**: 928–941, Dec. 1972.

of durables is the sum of past rates of change in durables and therefore does not require a separate explanation.

The behavior of pure consumption c_t^f is relatively easy to explain and understand. Simply put, pure consumption is a constant fraction Θ of wealth as measured by permanent income y_{Pt}:[13]

$$c_t^f = \Theta y_{Pt} \qquad\qquad [8.9]$$

Equation [8.9] contains two substantive empirical generalizations: (1) pure consumption depends on permanent income not current income, and (2) the fraction of permanent income devoted to pure consumption neither rises nor falls as permanent income increases over time.

Good or bad luck as measured by transitory income y_{Tt}, the difference between actual income and permanent income, affects both present and future consumption. It does this, however, only by affecting the basic constraint of wealth which is measured here by permanent income. The present value of planned present and future consumption will just equal the amount available to spend—current wealth. A windfall gain or loss due to current income differing from expected income y_{Pt} will generally increase or decrease, respectively, planned consumption in all periods, not solely the one in which the windfall occurs.

It is sometimes argued[14] that the fraction of income consumed will decrease as wealth increases because "needs" or wants become less pressing as wealth increases. This is bad logic however, because the consumption-saving decision involves the comparison of the values of current and future consumption. A poor man may in some sense place a greater psychological value on present consumption than a rich man, but he will also put a greater value on increasing next year's consumption than will the rich man. There is no reason to expect the relative valuation of present to future consumption to be any greater in the one case than in the other.

From the point of view of the individual, his stocks of durable goods are just one way to hold wealth. In full equilibrium, there will be a desired ratio of these stocks to wealth or permanent income since they are sources of consumption services. If, however, an individual finds himself in disequilibrium because of windfall gains or losses (transitory income) or excess money holdings, he will alter the rate of change in durables from that which just covers the desired increase due to growth of permanent income. Possibly offsetting or reinforcing these influences on the rate of change of durables would be the gradual elimination of any excess or deficiency of actual compared to long-run desired stocks of durable and semidurable goods.

---

[13] Permanent income was introduced in Chap. 4 as the product of a constant long-run expected yield r_p' on all (human and nonhuman) wealth v_t; thus, $y_{Pt} = r_p' v_t$.

[14] As, for example, by John Maynard Keynes, *The General Theory of Employment, Interest, and Money,* New York: Harcourt, Brace & Company, 1936, p. 97.

These influences can be summarized by a function

$$\Delta cd_t = \Delta cd(y_{Pt}, y_{Tt}, m_t - m_t^d, cd_t) \qquad [8.10]$$

The rate of change of durables will increase if permanent income y_{Pt}, transitory income y_{Tt}, or excess real money holdings $m_t - m_t^d$ are increased and decrease if they are decreased. Increases in the stock of consumers' durable and semidurable goods cd_t will decrease the rate of change in durables and vice versa.

Equations [8.8], [8.9], and [8.10] can be combined to obtain a general *consumer expenditure function:*

$$c_t = c(y_{Pt}, y_{Tt}, m_t - m_t^d, cd_t) \qquad [8.11]$$

Again, total consumer expenditures increase with increases in permanent income, transitory income, and excess real money holdings, but with decreases in the current stock of consumers' durables.

For situations of full equilibrium, transitory income and excess money balances are zero and stocks of consumers' durables and permanent income increase in constant proportion. In that case,

$$c_t = (1 - \sigma^*)y_{Pt} \qquad [8.12]$$

Or since current and permanent income then are equal,

$$c_t = (1 - \sigma^*)y_t^n \qquad [8.13]$$

which is the average relationship actually observed over long periods of time. This is *not* a behavioral relationship which explains how changes in current real private income affect consumer spending however. An increase in real private income immediately affects only the transitory income $(y_{Tt} = y_t^n - y_{Pt})$ argument of the consumer expenditure function. But each dollar change in transitory income causes only about a \$0.40 change in consumer expenditures—much less than would be predicted from [8.13] and $1 - \sigma^*$ of about 0.9.

Since a temporary tax reduction increases transitory income immediately and permanent income only slowly over time, the direct effect on consumer spending of each base-year dollar of tax reduction would be an increase of about 0.4 base-year dollars initially, rising to about 0.45 base-year dollars at the end of a year's time.[15]

It is argued by some economists that the direct effect on consumer spending will be even smaller because the current tax cuts are correctly believed by individuals to mean higher taxes later. As a result these individuals will save more and consume less. The difficulty with this argument is that pure consumption is increased only trivially by the tax reduction, most of the effect

---

[15] This computation assumes that at the end of a year, the tax reduction will be treated as 90 percent transitory income and 10 percent permanent income (see Chap. 4) and that $1 - \sigma^* = 0.9$. Then $(0.1)(0.9) + (0.9)(0.4) = 0.45$.

on consumer spending being represented by quasi-saving in the form of increasing stocks of durable goods. Thus, it would be very hard to detect any difference in observed behavior over the life of a temporary tax reduction.

In summary, the direct effect of a tax reduction on consumer spending for given total income is to increase spending by somewhat more than one-quarter of the reduction but by less than one-half.

Effects of a Temporary Tax Change on Nominal Income

Traditionally, macroeconomists have argued that a tax reduction will have generally the same effects on total nominal income—though not how it is spent—as a somewhat smaller temporary increase in government spending, where both are financed by increased government borrowing. The portion of the tax reduction that is saved finances an equal amount of new government borrowing and so washes out of the picture. The portion that is spent on consumers' goods and the corresponding amount of borrowing can be substituted into the analysis for increased government spending and borrowing. Conversely, an increase in taxes will have the same effects on nominal income as a smaller decrease in government spending, both involving equal reductions in government borrowing.

Recent empirical studies[16] have been notably unsuccessful at finding the expected effect (or much of any other). This may simply reflect the relatively small size of variations in real taxes around their trend growth path. If the peak effect on nominal income is no more than half the amount of a change in taxes, then even a 10 percent change in federal taxes (from 9 percent to 8 percent or 9.9 percent of total income) would change nominal income by less than 0.5 percent ($0.009 \times 0.5 = 0.0045$). It is very difficult to detect and measure effects which are so small even for quite large changes in taxation. The current state of knowledge does not permit any strong statements about the process of dynamic adjustment to changes in taxes. Patterns analogous to those summarized in Figs. 8.5 and 8.6 are traditionally expected but have not been reliably demonstrated. There is at least a hint that the initial effect of a tax decrease may be to perversely increase fluidity as people hold on to unexpectedly higher cash receipts while deciding how to use them.[17] In that case, nominal income at first falls with a tax decrease or conversely rises with a tax increase. Presumably the short-term interest rate initially rises sufficiently to decrease investment by more than the increase in consumer spending—if

---

[16] See the studies cited in footnote 9 in connection with the effects of government spending.

[17] This perverse effect would persist to some extent if an increase in private income for given total income increases the demand for money. If private wealth as measured by permanent income is a determinant of the demand for money, this influence would become increasingly important as the tax change effects permanent income over time. A related analysis is contained in James M. Holmes and David J. Smyth, The Specification of the Demand for Money and the Tax Multiplier, *Journal of Political Economy*, **80:** 179–185, January/February 1972.

these perverse effects are more than statistical vagaries. Only brave or fool-hardy souls can draw firm conclusions from the current meager empirical evidence, however.

Adjustment of Taxation and Borrowing to Desired Levels

As with the use of changes in the growth path of government spending, changes in taxation must be reversed and for a time more than reversed[18] in order to return to the desired growth paths of real taxes and government debt. On the traditional analysis, a stimulative policy (tax reduction) would be followed by a more restrictive policy (greater tax increase to pay off excess government debt) which would be followed by a stimulative policy (tax reduction to the desired steady-state growth path). Alternatively, an initially restrictive policy would be followed by a more stimulative policy and then a final restrictive policy.

For both real taxation and real government spending, the basic difficulty is that a fiscal policy which has a detectable impact on nominal income involves substantial deviation of actual from the desired levels of taxation or spending. Further, this impact does not appear to persist for more than a year to a year and a half. So to obtain a continuing increase, say, in nominal income above its original growth path, there must be continuing reduction in taxes or increases in government spending as a fraction of income with associated acceleration in the rate of government borrowing. Merely maintaining taxes permanently below desired levels is not enough. Those economists who read the lack of evidence for the traditional view of the effects of changes in real taxes as evidence for no impact of changes in taxes on nominal income would consider that changes in the growth path of taxes have no effects on nominal income and simply move the ratio of investment to consumption from its desired level.

The Burden of Deficit Finance

The main burden of deficit finance—of borrowing instead of taxing[19]—arises from the induced shift from private investment to consumption. In the terms of the growth model of Chap. 6, a continued policy of deficit finance would cause a reduction in the fraction σ of income which is invested. This would produce a lower equilibrium capital-labor ratio and a growth path of real

---

[18] Alternatively, too high a government debt could be eliminated by temporarily reducing government spending after returning taxes to their desired level and vice versa for too low a government debt. The empirical results suggest that this policy would be more disruptive than a temporary overcorrection of the rate of taxation, however.

[19] Revenue from money creation is not considered here, but see Sec. 6.3.

income parallel to but below the growth path associated with a balanced budget.[20]

Advanced treatments[21] have shown that if the capital accumulation–income ratio is so high that the real rate of interest is less than the growth rate of real income, a lower ratio would result in a higher level of private plus government consumption at every point in time. In that case an increase in the ratio of government borrowing to income will have beneficial effects by reducing income less than saving in every period. On both theoretical and empirical grounds, the probability of this special case actually occurring appears to be negligible. In fact many countries follow precisely the opposite policy of increasing the ratio of capital accumulation to income by running a budget surplus of taxes over government expenditures. These countries use the surplus to retire the government debt, to finance private securities, or to invest directly through government-owned enterprises.

If an increase in government borrowing is only temporary, the investment-income and capital-labor ratios will eventually rise back to their original equilibrium levels after a period of reduced real income. Higher consumption levels in the earlier period are traded for temporarily lower levels later. If the accumulated extra debt remains without offset, additional government interest payments must be financed either by an increase in taxes—or a reduction in other transfer payments—or a permanently increased rate of borrowing. As neither alternative is attractive, debt accumulated through budget deficits has usually been slowly offset by budget surpluses net of revenue from money creation and by inflation.

This analysis does not imply that government borrowing is always bad. There are instances in which it is appropriate to consume more now even if it causes less capital to be available to us and our children in the future. The most obvious example is war. Table 8.2 shows that war is the main source of real federal debt and that the ratio of this debt to income has been steadily reduced in peacetime. A more prosaic example is the debt financing of local government facilities so that future residents will pay for the services that they receive. Nevertheless, the higher current consumption levels due to government borrowing imply reduced consumption in the future.

Balanced-Budget Fiscal Policies

The budget of the federal government is said to be *balanced* if the federal deficit (borrowing plus money creation) is zero. This concept can also be applied to the aggregate of all governments. Fiscal policy which leaves the

[20] Depending on the elasticities of the demand for money with respect to real income and the interest rate, the growth path of nominal income would shift up or down or stay the same. In any case, the equilibrium level—but not the growth rate—of the price level would be higher under the policy of deficit finance.
[21] See particularly Edmund S. Phelps, *Golden Rules of Economic Growth*, New York: W. W. Norton, 1966, pp. 56–61; Peter A. Diamond, National Debt in a Neoclassical Growth Model, *American Economic Review*, 55: 1126–1150, Dec. 1965; and Earl A. Thompson, Debt Instruments in Both Macroeconomic Theory and Capital Theory, *American Economic Review*, 57: 1196–1210, Dec. 1967.

TABLE 8.2 Government debt in the United States

Year	Nominal Debt, Billions of Dollars			Real Debt, Billions of 1958 Dollars[b]			Debt-Income Ratios[c]		
	Federal[a]	State & Local	Total	Federal	State & Local	Total	Federal	State & Local	Total
1902	1.2	2.1	3.3	4.6	8.0	12.6	0.06	0.11	0.17
1913	1.2	4.4	5.6	3.7	13.5	17.1	0.03	0.13	0.16
1922	22.0	10.1	32.1	42.6	19.5	62.1	0.32	0.15	0.47
1932	16.8	19.2	36.0	41.8	47.8	89.6	0.33	0.38	0.71
1940	40.6	20.2	60.8	92.5	46.0	138.5	0.44	0.22	0.66
1946	202.0	15.9	217.9	302.8	23.8	326.7	1.02	0.08	1.10
1950	209.3	24.1	233.4	261.0	30.0	291.0	0.79	0.09	0.88
1955	214.0	44.3	258.3	235.4	48.7	284.2	0.58	0.12	0.70
1960	189.2	70.0	259.2	183.2	67.8	250.9	0.41	0.15	0.56
1965	197.8	99.5	297.3	178.4	89.7	268.1	0.32	0.16	0.48
1970	202.1	143.6	345.7	149.5	106.2	255.7	0.23	0.16	0.39
1972	233.6	175.0	408.6	159.9	119.8	279.7	0.22	0.17	0.39

Totals may not add due to rounding. 1902–1932 data are for June and 1940–1972 data are for December.

[a] Debt held by the public; excludes securities held by the Federal Reserve System and other federal agencies and by state and local governments.

[b] Deflated by the implicit price deflator for GNP for the indicated year. Deflator for 1902 and 1913 estimated from 5-year averages.

[c] Ratio of indicated concept of government debt to net national product for the year. Net national product for 1902 and 1913 estimated from 5-year averages.

Sources: Historical Statistics of the United States, Colonial Times to 1957 (1902–1922); *Federal Reserve Bulletin,* various issues (1932–1972); *The National Income and Product Accounts of the United States,* 1929–1965; *Statistical Abstract of the United States,* various issues; and *Survey of Current Business,* various issues.

deficit unchanged—that is, equal changes in government spending and taxation—is called *balanced-budget fiscal policy* whatever the actual level of the deficit.

Balanced-budget fiscal policy has the advantage of not altering the growth path of government debt. A balanced-budget increase in government spending and taxation can be decomposed into an increase in government spending financed by increased borrowing and an equal increase in taxation that finances decreased borrowing. Similarly, a balanced-budget decrease in government spending and taxation consists of a decrease in government spending that finances decreased borrowing and of an equal decrease in taxation financed by increased borrowing. The effects are therefore obtained by combining the previous analysis of this section (8.3) with that of Sec. 8.2.

On the traditional view, an increase in taxes that finances reduced borrowings would reduce (temporarily) nominal income by less than an equal reduction in government spending that finances reduced borrowing. Now the effects of an increase in government spending financed by increased borrowing are opposite in sign and of approximately the same magnitude as the effects of an equal decrease in spending and borrowing. So the net effects on nominal income of a balanced-budget increase in spending and taxation would be smaller than, but similar to, the effects of the same increase in spending financed by borrowing. This can also be seen directly. The decrease in consumer spending due to the decrease in private income implies a smaller required reduction in investment to offset a given increase in government spending. Therefore the short-term interest rate will not rise by as much and hence the quantity of money demanded at the initial level of total income will fall less and income will be increased less. A Keynesian phrasing of this result would be that the increase in government spending is partially offset by a decrease in consumer spending so that the increases in income and the interest rate required to reestablish equilibrium are less than if the government spending had been financed by increased borrowing. Adjustments in the interest rate paid on bank deposits, the long-term interest rate, and investment projects underway would tend to reduce or eliminate these effects over the course of a year to a year and a half. Economists who doubt the traditional view of the effects of taxation would argue that the reduction in consumer spending is trivial and, perhaps, that the decrease in private income decreases the demand for money at the initial levels of total income and interest rates.

The converse case of a decrease in government spending and taxation would be approximately equivalent in effects to a smaller decrease in government spending financing reduced borrowing. The traditional argument is that there will be an increase in consumer spending because of the tax reduction and that this increase in consumer spending will reduce the required increase in investment and the decrease in the short-term interest rate required to offset the decrease in government spending. As a result, there is a smaller increase in desired fluidity and a smaller decrease in nominal income.

For balanced-budget fiscal policies, a restrictive policy equivalent to the initial stimulative policy (or vice versa) is sufficient to return government spending, taxation, and debt to their desired growth paths. This occurs because government debt remains on the desired growth path so that no corrective "overshooting" is required. On the other hand, greater divergences of spending (and taxation) from the desired growth path are required—on the traditional view—to achieve any given impact on nominal income.

Separation of Impacts of Fiscal and Monetary Policies

As will be seen in Chap. 10, pure fiscal policy with a constant growth rate in the money supply is actually quite rare. A stimulative fiscal policy is normally combined with a stimulative monetary policy (increased growth rate of the money supply) which finances part of the increased government spending or decreased taxation. The exceptions, though rare, in which only pure fiscal or monetary policy is operative or in which monetary and fiscal policies operate in opposite directions provide the best evidence we have on the separate effects of monetary and fiscal policies.

The usual pattern of reinforcing monetary and fiscal policies has led to an understandable confusion of the *effects* of monetary and fiscal policies. Changes in government spending or taxation are debated in Congress and widely publicized. Much less publicity accrues to the Fed's administrative decisions which determine the rate of growth of the money supply. A purely discretionary Fed decision to partially finance an increase in government spending or reduction in taxation by say, increasing the growth rate of the money supply by 3 percentage points may have a much greater effect than the original fiscal policy. If the distinction between the two effects is not kept carefully in mind, it is natural but erroneous to attribute the sum of the effects of monetary and fiscal policies to the much more dramatic change in fiscal policy.

8.4 OTHER POTENTIAL DOMESTIC MACROECONOMIC SHOCKS
Shifts in Behavioral Functions as a Source of Macroeconomic Shocks

So far we have discussed macroeconomic shocks connected with government decisions: changes in the growth rate of the money supply or, more precisely, changes in the growth rate of high-powered money, and changes in the growth paths of government spending and taxation. This section considers macroeconomic shocks which might arise in the private sector of the economy. These shocks would involve sudden changes in the basic behavioral relationships: the money multiplier, the demand for money function, the aggregate production function, the supply function for labor, the investment function, and the consumption function.

A change in the value of a behavioral function—for example, the observed level of real consumer spending—can reflect changes in the determinants of the function or a change in the function itself. An example of the former sort of change, *a movement along the function*, would be the increase in real consumer spending due to an increase in transitory income with the other arguments of the consumption function—permanent income, excess real money balances, and the real stock of consumers' durables—unchanged. An example of the latter sort of change, *a shift in the function*, would be a change in real consumer spending with *all* the arguments of the consumption function— permanent income, transitory income, excess real money balances, and the real stock of consumers' durables—unchanged.

A difficulty with this distinction is that one economist's shift in a behavioral function is simply a movement along another economist's more complete behavioral function. Carrying the consumption function example a step further, an economist who omits excess real money balances from his specification (or mathematical description) of the consumption function will note a shift in his estimated consumption function whenever excess money balances change. Economists who include excess real money balances in their estimated consumption function will call these changes in real consumer spending a movement along the consumption function. More generally, as a philosophical matter, stating that there was a shift in one of our behavioral functions is the same thing as saying that there was a movement along the true, complete behavioral function due to a change in an argument of which we are unaware or neglectful because of our ignorance or inability to measure.

From the standpoint of macroeconomic shocks we are interested in sudden shifts in behavioral functions which occur because of changes in any factor which is not systematically determined within the macroeconomic model. Much of the current debate among macroeconomists questions whether or not apparent shifts in behavioral functions—particularly the investment function—are due to changes in factors properly determined within the macroeconomic model. Particularly important for decisions about investment in a capital commodity yielding services over many years are expectations of the future real rental rates to be received. If these expectations only change in response to changes in such factors as present and past rental rates on capital, real income, and nominal money supply growth, these apparent shifts in the investment function are induced by macroeconomic shocks and are not themselves sources of macroeconomic shocks. The apparent shifts just pinpoint part of the model requiring more work to explain the details of the way in which, say, monetary and fiscal policy changes affect real income and the price level. If, however, there are important factors affecting expectations which are not given or determined in macroeconomic models, then changes in those factors will be sources of macroeconomic shocks. The only ultimate way to settle this debate is to find a reliable way to measure and explain expectations and see whether or not there are important neglected factors.

We now turn to a discussion of the potential size of shifts in the individual behavioral functions and, where appropriate, the effects of such shifts.

Changes in the Money Multiplier

The money multiplier μ_t was derived in Chap. 3 as

$$\mu_t = \frac{(F_t)/(BD_t) + 1}{(F_t)/(BD_t) + (R_t)/(BD_t)} \qquad [8.14]$$

where F_t is currency and coins held by the public, BD_t is bank deposits held by the public, and R_t is bank reserves. The money supply is equal to the money multiplier times the monetary base (stock of high-powered money):

$$M_t = \mu_t B_t \qquad [8.15]$$

Except for seasonal fluctuations, the cash-deposit ratio and reserve-deposit ratio normally change only according to rather slow trends. There are, however, some important exceptions.

The Federal Reserve System can change the fraction of bank deposits which member banks must hold as reserves. This directly alters the observed reserve-deposit ratio for the banking system. Increases in this ratio decrease the money multiplier and vice versa. The Fed uses this power infrequently and normally offsets the effect on the money supply of the changes in the money multiplier. This is done by simultaneously changing the monetary base through open market purchases or sales of government bonds. The important exception occurred between August 1936 and May 1937. During this period, the Board of Governors of the Federal Reserve System used its newly acquired power to set reserve requirements to double them in a series of steps. The resulting sharp decline in the growth rate of the money supply as the money multiplier fell was sufficient to stop the recovery from the Great Depression and begin the severe recession of 1937–1938.[22]

Through the 1930s, banking panics were the most important source of macroeconomic shocks. Banking panics started when, through mismanagement or mischance, a major bank went bankrupt. Rumors would spread that other banks which had held deposits in the closed bank would go bankrupt as a result. A *run* on these banks would occur in which depositors would line up demanding their funds in high-powered money. Since banks held only a small fraction of their deposits in reserves of high-powered money, they could pay off their depositors only if they could borrow or buy high-powered money

---

[22] Because of effects on the demand for money (by altering the ratio of interest rates paid on bank deposits to those on short-term bonds), changes in the money supply achieved through changes in the reserve-deposit ratio will have smaller effects on aggregate demand than would the same changes caused by changes in high-powered money. A thorough analysis of these differential effects must be left to courses in money and banking. Similar changes can be achieved by varying the amount of U.S. Treasury deposits at commercial banks, since they affect required reserves but are not part of the money supply.

from others on the strength of their loans and investments. In a panic, this was often not possible and the bank would have to close, which threatened other banks in turn.

It is easiest to see what happens during banking panics by reference to [8.14]. The public wants a higher cash-deposit ratio because of doubt about the safety of bank deposits. This increases the denominator of the money multiplier proportionately more than the numerator, so that the money multiplier falls. If the central bank does not step in and supply more high-powered money, the money supply must fall. This reduction in the money supply is spread over time as banks at first dip into their reserves and the reserve-deposit ratio is temporarily reduced. Bankers try to liquidate their loans and investments as rapidly as possible to achieve the desired reserve-deposit ratio. In severe panics, banks as a group would suspend payments of deposits in high-powered money to give themselves time to liquidate their loans and investments, and then reopen with reduced deposits (loans would be paid off in or sold for deposits) commensurate with their abilities to pay out high-powered money.

As a result of a panic, there would be a very large decrease in the rate of growth of the money supply (which would average a negative number of large size) over a few months. After that, monetary growth would resume. Over a period of some years, doubts about the ability of banks to pay depositors recede and the money multiplier returns to its original growth path. Although the data are very imprecise for the periods in which panics occurred in the United States, the broad effects are quite clear and are as expected from the discussion in Chap. 7. Soon after the start of the panic, nominal income fell sharply in response to the fall in the money supply. The dramatic fall in nominal income affected both real income and the price level, though the effect on real income was apparently considerably smaller when the country was primarily agrarian than it would be today. Real income would recover to its steady-state growth path over the next few years, with slower recoveries in money supply, nominal income, and the price level.[23]

Recurrent episodes of panic and its aftermath no longer occur in the United States or most other industrialized countries. In the United States, bankruptcies of even large banks no longer lead to panics because the Federal Deposit Insurance Corporation was established in 1934. The FDIC nominally insures deposits up to $40,000, but in fact effectively insures all deposits—with rare exceptions—in order to avoid providing large depositors with an incentive to start a run on a bank. Some other countries prevent panics by instructing the central bank to lend freely as an emergency "lender of last resort" so that increases in high-powered money offset decreases in the money multiplier.

---

[23] In practice, this process was speeded by increases in the stock of high-powered money under the international gold standard then operative. International complications are discussed in Chap. 9.

The Federal Reserve Act of 1913 which established the Federal Reserve System instructed our central bank to do the same, but it nevertheless failed to do so in the banking panics of 1930, 1931, and 1933. As a result of the unreliability of the Fed, Congress established the FDIC.

Sudden changes in the money multiplier other than those due to changes in Fed policy are no longer a major source of macroeconomic shocks.

Changes in the Demand for Money

Instability in the demand function for money balances is a possible though surely unusual source of macroeconomic shocks. The steady-state growth path of fluidity reflects the growth of real income, of communications and payment technology, and of substitutes for the use of money. A radical technological or institutional innovation could cause a sudden change in the steady-state growth path of fluidity. Since we can write

$$\log Y_t = \log M_t - \log \phi_t \qquad\qquad [8.16]$$

a change in the steady-state growth path of fluidity would have the same effects as a change in the growth path of the nominal money supply of the same size but opposite sign.

It has been suggested that the rapid growth of savings and loan associations and the spread of credit cards during the last 25 years have reduced the steady-state growth rate of fluidity. This may be the case since the trend growth rate of fluidity has been much lower than it was before World War II. The trend growth rate of fluidity has been remarkably steady within this period, however.

Although sudden changes in the steady-state growth rate of fluidity may be an occasional source of macroeconomic disturbances, they are exceptional. For long periods of time no such major technological or institutional innovations occur, and changes in the steady-state growth rate of fluidity are negligible.

Changes in Investment Demand

Keynesian economists have argued that investment demand is very unstable because the expectations of businessmen about future returns from investment are very fragile and unstable. If there is a general feeling of optimism in which future prospects are viewed through rose-colored glasses, investment demand will be high. If, conversely, entrepreneurs are generally gloomy, then investment demand would be lower. Increases in confidence would drive up interest rates. This would—just like an increase in government spending—at least temporarily decrease desired fluidity and increase nominal income. Conversely, a fall in investment demand due to a new mood of pessimism would decrease interest rates, and at least temporarily increase fluidity and decrease nominal income.

A peculiarity of this argument is that increased optimism leads to a growth rate of capital greater than the growth rate of labor. It was seen in Chap. 5 that this means that the real rental rate of capital will decline. Similarly, waves of pessimism would lead to rising rental rates on capital. There is always some doubt about an economic theory which is based on consistently wrong expectations—the reward to learning is too great.

One of the major questions in macroeconomics is whether substantial shifts in expectations occur frequently because of unexplainable changes in mood or whether such changes in expectations as occur are due to other macro-economic shocks. The challenge to Keynesians is to find some periods in which investment demand appears to change in the absence of other macroeconomic shocks. This challenge has not yet been met. Some of the empirical evidence will be discussed in Chap. 10.

Changes in Other Behavioral Functions

The aggregate production function, the supply function of labor, and the consumer expenditure function do not appear to be sources of macroeconomic shocks in the United States.[24]

The aggregate production function could significantly vary from year to year in a small agricultural country. Those complications due to the random effects of weather can be safely neglected when averaged over the United States as a whole. For certain states, weather conditions may nevertheless have a greater impact in determining state real income than moderate monetary and fiscal policy actions.

Though expected nominal wages enter the short-run supply of labor function, there is no suggestion that these expectations are determined by anything other than present and past conditions. Changes in the trend growth rate of the labor supply occur much too gradually to count as a macroeconomic shock.

The consumer expenditure function was originally difficult for economists to describe well. Steady work over the last 40 years has culminated in recent advances which leave little room for any significant shifts in the consumer expenditure function.

Summary of Behavioral Shifts as Sources of Macroeconomic Shocks

There are only three behavioral functions which have been—at least arguably —significant sources of macroeconomic shocks: (1) the money multiplier, (2) the money demand function, and (3) the investment function. The money

---

[24] Minor exceptions to this statement will be noted in Chap. 10.

multiplier was formerly a major source of shocks because of the instability of the fractional reserve banking system, but the FDIC changed all that. Now sudden changes in the money multiplier reflect Fed policy actions. There appear to be rare changes in the trend rate of growth of fluidity. Whether these changes occur suddenly enough to cause noticeable disequilibrium is unclear. Changes in the money multiplier and in the demand for money operate in a manner closely analogous to changes in high-powered money which are offset by changes in government borrowing. However, decreases in the demand for money have effects on aggregate demand which are equivalent to those caused by increases in the supply of money. Changes in the investment function due to random changes in expectations would have short-run effects on aggregate demand equivalent to a temporary change in government spending and borrowing. An increase in investment demand increases investment, however, while an increase in government spending decreases investment.

With the exception of policy effects on the money multiplier, we are discussing shocks due to random or unknown causes. The only effective way to get an idea of the relative importance of such shocks is to examine the empirical record as in Chap. 10.

□ **SUMMARY**
There are desired growth paths of real government spending and taxation determined by the alternatives, institutions, and tastes of society. Temporary shifts in the growth paths of government spending, taxes, or both are called fiscal policy. Increases in government spending financed by borrowing reduce private investment through increases in short-term interest rates. These reduce desired fluidity so that nominal income rises by perhaps as much as the increase in government spending. In percentage terms, the effect on nominal income is much smaller than the percentage change in real government spending. This effect appears to last only for 1 to $1\frac{1}{4}$ years as interest rates paid on bank deposits and long-term bonds adjust upward and investment projects underway are reduced. The initial change in government spending and the accumulated extra government debt must be eliminated by a cyclical adjustment in government spending. Symmetric effects are observed for reductions in government spending and borrowing. Traditionally, a tax decrease financed by borrowing is argued to have effects on nominal income equivalent to a smaller increase in government spending and borrowing. This is because the tax cut increases consumer spending. Statistical evidence to support this view is hard to find. This difficulty may reflect an increase in the demand for money due to increased private income. Readjustment of taxes and government debt to desired levels also involves cyclical adjustments of taxes. Government borrowing reduces private capital accumulation and future levels of real

income and is not generally an attractive alternative to taxation. Balanced-budget fiscal policies in which government spending and taxes change together have effects on nominal income similar to a (perhaps) smaller change of government spending and borrowing. Macroeconomic shocks due to shifts in behavioral functions have been concentrated in the money multiplier, demand for money function, and investment function. Whether or not shifts in the investment function are sources of macroeconomic shocks is the subject of a continuing debate.

☐ QUESTIONS AND EXERCISES

1 Why does the government budget identity include the *levels* of government spending and taxes and the *rates of change* of base money and government debt?

*2 If nominal income is increased by 80 percent of an increase in government spending 6 months after the beginning of a pure fiscal policy, and at that time federal government spending is $110 billion instead of the $100 billion that it would have been spending otherwise, how much will nominal income be if it would have been $1,000 billion in the absence of the policy? This is a _____ percent increase in government spending and a _____ percent increase in nominal income.

3 How would the federal government temporarily increase its real spending on *goods and services* by 10 percent over what it would otherwise be? How much time do you think that it would take to get these programs started? Does it seem sensible to shift resources into producing these goods and services and then a year or two later stop buying these goods and services?

4 How would a Keynesian economist describe the initial effects of a decrease in government spending and borrowing?

5 "If people have more money than they want, they will only use it to buy financial assets, not consumers' durable goods." Is this a reasonable description of consumer behavior? Explain.

*6 Why would we expect the effect of a tax decrease financed by borrowing to have smaller effects on nominal income than an equal increase in government spending and borrowing?

7 Why might the increase in private income associated with a tax cut financed by borrowing increase the demand for money in the short run? In the long run?

8 For much of its existence, Federal Reserve policy was couched in terms of maintaining a certain interest rate on short-term securities until a new interest rate was chosen. This was done by buying back government bonds (issued by the Treasury) with new high-powered money if the interest rate rose above target and selling government bonds and so withdrawing high-powered money if the interest rate fell below target. What would this policy do to growth of the money supply if government spending and borrowing were increased? Reduced?

*9 (a) The burden of the government debt on real income is a function of the rate of change of the debt, not its level. Why is this so?

(b) If a country were to finance a brief period of high government expenditures by borrowing (as during a war) and thereafter maintain the *level* of the real government debt constant, what would this do to the steady-state equilibrium real income? Who will pay for the temporary increase in government expenditures? An increased real debt requires higher interest payments and so higher taxes or lower levels of other transfers; what will this do to the distribution of income within the country?

10 Why are gradual shifts in behavioral functions incorporated in the analysis of steady-state equilibrium instead of being treated as macroeconomic shocks?

11 Banking panics often increased the desired reserve-deposit ratio of bankers who felt the threat of panics more keenly for some years afterwards. As the actual reserve-deposit ratio was adjusted to the new desired reserve-deposit ratio, what would be the effect on the money multiplier?

12 Detail the process by which an increase in investment increases interest rates and nominal income. Explain why the real rental rate on capital must fall over time if investment is increased as a fraction of income.

☐ REFERENCES FOR FURTHER READING

Andersen, Leonall C., and Jerry L. Jordan: Monetary and Fiscal Actions: A Test of Their Relative Importance in Economic Stabilization, *Federal Reserve Bank of St. Louis Review*, **50** (11): 11–24, Nov. 1968.

Darby, Michael R.: Postwar U.S. Consumption, Consumer Expenditures, and Saving, *American Economic Review*, **65:** 217–222, May 1975.

Friedman, Milton: *A Theory of the Consumption Function*, Princeton: Princeton University Press for NBER, 1957. This book is the original statement of the permanent income theory of consumption. See especially chaps. 1, 2, 3, and 9.

Haberler, Gottfried: Monetary and Real Factors Affecting Economic Stability: A Critique of Certain Tendencies in Modern Economic Theory, as abridged in Robert Aaron Gordon and Lawrence R. Klein (eds.), *Readings in Business Cycles*, Homewood, Ill.: Irwin for the American Economic Association, 1965.

Modigliani, Franco: Long-Run Implications of Alternative Fiscal Policies and the Burden of the National Debt, *Economic Journal*, **71:** 730–755, Dec. 1961.

Schmidt, Peter, and Roger N. Waud: The Almon Lag Technique and the Monetary Versus Fiscal Policy Debate, *Journal of the American Statistical Association*, **68:** 11–19, Mar. 1973.

U.S. Council of Economic Advisers Staff Memorandum: Financing a Federal Deficit, in Warren L. Smith and Ronald L. Teigen (eds.), *Readings in Money, National Income, and Stabilization Policy*, 3d ed., Homewood, Ill.: Irwin, 1974.

International Trade and Financial Arrangements

Chapter 9

9.1 FOREIGN EXCHANGE MARKETS

Why Do We Have International Financial Arrangements?

The basic function of money is to eliminate barter. This works very well when sellers and buyers are residents of the same country. If commodities are exchanged for money, the most willing buyers can always buy from the most willing sellers, regardless of whether the sellers want to buy what the buyers sell. Sometimes the buyers who value a commodity most and the sellers who can produce it most cheaply are in different countries. Simple monetary exchange is impossible because the buyer's money, say dollars, is not money to the seller and the seller's money, say pounds, is not money to the buyer. So they must either engage in barter or not trade at all.

International financial arrangements arose as a means of extending the benefits of money in eliminating barter to international transactions. This is done by making it possible for the buyer to pay in his money and the seller to receive payment in his money. Do international exchange markets actually transform dollar bills into pound notes by some magic process? No, they just make individuals in each country who buy from foreigners pay those who sell to foreigners. This section and the next will discuss the mechanics of this process and how it is that these two totals happen to be equal. When looked at from this point of view, international finance turns out to be not so mysterious as it would appear from romanticized newspaper stories. Although they are not mysterious, the details of international finance are numerous and must be left largely to specialized works.[1] This chapter emphasizes only the key facets for macroeconomic analysis.

Trade between Two Countries

Most of the basic principles of international finance are illustrated by a simple world of only two countries trading with each other. This example will serve

---

[1] Such as the book by H. Robert Heller listed in the references for this chapter.

as an introduction to the discussion of many countries trading in the complicated patterns observed in the real world. The two countries will be called America and Britain and their moneys are called dollars ($) and pounds (£), respectively. The exchange rate E_t between pounds and dollars is £0.40/$; that is, $1 can be purchased with or can purchase £0.40. How this exchange rate is determined will be discussed later.

A British chemical firm wishes to buy a computer and finds that the best combination of characteristics and price is offered by an American manufactured machine priced at $2,500,000. The British chemical firm would like to make a payment of the equivalent sum in British money, £1,000,000 [$2,500,000 × (£0.40/$)]. The American computer manufacturer would like to receive payment in American money, $2,500,000. The transaction is completed by the chemical firm writing a check for £1,000,000 on its British bank. Either the chemical firm or the computer firm (depending on the sales contracts) pays a tiny commission to sell the £1,000,000 deposit at a British bank for a $2,500,000 deposit at an American bank. The deposit at the American bank is then transferred through the American banking system to the account of the computer firm.

This transaction is all very simple, except that one not-so-minor point was left out: Who sold the $2,500,000 for £1,000,000? Say at the same time an American department store bought £1,000,000 worth of sweaters from a British woolens firm. Just as with the computer sale, each firm would like to exchange goods for the firm's own money. Since the moneys are different, $2,500,000 of the department store's bank deposit must be sold for a £1,000,000 British bank deposit which can be transferred to the account of the woolens firm. This sweater sale provides the seller of the $2,500,000 for £1,000,000. In effect, the department store pays $2,500,000 to the computer firm and the chemical firm pays £1,000,000 to the woolens firm.

This offsetting of amounts due to foreigners against amounts due from foreigners is what foreign-exchange markets are all about. *Foreign exchange markets* are places where the money of one country is exchanged for the money of other countries. Most exchanges involve transfer of rights to bank deposits, though actual currency is also traded. With modern telegraphic communications, such markets are effectively combined into a single worldwide foreign exchange market. As illustrated in Fig. 9.1, goods and services flow from each country's exporters (sellers) to the other country's importers (buyers). Money flows from each country's importers to its own exporters.

It may be that the value owed American exporters exceeds the value owed by American importers, that is nominal net exports or the balance of trade is positive. Since the British importers owe the amount due to American exporters and the British exporters are owed the amount due from American importers, British nominal net exports are equal to minus American nominal net exports when converted into the same monetary units by the exchange rate.

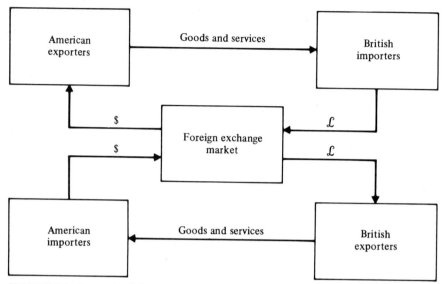

FIGURE 9.1 International flows of goods and payments. Amounts owed to foreigners are matched with amounts owed by foreigners in the foreign exchange market. This permits payments of dollars to be made from American importers to American exporters and payments of pounds to be made from British importers to British exporters. Commodities are shipped from American exporters to British importers and from British exporters to American importers.

In the assumed situation of a positive American balance of trade (or *trade surplus*) and a negative British balance of trade (or *trade deficit*), more dollars appear to be received than paid and fewer pounds paid than received. The difference arises because an important class of international transactions has been omitted: international capital flows. *International capital flows* refer to the purchase by the residents of one country of securities owned or newly issued by residents of another country. This may be in the nature of a long-term loan to finance a sale of real capital goods, such as machines for a new automobile plant, but there is no necessary or usual connection. The term *international securities flows* would be more descriptive, but is not used in the literature. Figure 9.2 illustrates both types of international transactions, the sales of real goods and services and the sales of securities representing rights to future payments. *Net capital outflows*, CO_t, the value of securities bought less the value of securities sold, must exactly equal net exports for each country. If this is true, the total amount of dollars paid by American buyers will just equal the total amount of dollars received by American sellers. Similarly, the total pounds paid and received by British buyers and sellers will be equal.

The basic question concerns how the foreign exchange market equates net

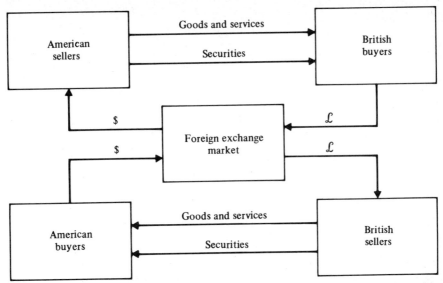

FIGURE 9.2 International finance of trade and capital flows. Both commodities and securities are traded. Net international capital outflows must exactly equal net exports so that the total value of goods, services, and securities sold exactly equals the total value of goods, services, and securities bought.

exports with net capital outflows. Since foreign exchange transactions always involve a seller and buyer, the transactions of sellers of dollars for pounds must always equal those of the buyers of dollars for pounds after all is said and done. The question is more basically why people will desire to sell and buy exactly equal amounts. As with the case for the demand and supply of peanut butter or any other commodity, the price will adjust until the amount willingly sold exactly equals the amount willingly bought at the market price. The price in the foreign exchange market is the exchange rate E_t.

Determinants of Nominal Net Exports

American nominal net exports are a decreasing function of the exchange rate.[2] This is so because a fall in the exchange rate makes American goods cheaper to the British in terms of pounds while British goods are made more expensive

---

[2] British net exports are an increasing function of the exchange rate, but a decreasing function of the British exchange rate defined as the number of dollars per pound $(1/E_t)$.

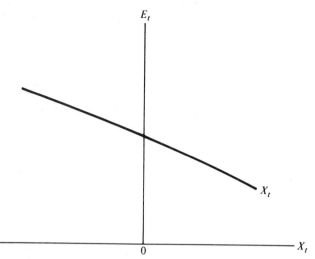

FIGURE 9.3 Relationship of nominal net exports to the exchange rate. A decrease in the exchange rate (£/$), other things being equal, will increase American nominal net exports because American goods are cheaper to British buyers and British goods are more expensive to American buyers. Similarly, higher exchange rates reduce nominal net exports. The level of nominal net exports will be more responsive to exchange rate changes (that is, the net export curve will be flatter) in the long run, when sellers and buyers have had time to adjust fully, than in the short run.

to American buyers in terms of dollars.[3] Such a relation is illustrated in Fig. 9.3. The net export curve has a negative or downward slope to show that net exports are a decreasing function of the exchange rate. The net export curve can be drawn either for short-run changes in the exchange rate or for long-run adjustments to changes in the exchange rate continuing over extended periods of time. Net exports will be more responsive in the long run because this will allow time for the establishment of commercial relationships (for example, automobile dealerships selling foreign cars) and construction of plants in the country with increasing exports and the depreciation of plants in the country with reduced exports.

Among the most important "other things constant" which underlie the

[3] These facts alone are not enough to unambiguously indicate that nominal net exports will increase with a decrease in the exchange rate. This ambiguity arises because the induced increase in import prices in dollars conceivably could be sufficiently great to offset the fall in the quantity of imports and the rise in the dollar price and quantity of exports. This does not appear to be more than a hypothetical curiosity judging from the actual behavior of nominal net exports.

nominal net export curve are the levels of prices and real income in America and Britain. Using functional notation,

$$X_t = P_t x \left(\frac{E_t P_t}{P_t^F}, y_t, y_t^F \right) \qquad [9.1]$$

The function $x(\ \ )$ determines real exports measured in base-year dollars per annum. Multiplication by the American price level converts this into the nominal net exports measured in dollars per annum. The discussion in the previous paragraph of the effects of changes in the exchange rate applies to any change in the relative prices of domestic and foreign goods, and this is measured more generally by $E_t P_t / P_t^F$; so $x(\ \ )$ is a decreasing function of this ratio. An increase in American real income y_t will decrease net export demand by increasing domestic demand for foreign goods (imports). An increase in British real income y_t^F will similarly increase British imports and British imports are American exports. So real net exports are a decreasing function of American real income and an increasing function of foreign real income.

Determinants of Nominal Net Capital Outflows

Nominal net capital outflows are an increasing function of exchange rates, other things being equal. The most important other things equal are the domestic price level (to convert real capital flows into nominal amounts), American and British interest rates r_t and r_t^F, and expectations of future exchange rates. If expectations of future exchange rates are unchanged, a rise in the exchange rate means that British securities can be purchased cheaply now in terms of dollars and sold back later at a more favorable exchange rate. Similarly a fall in the exchange rate makes American securities more attractive and British securities less attractive. This is illustrated in Fig. 9.4.

The influence of expectations of future exchange rates through time into the future does not lend itself well to an algebraic summary. If only one expected future exchange rate is considered, say E_{t+h}^*, then it is expected that the proportionate change at annual rates in the exchange rate over the period from t to $t + h$ will be $(E_{t+h}^* - E_t)/(E_t \cdot h)$. If h is arbitrarily small, this is the expected growth rate of the exchange rate, g_{Et}^*. This is the expected growth rate of the value of the dollar relative to the pound. A dollar invested in an American security grows at the American nominal, after-tax, interest rate r_t^*. A dollar invested in a British security is expected to grow *in terms of dollars* at the British nominal, after-tax interest rate r_t^{F*} less the expected growth rate of the exchange rate g_{Et}^*.[4] The difference between these two alternative yields

---

[4] The reasoning is perfectly analogous to the derivation of the relation of the real interest rate in terms of base-year dollars to the interest rate in terms of dollars and the expected growth in the price level which is the exchange rate of dollars per base-year dollar. The derivation is essentially identical to that used for [4.50] and [4.51].

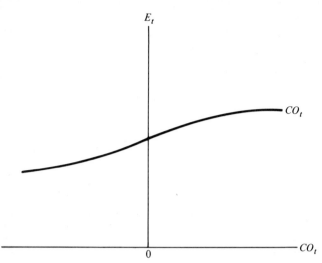

FIGURE 9.4 Relationship of nominal net capital outflows to the exchange rate. An increase in the exchange rate E_t, for given expected future exchange rates and domestic and foreign interest rates, makes foreign securities more attractive when they are compared to American securities. This occurs because the expected fall in the exchange rate provides an extra return to foreign securities in terms of dollars.

$r_t^* - (r_t^{F*} - g_{Et}^*)$ or $r_t^* + g_{Et}^* - r_t^{F*}$ summarizes the relative attractiveness of American and British securities. Since the higher this amount is, the less attractive British securities are to Americans and the more attractive American securities are to the British, real net capital outflows would decrease. That is, real net capital outflows are a decreasing function of $r_t^* + g_{Et}^* - r_t^{F*}$; so it can be converted to nominal net capital flow by multiplying by P_t:

$$CO_t = P_t co(r_t^* + g_{Et}^* - r_t^{F*}) \qquad [9.2]$$

As can be seen from the definition of the expected growth rate of the exchange rate g_{Et}^*, increases in the current exchange rate E_t decrease g_{Et}^*, given future expected exchange rates E_{t+h}^*. An alternative functional notation is therefore

$$CO_t = P_t co(E_t, E_{t+h}^*, r_t^*, r_r^{F*}), \qquad [9.3]$$

with nominal net capital outflow CO_t an increasing function of the domestic price level, of the exchange rate, and of foreign interest rates, and a decreasing function of the expected future exchange rates and of domestic interest rates.

An example will help illustrate the nature of the decisions concerning net capital flow. Assume that the exchange rate is expected to be £0.42/$ in one year. If the domestic interest rate is 4 percent per annum, compounded annually, $100,000 lent in the U.S. would pay back $104,000 in a year (1.04 × $100,000). If the interest rate in Britain is 9 percent per annum, it might seem much more attractive to lend there. The amount actually lent is £40,000 [$100,000 × (£0.40/$)]. The amount paid back is £43,600 (1.09 × £40,000). This must be converted back to dollars to be compared with the $100,000 lent. The amount of dollars expected to be repaid is $103,809.52 (£43,600/(£0.42/$)), which is actually a bit less than would be earned on the American loan at "only" 4 percent per annum. If the exchange rate were only £0.01/$ higher, or £0.41/$, and other things equal, the net repayment in dollars would be $106,404.76 since $100,000 × (£0.41/$) × 1.09/(£0.42/$) = £44,690/(£0.42/$) = $106,404.76. Clearly a small rise in the current exchange rate can drastically change the relative attractiveness of American and British securities.

Equilibrium for Two-Country Trade

If the dollars willingly offered in exchange for pounds are to equal the dollars demanded in exchange for pounds, the exchange rate must be such that desired nominal net exports equal desired capital outflows. This occurs at the point of intersection in Fig. 9.5 of the nominal net export and nominal capital outflow curves. At the equilibrium exchange rate E_t^e, the values of desired nominal net exports and nominal capital outflows are equal at $X_t^e = CO_t^e$. In the case illustrated, there is a positive balance of trade (trade surplus) and positive capital outflows (positive net purchases of foreign securities). In this case, Americans on net find it advantageous to provide some current goods and services to the British in return for claims on future British goods and services. This position could as easily be reversed with the British acquiring securities from Americans on net.

The direction of the net capital outflows and balance of trade will be determined in full steady-state equilibrium by the marginal productivity of capital in each country as well as any barriers or risks involved in purchasing securities of other countries. Such barriers aside, international capital flows are the means by which countries with above average saving-income ratios shift investment to countries with low saving-income ratios.[5] Such foreign investment raises the domestic income of countries with low saving-income ratios because the increase in total wages exceeds the fall in the income on domestically owned capital.[6] A full discussion of the steady-state equilibrium is the subject

---

[5] If the stock of foreign securities held is significantly positive (or negative), the real income from these securities should be added to (subtracted from) the real income produced by domestic capital and labor. This complication has been omitted as of negligible importance (see Table 2.3) throughout this book.

[6] Not surprisingly, domestic capital owners frequently support attempts to exclude foreign investment.

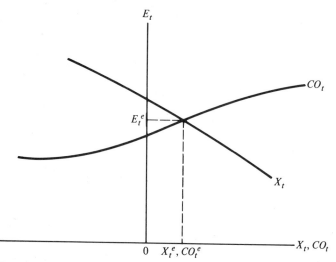

FIGURE 9.5 Determination of the values of the exchange rate, nominal net exports, and nominal capital outflows. The exchange rate adjusts to equate the desired levels of nominal net exports and nominal net capital outflows. The equilibrium exchange rate is E_t^e and equilibrium nominal net exports are X_t^e. Equilibrium nominal net capital outflows are $CO_t^e = X_t^e$. The value of $X_t^e = CO_t^e$ can be positive, zero, or negative in steady-state equilibrium.

for books on international economics, but one useful property should be noted. This is that the actual and expected growth rate of the exchange rate, $\bar{g}_E$, will equal the differences in foreign and domestic rates of inflation, $\bar{g}_P^F - \bar{g}_P$. This means that the exchange rate will adjust so that alternative inflation rates affect neither E_t, P_t/P_t^F or $r_t^* + g_{Et}^* - r_t^{F*}$. The growth paths of the real balance of trade and real net capital outflows are therefore unaffected by the domestic and foreign rates of inflation in steady-state equilibrium.

Trade among Many Countries

More complex patterns of trade are possible when the number of countries involved is increased beyond two. The reason for this is that the most willing foreign buyers of American goods, services, and securities and the most willing foreign sellers of goods, services, and securities to Americans are not evenly distributed throughout the world. Instead, Americans may buy automobiles from Japan and stock certificates from Brazil and pay for these by selling computers to Britain and wheat to India. Each of these countries will in turn be net buyers from some countries and net sellers to other countries.

For each country, however, the foreign exchange market permits such variation so long as the nominal value of net exports to all countries equals the nominal value of net capital outflows to (security purchases from) all countries. This can be alternatively stated as requiring only that the value of all sales to foreigners of goods, services, and securities equal the value of all purchases from foreigners of goods. This is because total sales of each money must equal total purchases, but it is not necessary that total sales of each money equal total purchases in exchange for each of the other moneys individually.

An example for three countries will make the situation clear. Assume trade takes place among America, Britain, and Japan. The exchange rate of pounds for dollars is $E_t^B = £0.40/\$$ and the exchange rate of Japanese yen ($\mathcal{Y}$) for dollars is $E_t^J = \mathcal{Y}300/\$$. Note that it is not necessary to state the exchange rate of yen for pounds explicitly as this can be computed as $E_t^J/E_t^B = (\mathcal{Y}300/\$)/(£0.40/\$) = \mathcal{Y}300/£0.40 = \mathcal{Y}750/£$. Table 9.1 presents hypothetical data for each country on nominal net exports and nominal net capital outflows for each country both on an overall basis and in terms of trade with each country. For example, overall America has a trade deficit of $15 billion paid for by a net capital outflow of $-\$15$ billion. That is, Americans are selling less goods and services to foreigners than they are buying. These goods are paid for by, on net, selling more American securities to foreigners in the amount of $15 billion. Since these two amounts are equal, the total amount of dollars offered for foreign moneys by buyers from foreigners is equal to the total amount of dollars received for foreign moneys by sellers to foreigners. American net exports can be broken down into $-\$5$ billion with Britain and $-\$10$ billion with Japan. Net capital outflows are $+\$25$ billion and $-\$40$ billion respectively; that is, America is a net buyer of British securities while Japan buys even more American securities. The

TABLE 9.1 **Three-country example of international payments**

Country		Overall	To America	To Britain	To Japan
America	Net exports	−$15	...	−$ 5	−$10
	Net capital outflows	−$15	...	+$25	−$40
	Difference	0	...	−$30	+$30
Britain	Net exports	−£18	+£ 2	...	−£20
	Net capital outflows	−£18	−£10	...	−£ 8
	Difference	0	+£12	...	−£12
Japan	Net exports	+$\mathcal{Y}$18,000	+$\mathcal{Y}$ 3,000	+$\mathcal{Y}$15,000	...
	Net capital outflows	+$\mathcal{Y}$18,000	+$\mathcal{Y}$12,000	+$\mathcal{Y}$ 6,000	...
	Difference	0	−$\mathcal{Y}$ 9,000	+$\mathcal{Y}$ 9,000	...

Note: All amounts in billions. Exchange rates are £0.40/\$, $\mathcal{Y}$300/\$, and $\mathcal{Y}$750/£.

differences of $-\$30$ billion and $+\$30$ billion are the excess of dollars demanded over dollars supplied in exchange for pounds and the excess of dollars demanded over dollars supplied in exchange for yen, respectively. Their sum is of course zero as required for the total amount of dollars demanded to equal the total amount of dollars supplied. Note that each amount in the by-country breakdown of any country is necessarily repeated with opposite sign and converted by the exchange rate in the by-country breakdown of the other country. Thus net exports of Britain to America are $-(-\$5 \text{ billion}) \times (£0.40/\$) = +£2$ billion. This must happen because a sale from one country to another is by definition a purchase by the second country from the first.

In this example, Americans are offering on net ¥9,000 billion for $30 billion and offering $30 billion for £12 billion. The dollar amounts are equal, but who will take the yen and provide the pounds? Since total net exports equal total net capital outflows, there must be a demand for exactly the amount of yen supplied and a supply of exactly the amount of pounds demanded.[7] This is shown in Table 9.1 by the differences of $-£12$ billion and $+¥9,000$ for Japanese-British payments. British purchasers and Japanese sellers are offering on net £12 billion for ¥9,000 billion. Specialists, called *arbitrageurs*, buy the ¥9,000 for $30 billion and simultaneously both sell the ¥9,000 for £12 billion and sell the £12 billion for $30 billion. The incentive for this transaction is in fact offered by the exchange rate of yen for pounds being slightly lower than implied by E_t^J/E_t^B, say ¥749.9/£ instead of ¥750/£. That difference of 0.013 percent would provide an annual gross income to arbitrageurs of $4,000,000.[8] Compared to the billions involved, $4,000,000 is negligible, but it can pay for the salaries, telephone bills, and paperwork to keep enough arbitrageurs in business to make the foreign exchange market work quite smoothly.

Broadening trade to all the countries in the world changes none of these principles. So long as the nominal net exports of each country equal the nominal net capital outflows, there will always be a sequence of transactions by which arbitrageurs can eliminate any inequality of a country's payments to other countries individually.

Equilibrium for Trade among Many Countries

With many countries equality of nominal net exports with nominal net capital outflows for each country is achieved by the simultaneous adjustment of all

---

[7] This must be true because the overall difference for each country is zero and the difference between each pair of countries enters both country's accounts.

[8] This is found by computing the profit on the pounds for yen transaction: ¥9,000 billion/(¥749.9/£) $-£12$ billion $= £12.0016$ billion $- £12$ billion $= £1.6$ million. In dollars, this is £1.6 million/(£0.40/\$) = $4 million. All these amounts are flows measured at annual rates.

exchange rates. For macroeconomists interested in analyzing only the influence of the "rest of the world" on a single economy, this detail is superfluous and aggregate measures of real income, average price level, and average exchange rate for the rest of the world will serve quite well. The symbols y_t^F, P_t^F, and E_t^F will be adopted for these "rest of the world" aggregates. Thus Fig. 9.5 serves to illustrate the determination of net exports and the average exchange rate in this more general case also. The statements made about "Britain" in the two-country case apply more generally to America and the aggregate "Rest of the World."

9.2 EXCHANGE RATE SYSTEMS

Types of Exchange Rate Systems

The term *floating exchange rates* is applied to exchange rates determined in markets free of government intervention. The main elements of this system were presented in the previous section. Starting in 1973, the international financial arrangements among major trading nations can be generally characterized as a floating exchange rate system.[9] Smaller countries still generally link their currencies to the currency of a major trading nation through the other exchange rate systems discussed below.

Floating exchange rates were exceptional during the period from World War II to 1973.[10] During this period there was an international agreement to maintain exchange rates in terms of dollars at certain announced levels, plus or minus 1 percent. These levels were changed from time to time. This agreement was usually referred to as the Bretton Woods Agreement because it was signed at Bretton Woods, New Hampshire (1944). The Bretton Woods Agreement established a system of *pegged exchange rates* because foreign governments took actions—explained shortly—to assure that the exchange rate for their currency would fluctuate around the announced or pegged exchange rate.

Some countries are linked by *fixed exchange rates* or a *unified monetary system*. Fixed exchange rates are similar to pegged exchange rates in the sense that exchange rates fluctuate only within a very narrow band around an announced exchange rate. They differ fundamentally however in two ways: (1) a unified monetary system has an automatic device linking the money supplies of the countries involved; and (2) the exchange rates cannot be changed so long as the system exists.

---

[9] Intervention by central banks has continued to some extent in an attempt to "moderate day-to-day fluctuations" in exchange rates. This speculative activity by the government has led to the characterization of the system as a "dirty float." (See the discussion of speculation at the end of this section.)

[10] The most important exception in terms of length of time and size of country was Canada. Details of the more remote history of international financial arrangements are beyond the scope of this book.

Equilibrium under Unified Monetary Systems

The principal difference between a unified monetary system and a system of pegged or floating exchange rates is that it is indeed possible to convert the money of one country into the money of another country at a fixed exchange rate. If, for example, there are only two countries involved, there is no reason that the total sales of each country to the other should equal the total purchases from the other country. The difference can be made up by converting one money to the other and shipping it.

A trivial but illuminating example arises from treating California as one country and the rest of the United States as another country. If Californians purchase more from other Americans than they sell at the exchange rate of one Californian dollar to the dollar, the exchange rate will not rise. Californians will simply transfer Californian dollars out of the state to pay their bills. The transfer is made by shipping base money. Note that this will not continue indefinitely however, since Californians would run out of money. Instead the reduction of the California money supply will lead to a bit higher interest rates in California in the short run, attracting loans from out of state. In the longer run California aggregate demand will be a bit lower than it otherwise would have been so California prices will drop slightly relative to other American prices and California's nominal net exports curve will shift up until the California money supply stops decreasing relative to the total American money supply. These adjustments take place so quickly and automatically that no one has cause to remark on them. They serve to keep the value of the dollar similar throughout the country.

Precisely the same situation applies less trivially for Panama and Liberia. The currency units of these countries are defined in terms of American dollars and, except for coinage, dollars actually circulate there. The same is true for the British pound in the Republic of Ireland.

An historically important unified monetary system existed under the gold standard. National monetary units were defined as certain weights of pure gold. The value of an ounce of gold would be kept constant throughout the system by melting of gold coins of one country where prices were high and shipping them to a place where prices were lower. The system could be broken if the government of a country redefined the weight of gold equal to a unit of its currency.

Under most unified monetary systems there are slight fluctuations of exchange rates around the conversion or *central rate* to cover the cost of shipping and converting one money to another. The Federal Reserve System subsidizes these costs in the United States, so there are no longer domestic exchange rates between, say, Chicago and New York. But the right to a dollar in a Panamanian bank can and does exchange for slightly more or less than the right to one dollar in a New York bank. Under the gold standard, the costs of converting and shipping gold from one country to another could amount to 1 to 2 percent of the amount shipped.

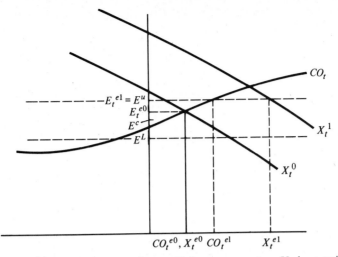

FIGURE 9.6 Equilibrium under a unified monetary system. Under a unified monetary system, money is converted and shipped whenever the exchange rate would otherwise rise above the upper rate E^u or fall below the lower rate E^L. This occurs because, outside of these rates, it is cheaper to convert and ship money than to pay for net purchases by buying foreign exchange. In case 0, the equilibrium exchange rate E_t^{e0} is determined in the usual way with nominal net exports X_t^{e0} equal to nominal net capital outflows CO_t^{e0}. In case 1, with a higher net export curve the exchange rate would rise above the upper rate E^u if no money were converted and shipped by foreigners. In this case, nominal net exports X_t^{e1} exceed nominal net capital flows CO_t^{e1} at the equilibrium exchange rate $E_t^{e1} = E^u$. The difference or balance of payments surplus is paid by foreigners' shipping $X_t^{e1} - CO_t^{e1}$ in money. The balance of payments can be zero, positive, or negative.

The determination of exchange rates where there are shipping and conversion costs is illustrated in Fig. 9.6. The central rate E^c is determined by the ratio at which one money can be converted into another. The *upper rate E^u* equals the central rate plus shipping and conversion costs measured in foreign monetary units per domestic unit. The *lower rate E^L* is the central rate less these shipping and conversion costs. If, as for nominal net export curve X_t^0, the exchange rate determined by the equality of net exports and net capital outflows lies between E^u and E^L, that rate, here E_t^{e0}, will be the exchange rate. If that rate is above the upper rate, the exchange rate will equal the upper rate, as for the net export curve X_t^1. Nominal net exports will exceed nominal net capital outflows and the difference $X_t - CO_t$ is called the *balance of payments*. In this case the balance of payments is positive (or *in surplus*) and it is paid by importing base money from the foreign country. If the exchange rate at $X_t = CO_t$ happens to be less than the lower rate E^L, the balance of payments will be negative. The excess of nominal net capital outflows over nominal net exports will be paid by exporting monetary base to the foreign country.

Equilibrium under the Pegged Exchange Rate System

The pegged exchange rate system was aimed at approximating the unified monetary system which existed under the gold standard. Indeed the system was euphemistically called the "gold exchange standard." Central, upper, and lower rates were announced and central banks in foreign countries would sell dollar securities for their own money if the upper rate was reached and buy dollar securities with their own money if the lower rate was reached. The foreign central banks thus provided whatever capital flows were necessary to equate net capital outflows and net exports between the upper and lower rate. Net capital outflows on private and central bank accounts were accounted separately with the American balance of payments equal to net purchases by foreign central banks of dollar-denominated securities plus any net sales by the American monetary authorities of foreign securities or gold to assist foreign central banks.

Gold entered the picture because between 1946 and 1968 the United States would buy gold from foreign central banks or sell it to them at $35 per ounce. Central banks could use dollars to buy gold from the Fed instead of dollar-denominated securities. The idea was that the requirement to buy or sell gold would keep the dollar's value fixed in terms of gold while other moneys were fixed in terms of dollars.

The determination of equilibrium under the pegged exchange rate system is identical to that under a unified monetary standard if nominal net capital outflows CO_t are interpreted as referring to private capital flows only, and the balance of payments are interpreted as net central bank capital and gold outflows. The two main differences between the pegged exchange rate system and a unified monetary system are: (1) Countries could offset (*sterilize*) the effects of their balance of payments on their monetary base by selling their own securities for their own money if they were buying dollar securities with their own money, and vice versa. (2) Countries could change announced exchange rates whenever a balance of payments surplus or deficit became too bothersome. Consequently, foreign central banks would not let their money supplies passively adjust to the American balance of payments. Some would desire a faster rate of monetary growth and raise the pegged exchange rate (depreciate their currency) from time to time (most notably Britain). Others would desire a lower rate of monetary growth and lower the pegged exchange rate (appreciate their currency) on occasion (notably Germany). This led to huge private capital flows whenever it became obvious that the rates would soon be changed. These huge capital flows can occur only under a pegged exchange rate system. Under either a unified monetary system or a floating exchange rate system, small, frequent adjustments in the relative money supplies or exchange rates, respectively, keep the system in equilibrium.[11] The delayed adjustments of the pegged exchange rate system presented private individuals with a "sure bet" and the resulting capital flows led to the eventual destruction of the system.

9.3 EFFECTS OF INTERNATIONAL SHOCKS ON AGGREGATE DEMAND

Response of Net Exports to an International Shock under a Floating Exchange Rate System

Since foreign real income and price level enter into the determination of the American net export curve, foreign macroeconomic shocks can have an effect on the U.S. economy. All such shocks to an economy arising from its international trade are termed international shocks. Thus, one country's domestic shock, say a change in the money-supply growth rate, causes an international shock to each of its trading partners.

The impact of international shocks is easy to illustrate. First consider the current situation of a floating exchange rate system. A foreign monetary shock which increases y_t^F relative to its steady-state growth path will shift the nominal and real net export curves upward. This occurs because of the resulting increased foreign demand for American goods. This is most conveniently illustrated by graphing the real net export curve and the real capital outflows curve as shown in Fig. 9.7. In this figure, the curve labeled x_t^0 indicates what the real net export curve would have been in the absence of the international shock. The curve labeled x_t^1 indicates the real net export curve. Real net exports are increased by the amount $x_t^{e1} - x_t^{e0}$ and real capital outflows (or net borrowing by foreigners) are increased by the equal amount $co_t^{e1} - co_t^{e0}$. This is nearly equivalent to an equal increase in real government expenditures financed by increased government borrowing.

The analysis of international shocks is somewhat different from that presented for government spending because of their more gradual nature. The government can fairly suddenly shift spending above (or below) its previous steady-state growth path. This is not characteristic of the response of real income to macroeconomic shocks, however. Since international shocks are a reflection of the response of foreign real income to foreign macroeconomic shocks, a gradual rise in net export demand relative to normal is to be expected. This increase in net export demand, it was seen in Fig. 9.7, leads to a temporary increase in capital outflows. As this change in capital outflows continues over time, net holdings by Americans of foreign securities increase.

---

[11] A banking panic which suddenly reduced the money supply and raised the interest rates in one country would cause large net capital *inflows* to finance a large balance of payments surplus needed to restore the money supply under the gold standard.

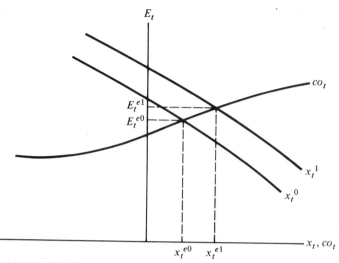

FIGURE 9.7 **Effect of an increase in real net export demand on real net exports.** An outward shift in the real net export curve due to an increase in foreign real income increases the exchange rate from E_t^{e0} to E_t^{e1} and real net exports from x_t^{e0} to x_t^{e1}. The increase in real net capital outflows (net foreign borrowing) will equal the increase in real net exports.

This increase in the net stock of foreign securities will make further increases less desirable, other things equal, and the net capital outflows curve will begin to shift back to the left, as illustrated in Fig. 9.8. This reduces net exports for given net export demand and further increases the exchange rate. Eventually, net exports must be reduced below their steady-state level for a while so that the excessive net holdings of foreign securities can be worked off. This repeats the complete pattern of fiscal policy: Increased government spending and borrowing for a while followed by decreased spending and borrowing for a while. The difference arises because of the more gradual adjustment seen in market-determined magnitudes such as net exports compared to government policy changes. A typical complete pattern of real net exports (and capital outflows) is illustrated in Fig. 9.9.

The analysis of the effects of changes in government spending and borrowing would appear to apply directly, although there is relatively little direct empirical evidence.[12] The application of this analysis to an international shock which initially increases net export demand runs as follows: The increase in net export demand temporarily increases net exports and net capital

---

[12] The paucity of empirical work may reflect both considerable statistical difficulties and the relative unimportance of international shocks in the American economy. Indirect evidence is consistent with the adjustment pattern outlined, but cannot be conclusive.

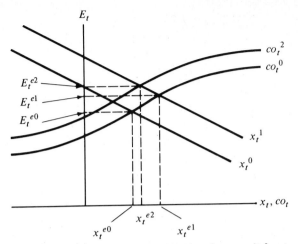

FIGURE 9.8 Induced upward shift in real net capital outflows curve reduces real net exports. Unusually large net capital outflows as at x_t^{e1} will shift the real net capital outflows curve upward over time, as from co_t^0 to co_t^2. This initiates a reduction in real net exports back toward the level x_t^{e0} which would have existed in the absence of the shock and, for a while, below it.

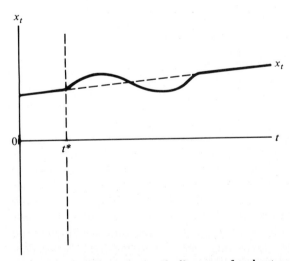

FIGURE 9.9 Typical pattern of adjustment of real net exports to international shock. In the instance of an initially stimulative international shock beginning at t^*, real net exports x_t at first rise, relative to trend, and then fall below trend for a while to return foreign securities holdings to equilibrium. Logarithmic scaling is inappropriate here since net exports can as easily be negative as positive.

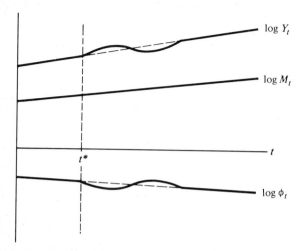

FIGURE 9.10 Effects of initially stimulative international shocks on nominal income. The increase in net exports and net capital outflows drives short-term interest rates up relative to interest rates on money and long-term bonds. This reduces desired fluidity so that nominal income rises. Over time, interest rates on money and long-term bonds adjust upward so that desired fluidity rises toward its original growth path and nominal income falls toward its original growth path. This adjustment is continued as net exports fall below the levels that would otherwise exist because of the upward shift in the net capital outflows curve. This shift is induced by the increase in net holdings of foreign securities as compared to normal holdings during the period in which net exports are higher than normal. Eventually net holdings of foreign securities, net exports, and the various interest rates return to their steady-state values and the effect on fluidity and nominal income is eliminated.

outflows. This drives short-term interest rates up relative to the interest rates paid on bank-issued money and long-term bonds. This rise in interest rate reduces investment by less than the increase in net exports because desired fluidity is decreased. This decrease in desired fluidity cause excess money balances at the levels of real income and prices which would otherwise exist, so aggregate demand is increased and nominal and real income rise above their steady-state path. As the lagging interest rates on money and long-term bonds adjust over time, this increase in aggregate demand is partially or entirely eliminated. Soon real net exports begin to fall back toward and even below their steady-state growth path and the interest rate on short-term bonds falls relative to the interest rates on money and long-term bonds. This reverses the process and aggregate demand falls below the steady-state aggregate demand. This, too, does not continue indefinitely, and nominal and real income catch up with their steady-state level. This pattern of adjustment is illustrated in Fig. 9.10.

This pattern of adjustments is just reversed for an international shock which initially decreases net export demand. The original fall in aggregate demand is later offset by a rise in aggregate demand above steady-state aggregate demand. Details are left to the reader (see question 12 at the end of this chapter).

Adjustment to International Shocks under Pegged Exchange Rates and Sterilization

Under a pegged exchange rate system, the impact of international shocks on net exports and hence aggregate demand will be, if anything, larger than under floating exchange rate systems. This occurs because whenever the shift in net export demand would increase the exchange rate E_t above the upper rate E^u (or decrease it below the lower rate E^L), the central banks step in and supply whatever government net capital outflows are needed over private net capital outflows to equate net capital outflows to net exports at E^u (or E^L). This permits a greater expansion (or contraction) of net exports than would occur under floating exchange rates (see Fig. 9.6). Complete adjustment must involve a more substantial period of real net exports below (above) their steady-state level to make up for this. The complications of governmental decision making and possible changes in the pegged exchange rate make a complete analysis beyond the scope of this book.

It should be noted that sterilization of Fed purchases of foreign securities with newly issued base money is assumed in this section. That is, the Fed simultaneously sells an equal amount of U.S. Treasury securities so that *net* borrowing and *net* base money creation by the government is unchanged. In effect, the Fed and foreign central banks buy foreign securities and sell American securities. This situation of a balance of payments surplus could be maintained by the Fed indefinitely if it is willing to hold an ever-increasing amount of foreign securities. On the other hand, foreign central banks could not maintain the pegged exchange rate by themselves because they would eventually run out of American securities to sell.

Quite generally, a country running a balance of payments surplus can maintain its exchange rate at an artificially low level so long as the government is willing to ship real goods in return for foreign securities. Countries often do this for remarkable periods of time in order to put off the costs of shifting workers from industries producing internationally traded goods to industries producing domestically traded goods. Because of this tendency to put off adjustments, the adjustments, when they are actually made, can be quite devastating. For example, the Japanese were among the last to adopt floating exchange rates in 1973 because they feared the political repercussions from eliminating the undervaluation of the yen. The effects on the Japanese electronics and automobile industry of the change in exchange rate were especially severe because previously there had been years of increasing investment and employment resulting from the undervalued yen.

Pegged Exchange Rates without Sterilization

Under a unified monetary system, an American balance of payments surplus would imply an increase in the rate of change of base money in America by the amount of that surplus and a similar decrease in the rate of change of foreign base money. Under the pegged exchange rate system, even if there is no sterilization at all, the effect on monetary growth is less. If the balance of payments surplus was $2 billion, it could be met by the Fed buying $1 billion in foreign securities with new base money and the foreign central banks selling $1 billion of American securities from their holdings, thus destroying that much of their base money. In this way, the increase in base money in America and decrease of base money in foreign countries would equal only half the balance of payments. For this reason, it was at times argued that the "gold exchange standard" was a milder form of the gold standard.

This claim would not be without merit if there had been some automatic way of affecting the rate of change of the money supply so that sterilization did not occur. In the absence of sterilization, balance of payments deficits would reduce the growth rate of the money supply and balance of payments surpluses would increase the growth rate of the money supply. This would greatly strengthen the impact of an international shock, just as the impact of changes in government spending financed by changes in the rate of creation of base money is much greater than changes in government spending financed by changes in the rate of borrowing.

This greatly strengthened impact of international shocks seemed rather foolish where the shocks were of a "temporary" rather than "basic" nature. Under floating exchange rates private investors have an incentive in terms of their own wealth to provide changes in net capital outflows sufficient to offset much of any temporary international shock. If an individual forecasting or *speculating on* future exchange rates does not do a good job distinguishing temporary shocks from more basic shifts, his wealth will soon be eliminated. This is not the case for central bank officials speculating on behalf of the government, rather than for their own benefit. There was apparently a strong incentive to treat all balance of payments deficits or surpluses as reflecting temporary shocks which should be sterilized (not allowed to affect the growth rate of the money supply). Most of the time this bias was right, but the cumulative effect of the exceptions over time would lead to the type of international financial crisis and changes in pegged exchange rates previously discussed.

9.4 MONEY SUPPLY GROWTH AND LONG-RUN INTERNATIONAL EQUILIBRIUM UNDER ALTERNATIVE EXCHANGE RATE SYSTEMS

Money Supply Growth under a Unified Monetary System

There is an intimate connection between the exchange rate system adopted by a country and the ability of its government to choose among trend growth rates of the money supply. Among the different countries joined by fixed exchange rates, independent decisions about the money supply can be made by only one country or for the entire unified monetary system. But no more than one independent decision can be made. The decision must be made by a single central bank under a fiat (paper) standard, but would be made by impersonal market forces under a commodity standard such as the gold standard.

The reason why the growth rate of only one money supply total can be independently determined under a unified monetary system is easiest to see by showing that the alternative is impossible. Suppose that the United States and Canada were to create a unified monetary system with the American money supply determined by the Fed and the Canadian money supply determined by the Bank of Canada. Assume that the steady-state growth rate of real money balances is 1 percent per annum in the United States and 2 percent per annum in Canada. If the Fed chose a 3 percent money-supply growth rate and the Bank of Canada a 4 percent growth rate, inflation in both countries would be at a rate of 2 percent per annum. Starting from a position at which the American and Canadian dollars had equal value in purchasing real goods and services, this would persist over time, since the value of each is falling by 2 percent per annum. Thus an exchange rate of one Canadian dollar (C$) per American dollar ($) could persist indefinitely.

Suppose instead that the Bank of Canada desired to have a constant price level and accordingly selected a 2 percent trend rate of growth of the Canadian money supply. If the Canadian and American dollar were initially of equal value, this policy would appear to have the American dollar drop in value relative to the Canadian dollar by 2 percent per annum. But this cannot happen because Canada will begin to run a balance of payments surplus as American goods become more expensive than Canadian goods at the assumed fixed exchange rate of C$1/$. Since this is a unified monetary system, this balance of payments must increase the growth of the Canadian money supply automatically and decrease the growth of the American money supply. Thus the inconsistent, independent decisions of the Fed and the Bank of Canada cannot be maintained.

Money Supply Growth under a Pegged Exchange Rate System

Under a pegged exchange rate system, countries can independently choose their trend rates of inflation if from time to time they change the pegged exchange rate. Independent choices of trend monetary growth rates (and thereby trend rates of inflation) are impossible without changes in the pegged exchange rate.

This can be seen by a slight alteration in the United States–Canada example. Suppose that the countries are joined by a pegged rate of C$1/$ instead of a fixed exchange rate. In that case, Canada can maintain a 2 percent growth rate of the money supply while the Fed maintains a 3 percent growth rate of the money supply. This is done by the Bank of Canada sterilizing the balance of payments. That is, the Bank of Canada sells as much in Canadian dollar bonds as it buys in American dollar bonds. The difficulty arises because the balance of payments will increase without limit. This happens because American real net exports are a decreasing function of $E_t P_t/P_t^F$. In this instance, the exchange rate E_t and the Canadian price level P_t^F are constants, but the American price level will grow at a rate of 2 percent per annum so that year after year the American net exports will become more and more negative and the Canadians will be financing more and more American investment and less and less of their own. Because its Canadian securities will soon be exhausted, the Fed is in no position to help the Bank of Canada by selling these securities.

The only way out is to change the pegged exchange rate to reflect the changed relative values of the moneys. If this is about to happen, private investors see that by purchasing Canadian securities they can make an overnight killing. As they attempt to get out of American securities and into Canadian securities, the pressure to lower the exchange rate is increased because of the further increase in the Canadian balance of payments. If the Bank of Canada puts off changing the exchange rate by buying yet more American securities, private buyers of Canadian securities have not lost much. If the Bank of Canada were to lower the pegged rate by 10 percent, that much profit would accrue to private investors literally overnight. This sort of one-sided potential led to huge capital flows in anticipation of changes in exchange rates and forced central banks to accept exchange rates consistent with the relative values of the moneys.

If there were no change in the different rates of inflation, an exchange rate which reflected relative values in one year would soon become inconsistent with relative values. The combination of mounting balance of payments surpluses in countries with low rates of inflation and rising balance of payments deficits in countries with high rates of inflation would continue until another international financial "crisis" forced central banks to adjust exchange rates again.

Money Supply Growth under Floating Exchange Rate Systems

The inherent instability of pegged exchange rates led to the complete breakdown of the Bretton Woods system in 1973. Under the floating exchange rate system that replaced it, each country can select a rate of growth of its money supply consistent with its own desired rate of inflation. The value of its money will rise in terms of the money of a country with more rapid inflation and fall in terms of a country with less rapid inflation. The differences in the rate of inflation will be reflected in both the expected rate of change in the exchange rate and the differences in nominal interest rates so that there is no net effect on real capital flows.

The great advantage of the floating over the pegged exchange rate system is that the exchange rate moves gradually under the former instead of in the large jumps characteristic of the latter. The problem with large jumps is that they require sudden shifts of resources between internationally and domestically traded goods in response to sudden shifts in their relative values. That is, pegged exchange rates have a *microeconomic* cost because most of the time either too many or too few resources are devoted to producing internationally traded goods.

Alternative Goals: Inflation Rate and Growth Rate of the Exchange Rate

It is now clear that in the long run a nation can choose to maintain either a desired trend inflation rate or a desired trend growth rate[13] of the exchange rate with one or more countries. In order to maintain fixed exchange rates, a unified monetary system with harmonized monetary policy is necessary— there can be only one independent determination of money-supply growth rates. If independent choices of trend inflation rates are to be made, the trend growth rate of the exchange rates must reflect the differences in the inflation rates chosen. The only choice is whether the changes in exchange rates are to occur gradually (floating exchange rates) or in sudden jumps (pegged exchange rates).

The long-run independence of monetary policy under floating or pegged exchange rates does not imply that international shocks cannot have significant temporary effects. It is true that international shocks, other things being equal, are likely to have the least impact under floating exchange rates, intermediate impact under pegged exchange rates and the greatest impact under fixed exchange rates because of differences in the impact on monetary growth. Nevertheless, as was seen in Sec. 9.3, in each case there will be some effect due to changes in net exports. Floating and sterilized pegged exchange rates prevent this shock from being amplified by a change in money supply growth.

---

[13] In practice, a $\bar{g}_E$ of zero is the only growth rate of the exchange rate chosen—that is, a fixed exchange rate.

□ SUMMARY

Foreign exchange markets eliminate barter in international transactions by canceling amounts due to foreigners against amounts due from foreigners. In effect, a country's buyers from foreigners pay its sellers to foreigners. There are three main alternative foreign exchange rate systems: (1) floating exchange rate systems, (2) pegged exchange rate systems, and (3) unified monetary systems or fixed exchange rate systems. A floating exchange rate system is currently dominant. Under this system, exchange rates adjust so that a country's desired nominal net exports equal its desired nominal net capital outflows. Under a unified monetary system these amounts need not be equal if at the exchange rate it is feasible to convert and ship base money from one country to the others to make up for any difference (balance of payments). Under a pegged exchange rate system, central bank capital flows provide a means of bridging a difference between private nominal net capital outflows and nominal net exports. Foreign booms and recessions cause international shocks to the domestic economy by shifting the nominal net export curve up or down, respectively. The effect is similar to a gradual increase (or decrease) in the growth rate of government spending followed by a gradual decrease (increase) in the growth rate of government spending with offsetting changes in government borrowing. These impacts can be amplified under pegged exchange rate systems and will be amplified under fixed exchange rates systems by a similar change in the growth rate of the money supply. A country can choose and achieve either a rate of inflation goal or a growth rate of the exchange rate goal, but not both independently.

□ QUESTIONS AND EXERCISES

1 In the absence of foreign-exchange markets, why would there be barter involved in a sale of woolens by a British firm to an American firm for $1,000,000?

2 Why is the equality of nominal net exports and nominal net capital outflows equivalent to the equality of the quantities of dollars supplied and demanded in the foreign-exchange market?

*3 What are the units of the expression $E_t P_t / P_t^F$? In what sense is this a measure of the relative quantity of real goods and services which could be bought abroad compared with the quantity that could be bought in America for a given amount of money? Why would increases in this ratio tend to increase American imports and reduce American exports?

4 Other things being equal, what would be the effect of an increase in the expected future exchange rate on the current exchange rate and net exports under floating exchange rates? Under pegged exchange rates? Why is the expected growth rate of the exchange rate subject to sudden, large changes under pegged exchange rates but not under floating exchange rates?

5 In Table 9.1, are the figures given for Japanese net exports and net capital outflows to Britain consistent with the British figures for Japan? Why or why not?

*6 Is it a cause for any particular notice or concern under floating exchange rates if Japan exports more to America than it imports from America? Why or why not? Is it a cause for any particular notice or concern if you buy more from your local supermarket than you sell to it? Why or why not?

7 (*a*) Under floating exchange rates, the balance of payments is always zero. Why? Why is it impossible to have a "balance of payments problem" under floating exchange rates?

   (*b*) In what sense are two or more central banks necessary for a balance of payments problem? Why don't nonzero balances of payments under fixed exchange rates cause problems?

8 If the city of Columbus, Ohio, were to secede from the United States and establish its own money, there would be a great deal of "international trade" between Columbus and the United States. Under floating exchange rates, would changes in the American money-supply growth rate cause significant macroeconomic shocks for Columbus? Would changes in the Columbus money-supply growth rate cause significant macroeconomic shocks for the United States? Why would the absolute size of the shocks be similar but the sizes relative to income be dissimilar? Does this have any application to the United States and Canada?

9 (*a*) Show that large shifts in the (private) net capital outflows curve have less effect on net exports under pegged exchange rates than under floating exchange rates.

   (*b*) Show that large shifts in the net exports curve have less effect on net exports under floating exchange rates than under pegged exchange rates.

   (*c*) Why is it that discussion of the advantage of pegged exchange rates over floating exchange rates in the face of large shifts in the private net capital outflows curve receives such scant attention?

10 Why do international shocks lead to a *cyclical* adjustment of log Y_t around its growth path?

11 American net exports are affected by domestic as well as international shocks; show why. If this were not true, there would be no international shocks. Why? Why are data on actual real net exports insufficient to pinpoint international shocks?

12 Analyze the effect of a reduction in the growth rate of the Canadian money supply on American real income under floating exchange rates.

*13 Can monetary policy be used to select the trend rate of inflation in a small, open economy under floating exchange rates independent of the rates of inflation in its large trading partners?

☐ REFERENCES FOR FURTHER READING

Friedman, Milton: The Case for Flexible Exchange Rates, in *Essays in Positive Economics*, Chicago: University of Chicago Press, 1953.

————:   Free Exchange Rates *and* The Political Economy of International Monetary Arrangements, in *Dollars and Deficits*, Englewood Cliffs, N.J.: Prentice-Hall, 1968.

Heller, H. Robert: *International Monetary Economics*, Englewood Cliffs, N.J.: Prentice-Hall, 1974.

Machlup, Fritz: The Theory of Foreign Exchanges, as reprinted in Howard S. Ellis and Lloyd A. Metzler (eds.), *Readings in the Theory of International Trade*, Homewood, Ill.: Irwin, for the American Economic Association, 1950.

Yeager, Leland B.: *International Monetary Relations: Theory, History, and Policy*, New York: Harper & Row, 1966.

The Impact of Macroeconomic Shocks on the American Economy

Chapter 10

10.1 THE HISTORICAL RECORD: THE GREAT DEPRESSION THROUGH WORLD WAR II

Setting the Stage

The tools of macroeconomic analysis can most fully be appreciated by applying them to the study of recent macroeconomic experience. This study will provide a grasp of the effects of simultaneous and serial macroeconomic shocks and of the relative importance of different types of macroeconomic shocks. Dates are provided to illustrate the timing relationships rather than for any historical interest.

A study of macroeconomic experience is limited by data—as well as space—to relatively recent times. Before 1929, data series exist only for the broadest macroeconomic variables and are unreliable for detailed information. The early data that are available are consistent with the macroeconomic model presented in previous chapters,[1] but a discussion of them would add little in the way of understanding. The data on the national income accounts of the federal government, drawn from basic source records, begin in 1929. Complete quarterly data as described in Chaps. 2 and 3 are available beginning with 1947.

This section will concentrate on the period of reliable data from 1929 through 1946. This very interesting period includes the Great Depression of 1929–1933, the recovery of 1933–1937, the severe recession of 1937–1938, the subsequent recovery and World War II. The next section will discuss the economy in the postwar era.

The dynamic nature of macroeconomic problems requires that some infor-

---

[1] This is shown in Milton Friedman and Anna Jacobson Schwartz, *A Monetary History of the United States, 1867–1960*, Princeton: Princeton University Press for NBER, 1963. Much of the discussion in this section and the next depends on this book. Other data sources for figures given in the text are Milton Friedman and Anna Jacobson Schwartz, *Monetary Statistics of the United States*, New York: NBER, 1970; *The National Income and Product Accounts of the United States, 1929–1965*, 1966 Supplement to *The Survey of Current Business;* and U.S. Bureau of Economic Analysis, *Long Term Economic Growth, 1860–1970*, Washington: GPO, 1973. Nominal income is measured here—for reasons of consistency over the whole period—by gross national product and the price level by the GNP deflator.

mation be given about what was going on before 1929. The period from 1923 through 1928 was characterized by moderate fluctuations in the growth rate of the money supply around an average rate of 4.4 percent per annum. The definition of money supply used in this section is the broad money supply (M_2) because the distinction between demand and time deposits was blurred by banks until the Banking Acts of 1933 and 1935;[2] so M_2 is the only consistent money supply definition throughout the period.

Between 1923 and 1928, there were two sequences consisting of a significant decrease in the money-supply growth rate followed in about a year by an increased growth rate. The decreases in growth rates started near the beginning of both 1923 and 1926 and caused the contractions of 1923–1924 and 1926–1927, respectively. Nevertheless, the fluctuations were small by previous standards, and the period as a whole was thought to reflect improved skill and ability on the part of the Federal Reserve System.

The average growth rate of fluidity during the period was nearly zero $(-0.1$ percent per annum). The average growth rate of nominal income (4.5 percent per annum) differed from the growth rate of the money supply (4.4 percent per annum) by only this small amount. The average growth rate in real income was 4.2 percent per annum and that in the price level was 0.3 percent per annum.[3] The period immediately preceding the Great Depression closely resembled the same years in the 1950s. Money-supply growth rate fluctuations were large enough to cause recessions, but not so large as to cause any widespread, continuing macroeconomic problems.

There have been frequent attempts by noneconomists to find reasons for the Great Depression in the period leading up to 1929. Some of these specious arguments will be discussed below, but it should be stated here that there was no basic unsoundness in the economy in 1929 any more than there was in 1959. An argument can be made that the 1920s led to the 1930s in another way however: The Federal Reserve System misunderstood what was happening in the 1920s and applied that faulty understanding to dealing with the 1930s. The results were nothing short of disastrous.

The Start of the Great Depression

The Great Depression started in a very undramatic fashion. The Fed had become concerned with what it supposed was undue speculation in the stock market. This was attributed to unsound "speculative fever" and "easy credit," and the Fed became determined to purge these supposed evils from the system. In early 1928, the Fed embarked on a restrictive monetary policy by selling government securities and raising the discount rate at which it would

---

[2] See Sec. 3.3 for details.
[3] This average growth rate of real income exceeds the trend growth rate of about 3.1 percent per annum because the recovery from the severe 1920–1921 recession is included.

buy the promissory notes of member banks. This resulted in slight declines in base money and in the money supply from April 1928 through November 1930—the latter at an average growth rate of −1.4 percent per annum.

This decrease of almost 6 percent in the growth rate of the money supply compared to the previous average should, after a lag, cause a sharp decrease in the growth of aggregate demand. The contraction began, in fact, during the summer of 1929, as the decline in fluidity due to the initial monetary shock slowed and reversed. This early part of the contraction from 1929 to 1930 was in no way different from the sharp recession that would be expected from a 6 percent decrease in the money-supply growth rate.

What of the famous stock market crash of October 1929? There is little to choose between it and similar falls such as those occurring near the beginning of the 1937–1938 and 1969–1970 recessions. It is mainly remarkable for having marked the peak in view of the large fall in stock prices which occurred during 1931 and 1932. During 1930, the average stock price was about 5.5 percent *higher* than it had been in 1928 and only 19.2 percent lower than the 1929 average.

The Collapse of the Banking System

Through November of 1930, the recession was severe, but certainly not so severe as to be classed as a depression. The Fed had begun a mild reversal of policy in October 1929 by lowering discount rates and purchasing government bonds in the open market. In addition, gold was flowing into the country from abroad as net exports rose. The decline in discount rates was not as large as the decline in market interest rates on short-term government bonds, however. So the net effect was a reduction in member bank borrowing even greater than the increased holdings of government bonds and gold. This mild reduction in base money was the source of the mild reduction in the money supply.

In November and December of 1930, the whole character of the contraction was changed by the emergence of a genuine banking panic of the type which the Fed was established to prevent.[4] During November, a rash of rural bank failures in the midwest shook confidence in the banking system. The cash-deposit ratio began to rise, causing the money supply to fall and interest rates to rise as banks sold bonds and other earning assets to reduce deposits. Runs became common and banks could turn only to the Fed when holdings

---

[4] See pages 203–205 for an analysis of a bank panic. In essence, the bulk of bank assets consists of non-marketable loans which cannot be sold to pay off depositors after base-money reserves and marketable securities are exhausted. Selling of marketable securities by money banks during a crisis lowers the price of the securities and makes all banks more prone to failure. Most, if not all, of the deposits in closed banks were eventually paid off under bankruptcy proceedings as the nonmarketable loans were collected, but the delay was costly and well worth avoiding. The costs of bankruptcy proceedings and sacrifice sales of assets could easily absorb enough assets of a sound bank that depositors were not repaid in full. Further, the contraction caused by a panic can bankrupt otherwise sound borrowers from the bank.

of readily marketable securities were exhausted and only loans to customers were left as assets. Amazingly, the Fed displayed little understanding of the "lender of last resort" role of a central bank in preventing the cumulative psychology of panic. Instead, banks were viewed as failing because of "bad management" and the Fed did not encourage banks to borrow during a run. As a result, 256 banks with deposits of $180,000,000 failed during November 1930. The panic became severe after the failure on December 11, 1930, of the Bank of United States.

The Bank of United States was a commercial bank, but the name was suggestive of some sort of official status to many people. It had deposits of over $200,000,000 and was a member of the Federal Reserve System and the New York Clearing House. For a while, the Fed and the other Clearing House banks supported a plan to save the Bank of United States, but once the Clearing House banks withdrew, the Fed chose to allow the Bank to fail. The failure shook confidence in both banks and the Fed, and a total of 352 banks with deposits of $370,000,000 failed during December.

The important impact of the banking panic was the increase in the cash-deposit and reserve-deposit ratios. This caused the money multiplier to drop sharply so that the small increase in base money permitted by the Fed was insufficient to offset the decline in the money multiplier. The money-supply growth rate during November, December, and January averaged -12 percent per annum.

The situation appeared to stabilize in January 1931 and the Fed reduced base money during February by selling government securities. The money multiplier stopped falling and even rose slightly so that the money supply rose during February.

In March 1931, runs and bank failures resumed and continued intermittently until March 1933. The Fed took little corrective action, and the cash-deposit and reserve-deposit ratios fell as crisis followed crisis. Between March 1931 and March 1933, the cash-deposit ratio rose from 0.0964 to 0.2252 and the reserve-deposit ratio rose from 0.0807 to 0.1188. As a result, the money multiplier μ_t fell from 6.278 to 3.720, a fall of some 41 percent. The Fed increased high-powered money over the same period by only 18.7 percent. The net fall in the money supply was 29.7 percent, that is, at an average annual growth rate of -17.6 percent per annum.

Through March 1933, the pattern of monetary policy was one of falling money-supply growth rates. As would be expected, the cumulative effect on the economy of this series of restrictive shocks was devastating. Over the period from the money supply peak at April 1928 to the money supply trough of April 1933, the average growth rate of the money supply was -8.2 percent per annum. Table 10.1 illustrates the pattern of deceleration concealed by this average. The growth rate of the money supply drops from -0.9 percent per annum over the first two years to -4.3 percent, -19.0 percent, and -15.9 percent per annum over the next three years. On the basis of

TABLE 10.1 Growth rates of the broad money supply (M_2), 1928–1933

$t-1$ t	$\log M_t - \log M_{t-1}$
April 1928 to April 1929	-1.0%
April 1929 to April 1930	-0.9%
April 1930 to April 1931	-4.3%
April 1931 to April 1932	-19.0%
April 1932 to April 1933	-15.9%

Source: Calculated from data in Milton Friedman and Anna Jacobson Schwartz, *Monetary Statistics of the United States*, New York: NBER, 1970, pp. 24–29.

the available annual data, the average growth rate of nominal income from 1928 to 1933 was -11.1 percent per annum. This was divided between an average growth rate of real income of -6.0 percent and an average rate of inflation of -5.1 percent. As the monetary growth rate did not fall further and even increased slightly between April 1932 and April 1933—though it was still at an unexpectedly low rate—the restorative powers of adjustment in the economy began to emerge. In the summer of 1932, the growth rate of real income apparently rose to about zero, and by March 1933 was strongly positive.[5] Such a huge, cumulative fall in real income reflected a drastic fall in employment. Available estimates of the unemployment rate increase from about $3\frac{1}{4}$ percent in 1929 to 24–25 percent in 1932 and 1933. The behavior of fluidity also was as would be expected. During the first year or so after the April 1928 decrease in g_{Mt}, fluidity fell. Then, as real income fell below permanent income, the demand for money fell at a rate that was much less than proportional to the fall in real income, and desired and actual fluidity rose.[6] The rise in fluidity intensified the reduction in nominal income due to the reduction in g_{Mt} (refer back to Fig. 7.5).

No mention has been made of fiscal policy or other nonmonetary macroeconomic shocks during this period. During 1930 and 1931, fiscal policy was actually very expansive due to a large increase in new government spending and borrowing relative to their low levels. In 1932, taxes were increased and government expenditures reduced, and then in 1933 real federal expenditures were sharply increased, but real state and local expenditures were reduced by more. The small effects through changing desired fluidity resulting from these

---

[5] This is inferred from such data as the index of industrial production, since only annual data on real income are available. Real income for 1932 was 71 percent of 1929 real income. For 1933, the figure was 69.5 percent.
[6] In 1929, fluidity was about 6 percent below the 1928 level. At the 1932 peak, fluidity rose to 44 percent above the 1928 level. Fluidity in 1933 was down to 33 percent above the 1928 level. These figures reflect relatively constant real money balances demanded and drastically falling real income.

and any other nonmonetary shocks are difficult to detect given the over-whelming monetary shock and the limited data. Some economists have emphasized falling investments as a macroeconomic shock, but given the relative constancy of consumer and government expenditures, monetary policy must operate primarily by reducing investment if real income is to fall.

A fascinating question which has been posed by Friedman and Schwartz[7] is "Why was monetary policy so inept?" As with any such question of "might have beens," there are many possible answers. Friedman and Schwartz suggested that the main cause was the power vacuum and struggle within the Federal Reserve System following the death of Governor Benjamin Strong in 1928. Other explanations include (1) the Fed's obsession with "unsound stock market speculation" and the general virtues of a "cleansing deflation"; (2) the Fed's practice of sterilizing gold flows so that gold inflows were not allowed to increase base money; (3) a general lack of understanding of monetary theory on the part of Fed officials; and (4) the Fed was accustomed to bank failures due to mismanagement in the 1920s and thought bank failures during the crises also reflected mismanagement. As fascinating as these arguments are, they are largely irrelevant to the goal of understanding how macroeconomic shocks affect the economy.[8]

The continuing 1930–1933 monetary crises pointed out a peculiarity of the banking system established by the Federal Reserve Act of 1913. Previous to the Act, crises were short-lived because all banks in concert temporarily restricted convertibility of deposits into currency until after the panic had subsided, but otherwise continued their usual financial operations. The banks did not close. The fall in the money supply was sharp but soon followed by a recovery. Under the Federal Reserve Act restricted convertibility was prohibited as outmoded so that this catharsis did not occur. This was fine so long as the Fed did what it was supposed to and lent freely to banks facing runs. But when the Fed failed in this duty, the contagion of panic easily spread from one bank to others.

The Banking Holiday of 1933

Another peak in the pattern of bank failures was reached in January 1933. As panic spread, many states declared bank holidays closing the banks in their states. By March 4, 1933, when the New York bank holiday began, most other states had already closed their banks. Finally on March 6, 1933, President Roosevelt closed all banks. Thus, the Fed—which was established to prevent panics from leading to restrictions on bank payments of currency—had, by

---

[7] Friedman and Schwartz, *Monetary History*, pp. 407–19.
[8] Chapter 15 on stabilization policy will return to the question of the ability of an independent central bank to stabilize the economy.

TABLE 10.2   Growth rates of the broad money supply (M_2), 1933–1937

$t-1$	t	$\log M_t - \log M_{t-1}$
April 1933 to April 1934		8.3%
April 1934 to April 1935		12.6%
April 1935 to April 1936		10.5%
April 1936 to April 1937		7.9%

Source: Calculated from data in Milton Friedman and Anna Jacobson Schwartz, *Monetary Statistics of the United States*, New York: NBER, 1970, pp. 28–31.

its failure to act, caused the most severe and widespread banking suspension in American history.

Beginning March 13th, banks were permitted to reopen upon license from the Secretary of the Treasury.[9] Only clearly "sound" banks were licensed to reopen. This certification by the newly elected administration restored some confidence in the banking system. On March 15, 1933, 68.6 percent of the banks with 87.3 percent of the nation's total deposits were licensed and open. About half of the unlicensed banks, with one-quarter of the unlicensed bank deposits in March 15, 1933, were reopened by the end of 1933.

The Banking Holiday and licensing served the same cathartic function that restriction of bank payments of currency had served before the Federal Reserve System was established. With a measure of public confidence in the banking system restored, the cash-deposit ratio began falling instead of rising.

The Expansion of 1933–1937

The bottoming out of real income begun during the summer of 1932 became a definite recovery by early 1933. The recovery was materially hastened by a stimulative monetary shock in the form of an increase in the growth rate of the money supply. Comparison of Tables 10.2 and 10.1 illustrates the large increase in g_{Mt}. The reasons for the reversal in the growth rate of the money supply were twofold: (1) an increased—though still negative—growth rate of the money multiplier and (2) an increased growth rate of base money.

The increased growth rate of the money multiplier is attributable to the changed growth rate of the cash-deposit ratio from positive to negative. Confidence in the reopened banks steadily grew, and as confidence grew the cash-deposit ratio desired by the public fell back toward its normal level.

---

[9] Licenses were issued by state banking officials for banks which were not members of the Federal Reserve System.

An important factor in restoring public confidence was the establishment of the Federal Deposit Insurance Corporation in 1934. The enormous value of the FDIC in preventing runs and panics is based more on its actual operation than on its legal contract with depositors. The federal government has no legal liability to bail out the FDIC if its reserves are exhausted by a bank panic, and this was a real possibility in the early years. Further, depositors are insured only up to a specified sum.[10] A very large fraction— usually between one-third and one-half—of bank deposits are thus uninsured. The holders of these deposits would appear quite sufficient to cause a run which could cause almost any bank to fail. In operation, the FDIC has eliminated most of the incentive for a run so that cumulative panics have become a thing of the past. This is true because the FDIC rarely allows a bank actually to go bankrupt so that the insurance limits apply. Instead, the FDIC arranges a merger of a mismanaged bank into a well-managed bank and compensates the good bank for any losses incurred in the take-over.

More than offsetting the fall in the cash-deposit ratio was the rise in the reserve-deposit ratio. Bankers had been rapidly increasing their reserve-deposit ratio since it became apparent that the banker who relied on the Fed for borrowing during a panic was very likely to fail, and this increase continued until the summer of 1935.[11] The net effect of the rising reserve-deposit ratio and falling cash-deposit ratio was an average growth rate of the money multiplier μ_t of -1.6 percent between April 1933 and April 1936. This compared to an average $g_{\mu t}$ of -20.7 percent between October 1930 and April 1933.

Between April 1933 and January 1934 the United States raised the price at which it would buy or sell gold from $20.67 per ounce to a maximum of $35. At this high price much gold was purchased. The Fed had lapsed into almost complete inactivity so that the gold purchases raised base money almost dollar for dollar. As a result the growth rate of base money between April 1933 and April 1936 was 12.2 percent per annum. The net effect on money supply growth is detailed in Table 10.2.

The resulting recovery in real income was highly dramatic. The average growth rate of real income between 1933 and 1937 was 9.0 percent per annum. Despite this very rapid recovery, real income in 1937 was only about the same as in 1929. If real income had grown at the long-run trend growth rate of about 3.1 percent per annum from 1929 on, real income in 1937 would have been about 28 percent higher than in 1929. That is, 1937 real income was about 22 percent below the estimated steady-state level. Four years of reductions

---

[10] This was $2,500 on January 1, 1934, raised to $5,000 on July 1, 1934, and maintained there until 1950. Currently the liability limit is $40,000.

[11] From October 1930 to April 1933 the reserve-deposit ratio rose at an average growth rate of 16.3 percent. From April 1933 to June 1935, the growth rate was 19.7 percent. From June 1935 through July 1936, there was no particular trend up or down. The Fed's published figures on bank reserves classified the large fraction which were not required as "excess" even though the evidence shows that they were not so regarded by the banks.

in real income were just made up by the increases of the next four years. So even a 43 percent rise in real income over only 4 years was disappointing. Alternatively, employment in 1937 had only recovered to the 1929 level while the labor force had increased by about 10 percent. So the unemployment rate—though much improved from 1932 and 1933—was still a very high 14 percent. In part the "slow" recovery can be attributed to certain ill-advised legislation which adversely affected the aggregate production function.[12] The analysis of these structural changes must be left to economic histories. A more generally operative factor played an important role, however. Between 1929 and 1933, there was a sharp reduction in investment in physical capital and considerable disinvestment in the intangible capital represented by a firm as a going organization. The fact that the capital stock was below equilibrium would cause capital to grow more rapidly than labor until the equilibrium labor-capital ratio was reachieved.[13] Until this adjustment was completed, however, real income (and real wages) would be below the steady-state growth path.

Summing up the Great Depression and Recovery

The Great Depression was primarily the result of a series of monetary shocks. In early 1928, Fed policy reduced the growth rate of the money supply because of concern over "undue speculation" on the stock market. The result had all the appearances of a classic recession beginning in the summer of 1929 and continuing into 1930. In October of 1930, the Fed permitted a banking crisis to get started which recurred in waves until the Banking Holiday of 1933. The Fed had both the power and responsibility to prevent banking panics, but it failed to do so. The resulting large negative growth rate in the money multiplier caused a further sharp fall in the growth rate of the money supply. Further decreases in real income resulted, and recovery did not resume in earnest until early 1933. Rising public confidence in banks after the Banking Holiday nearly offset the continuing efforts of banks to build up reserves in case of renewed crisis. The rise in the price of gold, from $20.67 to $35 per ounce, led to large government gold purchases. This caused base money to increase rapidly. The resulting large increase in the growth rate of the money supply greatly facilitated the rapid recovery of real income. By 1937, real income had returned to the level of 1929, but this was 20 to 25 percent below the steady-state value of real income. The difference can be attributed to both a level of capital that was below equilibrium—because of low investment during the Depression—and special factors related to New Deal legislation.

---

[12] The National Industrial Recovery Act, minimum wage laws, and similar legislation granted new or increased monopoly power to favored groups in the economy.
[13] Refer to the analysis of long-run equilibrium in a growing economy (Sec. 6.2).

The Recession of 1937–1938 and Recovery of 1938–1941

Incredibly, the Fed was finally stirred in 1936 by the specter of inflation. The "reinflation" caused by the restoration of the money supply was at an average rate of inflation of 2.8 percent per annum between 1933 and 1936. The price level was still 15.6 percent below the 1929 level. Nevertheless, because banks had accumulated supposedly "excess" reserves, the Fed felt moved to use its newly granted power to change reserve requirements. Reserve requirements were doubled in steps between August 1936 and May 1937. As a result, the average growth rate of the money supply between July 1936 and April 1938 was only 0.8 percent per annum.[14] In April 1938 reserve requirements were reduced and money supply growth increased to an average rate of 10.0 percent per annum through December 1941.

The recovery from the Depression was interrupted by the 1937–1938 contraction caused by the 1936–1938 reduction in money-supply growth. Nevertheless, by 1941 real income was 29.5 percent above the 1929 level or only 10.7 percent below the steady-state level of real income.[15] Taken as a whole, the average growth rate of real income from 1937 through 1941 was 6.5 percent per annum, about twice the steady-state growth rate.

The War Years, 1942–1946

The years of World War II present interesting problems for macroeconomists, but are not of much use for current illustrative purposes. Too many changes are combined with very unreliable data so that general principles are hopelessly veiled. For example, price controls and black markets make both price level and real income data very suspect. Price controls were removed in mid-1946 and a large jump in the price index measured the degree to which the price index was out of touch with reality. Nor is it safe to assume that the

---

[14] Since banks were holding more than the legal requirements in reserves, the rise in requirements caused a gradual adjustment in the reserve-deposit ratio. *Required* reserves could be used to meet a run only in proportion to reductions in deposits; so the excess of reserves over requirements provided the desired cushion against panics.

[15] As estimated by applying a 3.1 percent trend growth rate to 1929 real income. This reflected both a low capital stock and an unemployment rate of about 10 percent. [*Note added in press:* A major conceptual error has just been discovered in the Bureau of Labor Statistics estimates of the unemployment rate for 1934–1941 as quoted above and in the text. The emergency government labor force (employees of con- tracyclical government works programs such as the Works Progress Administration) were not counted as regular government employees and so were counted as unemployed when unemployment was estimated by subtracting employment from the labor force. Implicitly, a definition of unemployment as the difference between the labor force and "regular" (noncontracyclical) jobs was used instead of unemployment as the number of people without work who are looking for it. On this special definition, any contracyclical government employment which *increases* total employment by a smaller amount will increase reported unemployment! For the years indicated, unemployment was overstated in terms of the standard definition by about 2–3.5 million people and the unemploy- ment rate by 4–7 percentage points. This data masked the speed and strength of the return of the unemployment rate toward normal levels in the period after the 1933 reference cycle trough. Details are in Michael R. Darby, *Three-and-a-Half Million U.S. Employees Have Been Mislaid; Or, An Explanation of Unemployment. 1934–1941, Journal of Political Economy*, **84:** in press, Feb. 1976.]

composition of real income or the labor supply function were unaffected by the World War! War spending was financed in part by increased money creation as the Fed purchased government securities to the extent necessary to maintain low interest rates. The resulting price increases imposed an effective tax on holders of money.

10.2   THE HISTORICAL RECORD: THE POSTWAR ERA
An Overview

The postwar period can be divided into two distinct periods: (1) The first contains the period up to 1962 during which the country returned to a pattern of economic equilibrium disturbed by occasional recessions. During this period, there was no persistent tendency for the growth rate of the money supply to increase or decrease over time. (2) Since 1962, there has been a clearly rising trend in the growth rate of the money supply. During most of this period, the economy was experiencing a new stimulative monetary shock before adjustment to the previous one was completed.

The first period is mainly remarkable for a rather repetitive series of mild business cycles primarily related to moderate changes in the growth of the money supply. Each is independent but similar to the others. The second period is of especial interest because it has several dramatic points at which fiscal policy moves in one direction and monetary policy in the opposite direction.

In this section, the money supply definition used will be the narrow money supply (M_1). Very similar statements could be made about the broad money supply (M_2). As discussed in Chap. 3, the empirical and theoretical evidence presents no clear-cut choice between the two definitions.

Macroeconomic Trends, 1947–1962

The 16 years 1947–1962 are characterized by a constant trend growth rate of the money supply of 1.9 percent per annum. The actual growth path of the money supply fluctuated around its trend growth path but not by far. Variations in the growth rate occurred, but were always reversed within a year or two so that differences did not cumulate long.

The average growth rate of fluidity was −4.1 percent per annum and that of nominal income was 6.0 percent per annum. These trends are not consistent throughout the period, however. Fluidity had risen sharply during World War II, and it fell back at an average growth rate of −6.3 percent per annum between 1947 and 1951. Thereafter, the average growth rate of fluidity was −3.1 percent per annum and the average growth rate of nominal income was 4.8 percent per annum.

The growth in nominal income was divided between an average rate of inflation of 2.4 percent per annum and an average growth of real income of 3.6 percent per annum. The data are highly suspect in the middle of the period because of the Korean War and associated price controls which likely resulted in a temporary overstatement of real income and understatement of the price level.

The rapid average growth rate of real income can be most easily understood in terms of the growth model of Chap. 6. During the Great Depression, real income fell far below its steady-state growth path and was about 10 percent below it in 1941. Much of the capital goods purchased by the government during World War II was converted to producing private goods, but real income in 1947 was still 13 percent below its steady-state level as estimated by 1929 real income extrapolated at 3.1 percent per annum. This difference was due, not to unemployment of resources, but to the fact that resources—particularly physical and human capital—were below their steady-state growth paths because of low investment rates during the 1930s and World War II. As these resources grew more rapidly than normal to catch up with their steady-state growth paths, real income grew more rapidly to catch up with its steady-state growth path. By 1962, half of the percentage difference between real income and its steady-state growth path was eliminated.[16]

This discussion illustrates the difference between what has been called *full-employment real income* and steady-state real income. Full-employment real income refers to the level of real income which would exist if the current resources were employed with the expected distributions of wages and prices equal to the actual distributions.[17] Steady-state real income requires also that the level of resources currently available be on their long-run growth paths. The adjustment of real resources to long-term growth paths appears to be a very slow process compared to the adjustment of real income to full-employment real income.

The explanation of the negative growth rate of fluidity in the postwar period has been the subject of continuing controversy among macroeconomists. An important cause has doubtless been the introduction and steady growth of money substitutes such as savings and loan accounts. These substitutes have resulted mainly from the limitations on interest payment on commercial bank deposits. It is suggestive that fluidity has fallen at a much slower rate for the broad definition of money, for which the interest rate restrictions are less important. Another probable influence has been the rising trend of interest rates. Between 1947 and 1951 the average growth rate of interest rates on Treasury bills was 30.3 percent per annum; it was 4.6 percent per annum

---

[16] It will be seen later that all of the difference was eliminated by 1965, and since then the growth rate of real income has averaged about 3 percent per annum.

[17] This is the situation summarized in Chap. 5. There will still be some "unemployed" resources which are in effect employed in the activity of search on the basis of an accurate judgment of the available opportunities.

between 1951 and 1962—an overall increase from 0.38 percent per annum at the beginning of 1947 to 2.86 percent per annum at the end of 1962. Even though the long-run interest elasticity of the demand for money may be very low, an increase of interest rates to seven and one-half times the original level could significantly lower the growth rate of fluidity in the interim.

The Rebirth of Monetary Policy

The Fed came out of World War II with a continuing commitment to support the prices of government securities by buying and selling all the securities offered at certain *pegged interest rates*. A policy of maintaining pegged interest rates implies that money supply growth will be whatever is necessary, given other economic conditions, to maintain the peg. Such a policy can lead to runaway inflations if the peg is maintained below the interest rate which would otherwise exist, and to runaway deflations if the peg is too high.

As it happened, the pegged rates were generally about right up until the start of the Korean War. The interest rate peg for long-term government bonds was maintained until then at 2.5 percent per annum. This historically low nominal interest rate was acceptable because of widespread expectations of renewed, worsened depression. In view of a negative expected inflation rate, 2.5 percent was an attractive yield and average money supply growth was only a bit over 2 percent per annum.

The beginning of the Korean War in June 1950 eliminated these expectations quickly, and Fed purchases of securities and creation of base money increased rapidly. After a dramatic confrontation with the Treasury and the President, Fed freedom to determine monetary policy without regard to any support prices was announced in the Treasury–Federal Reserve Accord of March 1951.

Despite the accord, Fed policy up through the late 1960s continued to be formulated in terms of pegging the level of interest rates. The Fed also used such phrases as "credit conditions" and "feel and tone of the market," but it pretty much boiled down to an unannounced interest rate peg which the Fed changed from time to time. Unfortunately, the Fed judged its policy as stimulative or restrictive (or *easy* or *tight*) according to whether the pegged interest rates were low or high by historic standards. This will translate into high or low growth rates of money, respectively, only if the interest rate which would otherwise exist remains constant. If this does not roughly hold, particularly as during the 1930s and again in the late 1960s and early 1970s, the result can be rapid deflation or inflation.

Milder nonmonetary shocks will also affect the rate of interest which would exist for a given growth rate of the money supply. If money supply growth adjusts instead of interest rates because of pegging, changes in money supply growth will amplify the effects of nonmonetary shocks. This possible synchronization of shocks has led to much controversy in analysis of the effects of

TABLE 10.3   NBER reference cycle chronology, 1947–1962

November 1948	Peak	
October 1949	Trough	11 month contraction
July 1953	Peak	45 month expansion
August 1954	Trough	13 month contraction
July 1957	Peak	35 month expansion
April 1958	Trough	9 month contraction
May 1960	Peak	25 month expansion
February 1961	Trough	9 month contraction

stabilization policy during the postwar period.[18] For this reason, macro-economists particularly study points at which the Fed changed the interest rate peg by large amounts to offset the effects of fiscal policy or other macroeconomic shocks. These cases provide the clearest opportunity to measure the separate impact of monetary and other shocks in the postwar era.

Cyclical Changes, 1947–1962

The National Bureau of Economic Research (NBER) chronology includes four contractions between 1947 and 1962, as noted in Table 10.3. During each of these contractions the growth rate of real income not only slowed, but became negative.

The immediate cause of the 1948–1949 recession was a sharp decrease in the growth rate of the money supply engineered by Fed policy. The pattern of interest rates pegged by the Fed throughout World War II had been set on the basis of an anomalous pattern existing in 1941. The interest rate pegs varied from 0.375 percent per annum on 3-month Treasury bills up to 2.5 percent on long-term government bonds. This sort of spread can exist in the market only when short-term interest rates are expected to rise sharply. As a result, the Fed found itself selling off its long-term government bonds and buying short-term Treasury bills as fast as they were issued. Between the summer of 1947 and the autumn of 1948 the pegged interest rate on short-term government securities was gradually raised to a more realistic 1.125 percent per annum on 3-month Treasury bills. Although the longest-term government bonds were still pegged at 2.5 percent per annum, there had been a substantial increase in the average pegged rate.

At the higher average pegged rate, the equilibrium growth rate of the money supply was noticeably lowered. Between January 1948 and January 1949, the average growth rate of the money supply was only −1.1 percent

[18] See Chap. 15.

per annum compared to a 3.5 percent growth rate the previous year. Fiscal policy on the other hand was, if anything, stimulative through the third quarter of 1949 with rising federal expenditures and falling budget surpluses.

Monetary policy during this period is a bit obscured by increases in reserve requirements during 1948 and decreases during 1949. These changes have little effect under a pegged interest rate policy other than to determine how the growth of the money supply will be split between growth in base money and money multiplier. The net money-supply growth rate has to be whatever is consistent with the pegged interest rates and economic conditions.

The contraction (and the decrease in the growth rate of the money supply) was a bit milder than the 1929–1933 contraction in its first year. Unlike the earlier episode, the growth rate of the money supply did not continue to fall. Instead the Fed lowered interest rates below (raised security prices above) the officially pegged level a bit and money-supply growth rose slightly to 0.0 percent during 1949. The return of real income to its full-employment level was sufficiently strong to overcome a switch to restrictive fiscal policy beginning in the third quarter of 1949 and continuing until the start of the Korean War.

The Fed increased interest rates somewhat during the Korean War, but not by nearly enough to offset the rise in interest rates implied by the rise in the expected rate of inflation and government deficit financing. The average growth rate of the money supply was 4.5 percent per annum during 1950, 1951, and 1952. By the beginning of 1953, rising concern about inflation convinced the Fed to adopt a restrictive monetary policy, and it raised the pegged rate on long-term bonds from about 2.75 to 3.25 percent per annum. As a result, the growth rate of the money supply fell to about 1.1 percent per annum during 1953. This was combined with a restrictive fiscal shock due to the end of the Korean War in the third quarter of 1953, and the 1953–1954 recession followed.

The growth rate of the money supply increased in early 1954,[19] to an average rate of 2.7 percent per annum for the year. The combination of monetary stimulus and normal recovery from the recession made 1955 a boom year of rapid recovery. By mid-1955 the economy had apparently surpassed the full-employment level. Real income growth then slowed while the price level adjusted upward during 1956. This is the characteristic pattern of increased money supply growth followed with a lag by increased real-income growth, followed in turn by a more rapid rate of inflation.

The growth rate of the money supply gradually decreased to 2.2 percent for 1955, 1.2 percent for 1956, and −0.7 percent per annum for 1957 in the face

---

[19] The Fed had gradually reduced pegged interest rates since June 1953, but not by enough to offset the fall in the interest rate which would have accompanied the end of the Korean War spending. In January and February, the Fed pushed the Treasury bill rate down by almost two-thirds of a percentage point. The regularity with which Fed policy changes with the year is remarkable. Perhaps it reflects New Year's resolutions.

of rising interest rates. Growth slowed in 1956 and the recession of 1957–1958 began July 1957.

In November 1957, Fed policy was reversed, with interest pegs lowered through April 1958. The resulting growth rate of the money supply from January 1958 to August 1959 was 4.1 percent per annum. In May 1958 the Fed began to move the interest rate peg upward as the economy recovered. A strike in the steel industry during the summer of 1959 reduced the demand for credit as inventories were drawn down. In itself, the steel strike would have had transient effects. Combined with the Fed's suddenly "too high" interest rate peg, it led to a decline in the growth rate of the money supply to −1.7 percent per annum between July 1959 and June 1960. The recession beginning in May 1960, can thus be related to the unintended impact on the money supply of the previous year's steel strike. The Fed realized at the beginning of 1960 that its interest rate peg was incorrect for current conditions and lowered it sharply over the first half of the year. Money supply growth resumed in June 1960, strengthening the expansion begun the previous month. The recovery and expansion continued through and beyond 1962.[20]

Summing up the Experience from 1947 through 1962

The broad trend of real income growth was very rapid by long-term historical standards—a growth rate of 3.6 percent per annum compared to the historic trend for the century of 3.0 to 3.2 percent per annum. This meant that real income in 1962 was about 8 percent higher than it would have been had it grown from 1947 at the historic rates. Conversely, the capital-labor ratio in 1947 was very low because of low rates of investment between 1929 and 1946. An even higher rate of growth could have been hoped for during the period of increasing capital-labor ratios. Growth may have been slowed by recurrent mild recessions caused by a stop-go monetary policy which mainly resulted from the Fed's reacting with a lag to the ill effects of its previous policy. On occasion, changes in monetary policy were the unintended byproduct of determining policy in terms of interest rates instead of the growth rate of the money supply.

Macroeconomic Trends, 1963–1974

As a whole, the period 1963–1974 can be characterized as a period of increasing growth rates of the money supply. The acceleration was interrupted by three changes of direction: the second half of 1966, 1969, and 1973–1974. Table 10.4 presents the behavior of the growth rates of money and other macroeconomic variables. The average growth rate of the money supply for

---

[20] The NBER growth cycle chronology, however, records a downturn in April 1962 and an upturn in March 1963, corresponding with a lag to variations in money supply growth.

TABLE 10.4 Growth rates of major macroeconomic variables, 1963–1974

Year	Money	Fluidity	Nominal Income	Real Income	Price Level
1963	3.6%	−2.1%	5.7%	4.3%	1.4%
1964	4.5%	−1.8%	6.3%	4.6%	1.7%
1965	4.5%	−5.1%	9.6%	7.9%	1.7%
1966	2.4%	−5.8%	8.2%	4.8%	3.4%
1967	6.4%	0.7%	5.7%	2.3%	3.4%
1968	7.5%	−1.2%	8.7%	4.7%	4.0%
1969	3.5%	−2.9%	6.4%	1.2%	5.2%
1970	5.9%	1.4%	4.4%	−0.8%	5.2%
1971	6.1%	−2.7%	8.8%	5.4%	3.4%
1972	8.4%	−2.3%	10.6%	7.0%	3.6%
1973	6.0%	−5.0%	10.9%	3.8%	7.2%
1974	4.4%	−1.8%	6.3%	−5.1%	11.2%

Sources: Calculated from data in *1973 Business Statistics; Survey of Current Business,* July 1974 and March 1975; *NBER Data Bank,* April 1975.

the whole period, 5.3 percent per annum, was exceeded in no year before 1967 and in every year but two thereafter.

The average growth rates of fluidity and nominal income for the whole period were −2.4 percent and 7.6 percent per annum, respectively. The growth rate of nominal income was divided between a 3.3 percent growth in real income and a 4.3 percent rate of inflation. The high real income growth was concentrated in the early part of the period, and since 1966 this growth has been at a much slower average rate. The rate of inflation, in contrast, generally has been accelerating.

By the end of 1965, real income had finally achieved the steady-state growth path of real income extrapolated from 1929 at 3.1 percent per annum. This was achieved by reducing the unemployment rate to—and later less than— 4 percent when the rate corresponding to full employment was between 4.5 and 5 percent. As capital continued to rise, the steady-state real income growth path could be achieved with levels of unemployment nearer to the full-employment rate. It must be emphasized that a 3.1 percent per annum growth rate of real income is no more than a historical average used to estimate the underlying concept. Though it seems to work fairly well in explaining long-run trends in the economy, this may reflect historical accidents.

Data Problems, 1962–1974

There are two sources of difficulty in analyzing data on the national income accounts: the Vietnamese War and the price and wage control program of August 1971 through April 1974.

The Vietnamese War has no well-defined dates. In terms of the size of the armed forces and expenditures, the war started in 1966 and faded out during 1970 and 1971. During the interim, real income was probably overstated because of the shift in output mix.[21]

The price control program of 1971–1974 may have actually increased full-employment real income slightly by acting to temporarily reduce monopoly power of the unions. Most of the apparent impact in the data is probably due to cheating which reduced the price index relative to the true price level. Darby has estimated that the price index was reduced between 3 and 4.5 percent at the peak impact in late 1972.[22] This difference increased the rate of inflation during 1973 and the first half of 1974, as discussed below.

Cyclical Changes, 1963–1974

The relatively steady acceleration of money supply growth until 1969 provided no reference cycle peaks or troughs until November 1969.[23] Nevertheless, the adjustment period is of considerable interest.

The growth rate of the money supply increased by 2 percentage points in 1963 and by another percentage point in 1964. The growth rate of fluidity in these years was about 1 percent per annum higher than the -3 percent trend previously observed. Money growth was constant in 1965, and fluidity adjusted back to its trend level by the end of the year. The implied large increase in nominal income was primarily apparent in a large increase in real income. Money supply growth stopped during the last half of 1966, initially mainly reducing the growth rate of fluidity. Also reducing the growth rate of fluidity during this year was the normal decrease in desired fluidity during a boom and the stimulative fiscal policy implied by the United States entry in force into the Vietnamese War. At the end of 1966, fluidity was about 2.7 percent below its trend level as extrapolated from 1962 at -3 percent per annum.

The accelerating growth rate of the money supply had come about because the Fed pegged interest rates at a low level to stimulate the economy. As interest rates tended to rise, the Fed "leaned against the wind" by increasing the rate of money creation. The accelerating inflation that resulted finally convinced the Fed that it must tighten. As a result, the money supply was constant from June 1966 to January 1967. At the first evidence of slowing

---

[21] The unemployment rate was similarly lowered relative to similar economic conditions in peacetime by the practice of drafting teenage males, particularly those searching for a job. Teenage males normally provide a large fraction of unemployed persons. This lowering tends to occur whenever there is a war.

[22] Michael R. Darby, Price and Wage Controls: The First Two Years *and* Price and Wage Controls: Further Evidence, in K. Brunner and A. Meltzer (eds.), *Carnegie-Rochester Conference Series*, vol. II, Amsterdam: North-Holland, in press.

[23] The NBER growth cycle chronology records a downturn on June 1966 and an upturn on October 1967. The first half of 1967 is widely known as the minirecession although it is not an official reference cycle contraction.

industrial production, the Fed stepped on the money accelerator and the money supply grew at even a higher rate than before.

The pause in money supply growth caused the so-called "minirecession" during the first half of 1967. Real income declined slightly during the first quarter and then increased slightly during the second quarter of 1967 for an overall first-half growth rate of 0.3 percent per annum. The impact of the minirecession on the economy was trivial, but it did have a significant impact on economic thought. In the ferment following the publication of Friedman and Schwartz's *Monetary History of the United States, 1867–1960,* it provided a sharp contrast between the widely publicized predictions of Friedman, Schwartz, and other "monetarists" and those of prominent Keynesians who were labeled "fiscalists" because of their belief in the power of fiscal policy. The monetarists predicted a sharp drop in the growth rate of real income because of the previous drop in the growth rate of the money supply. Fiscalists predicted further rapid growth of real income because of further rapid increases in real government spending largely financed by borrowing. After the events, study of the views and evidence of the monetarists became more compelling.

During 1967, fluidity rose sharply, relative to the −3 percent trend, due to the effects of the minirecession and to the 4 percent per annum increase in the growth rate of the money supply. The relatively high growth rate increased fluidity to about 0.9 percent above its trend growth path. Put another way, the average growth rate of nominal income between the last quarters of 1962 and 1967 equaled the growth rate of the money supply plus 2.8 percent per annum due to a −2.8 percent per annum average growth rate of fluidity.

The growth rate of the money supply increased further during 1968 to 7.5 percent per annum. The acceleration of money supply growth during 1967 and the first half of 1968 had caused monetarists to predict continued rapid growth of nominal income in the last half of 1968. The fiscalists predicted a slowdown or recession because of a very large tax increase passed in June 1968. The tax increase, together with the cessation of growth of real government spending, did in fact stop the normal fall in fluidity during the second half of 1968, but this was not enough to outweigh the money supply acceleration. Monetarist views became more influential. In particular, the Fed which had engineered the money supply acceleration because of fears of fiscal "overkill," began a slow process of deemphasizing interest rate pegs and introducing money supply growth as the guide to open market operations.

Accelerating inflation was widely believed to have been an important issue in the Democratic loss of the Presidency in 1968. Beginning in January 1969, the Fed reduced the growth rate of the money supply to 3.5 percent per annum. Fiscal policy continued restrictive during 1969, and so had a neutral effect on the growth rate of fluidity. The NBER dates the beginning of the recession at November 1969. It is a measure of the acceleration of money supply growth since 1962 that by 1969 a 3.5 percent per annum growth rate of the money supply was a restrictive monetary policy.

The recession of 1969–1970[24] was widely viewed as further evidence of the dominance of monetary policy. This is, however, an overstatement since fluidity grew at a rate 4.4 percent greater than trend even though it started from a level of 2.8 percent above the trend level. Fiscal policy involved a −4.8 percent per annum growth rate of real government expenditures (compared with −3.0 percent for 1969) and also a much larger tax cut, reversing the 1968 tax surcharge so that the government deficit increased sharply. An apparently important influence was a sharp fall in the expected rate of inflation brought about by the Fed's willingness to reduce money supply growth and cause a recession. Many borrowers and lenders believed—erroneously as it turned out—the claims by federal officials that monetary restraint would be maintained until inflation was eliminated. In combination with the normal cyclical fall in real interest rates, short-term interest rates fell by over 3 percent per annum during 1970. The short-run effect on the demand for money apparently significantly worsened the recession.

Fluidity was reverting to trend at a growth rate of −4.2 percent per annum during the first half of 1971. The so-called Economic Stabilization Program (ESP) announced by President Nixon on August 15, 1971, stopped and for a while reversed that process, at least in the official data. Fluidity growth was a bit above trend for the rest of 1971 and 1972.[25]

Although popularly termed wage and price controls, the ESP controls generally permitted prices to rise in proportion to costs (just as in a steady-state inflation) and only applied to some wages.[26] The wage controls were effective only for union wages, so that the ESP turned out to be little more than an antitrust program for unions. As the normal loss of real income due to the monopoly power of unions is generally estimated to be somewhat less than 1 percent of GNP, an increase of $\frac{1}{2}$ percent of GNP is likely a high estimate of real income gains from ESP after allowance is made for the waste of misallocation in a few industries under special rules and for administrative costs.

Reported real income in the first quarter of 1973 was nevertheless about 4 percent higher than could be accounted for by normal growth and the 0.9 percentage point decline in the unemployment rate from the second (pre-ESP) quarter of 1971. Either alchemy had been at work or firms had responded to the incentives to lie downward about their prices and especially to reduce the quality of their goods. About $1\frac{1}{2}$ percentage points of this apparent understatement of the price level (and overstatement of real income) was worked off by

---

[24] The trough is dated at November 1970.

[25] This effect on the official data seems to be quite usual during price controls. See Juan T. Toribio, "On the Monetary Effects of Repressed Inflation," Ph.D. dissertation, University of Chicago, 1970.

[26] By July 1972, the wages of 56 percent of the labor force had been exempted from the controls program. This discussion summarizes the material cited previously in footnote 22.

TABLE 10.5 Growth rates of components of nominal income corrected for estimated misreporting due to ESP, 1971–1974

Year	Nominal Income	Real Income	Price Level
1971	8.8%	4.4%	4.4%
1972	10.6%	4.7%	5.9%
1973	10.9%	4.6%	6.3%
1974	6.3%	−2.7%	9.0%

Source: Computed from quarterly data in Michael R. Darby, Wage and Price Controls: Further Evidence, in K. Brunner and A. Meltzer (eds.), *Carnegie-Rochester Conference Series*, vol. II, Amsterdam: North-Holland, in press.

the third quarter of 1973 under Phase III. Controls were then reformulated to place a real constraint on prices as well as wages. The increasing economic dislocations quickly led business executives to join unionists in opposing the ESP. The controls were gradually removed beginning in January 1974, with final abolition in April 1974.

By using the normal relation of real income to changes in unemployment, estimates of real income have been made. These estimates are used in Table 10.5 to present a division of the growth rate of nominal income alternative to that in the official data reported in Table 10.4.

From December 1971 through June 1973, the Fed—apparently less concerned about inflation because of the ESP—accelerated money supply growth to an average rate of 8.0 percent per annum. As the ESP came unhinged in 1973 under this monetary pressure,[27] the Fed cut money supply growth to 4.6 percent per annum from June 1973 to December 1974, 6.0 percent per annum for the next six months, and 1.3 percent per annum from June 1974 to January 1975.[28] Thus, a recession would have been anticipated beginning about the second quarter of 1974 and worsening late in 1974 due to the near cessation of monetary growth in the last half of 1974.

The establishment in late 1973 of an oil cartel and a temporary embargo on Arabian oil sales to the United States somewhat complicated the picture. On the basis of the quarterly data underlying Table 10.5,[29] the oil embargo had about the same impact on the economy as a major strike. That is, the

[27] An almost 8 percent per annum steady-state inflation rate was implied.
[28] The erratic monetary growth rate in 1974 did not reflect policy but occurred because the Fed's operating instructions were formulated in terms of a monthly peg for the federal funds rate on interbank loans. The peg was estimated to imply the Fed's money-supply growth target. The risk premium on federal funds over Treasury bills rose from 2.5 to 5.4 percentage points from December 1973 to July 1974 because of fears for bank solvency after several large bank failures. As the risk premium rose, the federal funds rate peg was underestimated and money supply growth was above the Fed's goal. From July 1974 to January 1975, the risk premium declined to 0.9 percentage point and the federal funds rate peg was overestimated. Thus the money-supply growth rate was below target.
[29] Similar inferences are implied by such indicators as industrial production and employment which do not involve deflation by the estimated price index.

corrected real income data indicate that compared to the fourth quarter of 1973, real income was about 0.7 percent lower in the first quarter of 1974 but 0.1 percent higher in the second quarter. Two quarters growth would normally imply about a 1.5 percent increase in real income; hence, the second quarter of 1974 shows both some remaining effects of the establishment of the oil cartel and the beginnings of the recession due to the cut in money supply growth. The corrected data show real income growth rates of -1.5 and -9.5 percent per annum for the third and fourth quarters of 1974, respectively.

The official data show a 2.2 percent fall in real income from the fourth quarter of 1973 to the second quarter of 1974. This reflects in part the ending of the ESP and overstatement of real income. But even allowing for that, real-income growth was practically nil, mainly because of the oil embargo and cartel. The remainder of 1974 corresponds to the classical pattern of a monetary contradiction.

Looking Forward from 1974

This discussion of the dozen years 1963–1974 has concentrated on the wide variations in the money supply growth rate which were the dominant determinant of short-run fluctuations in the growth of real income and the price level. The question naturally arises whether the long-run equilibrating forces discussed in Part 2 have been operative in keeping the economy anywhere near the steady-state equilibrium.

A straightforward test is possible in terms of the Cambridge equation

$$M_t = \phi_t \, y_t \, P_t \qquad\qquad [10.1]$$

The actual values of this equation for the fourth quarter of 1974 can be compared with those predicted by long-run trends. If the differences are small, it can be concluded that the economic fluctuations were anchored by the long-run equilibrium.

The actual values of the Cambridge equation at the end of 1974 were[30]

$$\$282.9 \text{ billion} \approx (0.1997 \text{ year}) \ (R\$804.0 \text{ billion/year}) \ (\$1.7797/R\$) \qquad [10.2]$$

The steady-state value of fluidity was estimated by applying the -3 percent per annum trend growth rate to the end of 1962 value. The steady-state value of real income was estimated by correcting for the cyclical reduction in real income.[31] This corresponds to a 3.1–3.2 percent per annum trend growth rate from 1928. The corresponding price level is then computed for the given

---

[30] The equations are not exact due to rounding.
[31] The unemployment rate was 1.5 percentage points above the natural rate of about 5 percent (see Chap. 14). This would imply a full-employment real income some 4.5 percent higher.

nominal money supply. The estimated steady-state Cambridge equation for the end of 1974 is

$$\$282.9 \text{ billion} \approx (0.1844 \text{ year}) \ (R\$840.2 \text{ billion/year}) \ (\$1.8262/R\$) \qquad [10.3]$$

Compared to these estimated steady-state values, actual fluidity was about 8.3 percent high, real income about 4.3 percent low, and the price level about 2.5 percent low. So over these twelve years, the steady-state model has done very well in tracing the broad movements of fluidity, real income, and prices given the actual growth in the nominal money supply.

To the extent that these rough estimates provide information about the remaining level disequilibria at the beginning of 1975, they suggest a normal recovery after the 1974–1975 recession with only 2–3 percent more in catch-up price increases. An expected rate of inflation of 4–6 percent per annum has been built into the economy, however. Thus, monetary growth at a much lower rate would be associated with falling trend rates of inflation but persistent high unemployment for some years to come.

10.3 THE RELATIVE IMPORTANCE OF SOURCES OF MACROECONOMIC SHOCKS

A central issue in the monetarist-fiscalist controversy was the monetarist proposition that fluctuations in the growth rate of the money supply have been the major source of American business fluctuations.

Recall that the growth rate of nominal income equals the growth rate of money less the growth rate of fluidity,

$$g_{Yt} = g_{Mt} - g_{\phi t} \qquad [10.4]$$

The fiscalist position in the early years of the debate—roughly the 1950s and early 1960s—has been characterized as "money doesn't matter." The logical basis of this proposition will be discussed in Part 4 on the Keynesian model. The proposition implies that a change in the growth rate of money will be offset by a passive equal adjustment in the growth rate of fluidity. There is an element of truth in this, of course, but only for the first quarter or two. After that, fluidity adjusts back toward equilibrium.

As empirical evidence became available, the fiscalist position gradually shifted to "not only money matters." In this incarnation, changes in the growth rate of the money supply are not (entirely) offset by passive changes in fluidity but other shocks, particularly changes in investment demand and fiscal policy, can affect the growth rate of fluidity. This movement was a major victory for the monetarists, because it came down to a question of how great an effect these other shocks can actually have.

The limitations of continuing influences on fluidity from these other types of shocks have been discussed at length in Chaps. 8 and 9. As a matter of historic fact it seems clear that money supply fluctuations and war have been the major if not exclusive source of fluctuations in the annual growth rate of nominal income of 3 percent per annum or more. Conversely, fiscal policy and large sudden changes in the expected inflation rate have had quite noticeable short-run effects on the growth rate of fluidity and nominal income.

Because Keynesians emphasize very short-term questions, they tend to view this as a partial vindication of their position. Monetarists are interested in the behavior of the economy not just in this quarter and the next, but over the next several years. So they, too, can find their position of "mostly money matters" generally accepted.

A more detailed analysis of the basic differences between the monetary dynamic model and the Keynesian model is left to Chap. 13.

☐ **SUMMARY**

The Fed instituted a restrictive monetary policy in the spring of 1928 because of concern with high stock market prices. The resulting contraction started in the summer of 1929. The recession of 1929–1930 became a depression after the onset of a banking panic in late 1930 which recurred in waves until the Banking Holiday of 1933. Because the Fed abdicated its responsibility to stop panics, the growth rate of the money supply decreased sharply through spring 1932 and then recovered only slightly during the following year. Money supply growth resumed in 1933 and continued until the summer of 1936. The Fed then stopped money supply growth until the spring of 1938 by doubling reserve requirements. The rapid recovery since 1933 was then interrupted by the severe recession of 1937–1938. Recovery then resumed and continued until the start of World War II. Data through the war years are very unreliable, but it is clear that unemployment of resources was practically eliminated during the war. In 1947, the economy was characterized by a low capital-labor ratio because of reduced real investment during the 1930s and the war years. Though deflationary expectations kept unemployment very low—it was easy to find a "good job"—real income was also low compared to 1929 real income projected at the 3.1 percent per annum long-run trend. This provided a base for exceptionally fast growth through the mid-1960s. The growth of the economy between 1947 and 1962 was interrupted by four mild contractions due to monetary shocks and the Korean War. Nevertheless, the real income growth rate averaged 3.6 percent per annum during this period. Money supply growth fluctuated mildly around a 1.9 percent growth rate and the rate of inflation averaged 2.4 percent because of a negative trend growth rate in fluidity (−3.1 percent per annum). Between 1963 and 1974, the average growth rate of the money supply increased sharply with only mild fluctuations around the rising trend. In the early part of the period, the acceleration in money supply growth was reflected mainly in increased real income growth. As the economy adjusted to rapid increases in money the rate of inflation rose sharply and real income growth slowed. After 1965, real income fluctuated mildly around a 3.1 percent per annum trend line drawn from 1929. The 1960s provided several interesting situations of opposing monetary and fiscal policies in which the monetary policy was clearly dominant. The Economic Stabilization Program of 1971–1974 caused an understatement of the rate of inflation in 1971 and 1972 and a corresponding overstatement in 1973 and 1974. The overall increase in the price level from 1962 to 1974 was almost exactly what would be predicted from the actual growth in the nominal money supply and the secular trends underlying growth in real money demand. The historical record seems to indicate dominance of monetary shocks—and war—in determining macroeconomic behavior over periods of a year or more, but a considerable range of influence within a period of several quarters for other macroeconomic shocks.

□ **QUESTIONS AND EXERCISES**

*1 During the Great Depression, Fed officials claimed that the depression could not be blamed on them because the fall in the money supply was only as necessary to meet the fall in money demand due to falling income and to prevent credit conditions from becoming sloppy. Indeed, they claimed that monetary policy was easy because interest rates on Treasury securities were low and money was a larger fraction of income. What is wrong with this argument? (*Hint:* See Chap. 6, question 6.)

2 Why can a bank go bankrupt during a panic and then have sufficient assets to pay off all depositors with something left over for the stockholders?

3 A great advantage of Federal Deposit Insurance is that it reduces the probability of bank failure—the thing insured against. Why is it important to achieve this reduction that insurance limits are rarely applied?

4 The Fed's withdrawal between 1933 and 1937 from money creation—other than issuing base money to pay for Treasury gold purchases—temporarily put the United States on a quasi-gold standard. How would this cause rapid monetary growth between 1933 and 1936?

*5 If the Fed were to try to maintain a low interest rate peg with rapid base money creation, why would the growth rate of base money have to be increased over time? (*Hint:* What happens to the expected rate of inflation?)

6 If federal expenditures are rising and budget surpluses are falling, what can be inferred about federal taxes?

7 Use [10.4] to explain why nonmonetary shocks are analyzed as affecting the growth rate of fluidity.

☐ REFERENCES FOR FURTHER READING

Friedman, Milton, and Anna Jacobson Schwartz: *A Monetary History of the United States, 1867–1960,* Princeton: Princeton University Press for NBER, 1963, esp. chaps. 7–11.

────── **and Walter W. Heller:** *Monetary vs. Fiscal Policy,* New York: Norton, 1969.

Sprinkel, Beryl W.: *Money and Markets: A Monetarist View,* Homewood, Ill.: Irwin, 1971, esp. chaps. 1, 5, and 7.

Stein, Herbert: *The Fiscal Revolution in America,* Chicago: University of Chicago Press, 1969.

The Keynesian Model

Part 4

Parts 2 and 3 of this book have been devoted to the exposition of the modern quantity theory or dynamic model of income and the price level. Part 4 discusses the main alternative approach to macroeconomics: the income-expenditures or Keynesian model.

There are those who argue that "Keynesian" is a misnomer for the standard "IS-LM" macroeconomic model adopted by the followers of John Maynard Keynes along lines suggested by Sir John Hicks. It is, however, usual—and certainly less tedious—to refer to the Keynesian rather than the income-expenditures model. One should not assume, however, that all the weaknesses or strengths of the model also apply to Keynes' own thought.

The Keynesian model is a comparative statics model of aggregate demand. It explains in great detail certain aspects of short-run adjustment which are subsumed in the dynamic model. In order to focus such attention on some features of the economy, other features are assumed constant. If these other features are permitted to change too, the model becomes so unwieldy as to be effectively unusable.

Chapter 11 explains the basic elements used to build the Keynesian model. They are largely familiar from earlier chapters, but the emphasis is somewhat altered by the special assumptions of the model.

These elements are integrated into a model of income determination in Chap. 12. The model is used to analyze the short-run effects of fiscal and monetary policies and other macroeconomic shocks.

Chapter 13 compares the Keynesian and dynamic models. Important differences are to be found both in ideas about specific behavioral functions and in the overall approaches. Though the overall usefulness of the Keynesian model may be in doubt, its ability to illuminate certain features of macroeconomic adjustments is clear.

The Keynesian Building Blocks

11.1 UNDERLYING ASSUMPTIONS

The Keynesian Approach

The Keynesian approach to income determination is one of aggregate demand. Individual components of total expenditures are analyzed separately and then added together to obtain the total. Consistency of the total with conditions underlying the individual components and with the demand and supply of money is then obtained. This chapter undertakes the first part of the task—the analysis of the expenditure components. The basic elements are put together in Chap. 12.

There are three basic assumptions that underlie the Keynesian model: (1) There is a short period of time within which the economy adjusts to the equilibrium described by the model, a period which is so short that changes in the existing stocks are negligible. (2) The price level is given. (3) A quantity adjustment mechanism exists by which the comparative static equilibrium can be reached.

The Short Period Assumption

Strictly speaking, the Keynesian model is a model of comparative statics. A comparative statics analysis compares alternative equilibria at the same instant of time. In that instant, the effects of flows on stocks are nil. For example, it makes no difference to the stock of capital whether investment at that instant is $100 billion or $200 billion per annum. No time elapses so there is no change in capital. This greatly simplifies the analysis since the values of all stocks can be omitted from explicit consideration.

No one supposes that adjustment to changed conditions could in fact occur instantaneously. But it is assumed that the adjustment is completed over some short period—such as one-quarter or at most one-half year—in which the effects of different flows on stocks is negligible. The analysis can then be applied again in the next period. Large-scale computerized versions of the model take explicit account of the effects of some flows on stocks from period to period, but as a practical matter the properties of these models cannot be described analytically.[1]

Perhaps the shortness of the short period is a bit overdone in terms of other evidence on the timing of adjustments to macroeconomic shocks, but the idea is doubtless a usable approximation even for periods of a year.

The Constant Price Level

It is a matter of logical necessity that the price level is given for the analysis. Unless the price level or some similar variable—such as the nominal wage rate—is fixed, there are an infinite number of solutions to the Keynesian model. For expositional purposes it is easiest to assume that prices are given.

The assumption is not at all foolish for an instant of time. The growth rate of prices may well be sticky enough that the price level can be treated as if it were given for any single short period.

A useful way to view this assumption is that the Keynesian aggregate supply curve is a horizontal line at a height of $\bar{P}$. This means that the only interesting point on the aggregate demand curve is the one at $P = \bar{P}$. The Keynesian model analyzes what equilibrium income y^e will be associated with $\bar{P}$ on the aggregate demand curve as in Fig. 11.1.

The horizontal aggregate supply can be viewed as an extreme version of the aggregate supply curve discussed in Chap. 7. It is probably a reasonably accurate approximation for a very short period. In the strict Keynesian model, however, it makes no difference to the future positions of the aggregate supply curve where the current aggregate demand and supply curves intersect.

Because abundant unutilized resources are assumed, the Keynesian analysis has been called "depression economics." In particular, the horizontal aggregate supply curve was often rationalized by the assertion that prices are very sticky downward and do not fall in the face of unemployed resources.[2]

Since the price level is fixed, the distinction between nominal and real magnitudes becomes superfluous. No theory, just arithmetic, is required to relate nominal to real magnitudes.

The Quantity Adjustment Mechanism

The quantity adjustment mechanism is the means by which the quantity of output is adjusted to equality with total expenditures. The basic hypothesis is that firms will increase production if demand for their output at the fixed price

[1] The implications of a computer model are usually found by putting in alternative assumptions and waiting to see what the computer grinds out.
[2] Recall however that the price level fell by 22 percent from 1929 to 1933.

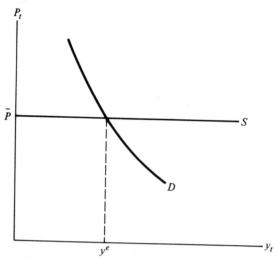

FIGURE 11.1 Graphical representation of the constant price level assumption. The Keynesian assumption of a constant price level is represented by a horizontal aggregate supply curve at height $\bar{P}$. Any amount demanded will be produced at the given price level by employing a corresponding amount of otherwise unemployed resources. Only the point $(y^e, \bar{P})$ on the aggregate demand curve is of interest, and so the model is solved for that point alone. It is sometimes assumed that there is some maximum level of real income at which the aggregate supply curve becomes vertical, but the Keynesian model is inapplicable if that level of income is reached.

exceeds the amount actually produced and will reduce production if the quantity demanded is less than the quantity produced.

Suppose, for example, that total *planned* expenditures are $1020 billion per annum when output is only $1000 billion per annum. Actual expenditures must always exactly equal output which is identical to income. But this means that actual expenditures are $1000 billion per annum, or $20 billion less than planned expenditures. Some plans are obviously being frustrated. The main frustrated plans are found in investment by firms.

Investment can be divided into investment in buildings, machines, and the like or *fixed investment* and changes in the stock of goods on hand or *inventory investment*. The $20 billion excess of planned expenditures over output will be met by selling out inventories. So inventory investment occurs at a rate $20 billion per annum less than planned so that other planned expenditures can be made.

Firms do not want their inventories to grow so slowly—or to decline—so they hire more workers and put idle capital to work to produce more goods. This increases output and income toward the planned level of expenditures. The higher level of income will generally raise expenditure plans but by an amount less than the increase in income. So the difference between planned expenditures and income narrows. The process continues until planned expenditures equal actual expenditures.

Consider the initial example in which planned expenditures exceed original output by $20 billion. Suppose that firms increase their output by the whole amount by which planned inventory investment exceeds the actual inventory investment. In the next round, output will be $1020 billion per annum. But the $20 billion increase in output may increase the desired level of planned expenditures. Suppose that they increase by 20 percent of the increase in output, that is, to $1024 billion per annum ($1020 billion + 0.2 × $20 billion = $1024 billion). Then, planned expenditures still exceed actual expenditures by $4 billion. This is noted as Round 1 in Table 11.1. If firms then again increase output by this difference, output increases to $1024 billion per annum and planned expenditures to $1024.8 billion per annum. This process continues as noted in Table 11.1 until planned and actual expenditures are equal at $1025 billion per annum.

An increase in income on net might, however, decrease planned expenditures. It will be seen in Chap. 12 that this can occur because an increase in income increases money demand relative to money supply. The process of quantity adjustment works much the same way. Table 11.2 records the process if planned expenditures *decrease* by 20 percent of any increase in income. In Round 1, output is increased to $1020 billion per annum, but this reduces planned expenditures to $1016 billion per annum ($1020 billion −0.2 × $20 billion = $1016 billion). As a result, there is an unplanned investment of +$4 billion per annum and output would be cut back. Eventually, actual and planned expenditures are equal at $1016.67 billion.

TABLE 11.1 **Example of the operation of the quantity adjustment mechanism**

Round Number	Output = Income = Actual Expenditures	Planned Expenditures	Unplanned Investment
0	1000	1020	−20
1	1020	1024	− 4
2	1024	1024.8	− 0.8
3	1024.8	1024.96	− 0.16
. . .	. . .	. . .	. . .
∞	1025	1025	0

Note: In this example it is assumed that an increase in income increases the level of planned expenditures by 20 percent of the increase in income.

TABLE 11.2 Example of the operation of the quantity adjustment mechanism

Round Number	Output = Income = Actual Expenditures	Planned Expenditures	Unplanned Investment
0	1000	1020	-20
1	1020	1016	$+4$
2	1016	1016.8	-0.8
3	1016.8	1016.64	$+0.16$
...	...	...	...
∞	$1016\frac{2}{3}$	$1016\frac{2}{3}$	0

Note: In this example it is assumed that an increase in income decreases the level of planned expenditures by 20 percent of the increase in income.

The process is reversed if planned expenditures are less than actual expenditures. So long as the change (whether an increase or decrease) in planned expenditures is less than the change in income, the process will converge from either direction to a single equilibrium in which planned expenditures equal actual expenditures.

This rigid step adjustment of output to the full amount of unplanned inventory changes is at best a caricature of the gradual adjustment process that actually occurs. The dynamic implications of such a mechanical approach should not be taken too seriously. For example, the oscillatory adjustment in Table 11.2 would not be likely to occur. As income gradually increased, planned expenditures would gradually decrease until the two were equal.[3] But some such quantity adjustment mechanism is indeed required.

A quantity adjustment mechanism is not explicit in a formal comparative statics analysis based on the Keynesian model. It is implicitly assumed, however, that some such mechanism is in operation and works with sufficient rapidity that the equilibria described by the formal analysis will adequately describe actual income over some short period.

11.2 THE CONSUMPTION FUNCTION
The Keynesian Short-Run Consumption Function

Aggregate expenditures can be divided into four main categories: consumer expenditures c, investment i, government expenditures g, and net exports x:[4]

$$y = c + i + g + x \qquad [11.1]$$

---

[3] Interestingly, gradual adjustment makes any negative impact of income changes on planned expenditures stable, but positive impacts are stable only if an increase in income of R$1 increases planned expenditures by less than R$1.
[4] This is a real-magnitude version of [2.3].

The time subscript is omitted because the Keynesian model is a comparative statics model. All variables refer to the instant—or short period—of time being analyzed. It was seen in Table 2.3 that consumer expenditures comprise a considerable majority of aggregate expenditures. The explanation of consumer expenditures is the first task of a macroeconomic model based on the explanation of individual expenditure components.

Keynes did not distinguish between consumer expenditures and consumption in the sense of the pure consumption of service flows. To avoid confusion in outside readings, Part 4 follows the Keynesian tradition in using "consumption" for consumer expenditures and "pure consumption" where the strict meaning is required.

Keynes hypothesized a consumption function of elegant simplicity:

> The fundamental psychological law . . . is that men are disposed, as a rule and on average, to increase their consumption as their income increases, but not by as much as the increase in their income.[5]

In functional notation, this is expressed as

$$c = c^s(y^n) \qquad\qquad [11.2]$$

where consumer expenditures are an increasing function of private income such that $(c_1 - c_0)/(y_1{}^n - y_0{}^n)$ is less than one. This ratio of algebraic differences in consumer expenditures and income is known as the *marginal propensity to consume* (MPC).

Note that it is assumed that private income y^n is the relevant income for determining consumers' expenditures. Private income measures the amount actually available to consumers for either spending or adding to wealth. Its value is found by subtracting taxes t from total income:

$$y^n = y - t \qquad\qquad [11.3]$$

Relationship of the Short-Run and Long-Run Consumption Functions

Keynes went further to hypothesize that the ratio of consumption to private income, c/y^n, declines as the level of private income increases. This ratio is known as the *average propensity to consume*, APC. This property requires that the APC exceed the MPC. As a short-run principle, it is certainly true. Over long periods it is demonstrably false.

This difference between the short-run and long-run properties of the consumption function arises because the short-run consumption function omits stock variables. Because of the short period of analysis, stocks are effectively fixed and can be implicit in the form of the consumption function. Over longer

---

[5] John Maynard Keynes, *The General Theory of Employment, Interest, and Money*, New York: Harcourt, Brace, 1936, p. 96.

periods of time, these stocks increase proportionally to income so that the APC does not fall. The increases in stocks cause shifts in the short-run consumption function but movements along a more complete long-run consumption function.

A long-run consumption function was introduced in [8.11] as:

$$c = c(y_P, y_T, m - m^d, cd) \tag{11.4}$$

Consumer expenditures are an increasing function of permanent income, transitory income, and excess real money holdings, and a decreasing function of the stock of consumers' durables. Permanent income (a measure of wealth) and the stock of consumers' durables are fixed from the short-period point of view of Keynesian analysis. Since private income is the sum of permanent income and transitory income, changes in private income are equal to changes in transitory income.

At a moment of time, then, private income is the only variable, except excess real money balances, which can affect consumer expenditures. It is explicitly assumed in Keynesian models that real money balances have no effect whatsoever on consumer expenditures. Thus a Keynesian analysis of the alternative incomes associated with alternative money supplies would make no provision for any effects of money on consumer spending. Further discussion of this difference between the Keynesian and dynamic models is delayed until Chap. 13.

The Treatment of Taxes in Keynesian Analysis

It is expositionally simpler if the definition of private income is substituted for private income in the short-run consumption function:

$$c_t = c^s(y - t) \tag{11.5}$$

This eliminates possible confusion of the two concepts of income.

The usual assumption is that the real burden of taxes (net of transfers) is held constant at $\bar{t}$ for purposes of analysis unless explicitly changed. An equally plausible assumption that taxes vary with total income is sometimes used. There is not much substantive difference in the analysis; consequently the simpler assumption of constant taxes will be followed.

One of the interesting questions considered in this framework is how fiscal policy in the form of tax changes will affect total income. The key point in this analysis is how alternative amounts of taxes affect consumer spending. That can be considered now.

Figure 11.2 illustrates the short-run consumption function for the alternative taxes $\bar{t}_0$ and $\bar{t}_1$ where $\bar{t}_1$ exceeds $\bar{t}_0$. Income must be $\bar{t}_1 - \bar{t}_0$ higher in Case 1

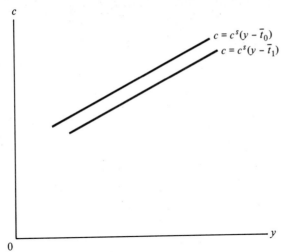

FIGURE 11.2 Alternative real taxes and the Keynesian consumption function. An increase in taxes from $\bar{t}_0$ to $\bar{t}_1$ shifts the consumption function to the right by $\bar{t}_1 - \bar{t}_0$. Since consumption is a function of private income $y^n = y - t$, income must increase by just enough to make up for the tax increase if consumption is to be unchanged.

than in Case 0 at the same level of consumer expenditures. This is clear in view of [11.5] and the fact that

$$(y + \bar{t}_1 - \bar{t}_0) - \bar{t}_1 = y - \bar{t}_0 \tag{11.6}$$

Thus, an increase in taxes shifts the consumption function that amount to the right in the yc plane.

The shift in the consumption function due to a change in taxes can also be described as a downward shift in the consumption function. The vertical distance between the curves is of interest in this regard because it measures the difference in consumer expenditures at the same level of total income. The MPC is by definition the slope of the short-run consumption function. Consider the triangle drawn in Fig. 11.3. Here y_1 exceeds y_0 by $\bar{t}_1 - \bar{t}_0$. Assuming taxes of $\bar{t}_0$, c_0 corresponds to y_0 and c_1 to y_1. Now

$$\frac{c_1 - c_0}{y_1 - y_0} = \text{MPC}$$

$$c_1 - c_0 = \text{MPC}\,(y_1 - y_0)$$

$$c_1 - c_0 = \text{MPC}\,(\bar{t}_1 - \bar{t}_0) \tag{11.7}$$

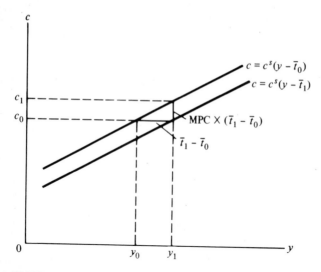

FIGURE 11.3 The vertical shift in the Keynesian consumption function due to a change in real taxes. The effect of a tax increase from $\bar{t}_0$ to $\bar{t}_1$ is to shift the consumption function to the right by $\bar{t}_1 - \bar{t}_0$. Therefore, if $c^s(y_0 - \bar{t}_0) = c_0$ and $y_1 = y_0 + \bar{t}_1 - \bar{t}_0$, $c^s(y_1 - \bar{t}_1) = c_0$. But by the definition of the marginal propensity to consume as the slope of the consumption function, $(c_1 - c_0)/(y_1 - y_0) = MPC$. So $c_1 - c_0 = MPC\,(\bar{t}_1 - \bar{t}_0)$. The vertical shift in the consumption function is $c^s(y_1 - \bar{t}_1) - c^s(y_1 - \bar{t}_0) = c_0 - c_1$ $= -MPC(\bar{t}_1 - \bar{t}_0)$. Hence, consumer spending for a given level of income changes by the marginal propensity to consume multiplied by minus the changes in taxes.

If taxes are $\bar{t}_1$ instead, c_0 corresponds to an income of y_1. And so, the vertical distance between the short-run consumption functions corresponding to $\bar{t}_0$ and $\bar{t}_1$ is equal to the MPC times the difference in taxes.[6] This is the *decrease* in consumption for a given income corresponding to an *increase* in taxes; therefore, consumption is a decreasing function of taxes.

The substantive implication of this result is that a tax cut of say $10 billion per annum would increase planned consumer expenditures by much less than that amount at a given level of total income. If the MPC were 0.4, planned consumer expenditures would increase by only $4 billion per annum (0.4 × $10 billion = $4 billion).

---

[6] This result holds exactly only if the short-run consumption function is a straight line with constant MPC in the region of interest. An equivalent result for the long-run consumption function was derived in Sec. 8.3.

11.3 OTHER EXPENDITURE COMPONENTS
Keynesian Investment Analysis

Investment is normally only about 8 percent of total income.[7] Keynes believed, however, that variations in investment demand were a very important cause of business fluctuations. It is certainly true that there are substantial variations in the investment-income ratio over the business cycle whether these variations are cause or effect.

There is a variety of approaches—largely overlapping—to deriving the Keynesian investment demand function. Almost all approaches are simple elaborations of the basic investment function presented in Sec. 5.2. Perhaps the simplest approach relates investment to changes in the desired stock of capital.

Investment is the rate of change in the stock of capital, so investment demand is derived from changes in the demand for capital.[8] The desired stock of capital, for given conditions, is that stock at which the real rental rate received on capital just covers the cost of financing capital. If the real rental rate on capital was greater than the cost of financing capital, firms would have an incentive to increase the capital stock. If the real rental rate was less than the cost of financing capital, firms would want to reduce the capital stock by not replacing worn-out machines. The higher the amount of capital relative to labor, the lower will be the real rental rate earned on capital, and vice versa. So these adjustments will tend, other things being equal, to move the stock of capital toward an amount at which the real rental rate on capital just equals the cost of financing capital.

In the aggregate, the cost of financing capital is measured by the real interest rate.[9] Given the expected rate of inflation, it is permissible to use changes in the nominal rate of interest as a measure of changes in the cost of financing capital. Since lower desired capital stocks are associated, other things being equal, with higher costs of financing capital, and vice versa, it follows that the stock demand for capital is a decreasing function of the nominal interest rate.

The most important "other thing" in determining the rental rate earned by a given quantity of capital is the amount of labor used with the capital. Within the short period of analysis, variations in the amount of labor employed are uniquely associated with the level of real income. So the level of employment can be measured by the level of real income—higher employment corresponding to higher real income. Given the nominal interest rate and other

---

[7] See for example Table 2.3.
[8] In microeconomic terms, the demand for capital is a demand to hold a stock, while investment demand is a demand to alter the stock held.
[9] In a strict Keynesian model, no explicit distinction is made between the nominal and real interest rate. It is nonetheless implicit in what Keynes referred to as the "state of long-term expectation" and is widely used by recent Keynesians.

factors, increases in real income will increase the desired capital stock and decreases in real income will decrease the desired capital stock. So the stock demand for capital is an increasing function of real income.

The nominal interest rate and real income are the only explicit arguments of the Keynesian investment demand function. In functional notation the desired capital stock k^* is determined as

$$k^* = k^*(r, y) \tag{11.8}$$

where k^* is a decreasing function of the nominal interest rate r and an increasing function of real income y. Changes in any other factor affecting the desired capital stock would be represented as a shift or change in the function $k^*(\ )$.

Investment is the rate of change in capital. The desired level of investment will reflect the expected rate of change in the desired capital stock and any difference between the current actual capital stock and desired capital stock.

The desired capital stock is expected to expand over time as the labor force and real income grow. Existing firms undertake expansion and new firms steadily enter. This normal growth in the capital stock provides a base or normal level of investment. Indeed, contracts are often made months or even years in advance, so that there is normally a cost involved in varying the actual rate of investment away from this normal rate in a short period, whether up or down.

If the currently desired capital stock differs from the actual capital stock, firms will want to increase or decrease the rate of investment from the normal rate.[10] The precise rate at which firms want to adjust actual capital stock toward desired capital stock will be affected by the costs of varying the rate of investment and the extent to which the current level of employment is extrapolated into the future.

The conclusion to be drawn is that investment is an increasing function of both the normal rate of investment and of desired capital stock minus actual capital stock. But, for the short period being analyzed, both the normal rate of investment and the actual capital stock are fixed by the existing conditions. Thus, for the purposes of Keynesian analysis, the only endogenous variables which affect investment are those which affect the desired capital stock: the nominal interest rate and real income. Increases in the desired capital stock increase investment, and decreases in the desired capital stock decrease investment. Therefore, the investment demand function can be stated as

$$i = i(r, y) \tag{11.9}$$

---

[10] If the difference between the current actual capital stock and desired capital stock were attributed to factors that would not extend to the next short period, this would not occur. A change in the expected rate of change in the desired capital stock would completely offset the effect of the difference between the current actual and desired capital stocks. In the text, expectations are assumed to extrapolate current conditions at least partially into the future.

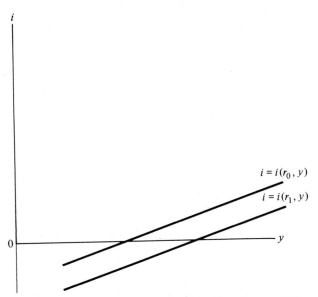

FIGURE 11.4 **The investment demand function.** Investment is a decreasing function of the nominal interest rate and an increasing function of real income. That investment is an increasing function of real income is illustrated by the positive slope of the investment function when graphed for a given nominal interest rate r_0 in the yi plane. That investment is a decreasing function of the nominal interest rate is shown by the fact that the investment demand function for r_1, where r_1 exceeds r_0, lies below the investment demand function for r_0.

where investment is a decreasing function of the interest rate r and an increasing function of the real income y.

The graphical representation of investment demand in the yi plane is shown in Fig. 11.4. The upward slope of the investment function for any given interest rate shows that investment is an increasing function of real income. For any level of income, investment is higher for r_0 than for r_1, because r_0 is less than r_1 and investment is a decreasing function of the nominal interest rate.

Government Expenditures

Government expenditures for real goods and services are currently about one-quarter of total income. Their determination in the Keynesian model presents no particular difficulties. Since government expenditures are subject to the discretion of government officials, they are treated as exogenously given by fiscal policy. That is, government expenditures are simply a constant:

$$g = \bar{g} \qquad [11.10]$$

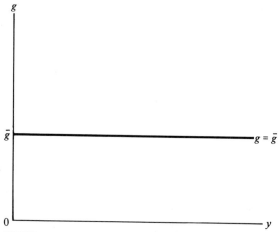

FIGURE 11.5 **The government expenditure function.** The government expenditure function is a constant function $g = \bar{g}$. This is graphed as a horizontal line in the yg plane at height $\bar{g}$.

A comparative statics analysis might be used to consider two alternative levels of government expenditures, however. Figure 11.5 illustrates government expenditures in the yg plane.

Net Exports

Real net exports make up a tiny, possibly negative fraction of total expenditures in the United States. The variability of net exports can be substantial, however, particularly in countries with an extensive international trade.

On the Keynesian view all prices are given, so the only factors affecting real net exports are domestic real income and foreign real income. Foreign real income is exogenous to the model, so foreign purchases (American exports) are fixed. American purchases from abroad (imports) increase with income, however, This happens because part of consumer expenditures and investment, which increase with real income, are for foreign goods.

Increases in real income decrease net exports (exports less imports), and decreases in real income increase net exports. In functional notation,

$$x = x(y) \tag{11.11}$$

where net exports are a decreasing function of real income. This is illustrated in the yx plane in Fig. 11.6.

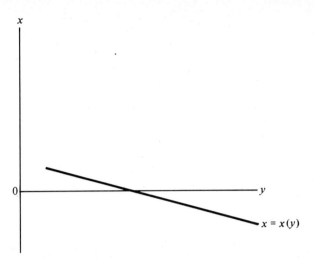

FIGURE 11.6 The net exports function. Net exports are a decreasing function of real income. This is illustrated by a negative slope for the graph of the net exports function in the yx plane.

The Aggregate Expenditure Function

Aggregate expenditures are the sum of consumer expenditures, investment, government expenditures, and net exports:

$$c + i + g + x = c^s(y - \bar{t}) + i(r, y) + \bar{g} + x(y) \qquad [11.12]$$

Using the symbol ax for aggregate expenditures $(c + i + g + x)$, the aggregate expenditure function is

$$ax = ax(y, r; \bar{g}, \bar{t}) \qquad [11.13]$$

The nature of the aggregate expenditure function is deduced from the component functions on the right-hand side of [11.12]. Consumption and investment are increasing functions of real income, while net exports are a decreasing function of real income. But net exports decrease with an increase in real income only because a *part* of the increase in consumer expenditures and investment is used to buy foreign goods. This part cancels out, and the remainder of the increase in consumer expenditures and investment causes aggregate expenditures to increase. Thus, aggregate expenditures are an increasing function of real income. The only effect of the nominal interest rate on aggregate expenditures is through the investment demand function. And so, aggregate expenditures are a decreasing function of the nominal interest rate. Real government expenditures and taxes are fixed for the model but

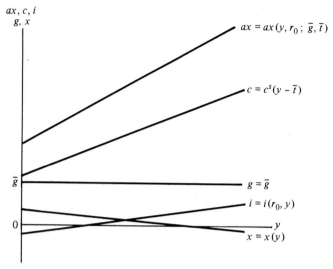

ax, c, i
g, x

$ax = ax(y, r_0; \bar{g}, \bar{t})$

$c = c^s(y - \bar{t})$

$\bar{g}$

$g = \bar{g}$

$i = i(r_0, y)$

0

y

$x = x(y)$

FIGURE 11.7 The aggregate expenditure function. The aggregate expenditure function for given values r_0, $\bar{g}$, and $\bar{t}$ is derived by vertically summing the expenditure functions corresponding to those values for consumer expenditures, investment, government expenditures, and net exports. This illustrates desired or planned aggregate expenditures as an increasing function of real income.

included explicitly in the function because they frequently figure in comparative statics problems. An increase in real government expenditures increases aggregate expenditures by the same amount, other things being equal. Similarly, an increase in real taxes decreases aggregate expenditures by the amount of the increase times the marginal propensity to consume.

The aggregate expenditure function can be derived graphically, as shown in Fig. 11.7. On the same axes, all four components of aggregate expenditures are graphed as functions of real income. They are then added vertically to obtain aggregate expenditures as a function of real income.

11.4 KEYNESIAN MONEY DEMAND AND SUPPLY
Keynesian Money Demand

Keynesian real money demand is determined by the level of real income and the nominal interest rate.[11] It is assumed that there is no interest paid on money—not even bank deposits—so that the nominal interest rate measures

---

[11] This can be viewed as a simplification of a more general money demand function such as that discussed in Parts 2 and 3 of this book. The effect of any omitted variables is implicit in the functional form of money demand.

the interest foregone if money is held instead of bonds. "Bond" is used as a collective term for all nonmoney financial assets.

In functional notation,

$$m^d = m^d(y, r) \tag{11.14}$$

Real money demand is an increasing function of real income. This is true because income is a measure of the level of transactions taking place and also of the wealth of moneyholders—that is, a measure of the work to be done by money and of the wealth constraint on asset holdings. The level of total income is clearly a better indicator of transactions than wealth, however. The interest rate measures the alternative return available on holding bonds instead of money. At higher rates of interest, bonds would be more attractive relative to money, so more bonds and less money would be held. The same transactions could be made with lower average money holdings, but only by undertaking the costs of more frequent buying and selling of bonds or otherwise synchronizing receipts and expenditures of money.[12]

Money demand can be graphed in the mr plane for a given value of y [see Fig. 11.8(a)] or in the my plane for a given value of r [Fig. 11.8(b)]. In the first instance, the effects of alternative levels of income are indicated by the placement of the demand curve: Higher incomes shift the demand curve to the right, since more money would be demanded at each level of interest. Similarly, lower incomes shift the demand curve to the left. In panel (b), lower interest rates shift the demand curve to the right, since more money would be demanded at each level of income. Higher interest rates would shift the graph to the left.

The Liquidity Trap

A very special hypothesis of Keynes, one still retained by some of his followers, is known as the liquidity trap. The hypothesis is that there is some positive interest rate at which the demand for money becomes infinitely elastic. This means that the money demand curve in the mr plane becomes horizontal at a minimum interest rate r^{min}, as illustrated in Fig. 11.9. The horizontal portion of the demand for money curve is called the *liquidity trap*.

It is supposed that if the interest rate declined at all below r^{min}, all bonds would be sold and people would want to hold money only. At exactly r^{min}, people are indifferent between any combination of money and bonds so long as they hold at least the minimum amount of money consistent with r^{min}.

Keynes attributed this minimum interest rate to the operation of the speculative motive for holding money. The *speculative motive* refers to the

---

[12] The classic analyses are William J. Baumol, The Transactions Demand for Cash: An Inventory Theoretic Approach, *Quarterly Journal of Economics*, **66**: 545–556, Nov. 1952; and James Tobin, The Interest-Elasticity of Transactions Demand for Cash, *Review of Economics and Statistics*, **38**: 241–247, Aug. 1956.

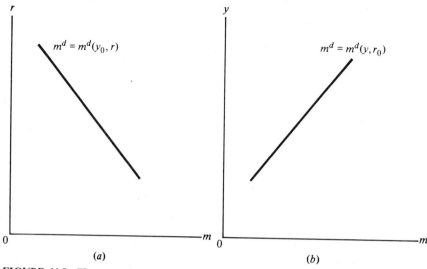

$$m^d = m^d(y_0, r)$$

$$m^d = m^d(y, r_0)$$

(a)   (b)

FIGURE 11.8   The money demand function. Keynesian money demand is an increasing function of real income and a decreasing function of the nominal interest rate; (a) illustrates the graph of money demand in the mr plane for a given real income y_0. It has a negative slope because increases in the nominal interest rate reduce the amount of real money demanded. In (b), money demand is graphed in the my plane for a given level of the nominal interest rate r_0. Since increases in real income increase the real quantity of money demanded, the graph is positively sloped.

desire to hold money instead of interest-bearing bonds because bond prices are expected to fall. There is some interest rate greater than zero, Keynes argued, below which everyone would agree that interest rates must rise and hence bond prices must fall. At any rate below that, no one would want to hold bonds, and so money demand would become unlimited.

However, unless expectations about interest rates are practically unanimous, there will not be a point at which everyone suddenly switches from money to bonds. Instead, a normal, downward-sloping demand curve for money would emerge for the community as a whole.[13] Consequently, this argument provided no logical necessity for the existence of the liquidity trap.

[13] A more convincing argument for a relatively interest-elastic demand for money function is based on the term-structure of interest rates. Long-term rates are identified as "the" interest rates and these interest rates are "little" affected by current short-term rates. This occurs because expected future short-term rates are the dominant factor in explaining long-term interest rates, and expected future short-term rates are little affected by current short-term rates. If the demand for money is a function of short-term interest rates and small variations in the long-term interest rate are caused by large variations in the short-term interest rate, large changes in the demand for money would be associated empirically with small, short-period changes in the long-term interest rate. Over time, long-term and short-term interest rates return to their normal relationship, so this is only a temporary phenomenon. See pages 185 and 186 for a further discussion of the term-structure of interest rates approach.

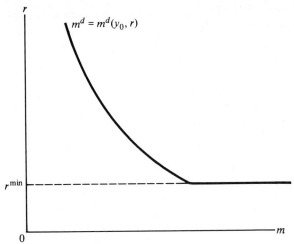

FIGURE 11.9   The money demand function with a liquidity trap.
If the liquidity trap exists, there is some low but positive nominal
interest rate r^{min} at which the elasticity of the demand for money
with respect to the nominal interest rate becomes infinite. This is
illustrated by a horizontal demand curve in the mr plane at r^{min}
and real income y_0. An increase in real income shifts the demand
function to the right but does not change r^{min}.

An alternative explanation of the speculative motive was proposed by James
Tobin.[14] He suggested that people have to be paid to accept the risk of
holding bonds which can fluctuate in price. Generally, the higher the interest
rate, the greater the risk that will be accepted. Only under special assumptions,
however, does this approach imply the existence of a liquidity trap.

Both Keynes' and Tobin's arguments provide reasons for people to shift from
long-term bonds as interest rates decline, but it is not clear why people
would shift into money instead of short-term bonds. Short-term bonds provide
a practically riskfree return, which, in the Keynesian model, money does not.
Perhaps the best argument for the liquidity trap at a positive rate of interest
is that short-term bond yields cannot decline to so low a level that they
do not cover the transaction costs of buying them and collecting the amount
due.

Keynes himself never claimed that the liquidity trap had ever been encountered in the real world. Nor is there any empirical evidence indicating
that it has ever been encountered. Perhaps the very short-run increase in
fluidity immediately following an increase in the money supply could be

---

[14] James Tobin, Liquidity Preference as Behavior Towards Risk, *Review of Economics Studies*, **25:** 65–86,
Feb. 1958.

viewed as a temporary liquidity trap. That interpretation is strained, because these increases reflect differences in actual money balances and long-run demand, or disequilibrium, rather than movements along the long-run demand for money function.

Nor is the existence of a liquidity trap necessary or sufficient for the major Keynesian propositions. It merely permits an expositional simplification and unduly extreme statements on the relative effectiveness of fiscal and monetary policy. Lacking neither necessity nor evidence, the liquidity trap has wisely been abandoned by many Keynesians.

The Supply of Money

Like real government expenditures, the nominal supply of money is determined by decisions of government officials. Therefore, the nominal money supply is treated as exogenously given by monetary policy. That is, the nominal money supply is simply a constant

$$M^S = \overline{M} \qquad\qquad [11.15]$$

The given price level assumption enters at this point. Since the price level is fixed at $\overline{P}$, it is possible to say that control over the nominal money supply is equivalent to control over the real money supply.

$$m^S = \frac{M^S}{\overline{P}} = \frac{\overline{M}}{\overline{P}} = \overline{m} \qquad\qquad [11.16]$$

Note that, in the Keynesian model, the rigidity of prices assures that supply conditions determine real money balances. This differs from the dynamic model in which adjustment in the price level allows conditions of money demand to determine real money balances.

□ SUMMARY

The Keynesian approach to macroeconomics investigates intensively the determinants of a single point on the aggregate demand schedule. There are three sorts of basic elements used in the Keynesian analysis: (1) Underlying assumptions set the framework within which the analysis is carried out. (2) Functions determining components and total aggregate expenditures explain aggregate expenditures as a function of real income, nominal interest rate, and some exogenously given variables. (3) Money demand and supply are also functions of real income, nominal interest rate, and some exogenously given variables. These elements will be combined into a unified model in Chap. 12. The underlying assumptions are that the analysis is a static one applied to a short period, that the price level is given for the period, and that a quantity adjustment mechanism moves the economy to the static equilibrium within the short period. The major components of aggregate expenditures are consumer spending, investment, government spending, and net exports. Consumer spending is an increasing function of private income or of total income less taxes. A change in the assumed level of taxes changes consumer spending for a given level of income by the marginal propensity to consume times minus the change in taxes. Investment is a decreasing function of the nominal interest rate, given the expected inflation rate, and an increasing function of real income. Government expenditures are exogenously given, like taxes, by fiscal policy. Net exports are a decreasing function of real income. Aggregate expenditures are an increasing function of real income and a decreasing function of the nominal interest rate. Some Keynesian economists hypothesize that a liquidity trap with infinitely elastic money demand exists at a positive rate of interest, but this is neither required for the Keynesian model nor observed empirically. Since the price level is given and the nominal money supply is subject to government control, monetary policy can be taken to determine the real money supply.

☐ QUESTIONS AND EXERCISES

*1 If investment is R\$100 billion per annum and the capital stock is initially R\$3000 billion, how much would the capital stock be worth after 1 year? After $\frac{1}{2}$ year? After $\frac{1}{4}$ year? Why does the assumption of a "short period" make a constant capital stock and positive rate of investment compatible?

2 "The Keynesian approach to macroeconomics investigates intensively the determinants of a single point on the aggregate demand schedule." Why can the aggregate supply schedule and all the other points on the aggregate demand schedule be neglected?

*3 (a) Suppose that the consumption function is $c = $ R\$500 billion/year $+ 0.3y$. If $i + g + x$ were somehow fixed at R\$500 billion per annum, at what level of real income would $c + i + g + x = y$?

(b) Suppose that $i + g + x$ were instead fixed at R\$600 billion per annum. At what level of real income would $c + i + g + x = y$?

(c) What is the value of the marginal propensity to consume in the assumed consumption function? Why might $1/(1 - \text{MPC})$ be called the simple income multiplier of changes in $i + g + x$?

4 (a) Omitting the units of coefficients, suppose the investment demand function can be written as $i = 20 + 0.1y - 500r$. If real income is measured in billions of base-year dollars per annum and the interest rate as a decimal fraction per annum, what units must be applied to the coefficients 20, 0.1, and 500?

(b) Complete the following table:

r	y	i
0.03	1000	
0.04	1000	
0.05	1000	
0.03	1100	
0.04	1100	
0.05	1100	

(c) Do the figures in the table in part (b) show the correct general properties for an investment demand function? Why?

5 Why is the effect of an increase in income on net exports less in absolute amount than the effect on $c + i$?

6 According to [11.1], aggregate expenditures equal real income. How then can aggregate expenditures be a function of real income? (*Hint*: The quantity demanded and supplied of a commodity are always equal. How can the demand and supply functions be different?)

*7 Why might short-period changes in real income be associated with smaller changes in real money demand than if they were to persist over a long period of time?

8 Why might short-period changes in the long-term interest rate be associated with larger changes in real money demand than if they were to persist over a long period of time?

☐ **REFERENCES FOR FURTHER READING**

References are given at the end of Chap. 12, as most of them refer to these topics in the context of the model presented there.

The Complete Keynesian Model

12.1 THE IS-LM MODEL

The IS-LM Approach

Sir John Hicks developed a useful graphical device for illustrating the equilibrium of the Keynesian model.[1] The approach is a familiar one for economists. Determinants of equilibrium are divided into two largely separate groups—the income-expenditures sector and the monetary sector. Each sector is summarized by a single equation or line in the yr plane. This can be done because the only variables which directly affect both the income-expenditures and monetary sectors simultaneously are real income and the nominal interest rate. One line shows all combinations of real income and the nominal interest rate for which the income-expenditures sector is in equilibrium. The other shows all combinations of the same variables in which the monetary sector is in equilibrium. So the intersection of the two lines is the only combination of real income and the nominal interest rate for which both sectors are in equilibrium.

This approach follows the familiar pattern of supply and demand analysis. There all the factors affecting the output of a particular commodity are grouped according to whether they affect the amount offered for sale (supply) or the amount purchased (demand).[2] Normally the only common factors are quantity and price. Therefore, the supply and demand curves are drawn in the quantity-price plane. Their intersection is the only combination of price and quantity at which the market is in equilibrium. The same mode of analysis was used in Chap. 5 to derive and use the labor market (LE) and capital market equilibrium (KE) curves.

---

[1] John R. Hicks, Mr. Keynes and the "Classics"; A Suggested Interpretation, *Econometrica*, **5**: 147–159, Apr. 1937.

[2] If this division cannot be made as when the same factors affect costs of production and demand for the product, the analysis is messy and inconclusive. It will be seen that the same is true for the Keynesian model.

The Basic Keynesian Equations

The Keynesian model can be summarized by a set of five equations:

$$ax = ax(y, r; \bar{g}, \bar{t})$$ [12.1]

$$ax = y$$ [12.2]

$$m^d = m^d(y, r)$$ [12.3]

$$m^s = \bar{m}$$ [12.4]

$$m^d = m^s$$ [12.5]

There are five unknown (endogenous) variables to be simultaneously determined by this system of five equations: y, r, ax, m^d, and m^s. The three exogenous policy variables—$\bar{g}$, $\bar{t}$, and $\bar{m}$—enter the system explicitly, but they are fixed in determining any particular solution of the model. All other factors which affect the solution do so by changing (shifting) either of the behavioral relations [12.1] and [12.3]. Since there are five equations and five unknowns, a unique solution is possible.

Equation [12.1] is the aggregate expenditure function. Equation [12.3] is the money demand function. Equation [12.4] sets money supply at the amount exogenously given by monetary policy. These three relations were considered in Chap. 11.

Equations [12.2] and [12.5] are the conditions of equilibrium in the income-expenditures sector and the monetary sector, respectively. In Chap. 2 it was seen that aggregate expenditures—the sum of consumer expenditures, investment, government expenditures, and net exports—are exactly equal to total income after all is said and done. Equation [12.2] assures that this occurs for the desired or planned level of aggregate expenditures determined in [12.1]. Similarly, [12.5] assures that the quantity of money demanded will equal the quantity of money supplied.

The model as stated explicitly assures that there is equilibrium in the markets for goods and money. But what about the third Keynesian market—the market for bonds? The equilibrium of this market is implied by equilibrium in the other markets. This is true because people can plan to buy more bonds than are issued only if they also plan to spend less income than they receive, decrease money balances below the amount supplied, or both. These are the only sources of funds to buy the bonds. Similarly, if people plan to buy fewer bonds than are issued, they must plan to spend more than they receive as income or increase money balances. But in the equilibrium defined by [12.1] through [12.5], people plan to spend just as much income as they receive and to hold just as much money as is supplied. Therefore, it must be true that the demand and supply of bonds are also in equilibrium. The aggregate expenditure and money demand and supply functions implicitly reflect the associated effects of bond demand and supply.

A unique solution to [12.1] through [12.5] is possible, but not necessary. To show that a unique solution in fact exists it is necessary to turn to a graphical analysis.

The Derivation of the IS Curve

Equations [12.1] and [12.2] can be combined to describe the equilibrium of the income-expenditures sector:

$$ax(y, r; \bar{g}, \bar{t}) - y = 0 \qquad [12.6]$$

This equation states that in equilibrium the excess demand for goods must be zero. This is true because $ax(y, r; \bar{g}, \bar{t})$ is the amount of goods demanded and y is the amount of goods actually produced. Equation [12.6] is called an *implicit function* of real income and the interest rate because the functional relationship between the two is implied by requiring y and r to vary so that the excess demand for goods remains zero. This equation defines the income-expenditures equilibrium or IS curve.[3]

The graphical derivation of the IS curve is a two-step procedure. The first step involves graphing the aggregate expenditure function in the y-ax plane for a given interest rate r_0, as shown in Fig. 12.1. The aggregate expenditure function is an increasing function of real income but with a slope less than unity. The only level of income consistent with the given interest rate r_0 and the condition that aggregate expenditures equal income is y_0. Consider a second interest rate, r_1, which is less than r_0. Since aggregate expenditures are a decreasing function of the nominal interest rate, the aggregate expenditures curve for r_1 will be everywhere above the curve for r_0 as drawn in Fig. 12.2. Consequently the equilibrium level of real income y_1 for r_1 is higher than the level y_0 for r_0. This statement is true for every combination of nominal interest rates.

This argument proves that the locus of all points in the yr plane for which the goods market is in equilibrium must be negatively sloping. Thus the IS curve, as defined by [12.6], has a negative slope, as shown in Fig. 12.3. The curve could actually be derived by finding the real income corresponding to every possible interest rate or by solving [12.6] for y as a (decreasing) function of r:

$$y = IS(r) \qquad [12.7]$$

Note that the greater the effect of a given change in nominal interest rates on aggregate expenditures, the less steeply sloped will be the IS curve. This happens because small decreases in r will be associated with larger increases in y.

---

[3] The name IS was adopted because of early Keynesian emphasis on the relation of investment and saving in a model excluding government spending and net exports.

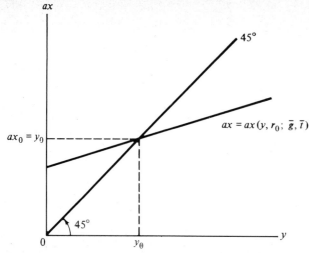

FIGURE 12.1 Determination of equilibrium real income for a given nominal interest rate r_0. The aggregate expenditure function for the given interest rate r_0 is graphed as $ax = ax(y, r_0; \bar{g}, \bar{t})$. The slope is less than 1 because a R$1 increase in real income increases aggregate expenditures by less than R$1, other things being equal. The other line, labeled 45°, is drawn through the origin with slope equal to 1. It is the locus of all points for which $ax = y$ —that is, all points with zero excess demand for goods. Real income $y_0 = ax_0$ is therefore the only level of real income consistent with a nominal interest rate of r_0 and equilibrium in the goods market.

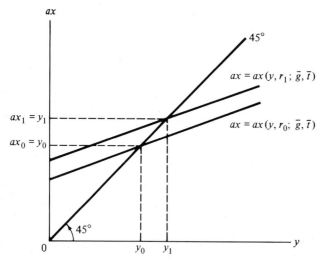

FIGURE 12.2 The effect of alternative interest rates on equilibrium real income. Interest rate r_0 is greater than r_1. Since aggregate expenditures are a decreasing function of the nominal interest rate, the aggregate expenditure curve for r_1 will lie everywhere above the one for r_0. So the level of equilibrium real income y_1 implied by interest rate r_1 exceeds the level y_0 implied by r_0. In terms of goods market equilibrium, lower interest rates are associated with higher levels of real income.

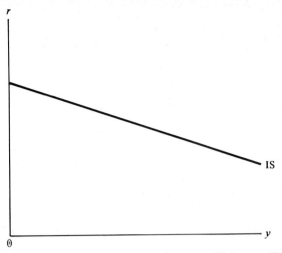

FIGURE 12.3 The income-expenditures equilibrium or IS curve. The IS curve plots all combinations of real income y and the nominal interest rate r for which income and expenditures are equal. This curve has a negative slope because lower interest rates are associated with higher levels of income. The IS curve is the graph of [12.6].

The Derivation of the LM Curve

Equations [12.3], [12.4], and [12.5] are combined to describe the equilibrium of the monetary sector

$$m^d(y, r) - \overline{m} = 0 \qquad [12.8]$$

Equation [12.8] states that in equilibrium the excess demand for money must be zero. The function $m^d(y, r)$ determines the demand for real money, and $\overline{m}$ is the amount of money supplied, as determined by the government. This equation implies a functional relationship for the values of real income and the nominal interest rate which are consistent with equilibrium in the money market. So [12.8] defines the monetary equilibrium or LM curve.[4]

The slope of the LM curve is established by a graphical technique similar to that used for the IS curve. The money demand function for a given real income y_0 is graphed in Fig. 12.4. The curve is negatively sloped because real money demand is a decreasing function of the interest rate. The supply of real money is a vertical line at $\overline{m}$. Supply and demand are equal—excess demand is zero—at the point $(\overline{m}, r_0)$ where the supply and demand curves intersect.

---

[4] This name arose because Keynes referred to the money demand function as the liquidity preference function (L) and the money supply as M.

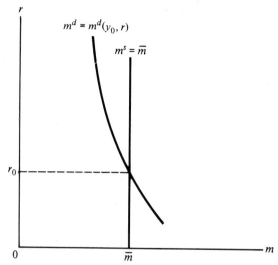

FIGURE 12.4 Determination of equilibrium nominal interest rate for a given real income y_0. If the money market is to be in equilibrium, money demand $m^d = m^d(y, r)$ must equal money supply $m^s = \bar{m}$. This occurs only at the intersection of the money demand and money supply curves. If real income were y_0, the money market would be in equilibrium only at an interest rate of r_0.

Consider a second real income y_1 which is greater than y_0. Since money demand is an increasing function of real income, the money demand curve for y_1 will lie everywhere to the right of the money demand curve for y_0. As shown in Fig. 12.5, this graph implies that the nominal interest rate r_1 associated with y_1 is greater than the nominal interest rate r_0 associated with y_0 and indicates that higher levels of real income are associated with higher interest rates if the money market is to remain in equilibrium.

Thus the locus of all points in the yr plane for which the money market is in equilibrium must be positively sloping. This is the LM curve, defined by [12.8] and illustrated in Fig. 12.6. The LM curve could be derived by plotting the nominal interest rate corresponding to every possible real income or by solving [12.8] for r as an (increasing) function of y;

$$r = LM(y) \qquad\qquad [12.9]$$

The greater the increase in money demand for a given increase in real income and the smaller the decrease in money demand for a given increase in the nominal interest rate, the steeper will be the slope of the LM curve. This follows because small increases in y will be associated with larger increases in the interest rate.

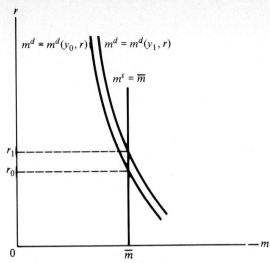

FIGURE 12.5   The effect of alternative real incomes on the equilibrium interest rate. Real income y_1 is greater than y_0. Since real money demand is an increasing function of real income, the demand curve for y_1 lies to the right of the demand curve for y_0. Hence, the equilibrium nominal interest rate r_1 implied by real income y_1 exceeds the rate r_0 implied by y_0. In terms of money market equilibrium, higher nominal interest rates are associated with higher levels of real income.

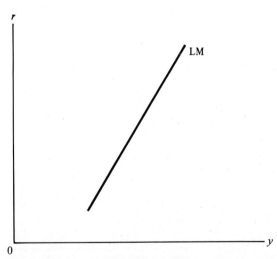

FIGURE 12.6   The monetary equilibrium or LM curve. The LM curve plots all combinations of real income y and the nominal interest rate r for which real money demand and real money supply are equal. This curve has a positive slope because higher levels of the nominal interest rate are associated with higher levels of real income. The LM curve is the graph of [12.8].

Special Cases of the LM Curve

Two extreme cases of money demand are often discussed: the liquidity trap and perfectly interest-inelastic money demand. If either of these occur in the relevant range of real incomes and nominal interest rates, the LM curve will not be positively sloped.

In the case of the liquidity trap, the money demand curve becomes infinitely interest elastic (horizontal) at some positive interest rate r^{min}. Although increases in real income still shift money demand to the right, the liquidity trap portions will partially overlap, as shown in Fig. 12.7(a). Consequently different real incomes may be associated with the same nominal interest rate r^{min} as long as the money supply is large enough to intersect both demand curves in their liquidity trap portions. This leads to an LM curve characterized [as in Fig. 12.7(b)] by a horizontal portion at r^{min} for low levels of real income and a positively sloped portion for higher levels of real income.

In the case of perfectly interest-inelastic money demand, changes in interest rates have no effect on money demand. So the money demand curve is a

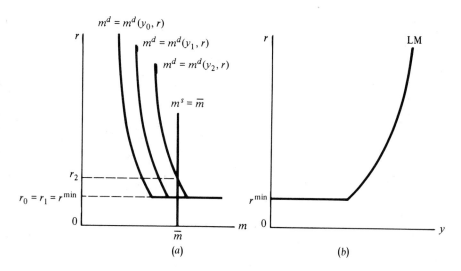

FIGURE 12.7   The LM curve in the presence of a liquidity trap. At real income y_0, the money supply curve in (a) intersects the liquidity trap portion of the money demand curve, and so $r_0 = r^{min}$. Any lower level of income would also be associated with r^{min}. An increase in real income from y_0 to y_1 shifts the demand curve to the right. In this instance, the shift is too small to change the interest rate, therefore $r_1 = r^{min}$. For sufficiently high levels of real income such as y_2, however, the supply curve intersects the demand for money out of the liquidity trap and higher levels of income are associated with higher nominal interest rates. In this region the LM curve has the characteristic positive slope. All real incomes sufficiently low for money supply to intersect money demand in the liquidity trap will be associated with a single interest rate r^{min}. Consequently, the portion of the LM curve corresponding to these lower levels of income is horizontal at height r^{min}. The LM curve in (b) is thus horizontal for low levels of real income and positively sloped for higher levels.

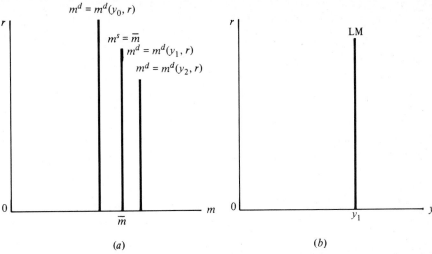

FIGURE 12.8 **The LM curve in the presence of perfectly interest-inelastic real money demand.**
If real money demand is perfectly inelastic with respect to the nominal interest rate, the real
money demand curve is a vertical line determined by the level of real income alone. For real
income y_1 in (a), this vertical line and the real money supply curve coincide, and so any
interest rate r whatsoever and real income y_1 imply equilibrium in the money market. If real
income were lower, say y_0, real money demand would be shifted to the left and there is no
interest rate at which real money demand and real money supply are equal. Similarly, levels
of real income higher than y_1, such as y_2, imply that real money demand is higher than real
money supply for all interest rates. Hence, the LM curve is a vertical line through y_1, as
illustrated in (b).

vertical line in the mr plane. For one and only one level of real income,
money demand and supply will coincide, regardless of the interest rate as
shown in Fig. 12.8(a). Thus, the LM curve will be a vertical line at that
level of real income, as shown in (b) of that figure.

Determination of Equilibrium Real Income and Nominal Interest Rate

The IS curve gives all possible combinations of real income and the nominal
interest rate for which the goods market is in equilibrium. The LM curve
gives all such combinations for which the money market is in equilibrium.
If both are graphed on the same axes, as in Fig. 12.9, their intersection
(y^e, r^e) is the only combination of real income and nominal interest rate at
which the goods market and money market[5] are simultaneously in equilibrium.

The complete solution values to the original set of five equations—[12.1]
through [12.5]—can now be given as y^e, r^e, $ax^e = y^e$, $m^s = \overline{m}$, and $m^d = \overline{m}$.
Given the negative slope of the IS curve and the positive (or nonnegative)

---

[5] And hence the bond market.

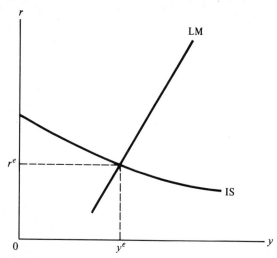

FIGURE 12.9 Determination of the equilibrium real income and nominal interest rate. The intersection of the IS and LM curves, (y^e, r^e), is the only point at which the goods market and the money market are simultaneously in equilibrium. So y^e and r^e are unique solution values for the set of equations [12.1] through [12.5].

slope of the LM curve, there cannot be more than one solution.[6] This one solution will in fact exist so long as there is either no liquidity trap or the IS curve intersects the vertical axis above r^{min}. The empirical evidence suggests that this has always been the case.

This solution shows the results of a particular set of given conditions. The strength of the model is its ability to provide definite comparisons of the results associated with alternative given conditions. These comparative static analyses are the subject of the following sections.

12.2 EFFECTS OF SHIFTS IN THE INCOME-EXPENDITURES SECTOR

Types of Shifts in the Aggregate Expenditure Function

Shifts in the aggregate expenditure function must be caused by shifts in one or more of the component expenditure functions explaining consumer expenditures, investment, government expenditures, and net exports. Most emphasis has historically been placed on shifts in the investment demand function, in government expenditures, and in the consumption function due to tax changes.

---

[6] More elaborate versions of the IS-LM model assume that it is possible that a R\$1 increase in real income might increase desired aggregate expenditures by more than R\$1 in which case the IS curve could be upward-sloping and multiple solutions could exist. These complications are neglected here on empirical grounds.

The position of the investment demand function was believed by Keynes to depend on the unstable state of long-term expectation. He argued that the psychology of businessmen was subject to sudden changes between optimism and pessimism over the future returns to current investments.

These changes in expectations might reflect changes in belief about future real rental rates on capital or about the expected rate of inflation by which the expected real interest rate is derived from the nominal interest rate. Higher expected future real rentals make current investment more attractive. So do higher expected rates of inflation for a given nominal interest rate, since this lowers the real interest rate. Increased optimism about future nominal returns to investment—whether because of higher real returns or inflation—will increase the desired amount of investment for given values of the nominal interest rate and real income. Conversely, increased pessimism will shift the investment function downward.

The empirical question is whether expectations of business executives concerning future returns to investment are largely ephemeral, as suggested by Keynes, or firmly rooted in reality, as suggested by Keynes' critics. The evidence is not sufficient to provide any clear-cut answer on the magnitude of exogenous shifts in investment demand.

Government expenditures are set by fiscal policy and can be changed at will. So it is in principle possible to offset a shift in investment demand by an opposite shift in government expenditure.[7]

An alternative form of fiscal policy is to change real taxes and so induce shifts in the consumption function. Higher taxes shift the consumption function downward and lower taxes shift the consumption function upward.

Exogenous shifts in the consumption function or net export function are conceivable, but they are not of much empirical interest for the United States. Such shifts affect real income through shifting the aggregate expenditure function in precisely the same way as a similar shift in the investment demand function; therefore, no separate exposition is necessary.

Summing up, higher levels of investor optimism and government expenditures and lower levels of taxes are associated with higher values of the aggregate expenditure function for any given combination of real income and nominal interest rates. All shifts in the income-expenditure sector operate through their effect on the aggregate expenditure function.

The Effects of Alternative Aggregate Expenditure Functions

Consider two alternative aggregate expenditure functions:

$$ax = ax^0(y, r; \bar{g}_0, \bar{t}_0) \qquad [12.10]$$

$$ax = ax^1(y, r; \bar{g}_1, \bar{t}_1) \qquad [12.11]$$

---

[7] As will be seen in Chap. 15, this in fact requires the ability to alter government expenditures instantaneously or to predict sufficiently in advance what future shifts in investment demand will occur.

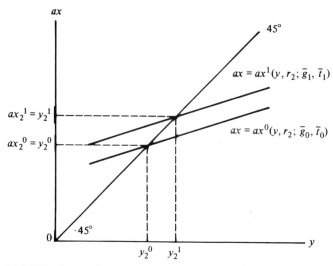

FIGURE 12.10   Effects of alternative aggregate expenditure functions on equilibrium real income for a given interest rate r_2. For any nominal interest rate r_2, the aggregate expenditure function denoted by 1 lies above the function denoted by 0 (zero). The condition for equilibrium in the goods market, that planned real aggregate expenditures equal real income, occurs where the aggregate expenditure function intersects the 45° line. So the equilibrium value of real income in case 1, $y_2{}^1$, is higher than the equilibrium value in case 0, $y_2{}^0$. In the simplest case of a parallel upward shift, it can be shown that the difference in equilibrium real income equals the difference in desired aggregate expenditures for $(y_2{}^0, r_2)$ divided by 1 minus the slope of the aggregate expenditure function.

Assume that for any given values of real income and the nominal interest rate, the aggregate expenditure function denoted by 0 implies lower desired aggregate expenditures than the alternative function denoted by 1. For the current analysis, it is irrelevant whether this difference arises because of differences in the functional relationships themselves, in the exogenous values of $\bar{g}$ or $\bar{t}$, or in some combination.

For any given value of the interest rate r_2 the aggregate expenditure function 1 will lie above the aggregate expenditure function 0 when they are graphed in the y-ax plane. This graph, shown in Fig. 12.10, implies that for any given interest rate there will be a higher equilibrium real income in case 1 than in case 0.

The IS curve is the locus of all points in the yr plane for which the goods market is in equilibrium. It was just seen that for any r, a higher equilibrium value of y occurs in case 1 than in case 0. Thus the IS curve for case 1 (IS_1) lies to the right of the IS curve for case 0 (IS_0), as shown in Fig. 12.11.

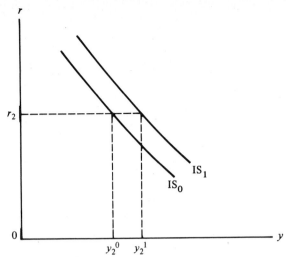

FIGURE 12.11 Implications of alternative aggregate expenditure functions for the IS curve. There is a higher equilibrium value of real income y in the goods market for any nominal interest rate r in case 1 than in case 0. It was seen, for example, in Fig. 12.10 that the interest rate r_2 implied equilibrium income y_2^0 for the lower aggregate expenditure function and y_2^1 for the higher aggregate expenditure function. By the definition of the IS curve as the locus of equilibrium points for the goods market, the IS curve for case 1 (IS_1) must lie everywhere to the right of the IS curve for case 0 (IS_0).

The effect of alternative aggregate expenditure functions on equilibrium real income and nominal interest rate is found by combining the alternative IS curves with the LM curve. Since the money market is unaffected by the factors altering the aggregate expenditure function, the LM curve is the same for either case. Figure 12.12 shows that Case 1 implies higher equilibrium values of both real income and the nominal interest rate than Case 0. The degree to which each changes reflects the magnitude of the shift in the IS curve and the slopes of both the IS and LM curves.

Summary of the Effects of Shifts in the Income-Expenditures Sector

Shifts in any of the functions determining the components of aggregate expenditures will alter the aggregate expenditure function. Keynesian economists believe that investment demand is subject to large shifts as a result of the state of expectations. Other important shifts occur because of fiscal policy: changes in government expenditures and in the consumption function due to tax changes. Higher levels of investor optimism and government expenditures

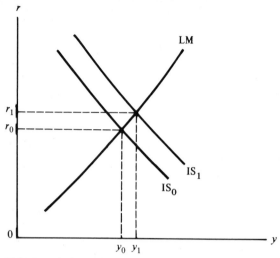

FIGURE 12.12 Implications of alternative IS curves for equilibrium real incomes and nominal interest rates. IS_1 lies to the right of and above IS_0 because the aggregate expenditure function for case 1 is greater than it is for case 0. Since the LM curve is positively sloped, the equilibrium point (y_1, r_1) for case 1 lies above and to the right of the equilibrium point (y_0, r_0) for case 0. For a given slope of the IS curves and horizontal distance between them, the flatter (more nearly horizontal) the LM curve, the greater will be the difference in real income and the less will be the difference in interest rates. For a given slope of the LM curve and a given horizontal distance between the IS curves, the flatter (more nearly horizontal) the IS curve, the less will be the differences in real income and the less will be the difference in nominal interest rates. For given slopes of the IS and LM curves, the greater the horizontal distance between the IS curves, the greater will be the differences in both real income and nominal interest rates. (See exercises 5, 6, and 7 for the proofs of these three propositions.)

or lower levels of taxes are associated with higher aggregate expenditure functions. A higher aggregate expenditure function shifts the IS curve to the right and thereby increases equilibrium real income and nominal interest rate.

12.3 EFFECTS OF SHIFTS IN THE MONETARY SECTOR
The Effects of Monetary Policy

Monetary policy is characterized by the choice of the real money supply $\bar{m}$. Alternative monetary policies can be represented by the alternative money supply functions

$$m^s = \bar{m}_0 \qquad\qquad\qquad\qquad\qquad\qquad [12.12]$$

$$m^s = \bar{m}_1 \qquad\qquad\qquad\qquad\qquad\qquad [12.13]$$

Assume that $\bar{m}_1$ is greater than $\bar{m}_0$.

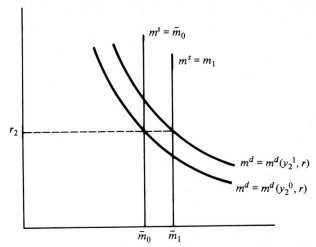

$m^s = \bar{m}_0$

$m^s = m_1$

r_2

$m^d = m^d(y_2{}^1, r)$

$m^d = m^d(y_2{}^0, r)$

$\bar{m}_0 \quad \bar{m}_1$

FIGURE 12.13 The effects of alternative monetary policies on the position of the LM curve. Consider any nominal interest rate r_2. There will be some real income $y_2{}^0$ for which real money demand $m^d(y_2{}^0, r_2)$ equals real money supply at $\bar{m}_0$. This is a point on the LM_0 curve corresponding to real money supply $\bar{m}_0$. There will also be some larger real income $y_2{}^1$ at which real money demand $m^d(y_2{}^1, r_2)$ equals money supply at $\bar{m}_1$. This is a point on the LM_1 curve corresponding to real money supply $\bar{m}_1$. So the LM curves for higher real money supplies lie to the right of the LM curves for lower real money supplies. If the liquidity trap exists, r_2 would have to be chosen greater than or equal to the minimum nominal interest rate $r^{\min}$. At $r^{\min}$, there would be a range of lower income levels at which LM_0 and LM_1 coincided.

The effects of the alternative monetary policies on the position of the LM curve are analyzed in Fig. 12.13. For a given nominal interest rate higher levels of real income must be associated with a money supply of $\bar{m}_1$ than with $\bar{m}_0$ if the money market is to be in equilibrium.[8] So the LM curve LM_1 for money supply $\bar{m}_1$ lies to the right of the LM curve LM_0 for money supply $\bar{m}_0$. The change in money supply has no direct effect on the aggregate expenditure function in the Keynesian model; therefore the IS curve is unchanged. Figure 12.14 shows that higher money supplies imply higher levels of real income and lower interest rates.

If, however, the IS curve were to intersect LM_0 in a horizontal portion corresponding to the liquidity trap, it would intersect LM_1 at the same point as seen in Fig. 12.15. This special case was important—if not dominant—in Keynesian thought as a working approximation until well into the 1960s. If real money demand were horizontal—or nearly so—in the relevant range, monetary policy would be impotent to increase real income. Desired fluidity, which played such an important role in the analysis of Parts 2 and 3, would

---

[8] An exception would be in the instance of the liquidity trap, in which case money demand and supply can be equal for different money supplies and the same real income and interest rate.

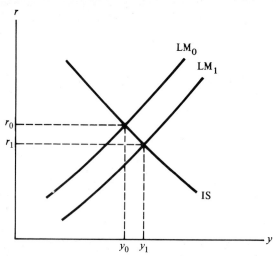

FIGURE 12.14   Effects of alternative monetary policies on real income and the nominal interest rate. A real money supply of $\bar{m}_0$ is associated with LM_0. A higher real money supply $\bar{m}_1$ would be associated with some LM curve LM_1, to the right of LM_0. The equilibrium points are (y_0, r_0) for $\bar{m}_0$ and (y_1, r_1) for $\bar{m}_1$. Consequently, higher money supplies correspond to higher levels of real income and lower levels of interest rates.

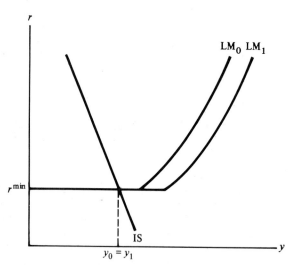

FIGURE 12.15   Effects of alternative monetary policies in the liquidity trap region. If the IS curve and LM_0 intersect in the horizontal or liquidity trap region, an increase in money supply from $\bar{m}_0$ to $\bar{m}_1$ would not alter either real income or the interest rate. This is true because the horizontal portion of LM_1 would include the entire horizontal portion of LM_0.

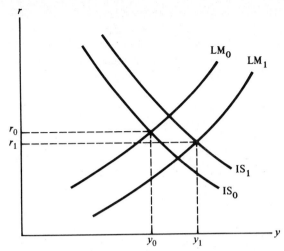

FIGURE 12.16 Effect of financing increased government expenditure by money creation. Increased government expenditure shifts the IS curve to the right from IS_0 to IS_1. Increased money supply shifts the LM curve to the right from LM_0 to LM_1. Real income must be increased from y_0 to y_1. Whether the equilibrium nominal interest rate increases or decreases is uncertain, depending on the precise shifts in the IS and LM curves.

adjust passively to offset any increases in the real money supply. Real income would be whatever equated desired aggregate expenditures and income at the fixed nominal interest rate r^{min}.

Effects of Shifts in the Money Demand Function

Instability in the money demand function has not been important in Keynesian analysis. A hypothetical decrease in the real money demand for any given combination of real income and nominal interest rate would be equivalent to an increase in the real money supply, however. The LM curve would shift to the right, real income would rise, and interest rates would fall. An increase in real money demand would have opposite effects.

Financing Increased Government Expenditures by Money Creation

It is normally assumed that changes in government expenditures, taxes, or (base) money creation are offset by changes in borrowing. Suppose a $10 billion increase in government spending over a short period were financed instead by $10 billion of base money. If the money multiplier were 2.5, this would cause a $25 billion increase in the money supply.

If the IS curve, in the absence of the spending increase, were IS_0, the new IS curve, IS_1, would lie to the right of IS_0. Similarly, the new LM curve, LM_1, would lie to the right of the LM curve, LM_0, which would otherwise exist. Figure 12.16 demonstrates that real income is unambiguously increased by the higher levels of government spending and money creation. Whether the nominal interest rate increases or decreases is uncertain, depending on the size of the slopes and shifts in the IS and LM curves.

The possible number of combinations of different sources of shifts in the IS and LM curves is large and need not be worked through here. The solutions always follow the same pattern: First determine the shifts, if any, in the IS and LM curves and then compare the two equilibria.

□ **SUMMARY**

The IS-LM model is used to find the values of real income and the nominal interest rate at which the goods market and the money market are simultaneously in equilibrium. This is done by graphing in the same yr plane the IS and LM curves. The negatively sloped IS curve gives all combinations of real income and the nominal interest rate for which desired expenditures equal real income. The positively sloped LM curve gives all combinations of real income and the nominal interest rate for which real money demand equals the amount supplied. Their intersection is the unique point at which both the goods market and the money market are in equilibrium. Any factor tending to increase aggregate expenditures for each combination of real income and the nominal interest rate tends to shift the IS curve to the right. The most important of these factors, from the Keynesian point of view, are increases in investor optimism, increases in government expenditure, and decreases in taxes. Any factor shifting the IS curve to the right tends to increase both real income and the nominal interest rate. Just the opposite is true for decreases in investor optimism or government spending and increases in taxes. Increases in the real money supply shift the LM curve to the right. Such a shift increases real income and decreases the nominal interest rate. In the special case of the liquidity trap, increases in the real money supply can leave real income and the nominal interest rate unchanged. Decreases in the money supply decrease real income and increase the nominal interest rate, except perhaps for the case of the liquidity trap. Shifts in various functions or policy variables may be combined to achieve offsetting or reinforcing effects.

□ **QUESTIONS AND EXERCISES**

*1 (a) In Chap. 11, it was asserted that either the assumption of a given price level or some substitute was required for the logical completeness of the Keynesian model. Suppose that this assumption was abandoned so that Fed control over the nominal money supply was not equivalent to control over the real money supply. Then [12.4] would be replaced with $M^s = \overline{M}$. Could the model be solved for a unique solution? Why?

(b) Suppose that the equation $m^s = M^s/P$ is added also. Can the model be solved for a unique solution? Why? Can the model be solved for real income as a function of the price level? Why? What would such a functional relationship between real income and the price level be called in the terminology of Chap. 7?

2 (a) Suppose that the aggregate expenditure function is

$$ax = 1000 + \overline{g} - 0.4\overline{t} + 0.6y - 100r$$

where ax, $\overline{g}$, $\overline{t}$, and y are in R\$ billions per annum and r is in percentage points per annum. If $\overline{g} = $R\$105 billion per annum and $\overline{t} = $R\$100 billion per annum, complete this table of points on the IS curve:

r	1%	2%	3%	4%	5%
y					

(b) Use the points in the table to draw an IS curve on graph paper.

3 Why is the IS curve flatter, other things being equal, if given changes in the nominal interest rate cause larger changes in investment demand? (*Hint:* An example may help. Substitute

$$ax = 1250 + \overline{g} - 0.4\overline{t} + 0.6y - 200r$$

for the aggregate expenditure function of question 2. Compare the implied IS curves.)

*4 (a) Show the effects of a decline in investor optimism on real income and the nominal interest rate.

(b) What would happen to the nominal interest rate if monetary policy could be and was used to offset the effect on real income? What about the use of fiscal policy?

5 Suppose a \$10 billion increase in real government spending would shift the IS curve to the right by \$20 billion. Compare the effects on real income and the nominal interest rate according to whether the LM curve is flat or steep. What is the common sense reason for these differences?

6 The same increase in government spending considered in question 5 is assumed. Compare the effects on real income and the nominal interest rate according to whether the IS curve is flat or steep. What is the common-sense reason for these differences?

7 The \$10 billion increase in government spending of problem 5 and a \$20 billion increase are both being considered. Compare the effects on real income and the nominal interest rate of the two policy changes. What is the common-sense reason for these differences?

8 Along the lines of Fig. 12.13, derive the effects of alternative real money supplies on the LM curve with a liquidity trap portion.

9 Show that a decrease in money demand for any given level of real income and the nominal interest rate would shift the LM curve to the right.

*10 In a *strict* comparative statics model, it makes no sense to talk about a $10 billion increase in real base money financing a $10 billion increase in the rate of government expenditure. Why? Why might it be permissible to consider changes in the stock of money over the "short period" even though the effects of investment on capital are neglected as trivial?

☐ **REFERENCES FOR FURTHER READING**

Dernburg, Thomas F., and Duncan M. McDougall: *Macroeconomics*, 4th ed., New York: McGraw-Hill, 1972. [This is one of the most popular, purely Keynesian textbooks.]

Hicks, John R.: Mr. Keynes and the "Classics"; A Suggested Interpretation, *Econometrica*, **5:** 147–159, Apr. 1937.

Keynes, John Maynard: *The General Theory of Employment, Interest, and Money*, New York: Harcourt, Brace, 1936.

Smith, Warren L.: A Graphical Exposition of the Complete Keynesian System, *Southern Economic Journal*, **23:** 115–125, Oct. 1956.

Comparison of the Keynesian and Dynamic Models

13.1 INTRODUCTION

The basic outlines of the two major approaches to macroeconomics have been presented in the previous seven chapters. Part 2 presented the comparative static and dynamic analysis of full-employment equilibrium. Part 3 was concerned with the modern quantity theory or dynamic model of temporary departures from this equilibrium due to shocks to the growth rates of the nominal money supply and fluidity. Chapters 11 and 12 were devoted to an exposition of the income-expenditures or Keynesian model of comparative statics.

There are two broad classes of differences between the dynamic and Keynesian models. One group of differences concerns the individual Keynesian building blocks. There are some substantial differences in views on both the proper variables to include in the basic behavioral relations and on the empirical magnitudes of the effects of changes in certain arguments of these behavioral functions. These differences need not cause the rejection of the basic IS-LM model however, but merely its emendation. More important differences arise over the underlying assumptions and conceptions of the economy. If one is interested in the effects of macroeconomic shocks, not just this quarter and perhaps the next but over several years, effects which are initially negligible become crucial. The different perspectives imply that different models are more useful for discussing particular issues and suggesting interesting new questions. A very elaborate modified IS-LM analysis which takes account of past values in determining present values could doubtless be used to trace out the growth paths over time of the dynamic model. However, like the speech of a talking dog, the wonder is not that it is done so well but that it can be done at all.

At the heart of the difference between Keynesian and monetarist or dynamic economists is a difference in viewpoint on the basic strength of equilibrating forces of the economy. A dynamic economist emphasizes the tendency of the economy to return to full-employment equilibrium if it has been displaced and to stay there if it has not been disturbed by monetary or fiscal shocks. A Keynesian economist believes these equilibrating forces are so weak as to be negligible. If the economy does not tend to return to full-employment equilibrium over time, it is acceptable to use a model which ends the analysis with the economy away from full employment. This difference in pre-conceptions explains why a dynamic economist might ask questions—and find answers—which would never occur to a Keynesian economist.

The next section discusses the debate about the basic Keynesian building blocks. The issues here can be generally expressed within the IS-LM framework. The more important differences concerning the basic models are then considered in Sec. 13.3.

13.2 DIFFERENCES CONCERNING THE INDIVIDUAL KEYNESIAN BUILDING BLOCKS

The Debate about the Marginal Propensity to Consume

The main problem with the simple Keynesian consumption function is that it squares relatively poorly with the data. Keynes' "fundamental psychological law" explains only part of the actual changes in consumer expenditures. The debate over the consumption function has revolved around two issues: the size of the marginal propensity to consume and the impact of real money balances on consumption. The former is discussed here and the latter below.

Early Keynesians thought the marginal propensity to consume (MPC) was quite high—well over 0.5 and in the range of 0.6 or 0.7. This view arose from fitting a simple linear consumption function to the available national income accounts data from 1929 up to the beginning of World War II. Figure 13.1 shows the data for real consumer expenditures c and real disposable personal income dpy[1] for 1929 through 1941. A typical consumption function, as estimated from these data, is

$$c = 31.4 + 0.73dpy \qquad [13.1]$$

This consumption function is the straight line in Fig. 13.1.

As more data became available both back into the nineteenth century and in the post-World War II era, it was apparent that the simple linear consumption function was an inadequate description of consumer expenditures over time. A more accurate description would be $c = 0.9dpy$. This disparity between the long-period time series and the data for the 1930s was shown to reflect statistical biases caused by the omission of wealth or permanent income from the consumption function.[2] The estimated coefficient of current income is an

---

[1] Disposable personal income measures only cash income receipts of individuals and not accrued income such as undistributed corporate profits. It was nevertheless widely used until recently in estimating consumption functions.

[2] Milton Friedman, *A Theory of the Consumption Function*, Princeton: Princeton University Press for NBER, 1957; and Franco Modigliani and Richard Brumberg, Utility Analysis and the Consumption Function: An Interpretation of Cross-Section Data, in Kenneth K. Kurihara (ed.), *Post-Keynesian Economics*, New Brunswick: Rutgers University Press, 1954.

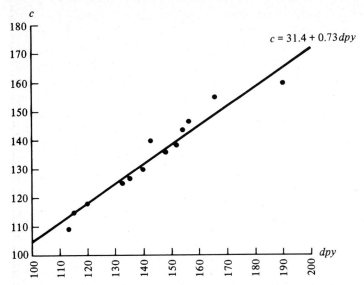

FIGURE 13.1   Real consumer expenditures and real disposable personal income, 1929–1941. The dots represent the values of real consumer expenditures and real disposable personal income for the 13 years 1929–1941. The linear Keynesian consumption function fitted to this data is shown by the solid line $c = 31.4 + 0.73dpy$. Because variations in measured dpy were partly due to variations in transitory income, and because changes in transitory income have smaller effects on consumer expenditures than change in permanent income, the estimated MPC is less than the long-run value of 0.9. It is, however, greater than the short-run value of 0.3 or 0.4. Both c and dpy are measured in billions of 1958 dollars. *Data source:* U.S. Bureau of Economic Analysis, *Long Term Economic Growth, 1860–1970*, Washington: GPO, 1973, pp. 184, 188.

average of the coefficients of permanent income (0.9) and transitory income (0.3 or 0.4). This explanation was questioned by some Keynesians in a series of papers. The papers were shown by Darby to suffer from a statistical bias also.[3]

The inclusion of permanent income in the consumption function poses no basic difficulty for the Keynesian model. Permanent income—as a measure of wealth—can be taken as fixed for the short period of analysis so that variations in current income correspond to variations in transitory income. There will be some effect of income during the current period on future consumption—so that a dynamic element is introduced—but this is not of great concern for most problems.[4]

---

[3] Michael R. Darby, The Permanent Income Theory of Consumption—A Restatement, *Quarterly Journal of Economics*, **88**: 228–250, May 1974.
[4] Further discussion of the consumption function is found in Sec. 8.3.

The fact that the ratio of consumer expenditures to income does not decline over time is fatal to one of the predictions of early Keynesians. They argued, following Keynes, that saving would become a larger and larger fraction of income as income rose. The interest rate would have to decline progressively to increase investment sufficiently to maintain full employment. Eventually, the interest rate could fall no further because of the liquidity trap and full employment could no longer be maintained. This *secular stagnation thesis* was the basis of Keynesian predictions of worsened post-World War II depression. The fault lay, of course, in confusing the short-period and long-run consumption functions.

In terms of short-period analysis, the effect of a lower MPC is to reduce the slope of the aggregate expenditure function in the *y-ax* plane. This happens because a R\$1 increase in real income induces a smaller increase in consumer expenditures. The lower the slope of the aggregate expenditure function, the less does a given shift in the function shift the IS curve, as shown in Fig. 13.2. Conversely, the IS curve is also steeper, a condition which reduces the effects on real income of monetary shocks. The reduced estimate of the MPC thus increases the estimated stability of the economy in response to various macroeconomic shocks. But the basic structure of the Keynesian IS-LM model is unchanged in the short period.

Real Money Balances in the Consumption Function

The most basic criticism of the Keynesian building blocks concerns the exclusion of real money balances from the consumption function. It is implausible and inconsistent with the evidence that the size of real money balances, given permanent and transitory income, should not affect consumer expenditures. The increase in consumer expenditures due to an increase in real money balances is called the *real balance effect*.[5]

---

[5] There are two main reasons to expect real money balances to affect real consumer expenditures in this way. The traditional view is that real money balances are a component of wealth which does not yield a stream of market income and so is excluded from such measures of wealth as permanent income. Consumer expenditures are a function of this total wealth. The balance-sheet view observes that many items of consumer expenditure are durable and semidurable goods which are substitutes for money in the allocation of wealth of a household. Though the implicit yields on automobiles, refrigerators, and the like are not recorded in any newspaper, they too vary as individuals shift out of real money and into real goods. (See pages 145 and 147 for further discussion.) This approach was suggested by Milton Friedman and Anna Schwartz and pursued by Karl Brunner and Alan Meltzer in numerous articles. The earliest discussions of the traditional real balance effect were by Gottfried Haberler, *Prosperity and Depression*, 2d ed., Geneva: League of Nations, 1939; and Arthur C. Pigou, The Classical Stationary State, *Economic Journal*, **53**: 343–351, Dec. 1943. The theoretical implications were worked out in detail by Don Patinkin, *Money, Interest, and Prices*, Evanston: Row, Peterson & Company, 1956. Some recent empirical estimates of the effect of real money balances on consumer expenditures are in Michael R. Darby, Postwar U.S. Consumption, Consumer Expenditures, and Saving, *American Economic Review*, **65**: 217–222, May 1975. The estimates there suggest that—for given values of permanent income, transitory income, and the stock of consumers' durables—an R\$1 billion increase in real money balances will cause an increase in real consumer expenditures of some R\$650 millions to R\$800 million per annum.

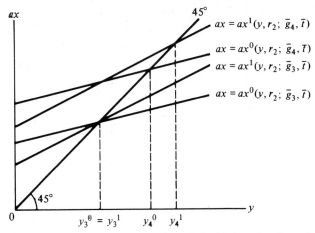

FIGURE 13.2 Shifts in and the slope of the IS curve for alternative slopes of the aggregate expenditure function. The two aggregate expenditure functions $ax = ax^0(y, r; \bar{g}, \bar{t})$ and $ax = ax^1(y, r; \bar{g}, \bar{t})$ differ only in their slope. For purposes of comparison, it is assumed that for r_2, $\bar{g}_3$, and $\bar{t}$, equilibrium real income is the same for both functions at $y_3{}^0 = y_3{}^1$. Suppose that real government expenditures were instead $\bar{g}_4$, which is greater than $\bar{g}_3$. This would shift the aggregate expenditure curves up vertically by $\bar{g}_4 - \bar{g}_3$. Note that the new equilibrium real income for case 0, $y_4{}^0$, is less than $y_4{}^1$ for case 1. Hence, the lower the slope of the aggregate expenditure function the smaller is the change in the equilibrium real income. The conclusion is that any shock which shifts the aggregate expenditure function causes a smaller shift in the IS curve if the slope of the aggregate expenditure function is low than that caused if the slope were high. This same diagram can be used to show that the lower the slope of the aggregate expenditure function, the steeper is the IS curve. If the upward shift in the aggregate expenditure function occurred because the interest rate was reduced from r_2 to r_4 rather than because of higher government expenditures, $(y_3{}^0, r_2)$ and $(y_4{}^0, r_4)$ would be points on the IS curve for case 0 and $(y_3{}^1, r_2)$ and $(y_4{}^1, r_4)$ would be points on the IS curve for case 1. Thus, a larger change in income occurs for a given interest rate change if the slope of the aggregate expenditure curve is higher. This means that the IS curve is steeper if the slope of the aggregate expenditure curve is low than it is if the slope is high.

This is a basic criticism of the structure of the IS-LM model. It implies that changes in monetary policy affect not only the LM curve but also the IS curve. If increases in real money balances in fact lead people to increase real consumer expenditures at a given level of real income and the nominal interest rate, they cause an upward shift in the aggregate expenditure function and hence a shift to the right in the IS curve. The effects on real income and the nominal interest rate of an increase in the real money supply, including the direct effect on consumer expenditures, are illustrated in Fig. 13.3. The effect

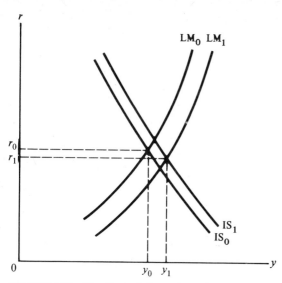

FIGURE 13.3 The effects of alternative real money supplies in the presence of direct effects on consumer expenditures. The real money supply is higher in case 1 than it is in case 0. The LM curve for case 1 (LM_1) lies to the right of the LM curve for case 0 (LM_0) for the usual reasons. The IS curve for case 1 (IS_1) also lies to the right of the IS curve for case 0 (IS_0). This is true because increased real money balances shift the aggregate expenditure function upward. Equilibrium real income y_1 is higher in case 1 than equilibrium real income y_0 in case 0. The effect on the nominal interest rate is ambiguous, depending on the relative size of the shifts in the IS and LM curves. In the case illustrated for example, the equilibrium nominal interest rate declines with increased real money balances. If the shift in the IS curve exceeded the shift in the LM curve, however, the nominal interest rate would rise.

on real income is reinforced by the shift in the IS curve, so that monetary policy is stronger than would otherwise be the case. The effects on nominal interest rates become ambiguous, however, since r rises or falls as the IS curve shifts more or less than the LM curve.

These ambiguous results for nominal interest rates are not surprising. Clear results in comparative statics usually occur only when changes in conditions affect only one of the two separate groups of determinants. Since changes in the real money supply affect both the money market and the goods market, offsetting effects can occur.

Allowance for the real balance effect on consumer expenditures complicates the short-period IS-LM model but does not make it unusable. The key implications concern the operation of the model over time, as will be seen in Sec. 13.3.

The Controversy over Investment Demand

Undoubtedly, over the course of a business cycle, real investment displays the greatest relative fluctuation of any expenditure component. There is considerable controversy over whether this fluctuation is basically a cause or an effect of the business cycle.

The Keynesian position is that investment demand is very unstable, shifting with ephemeral waves of optimism and pessimism among investors. If monetarists can be caricatured to show them viewing the business cycle as of mainly monetary origin—largely a dance of the dollar[6]—then Keynesians can justly be said to attribute the business cycle to shifts in investment demand—largely a dance of investment. The hypothesis of an unstable investment demand function is combined with a relatively small interest elasticity of investment demand.

The modern quantity theorists interpret the fluctuations in investment quite differently. To them, the cyclical variations in investment are primarily movements along a stable, interest-elastic, investment demand function. Further, changes in investor psychology do not just happen, but reflect changes in objective conditions in the economy. Consequently, such shifts in the investment function as do occur are not random disturbances but one of the means by which the true disturbances—such as a change in the growth rate of the nominal money supply—affect the economy. For example, a reduction in the growth rate of the nominal money supply might cause investors to expect accurately that a recession would occur and that the rate of inflation would decrease. This would indeed reduce the current level of investment for a given nominal interest rate and real income, but this shift is in no way a random cause of business fluctuations.

The difference in views about the relative importance of shifts in the investment demand function is illustrated in Fig. 13.4. Small circles represent two hypothetically observed levels of real investment and the nominal interest rate for a given level of real income, y_0. The monetarist position would be that these points each lie on a relatively stable investment demand function: $i = i^1(r, y_0)$. Keynesians would argue that such a small reduction in the nominal interest rate could not cause such a large increase in investment. So the two points must be on two different investment demand functions: $i = i^2(r, y_0)$ and $i = i^3(r, y_0)$. These investment demand curves are supposed to be steeper—less interest elastic—and different because of different states of expectations.

The state of empirical research in the field of investment is at best unsettled.[7]

---

[6] See Irving Fisher, The Business Cycle Largely a "Dance of the Dollar," *Journal of the American Statistical Association*, **18:** 1024–1028, Dec. 1923.

[7] Complicated investment demand functions have been tried with limited success. The literature has been recently reviewed by Dale W. Jorgenson, Econometric Studies of Investment Behavior: A Survey, *Journal of Economic Literature*, **9:** 1111–1147, Dec. 1971. A rather different view of the state of the literature is presented by Robert Eisner, Econometric Studies of Investment Behavior: A Comment, *Economic Inquiry*, **12:** 91–104, Mar. 1974.

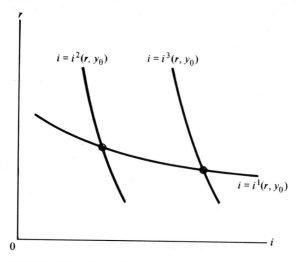

FIGURE 13.4 Alternative explanations of observed fluctuations in real investment. The two small circles represent hypothetically observed combinations of real investment and the nominal interest rate for a given real income y_0. These points could both lie on the same flat (highly interest-elastic) investment demand function $i = i^1$ (r, y_0) or on two steeper (less interest-elastic) investment demand functions $i = i^2(r, y_0)$ and $i = i^3(r, y_0)$. Keynesians tend to attribute changes in real investment to such shifts in the investment demand function, while monetarists are more likely to view the changes as movements along a stable, flatter investment demand function.

The basic question—Are fluctuations in investment an important cause or effect of business fluctuations?—has not yet been answered satisfactorily. Perhaps the best evidence on this question is that no significant business fluctuations have been observed in periods in which nominal money-supply growth has been constant. There are three alternative explanations of this fact: (1) Fluctuations in investor optimism are an important source of business fluctuations, but by chance there were no fluctuations during all these periods. (2) Fluctuations in investor optimism have no significant effect on investment demand, which is highly interest elastic. (3) Fluctuations in investor optimism have significant effects on investment demand; however, these fluctuations in optimism do not occur spontaneously but rather as a result of other macroeconomic shocks.

The related questions of the interest elasticity of the investment demand function and the magnitude of shifts in this function are important for the analysis of macroeconomic policy. On the one hand, if investment demand

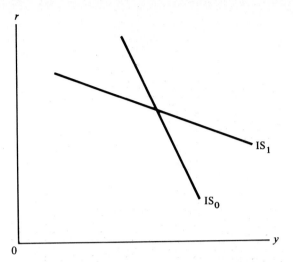

FIGURE 13.5 Effect of alternative interest elasticities of investment demand on the slope of the IS curve. The more elastic the investment demand function with respect to the nominal interest rate, other things being equal, the flatter is the IS curve. This is true because a given change in the nominal interest rate will cause a greater change in the value of the aggregate expenditure function the more interest elastic is investment demand. Thus, IS_0 is drawn according to the Keynesian view of small interest elasticity and IS_1 represents the monetarist position of a larger interest elasticity of investment demand.

is not very elastic with respect to the nominal interest rate, large changes in r will shift the aggregate expenditure curve up only slightly in the *y-ax* plane. Hence, smaller interest elasticities of investment demand are associated with smaller changes in the level of real income required for goods market equilibrium if there is a given increase in the nominal interest rate. This means that the IS curve is steeper as the interest elasticity of investment demand becomes smaller, as illustrated in Fig. 13.5. Later on, this will be seen to indicate that monetary sector shocks have a smaller effect on equilibrium real income and that income-expenditures sector shocks have a greater effect on real income than would be the case if the IS curves were less steep. Whether or not there are significant spontaneous shifts in investment demand is the key to whether or not government policy to offset these shifts might be desirable. If there are significant induced shifts in investment demand from other macroeconomic shocks, the model should be reformulated to take these influences into account.

The Money Demand Function

A long-standing dispute between Keynesians and monetarists has been about the interest elasticity of the demand for real money. Some Keynesians have viewed this as the principal difference of views, but this is not really the case, as will be obvious in Sec. 13.3. The original positions can be characterized as high or infinite interest elasticity of demand on the Keynesian side and low or zero interest elasticity of demand on the monetarist side.

The Keynesian position particularly emphasized the speculative motive for holding money balances as well as the incentive provided by the interest rate for economizing on money balances through closer synchronization of receipts and expenditures of money.

The theoretical basis for the speculative demand for money has been considerably weakened by subsequent analysis. Firmly held interest-rate expectations were seen to be theoretically invalid and were replaced with uncertainty. Even the uncertainty view does not imply the "speculative" effects of a decrease in the nominal interest rate if the variability of the interest rate is proportional to the level of the rate. In any case, the speculative motive applies to holdings of long-term versus short-term bonds—not money. Some sense can be made of the speculative effect by attributing it to fluctuations in the short-term interest rate which are only slightly reflected in movements of the long-term interest rate.

The theoretical basis of the interest elasticity of the demand for money is on sounder ground. The most important challenge here is to the view that the nominal interest rate on bank deposits is zero. If banks effectively pay interest on deposits,[8] then it is incorrect to view even the short-term nominal interest rate as the cost of holding money instead of bonds. A rise in short-term interest rates will be matched in whole or part by a rise in implicit interest rates on deposits so that the net change in the cost of holding money is trivial.

The empirical evidence is mixed. Most estimates of the demand for money have placed the interest elasticity of the demand for money between -1 and -0.1. These estimates may be subject to a statistical bias, however. A somewhat different result of essentially no interest elasticity arises in studies which (1) do not require that real money supply and demand be equated within a single quarter, and (2) permit permanent and transitory income to enter with different weights, as with consumer expenditures. These studies find no effect of the general level of interest rates.[9] Consequently, even the moderate interest elasticities estimated in earlier studies of the demand for money may reflect the correlation of the cyclical pattern of interest rates and these omitted

---

[8] See the discussion and references on pages 43–44.

[9] Models with separate variables for short-term interest rates and interest rates on money obtain significant but largely offsetting effects. References are to Sam Peltzman, The Structure of the Money-Expenditures Relationship, *American Economic Review*, **59**: 129–137, Mar. 1969; and Michael R. Darby, The Allocation of Transitory Income Among Consumers' Assets, *American Economic Review*, **62**: 928–941, Dec. 1972.

factors. The possibility that equilibrium in the money—and goods—market may not be achieved within the short period directly challenges the use of a comparative statics model and will be considered further in Sec. 13.3.

It should be observed that (M_1) fluidity declined by 59.9 percent from the end of 1946 to the end of 1974. During the same period, nominal interest rates on 3-month Treasury bills rose by 1836.8 percent and on long-term government bonds by 216.4 percent. Even if no allowance is made for the growth of money substitutes discussed in this context on page 248, there is not much room left for a large interest elasticity of the demand for real money.[10]

Let us recall, from Chap. 12, that for less interest-elastic money demand functions, the LM curve is steeper, since larger increases in the nominal interest rate would be required to offset the effect on money demand of a given increase in real income. A steeper LM curve will be seen to indicate that monetary sector shocks have a larger effect on equilibrium real income and that income-expenditures sector shocks have a smaller effect on real income than would be the case if the LM curve was less steep.

At this point, the discussion in Chap. 8 on the possible increase in the real demand for money caused by a tax reduction is apropos. The problem arises because total income is not clearly superior to private income in the determination of the demand for money. Indeed, private income would be more closely related to the wealth constraint on money holdings and perhaps to transactions to be made by private holders of real money. The money demand function could be rewritten as an increasing function of both total and private income

$$m^d = m^d(y, y - \bar{t}, r) \qquad\qquad [13.2]$$

This means that a tax reduction increases private income and therefore the demand for money. This shifts the LM curve to the left. A shift to the left in the LM curve and a shift to the right in the IS curve leave the effect on real income ambiguous, although the nominal interest rate must increase.[11] As with the real balance effect, this modification is not fatal to the IS-LM model. It does complicate it however.

13.3 COMPARISON OF THE COMPLETE MODELS
Differences concerning the Empirical Magnitudes within the IS-LM Model

The differences discussed in the previous section are primarily concerned with empirical magnitudes which define the precise nature of the IS and LM curves and how shocks shift them.

---

[10] Note that $-0.599/18.368 = -0.03$ and $-0.599/2.164 = -0.28$.
[11] See question 3 at the end of this chapter. A similar analysis is made by James M. Holmes and David J. Smyth, The Specification of the Demand for Money and the Tax Multiplier, *Journal of Political Economy,* **80:** 179–185, Jan./Feb. 1972.

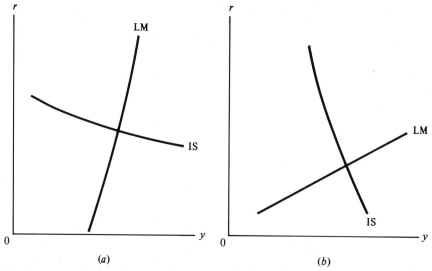

FIGURE 13.6   The slopes of the IS and LM curves from the monetarist and Keynesian viewpoint.
Monetarists generally suppose that the IS curve is flatter and the LM curve is steeper as in (*a*) than the Keynesian visualization of these curves (*b*). This distinction cannot always be made, however, and is not necessary to the positions taken. In the "monetarist" (*a*) a given horizontal shift in the LM curve will have a greater effect on real income than in the Keynesian (*b*). A given horizontal shift in the IS curve will have the greatest effect on real income in the Keynesian (*b*).

Figure 13.6 shows the standard comparison between the monetarist position (*a*) and the Keynesian position (*b*). The steeper slope of the monetarist LM curve reflects the monetarist view that money demand is less interest elastic than supposed by most of the economists who still consider themselves Keynesians. The slope of the monetarist IS curve is usually drawn to be less steep than that of the Keynesian IS curve. There is much more overlap here, however. Keynesians are likely to suppose that the interest elasticity of investment demand is less than the monetarists would expect.[12] This value would make for a steeper IS curve, of course. Conversely, monetarists generally suppose that there is a smaller slope of the aggregate expenditure curve and this notion also would make for a steeper IS curve, other things being equal.

Given the relative slopes of the IS and LM curves in panels (*a*) and (*b*), the following conclusions can be drawn. (1) A given horizontal shift in the IS

---

[12] Some of the early American followers of Keynes suggested that changes in the interest rate had essentially no effect on investment so that the IS curve was vertical! There are remaining influences of this view in Keynesian thought, but such naiveté is an unfair characterization of Keynesians as a whole.

curve has a larger effect on equilibrium real income in the Keynesian case than in the monetarist case. (2) A given horizontal shift in the LM curve has a larger effect on equilibrium real income in the monetarist case than in the Keynesian case.

This distinction is probably valid on average, but there is much overlap in the views of those who consider themselves monetarists or Keynesians; so the distinction is by no means essential.

A more basic disagreement is on the importance of shifts in the IS curve caused by spontaneous shifts in the investment demand function. Keynesian economists believe that large shifts in the IS curve do occur from time to time and are a significant cause of business fluctuations. Monetarists do not believe that this is true and await evidence to the contrary. This difference refers not to the nature of the model but to the nature of the real world which it is used to describe. The Keynesian model highlights the effects of shifts in the component functions of aggregate expenditures, but the question is whether there is much to highlight.

Put another way, monetarists observe the close relationship between money and income which seems to be able to explain—with occasional help from major fiscal or international shocks—essentially all the observed variation in income. Thus, when told that income fluctuations are at times largely caused by random shocks in this or that behavioral relationship, they are more likely to suspect that the behavioral relationship is not completely specified and that omitted variables are causing the apparent random "errors" in the estimated equation. After all, when there is nothing to explain, it is the explanations that require explaining.[13]

There are also differences concerning the shifts in the IS and LM curves which would be associated with a given shift in one of the basic functions. For example, Keynesians argue that a change in the money supply will shift only the LM curve; monetarists point out that the real balance effect causes the IS curve to shift also. Also, the less steep slope of the monetarist version of the aggregate expenditures curve suggests that a given shift in government expenditures or investment demand will cause a smaller shift in the IS curve than would occur if the slope were steeper.

These differences of view can be understood and accepted within the underlying assumptions and basic framework of the IS-LM model. In fact, many monetarist economists make use of such a modified IS-LM analysis for studying particular short-run problems. Important though these differences are, they do not form the basis for the rejection of the IS-LM model in favor of a dynamic model such as that presented in Parts 2 and 3. The reasons for that rejection can be examined now, however.

---

[13] This situation is exemplified by the wife who demands to know exactly why her husband suddenly brings home flowers for "no reason."

Differences about Equilibrating Forces

The dynamic model is based on the view that there is a full-employment, steady-state equilibrium and that there are powerful forces in the economy which tend to move the economy toward that equilibrium. At any moment of time the economy may move away from that equilibrium under the force of an economic shock, but over a period of time the tendency toward equilibrium will be dominant.

The Keynesian view of equilibrium is different. The short-period equilibrium is achieved quickly in response to any macroeconomic shock. Once an equilibrium is attained, the economy will stay in it unless some other shock happens to occur. If such an equilibrium, called an *underemployment equilibrium*, involves abnormally high levels of unemployed resources, that is just the way things are. According to the strictest Keynesian view, there is no reason for income-expenditures sector shocks to tend to cancel out over time, but they can simply accumulate one way or another according to the luck of the draw.

These are very different views of the way the world operates. If the equilibrating forces in the dynamic model were so weak as to take decades to operate, there would not be a substantial difference in practice, but this is not what is claimed. The effects of a single macroeconomic shock would not be expected to cause real income and employment to differ substantially from their full-employment equilibrium levels for more than 3 or 4 years at most. This period of adjustment cannot be approximated by either a quarter of a year or forever.

The hypothesized equilibrating forces differ in two major ways: (1) the importance of price changes and (2) the existence of inventory or search behavior.

In the Keynesian model, the real quantity of money—however large relative to income—has no effect whatsoever on desired aggregate expenditures. Neglecting the real balance effect is certainly an understandable oversight on the part of Keynes. However, inclusion of the real balance effect is fatal to Keynes' hypothesis of underemployment equilibrium.

In the Keynesian model a fall in the price level only increases the real supply of money. Now suppose that the nominal interest rate required to maintain aggregate expenditures at the full-employment level of real income y^* is less than the minimum possible interest rate r^{min}.[14] The IS and LM curves will intersect in the liquidity trap portion of a graph, and real income y_0 will be less than full-employment income, as shown in Fig. 13.7. If unemployed real resources cause the price level to fall over time, there is no effect on the equilibrium real income. To be sure, the LM curve shifts to the right, as shown in Fig. 13.8, but this does not affect real income which

---

[14] Perhaps no positive interest rate would be low enough to do it. The liquidity trap is not necessary for this viewpoint.

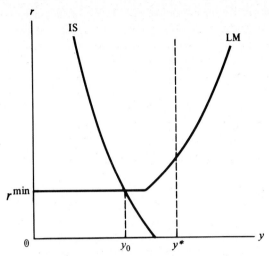

FIGURE 13.7 Keynesian underemployment equilibrium.
The IS curve intersects the LM curve in the liquidity trap
portion. Thus, the equilibrium nominal interest rate is r^{min}
and the equilibrium real income is y_0. But y_0 is less than
the full-employment level of real income y^*.

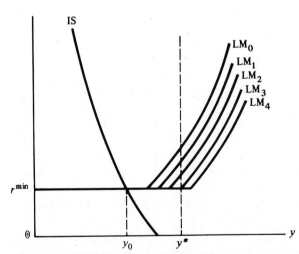

**FIGURE 13.8 The impotence of falling prices as a means of
restoring full employment in the Keynesian underemployment
equilibrium.** If unemployment causes prices to fall over time and
hence increase the real supply of money, the LM curve will shift
steadily to the right, to LM_1 in the first succeeding period, to LM_2
in the next, and so forth. However, they all coincide with the
liquidity trap portion of LM_0, and so equilibrium remains at the
point (y_0, r^{min}).

remains constant at y_0. Therefore, Keynes concluded, a fall in prices cannot get an economy out of a depression in which the liquidity trap—at least approximately—constrains the fall in the nominal interest rate. Hence it seemed harmless to treat prices as constant not only over a short period, but also in the long run, for purposes of analyzing an underemployment equilibrium.

If the liquidity trap is not effective however, and the nominal interest rate can fall, it is clear that falling prices—or prices rising less rapidly than the nominal money supply—could restore full-employment equilibrium. The impact of changing prices is more than that, however, because the real balance effect must be included.

Once the real balance effect is admitted, the impact of falling prices on the real supply of money takes on a different character. If prices fall, both the LM and the IS curves shift to the right. And so, as time progresses, equilibrium real income steadily increases until full-employment income is achieved, as shown in Fig. 13.9. Thus the real balance effect enables changes in the price level to eliminate underemployment of resources even in the presence of a liquidity trap.[15]

There is a second difference of opinion about the nature of equilibrating forces between the dynamic and Keynesian models. Search or inventory behavior which allows supply and demand to differ does not exist in the Keynesian model. It is true that there are discussions of unplanned inventory investment in regard to the quantity adjustment mechanism, but it ceases to exist in the formal model. Production is adjusted so fast that inventories are never really used. It is peculiar that firms presumably hold inventories to meet random fluctuations in demand but instead meet these fluctuations by changing output instead of the level of inventories.

The same comments can be applied to money balances. Excess money balances are not included in a Keynesian model because they are always adjusted so that the supply and demand of money is equal. Consequently, money serves no shock-absorber function in the Keynesian model.

The reason for this peculiar state of affairs may be attributed to the state of economic knowledge at the time of Keynes. All analysis was carried out under the assumption that information about market opportunities could be costlessly acquired. In this sort of world there can be no buyers or sellers who are not on their individual demand or supply curves, therefore inventory behavior is effectively nonexistent. Keynes believed that economists of his day assumed that changes in aggregate demand would mainly change

---

[15] In a dynamic framework another factor is important: The private income measure omits an element of income as perceived by individuals—capital gains or losses on holdings of real base money and, to some extent, of real government debt. These capital gains or losses transfer control over resources between the government and public in a way that is not recorded by our national income accountants. If prices are falling, people will receive capital gains on their holdings of government money and debt. This income effect will reinforce the effect on consumer expenditures of the level of real money balances.

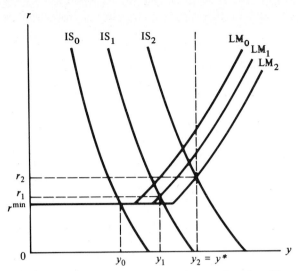

FIGURE 13.9 **Restoration of full employment by price adjustment and the real balance effect.** The presence of the real balance effect means that the increase in the real money supply due to falling prices shifts *both* the IS and LM curve to the right. The fall in the price level continues until the equilibrium real income equals full-employment real income, as at $y_2 = y^*$. Whether the interest rate rises above r^{min} depends on the relative sizes of the shifts in the IS and LM curves.

prices and not real quantities; that is, the aggregate supply curve was approximately vertical. This obviously was not the case in a depression, and so he reversed the effects by assuming a horizontal aggregate supply curve.

The dynamic model presents a more complex picture of adjustment to changes in aggregate demand. At first, inventories of goods adjust with no change in output so that aggregate demand exceeds aggregate supply. As time progresses, real output adjusts, but only because of the costs of information which lead to misinterpretation of the fluctuations in aggregate demand.[16] As information is adjusted to reality, the adjustment becomes entirely in prices. These stages are not discrete, but intertwined over time.

Differences about the Importance of Dynamics

While dynamic analysis is the essence of the dynamic model, it is inherently foreign to the IS-LM approach. This difference is a truly economic problem of allocating scarce resources—the ability of the human mind and electronic

---

[16] This process will be studied in depth in Chap. 14.

computer to comprehend a model. One can study a large number of variables over a short span of time or a smaller number of variables over a longer period of time.[17] In the final analysis, a decision must be made as to whether more variables or a longer time period are to be examined.

As a practical matter, Keynesian models with their many component expenditure functions are complex to begin with and become extremely unwieldy when dynamics are added. Normally only a few dynamic relations can be allowed, primarily stock-flow relations between investment and capital stock, current income and permanent income, and the like. Even with such limited dynamics, the only feasible means of analyzing the effects of a particular policy seems to be computer simulations. The models are just too complex for one to discover what will happen by direct analysis.

Many economists believe that these models leave out many essential dynamic elements of the behavioral functions. Especially important are the expected rate of inflation and the effects of past experience on the position of the aggregate supply curve. Since adding such elements to the IS-LM analysis results in models beyond our technical and technological ability to use, some severe pruning is required. This pruning precludes answering some questions of detail, but makes it possible to answer some of the most important ones.

This situation perhaps explains why different groups of economists can firmly support one model or the other in the face of mounting empirical evidence. Although both groups call themselves "macroeconomists," they mean much different things by that label.

Macroeconomists who have been developing dynamic models of the economy are interested in macroeconomics as defined by the questions in Chap. 1 of this book—basically what explains the behavior over time of real income, employment, and the price level. Macroeconomists who have been elaborating the IS-LM approach place much more weight on the value of disaggregation. Explaining real income is fine, but so is explaining consumer expenditures, or even consumer expenditures on automobiles, on housing, and so forth.

Whether a model is good or bad depends on the weights one puts on its strengths and weaknesses. Large scale, Keynesian macroeconomic models do very well at extrapolating income in the absence of monetary shocks and provide a wealth of disaggregative detail that no dynamic model could attempt. Dynamic models—though still in technical childhood if no longer infancy—do better at predicting turning points in response to monetary shocks. Their further development can be expected to result in a deeper understanding of the precise effects over the next decade of current policies on real income, employment, and the price level.

---

[17] Contrast, for example, the rich detail of the cross-section view of full-employment equilibrium in Chap. 5 with the comparative austerity and greater complexity of the dynamic view in Chap. 6.

☐ SUMMARY

Keynesians overestimated the size of the short-period marginal propensity to consume because of statistical biases. For the same reason the long-run MPC was underestimated. The actual short-period MPC is about 0.3 or 0.4. The specter of secular stagnation because of ever increasing saving-income ratios has not occurred because wealth, income, and consumption have grown proportionately over long periods. Keynes' omission of the effect of real money balances on consumer expenditures was a basic error. The inclusion of this real balance effect eliminates the theoretical possibility of an under-employment equilibrium continuing indefinitely. Increases in real money balances shift *both* the LM and IS curves to the right. Keynesians view cyclical fluctuations in real investment as due to spontaneous shifts in a relatively interest-inelastic investment demand function. These shifts are supposed to be an important cause of business cycles. Monetarists argue that the absence of such investment fluctuations in periods of stable money supply growth is to be explained by either a stable, interest-elastic investment demand function or by the hypothesis that shifts in the investment demand function are *induced* by other macroeconomic shocks. In either case, fluctuations in investment demand are an effect not a cause of business fluctuations. Monetarists generally suppose that the real demand for money is less interest elastic than Keynesians do, but this difference is not crucial as is sometimes suggested. The effects of a change in taxes on real income are ambiguous if the demand for money is an increasing function of private as well as total income. The differences of opinion between monetarists and Keynesians about issues within the context of the IS-LM model are summarized by two general observations: (1) Monetarists usually suppose the LM curve to be steeper and the IS curve flatter than most Keynesians do. (2) Monetarists do not believe that significant and spontaneous fluctuations in the investment demand function actually occur. Also, in the view of most monetarists, shifts in the income-expenditures sector effect the IS curve by less than Keynesians consider them to. However, from the monetarist view but not the Keynesian view, shifts in the monetary sector affect the IS curve as well as the LM curve. Their views concerning the nature of shifts in the IS and LM curves are a better means of distinguishing the two groups than are their views about the slopes of those curves. There are substantial differences of opinion about equilibrating forces in the economy. The dynamic model is based on the concept that there are powerful forces which tend to move the economy toward full-employment, steady-state equilibrium. Keynesians deny that such forces are significant over any period of reasonable length and propose that an underemployment equilibrium will persist in the absence of stimulative macro-economic shocks. Neglect of the real balance effect permitted Keynesians to conclude that changes in the price level in response to underemployment do not affect real income if the interest rate is fixed by the liquidity trap. The inclusion of the real balance effect reverses this conclusion and shows the importance of equilibrating forces. The Keynesian model assumes practically instantaneous adjustment to long-run equilibrium—given a horizontal aggregate supply curve. The dynamic model permits disequilibrium in the goods and money markets to be eliminated over time after a macroeconomic shock because of inventory behavior. Dynamic macroeconomists are primarily interested in the behavior of real income, employment, and the price level. Keynesian economists tend to be unwilling to sacrifice the detailed dis-aggregative information in the Keynesian model for an improved explanation of the behavior of these few variables.

☐ **QUESTIONS AND EXERCISES**

1 (a) Suppose the consumption function could be approximated by $c = 0.9y_P + 0.4y_T$. Suppose in year 0, current private income is $y^n = R\$100$ billion and permanent income y_P is the same amount. Transitory income is measured here as $y_T = y^n - y_P$. Suppose that in year 1, $y^n = R\$110$ billion and $y_P = R\$104$ billion. Compute $(c_1 - c_0)/(y_1{}^n - y_0{}^n)$. Why is this number not the short-period MPC? What would be the effect on consumer expenditures if y^n were R\$110 billion in year 0? What would be the effect on consumer expenditures if y^n were R\$104 billion in year 1?

(b) Can you suggest why over long periods of time the ratio of total change in consumer expenditures to total change in real private income would converge to 0.9?

2 Use the IS-LM model to derive the short-period effects on real income and the nominal interest rate of a decrease in the real money supply in the presence of the real balance effect.

*3 Show the effect of a tax reduction on real income and the nominal interest rate if the real demand for money is an increasing function of *both* private and total income. Suppose there is no net effect on real income, what happens to the level of consumer expenditures and investment? How is this implied by the consumption function and the investment demand function?

4 Show that a given horizontal shift in the LM curve has a greater effect on real income in panel (a) of Fig. 13.6 than in panel (b).

5 Show that a given horizontal shift in the IS curve has a smaller effect on real income in panel (a) of Fig. 13.6 than in panel (b).

*6 Why does the existence of a significant real balance effect make an enormous difference in views about the tendency of the economy toward full employment? Why do the dynamics of the response of the aggregate supply curve to underemployment become important?

7 Why are there no excess money balances in the Keynesian model?

☐ **REFERENCES FOR FURTHER READING**

Andersen, Leonall C.: The State of the Monetarist Debate, *Federal Reserve Bank of St. Louis Review*, **55** (9): 2–8, Sept. 1973; and Commentary by Lawrence R. Klein and Karl Brunner, *ibid.*, pp. 9–14.

Friedman, Milton: Interest Rates and the Demand for Money, *Journal of Law and Economics*, **9:** 71–85, Oct. 1966.

————, **et al.:** *Milton Friedman's Monetary Framework: A Debate with His Critics*, R. J. Gordon (ed.), Chicago: University of Chicago Press, 1974. Many of the basic issues of this chapter are involved in Friedman's "Comments on the Critics"; areas of particular interest may be pursued from the references cited there.

Leijonhufvud, Axel: *On Keynesian Economics and the Economics of Keynes*, London: Oxford University Press, 1968.

Stein, Jerome L. (ed.): *Monetarism*, Amsterdam: North-Holland, 1976.

Macroeconomic Goals and Policy

Chapter 15

15.1 MACROECONOMIC GOALS
Macroeconomics, Goals, and Policy

Macroeconomic policy refers to the whole range of government monetary and fiscal policy. This chapter investigates the possible ways in which macroeconomic policy might be used to achieve certain goals and the implications of such use for other goals.

Often goals conflict. For example, a goal of reduced inflation was seen in Chap. 14 to be possible only at the cost of a temporary increase in unemployment which would conflict with a goal of a zero cyclical unemployment rate. Decisions of how much of which goal to give up depend upon individual valuation of the goals. Different individuals will have different values and would make different choices. The author can make no special claims for his values, so appraisals of alternative policies are left to each reader.

Nevertheless, macroeconomics has much to say on these questions. People can place the same valuations on unemployment and inflation and yet come to radically different conclusions on macroeconomic policy if they disagree on the implications of policies for inflation and unemployment rates. A person who thinks that a stable quasi-Phillips curve exists is likely to prefer a higher inflation rate than a person with identical values who thinks that there is only a temporary reduction in the unemployment rate in exchange for a permanent increase in the inflation rate. Indeed, a deeper understanding of the process by which the cyclical unemployment rate is decreased may change a person's value judgment by altering the perceived implications of a reduction in unemployment.

Similarly, in appraising a particular macroeconomic policy actually selected by government, differences can arise either because of differences over the implications of possible policy alternatives or differences in the valuation of those implications. In this case, also, careful macroeconomic analysis can reduce the range of disagreement and even prevent the actual adoption of disastrous policies.[1]

Macroeconomic Goals

The first step in the analysis of alternative policies is to identify the macroeconomic variables which measure the main public concerns. The most important macroeconomic issues were summarized by the Employment Act of 1946 as "maximum employment, production, and purchasing power." Legislative and administrative history identifies other, subsidiary concerns which have in fact shaped macroeconomic policy—such as the balance of payments, interest rates, economic efficiency, economic growth, and environmental quality.

These concerns must be translated into much more specific goals. The actual goals cluster into three separate groups: those dealing with the stabilization of the economy in or near steady-state equilibrium, those dealing with the desired values of real steady-state variables, and those dealing with desired values of nominal steady-state variables.

A general definition of stabilization is keeping the economy in or near steady-state equilibrium. More simply, business cycles are to be reduced or avoided. Fluctuations in the growth rate of real income and the price level are to be reduced, as are the associated cyclical fluctuations in the unemployment rate, industrial production rate, interest rate, and the like. What is desired is a stable, predictable background of the aggregate economy. This permits individuals to make long-term plans and contracts without added risks of massive unemployment or unexpected changes in the price level. A general empirical measure of the degree of stability will be suggested and explained in Sec. 15.2 where the possibilities of stabilization policy are analyzed.

People are concerned not only with keeping the economy in steady-state equilibrium but also about *which* steady-state equilibrium. The key real macroeconomic variables are the growth path of real income and the natural unemployment rate. The main question is what—if anything—macroeconomic policies can do to raise the level or growth rate of real income or to lower the natural rate of unemployment. It is also important to consider the relation of the growth path of real income to other factors important to our well being such as leisure (the participation rate) and environmental quality.

Macroeconomic policies have a particularly important role in determining the steady-state values of nominal variables. The key nominal steady-state variable is the trend rate of inflation. The rise in the trend rate of inflation since the early 1960s has attracted much public attention and, indeed, outrage.

---

[1] Unfortunately, it is not always in the interest of either the political party in power or the party out of power to stick to a clear statement of the true implications of possible policy alternatives. It may be easier to make outrageous campaign promises.

In part, this reflects objection to any change in the inflation rate and so has to do with the stabilization goal. There is, however, a separate objection to high trend rates of inflation. The measurement of the rate of inflation is familiar to all readers by now.

Subsidiary goals with respect to the steady-state values of nominal variables involve the balance of payments and the level of nominal interest rates. Since balance of payments problems can occur only under pegged exchange rates, a more basic and general variable is the trend growth rate of the average foreign-exchange rate. Nominal interest rates will differ on securities with different maturities, risk of default, and other terms, but can generally be well represented in steady-state equilibrium by an average of key market rates.

15.2 STABILIZATION POLICY[2]
Measuring Macroeconomic Stability

In order to analyze possible stabilization policies, it is necessary to have a usable measure of the degree of macroeconomic stability. A good index for this purpose is the variance of the growth rate of nominal income, $\mathrm{var}(g_{Yt})$. *Variance* is a statistical measure of the expected average value of the squared difference between the actual and average value of a particular variable.[3] Using the *squared* difference has two desirable properties: (1) a negative or positive difference of similar absolute amounts each increases the variance by a similar amount; and (2) large differences increase variance proportionally more than small differences do. If the economy was always kept in steady-state equilibrium—so that the actual growth rate of nominal income always equaled its mean, steady-state value—the variance of the growth rate of nominal income would be zero. Positive values of the variance measure the degree of instability.

The variance of the growth rate of nominal income is a combined measure of instability in the growth rates of both real income and the price level since the growth rate of nominal income is the sum of those growth rates:

$$g_{Yt} = g_{yt} + g_{Pt} \qquad\qquad\qquad [15.1]$$

---

[2] The discussion of this section attempts to integrate a large number of basic sources, the most notable of which are Milton Friedman, The Effects of a Full-Employment Policy on Economic Stability: A Formal Analysis, in *Essays in Positive Economics*, Chicago: University of Chicago Press, 1953; Milton Friedman, The Role of Monetary Policy, *American Economic Review*, **58**: 1–17, Mar. 1968; William Poole, Optimal Choice of Monetary Policy in a Simple Stochastic Macro Model, *Quarterly Journal of Economics*, **84**: 197–216, May 1970; Board of Governors of the Federal Reserve System, *Open Market Policies and Operating Procedures—Staff Studies*, Washington: Board of Governors, 1971; J. Phillip Cooper and Stanley Fischer, Simulations of Monetary Rules in the FRB-MIT-Penn Model, *Journal of Money, Credit, and Banking*, **4**: 384–396, May 1972.

[3] In general, for any variable A_t, $\mathrm{var}(A_t) = \varepsilon(A_t - \bar{A})^2$ where ε means "the expected value of" and $\bar{A}$ is the average or mean value of A_t [so $\bar{A} = \varepsilon(A_t)$]. In this case, $\mathrm{var}(g_{Yt}) = \varepsilon(g_{Yt} - \bar{g}_Y)^2$.

Statistics provides a very useful theorem for analyzing the variance of a sum: For any two variables, say A_t and B_t, the variance of their sum is the sum of their variances plus twice the square root of their variances times the correlation coefficient:

$$\text{var}(A_t + B_t) = \text{var}(A_t) + \text{var}(B_t) + 2 \, \text{cor}(A_t, B_t)\sqrt{\text{var}(A_t) \, \text{var}(B_t)} \qquad [15.2]$$

The *correlation coefficient* $\text{cor}(A_t, B_t)$ is a number between $+1$ and -1 which measures the degree to which any two variables A_t and B_t move together.[4] A positive correlation coefficient near 1 means that high values of A_t are generally associated with proportionately high values of B_t and similarly for low values of A_t and B_t. If $\text{cor}(A_t, B_t)$ is near -1, then high values of A_t are generally associated with proportionately low values of B_t, and vice versa. Lower absolute values of the correlation coefficient indicate weaker associations and $\text{cor}(A_t, B_t) = 0$ indicates no such association. Thus a positive correlation indicates that fluctuations in A_t and B_t tend to reinforce each other and a negative correlation coefficient indicates that fluctuations in A_t and B_t tend to offset each other.

An expression for the variance of the growth rate of nominal income is found by applying this theorem to [15.1]:

$$\text{var}(g_{Yt}) = \text{var}(g_{yt}) + \text{var}(g_{Pt}) + 2 \, \text{cor}(g_{yt}, g_{Pt})\sqrt{\text{var}(g_{yt}) \, \text{var}(g_{Pt})} \qquad [15.3]$$

The growth rates of real income and the price level are positively correlated— though the correlation coefficient is far from 1.[5] Since the variances are both positive, the variance of the growth rate of nominal income is the sum of the variances of the growth rates of real income and the price level plus a term to reflect their mutually reinforcing effects. People may place somewhat different values on stabilizing the growth rate of real income and the growth rate of the price level than is implicit in the overall variance of the growth rate of nominal income. Nevertheless, it is difficult to think of policies which stabilize the growth rate of real income without also stabilizing the growth rate of prices—and vice versa—so the overall variance seems an acceptable measure.

Stabilizing aggregate demand—as indicated by reduced variance in the growth rate of nominal income—will automatically reduce the variance of the cyclical unemployment rate which is itself an important macroeconomic goal.

---

[4] The formal mathematical definition is

$$\text{cor}(A_t, B_t) = \frac{\varepsilon[(A_t - \overline{A})(B_t - \overline{B})]}{\sqrt{\text{var}(A_t) \, \text{var}(B_t)}}$$

Thus the correlation coefficient measures the degree to which A_t and B_t are simultaneously high or low or tend to move in opposite directions.

[5] This positive correlation is implicit in the characteristic negative slope of a short-run quasi-Phillips curve. See Robert E. Lucas, Jr., Some International Evidence on Output-Inflation Tradeoffs, *American Economic Review*, **63**: 326–334, June 1973.

The Conditions for Stabilizing Macroeconomic Policy

Fluctuations in the growth rate of nominal income occur because of macro-economic shocks. The shocks can be divided into two types: (1) shocks due to macroeconomic policy (or *policy shocks*) and (2) shocks due to all other reasons (*autonomous shocks*).

The variance computation is based on the deviation of the growth rate of nominal income around its average value, or $g_{Yt} - \bar{g}_Y$. Let us recall that the growth rate of nominal income equals the growth rate of the nominal money supply less the growth rate of fluidity:

$$g_{Yt} = g_{Mt} - g_{\phi t} \tag{15.4}$$

The growth rate of the nominal money supply equals the sum of the growth rates of nominal base money and the money multiplier, $g_{Bt} + g_{\mu t}$. Substituting in [15.4] yields,

$$g_{Yt} = g_{Bt} + g_{\mu t} - g_{\phi t} \tag{15.5}$$

The average or trend growth rate of nominal income is determined by the average or trend growth rates of nominal base money, the money multiplier, and fluidity,

$$\bar{g}_Y = \bar{g}_B + \bar{g}_\mu - \bar{g}_\phi \tag{15.6}$$

Subtracting [15.6] from [15.5],

$$g_{Yt} - \bar{g}_Y = (g_{Bt} - \bar{g}_B) + (g_{\mu t} - \bar{g}_\mu) - (g_{\phi t} - \bar{g}_\phi) \tag{15.7}$$

Deviations in the growth rate of nominal income from its trend must be due to deviations from their respective trends of the growth rates of nominal base money, the money multiplier, or fluidity.

Deviations of actual growth rate from trend growth rate of nominal base money can occur only because of monetary policy, since the Fed determines exactly how much base money is created. Such deviations would therefore be classified as a policy shock.

Deviations of actual growth rate from trend growth rates of the money multiplier and fluidity can occur because of either policy or autonomous shocks. For example, the growth rate of the money multiplier could deviate from trend because of a change in reserve requirements (a policy shock) or because of a banking panic (an autonomous shock). Similarly, the growth rate of fluidity could deviate from trend because of past or present changes in the growth rate of real government spending or base money creation (policy shocks) or because of shifts in investment demand or money demand (autonomous shocks).

Sum together all deviations in the growth rate of nominal income due to past and present policy shocks and denote the total pol_t. Similarly denote the total impact on the growth rate of nominal income due to autonomous shocks as aut_t. So the total deviation of the growth rate of nominal income is

$$g_{Yt} - \bar{g}_Y = \text{aut}_t + \text{pol}_t \qquad [15.8]$$

If stabilization policy is to occur, the total impact of policy shocks must generally offset—be of opposite sign from—the total impact of autonomous shocks. Nor can "stabilization" policy be carried so far that deviations due to policy are generally more than twice as large as the deviations due to the autonomous shocks which they offset.

This can be seen more clearly in terms of the formal measure of stability, the variance of the growth rate of nominal income $\text{var}(g_{Yt})$. By the definition of variance, this variance and the variance of the deviation of the actual and average growth rates of nominal income are identical:[6]

$$\text{var}(g_{Yt}) \equiv \text{var}(g_{Yt} - \bar{g}_Y) \qquad [15.9]$$

Applying the theorem on the variance of a sum to [15.8] and substituting in [15.9]:

$$\text{var}(g_{Yt}) = \text{var}(\text{aut}_t) + \text{var}(\text{pol}_t) + 2\,\text{cor}(\text{aut}_t, \text{pol}_t)\sqrt{\text{var}(\text{aut}_t)\,\text{var}(\text{pol}_t)} \qquad [15.10]$$

This is the basic equation for analyzing the effect of stabilization policy on the degree of stability of the economy.

If the government undertakes no stabilization policy other than that implicit in avoiding any policy shocks, there will be no deviations in the growth rate of nominal income due to policy shocks, so the variance of pol_t is zero $[\text{var}(\text{pol}_t) = 0]$. Consequently, if there is no active stabilization policy, the variance of the growth rate of nominal income is the variance of deviations due to autonomous shocks:

$$\text{var}(g_{Yt}) = \text{var}(\text{aut}_t) \qquad [15.11]$$

An active stabilization policy which introduces policy shocks [so that $\text{var}(\text{pol}_t) > 0$], is seen in [15.10] to necessarily increase instability unless the correlation coefficient of aut_t and pol_t is negative. This is so because the difference between the variance of g_{Yt} with active policy and without active policy is

$$\text{var}(g_{Yt}) - \text{var}(\text{aut}_t) = \text{var}(\text{pol}_t) + 2\,\text{cor}(\text{aut}_t, \text{pol}_t)\sqrt{\text{var}(\text{aut}_t)\,\text{var}(\text{pol}_t)} \qquad [15.12]$$

All the variances are positive, so instability must increase—in the sense $\text{var}(g_{Yt}) - \text{var}(\text{aut}_t) > 0$—unless $\text{cor}(\text{aut}_t, \text{pol}_t)$ is negative. This is the necessary condition for successful stabilization.

Successful stabilization requires that on average policy shocks and auton-

---

[6] By definition,

$\text{var}(g_{Yt} - \bar{g}_Y) \equiv \varepsilon[g_{Yt} - \bar{g}_Y - \varepsilon(g_{Yt} - \bar{g}_Y)]^2 \equiv \varepsilon(g_{Yt} - \bar{g}_Y - 0)^2 \equiv \varepsilon(g_{Yt} - \bar{g}_Y)^2 \equiv \text{var}(g_{Yt})$.

omous shocks at least partially offset each other and that policy shocks not be so large in terms of var(pol$_t$) that the net effect is worse than if there were no active policy at all.[7] The possibility that large changes in policy will destabilize the economy where small changes might stabilize it is a real possibility. The Fed for example has a long history of taking "dramatic action" against inflation by reducing the growth rate of base money, and then reversing itself to take "dramatic action" against the unemployment increase that results from the previous action. This cycle of slamming on the brakes and then the accelerator has been repeated so often that it is referred to as the Fed's *stop-go policy*. Good politics and good economics are not always the same, it appears.

A very lively debate rages among macroeconomists as to the extent and kinds of active stabilization policy that can actually improve the stability of the economy. There are two main areas of debate: (1) Is the optimal active stabilization policy for monetary authorities maintenance of a constant growth rate of the money supply, or is there a better alternative? (2) Is active fiscal policy feasible as a means of stabilization and—if so—is it worth the costs? The issues in each of these debates will be considered in turn.

Approaches to Stabilizing Monetary Policy

There appears to be nearly universal agreement that active monetary policy can in fact increase the stability of the economy, as compared to a policy of a constant growth rate of base money and no policy shocks to the money multiplier. The agreement breaks down over the question of precisely what sort of active monetary policy can do so best—or at all.

There are three main approaches to the determination of an active monetary policy: (1) Stabilize the growth rate of the money supply at some constant trend rate $\bar{g}_M$. (2) Stabilize the levels of nominal interest rates. (3) Vary the growth rate of the money supply around a trend growth rate $\bar{g}_M$ as warranted by conditions.

---

[7] Equation [15.12] can be rewritten as

$$\text{var}(g_{Yt}) - \text{var}(\text{aut}_t) = \sqrt{\text{var}(\text{pol}_t)}\left[\sqrt{\text{var}(\text{pol}_t)} + 2\,\text{cor}(\text{aut}_t, \text{pol}_t)\sqrt{\text{var}(\text{aut}_t)}\right]$$

Therefore, whether or not active stabilization policy is in fact stabilizing depends on whether

$$\sqrt{\text{var}(\text{pol}_t)} + 2\,\text{cor}(\text{aut}_t, \text{pol}_t)\sqrt{\text{var}(\text{aut}_t)}$$

is negative or positive. A negative value of this expression is called the "sufficient condition" for active policy. It can be negative only if policymakers are in fact able to offset autonomous shocks on average so that cor(aut$_t$, pol$_t$) is negative. Assuming that it is negative, $2\,\text{cor}(\text{aut}_t, \text{pol}_t)\sqrt{\text{var}(\text{aut}_t)}$ is a constant negative number regardless of the extent to which active stabilization policy is pursued. Large swings from stimulative to restrictive policies—as opposed to small swings—do however increase var(pol$_t$) and $\sqrt{\text{var}(\text{pol}_t)}$. So an overeager, heavy-handed approach to stabilization policy can decrease stability where a more restrained version of the same policy would increase stability.

The Constant Growth Rate Strategy

The idea behind the first approach of a constant money-supply growth rate is simple. The dominant variable affecting aggregate demand is the growth rate of the supply of money, and it makes very little difference as to how it is divided between the growth rate of base money and the money multiplier. If the growth rate of base money is varied so as to exactly offset autonomous shocks—such as banking panics—to the growth rate of the money multiplier, then there will be no net monetary shocks.

Formally the entire present and future effects of the policy shock are almost perfectly negatively correlated (-1) with the present and future effects of the autonomous shock. The effects are also of the same magnitude so they just cancel out. To illustrate the point, suppose the only source of autonomous shocks was deviations in the growth rate of the money multiplier. These will be matched by equal but opposite deviations in the growth rate of base money, so $\text{var}(\text{pol}_t) = \text{var}(\text{aut}_t)$. On the extreme assumption that deviations in the money multiplier do not induce fluctuations in the growth rate of fluidity, $\text{cor}(\text{aut}_t, \text{pol}_t) = -1$. So,

$$
\begin{aligned}
\text{var}(g_{Yt}) &= \text{var}(\text{aut}_t) + \text{var}(\text{pol}_t) + 2(-1)\sqrt{\text{var}(\text{aut}_t)\,\text{var}(\text{pol}_t)} \\
&= \text{var}(\text{aut}_t) + \text{var}(\text{aut}_t) - 2\sqrt{\text{var}(\text{aut}_t)\,\text{var}(\text{aut}_t)} \\
&= 2\,\text{var}(\text{aut}_t) - 2\,\text{var}(\text{aut}_t) \\
&= 0 \qquad\qquad\qquad\qquad\qquad\qquad\qquad\qquad [15.13]
\end{aligned}
$$

So, under these assumptions, the constant growth rate of the money-supply approach implies perfect stabilization. The assumptions are extreme, however, in excluding two sources of instability which would actually exist in the real world: deviations in the growth rate fluidity due to autonomous shocks other than deviations in the growth rate of the money supply, and any deviations in fluidity due to deviations of the money multiplier from trend. It will be seen that the monetary policy debate hinges on the magnitude of these other sources of shocks and the ability to formulate a policy negatively correlated with them.

The Constant-Interest-Rate Strategy

The traditional central bank policy has been to stabilize interest rates rather than the growth rate of the money supply. The traditional emphasis on attempts to moderate movements in the level of interest rates may be associated with a tendency for central bankers to model their behavior after that of commercial banks. This is natural because many central bank employees receive their basic training as employees of commercial banks. Commercial banks tend to follow a form of inventory behavior with infrequent changes in interest rates paid on deposits and charged on loans.

A stable-interest-rate policy works well so long as the only other macro-economic shocks are associated with the money demand function and the money multiplier. A constant level of interest rates in that case implies no effect on aggregate demand from monetary shocks. The growth rate of the money supply will adjust to that implied by the pegged level of interest rates and the growth in demand for money. Fluctuations in the growth of demand for money are met by fluctuations in the growth rate of nominal money so that growth in the money supply rather than nominal income adjusts to fluctuations in the growth rate of desired fluidity.

A stable interest-rate policy and stable policy for growth rate of the money supply are essentially identical in eliminating shocks due to deviations of the money multiplier from trend—though the explicit money supply policy works better with respect to banking panics.[8] A stable-interest-rate policy increases overall stability if shocks due to money demand alone are considered. However, we may recall from Chap. 10 that pegged interest rates lead to the growth rate of the money supply being adjusted to greatly strengthen any real sector shock—whether investment, fiscal policy, international trade, or consumption. A slowed increase in demand in any of these sectors would tend to reduce interest rates if the growth rate of money were constant. Instead, under pegged interest rates, the growth rate of money is reduced to keep the interest rate up. This can turn a minor "blip" into a full-scale recession.

Worse, the decreased growth rate of the money supply can increase the interest rate only temporarily. As it begins to fall after 6 to 9 months, further decreases in the growth rate of the money supply are required, and these further destabilize the economy. The process works in reverse if increased money supply growth is used in an attempt to hold the interest rate down to a pegged level. The explosive possibilities are closely analogous to those when monetary policy is used in an attempt to set the unemployment rate below or above the natural rate.

A pegged-interest-rate policy can be viewed as an alternative to a policy for constant growth rate of nominal money; such a policy is more stabilizing in the face of money demand shocks and less stabilizing—indeed explosive—in the face of real shocks. It is of course an empirical question as to which kinds of shocks are more important. For the United States, that question seems pretty well settled against the policy of attempting to peg interest rates. Autonomous fluctuations in the growth of demand for money seem very small indeed compared to the cumulative processes initiated by real shocks under pegged interest rates. In fact, the attempts to peg interest rates break down, and the pegs change—a macroeconomic shock. So the range of variation in interest rates under a strategy aimed at stabilizing interest rates appears paradoxically to be greater over a period of years than would occur under a constant growth rate of the money supply strategy. The Fed has been

---

[8] Changes in risk premiums on different types of loans make the operation of an interest rate peg uncertain during a panic.

gradually abandoning interest-rate stabilization in setting monetary policy since the late 1960s.

The Variable-Growth-Rate Strategy

A more robust contender with the constant growth rate of the nominal money-supply strategy is a constant trend growth rate with stabilizing deviations. The idea is to stimulate the economy when it is sluggish and restrain it when it is otherwise stimulated. If this is to work, it is necessary that the deviations of nominal income due to money-growth deviations be negatively correlated with deviations due to autonomous shocks. Further, the money-growth deviations must not be so large that they become a more important source of instability than the shocks they are to offset.

The ability to select money-supply growth deviations which are on average stabilizing is a matter of question because of the lags in the effect of monetary policy on aggregate demand. A monetary shock has significant effects on aggregate demand for a period beginning about 6 months later and continuing for 3 years or more. It is not an easy task to predict now what the autonomous shocks will be like over the next 3 or 4 years. If, however, autonomous shocks also tend to persist over a considerable period of time, it is possible to use current conditions to predict at least part of the future period. Since data are not available for truly current conditions but at best for conditions of 1 to 4 months ago, the task is yet more difficult. If, for example, autonomous shocks typically affected nominal income for a total of five quarters, offsetting monetary policies could cause negatively correlated, offsetting deviations in nominal income for one or two quarters. It is widely, though not universally, believed that this necessary condition for improvement over a constant money supply growth is met.

A second question is how great is the variance of nominal income remaining under a constant money growth strategy. If this variance is very small, there is little to be gained from further refinements and something to lose in allowing the Fed to deviate from the trend growth rate. The deviations in money-supply growth may easily be too large and cause net destabilization. The smaller the remaining variance under constant money supply growth, the smaller are the average deviations which can be stabilizing.

The Debate over Strategies for Monetary Policy

There are many economists who believe that given our current state of knowledge, the best that can be done by the way of active monetary policy is stabilizing the growth rate of the money supply. They argue that the main source of business fluctuations has been variations in the growth rate of the money supply and that, where such variations in money supply growth have been prevented, there have been in fact no significant business fluctuations.

In this view, "fine-tuning" of monetary policy is unnecessary and likely to be carried too far.

A great many other economists believe that it is possible to do somewhat better by varying money supply growth around a stable trend according to current conditions.[9] Under these plans the money-supply growth rate is decreased if nominal income is above its desired steady-state growth path and increased if it is below that growth path. As a matter of logic, it has been demonstrated that for *small* adjustments in the growth rate of the money supply this sort of strategy yields some improvement over a constant-growth-rate strategy in the stability of a statistical model of the economy.

The debate continues, however. Statistical models of the economy and the economy are two different things, critics of the variable-growth-rate strategy point out. In the real economy, policy shocks have been the main source of economic instability despite their stated goal of stabilizing the economy.[10] Critics of the constant-growth-rate strategy reply that past errors of heavy-handed policymakers are to be condemned, but should not prevent us from doing what can be done now.

A related question is the debate over "rules versus authorities." A constant growth rate of the money supply could be easily enacted by statute. If the Fed is instead given independent authority to determine the growth rate of the money supply—as is now the case—it is subject to many political pressures to stimulate the economy near election time, with disastrous results for economic stability. It would, however, be possible to frame an explicit law determining the growth rate of the money supply under a variable-growth-rate strategy, so this presents no real issues for that choice. The strength of an authority is that it can look more deeply into current circumstances, but the weakness is the potential for overemphasis of the "uniqueness" of current conditions and for political abuse.

The Feasibility of Active Fiscal Policy

Two possible tools of fiscal policy exist: government spending and taxation. The debate over the possible contribution to stability of active manipulation of these tools is quite as sharp as that over the possibility of increasing stability through varying the growth rate of the money supply.

Two separate issues are the subject of debate: (1) Do these tools of fiscal policy have a significant effect on the growth rate of nominal income? (2) If they do, can they be altered sufficiently rapidly that stabilization can in fact occur? If fiscal policy has no effect, even temporarily, on nominal income,

---

[9] This requires that stimulative policies and restrictive policies must eventually be canceled out so that the actual growth path of the nominal money supply does not drift away from the trend growth path.

[10] This apparently reflects the inability of policymakers to restrain their actions to the small variations which could do some good. See Levis A. Kochin, Judging Stabilization Policies, Research Paper No. 7211, Federal Reserve Bank of New York, December 1972.

then it certainly cannot be used to promote—or harm—the aggregate stability of the economy. If fiscal policy does have some effects on nominal income, it is possibly but not necessarily true that fiscal policy can stabilize the economy. The main issue of debate differs for the two policy tools.

Very few economists will disagree that deviations from the trend growth path in government spending for goods and services have significant, though perhaps temporary effects on aggregate demand.[11] The absolute size of the effect—the "bang per buck"—is still subject to considerable disagreement. The size of the effect is important to the evaluation of the efficiency but not of the possibility of stabilizing variations in government spending.

Unlike monetary policy which can be altered practically instantaneously, variations in the rate of government spending require considerable time to accomplish. After the decision is made to buy more or less goods and services, it takes time to decide precisely which ones, to increase or decrease orders accordingly, and so forth. This lag between decision and action may more than offset any advantages of fiscal policy in terms of the relatively short span of time over which the policy has effects. In order that the fiscal policy actually stabilize the economy, there must be reasonably accurate predictions of autonomous shocks occurring when the policy actually takes effect. If this is on the order of a year in the future, it is not surprising that this task may prove impossible. In that case, the required negative correlation between policy and autonomous shocks fails, and stabilizing policy based on varying government spending is impossible. Various schemes of standby projects have been proposed to reduce the lag between decision and action, but none have yet passed the test of political feasibility.

A considerable problem with active stabilization through variations in federal spending is the relatively large variations in federal spending required to obtain relatively small variations in nominal income. Such large variations in federal spending may themselves imply waste much greater than the value of any reduction in stability. There is no agreement yet on what—if any—magnitudes are involved. Politicians will undoubtedly continue to cut programs that they oppose in any case "in order to fight inflation" and to add programs that they support anyway "in order to fight unemployment."

Variations in taxation were long thought to offer an attractive alternative to variations in government spending. Since consumer spending is currently about 10 times as large as federal spending, tax-induced variations in consumer spending involve relatively smaller changes than do equal dollar changes in federal spending. They would therefore be likely to be accomplished more quickly and with less waste. The tax and transfer payment[12] laws indeed

---

[11] See the discussion of the empirical evidence on this point in Sec. 8.2.
[12] Remember that taxes are here counted net of transfer payments.

automatically adjust taxation to current conditions. This would all appear to make tax variation an effective instrument of stabilization policy. Unfortunately, there is a question about whether short-run variations in taxation affect nominal income. As was discussed in Chap. 8, there is neither theoretical nor empirical reason to expect an effect one way or the other. So the feasibility of stabilization through variation in taxes is not supported by the evidence.

Review of the Issues for Stabilization Policy

For stabilization policy to be effective, it must be possible to take policy actions which will offset fluctuations in nominal income that are due to autonomous shocks. This presents policymakers with the severe problem of predicting the effects of autonomous shocks over the period during which the effects of current policy decisions on nominal income occur. This task is relatively easy for autonomous shocks to the money multiplier. These shocks have effects almost entirely through their effects on the growth rate of the nominal money supply. Monetary policy which eliminates the resulting effects on the growth rate of the money supply automatically cancels their effects and stabilizes the economy.

Other sources of autonomous shocks have no such reliable early warning system. Policymakers must either successfully predict—on average—the net influence of these shocks and other policy shocks in the period over which current policy takes effect or else abandon further stabilization entirely.

Some economists argue that as a practical matter instability in the growth rate of the nominal money supply has been the only reason for significant fluctuations in the growth of aggregate demand. The small fluctuations—no more than 1 or 1.5 percent per annum—that would remain under a constant growth rate of the nominal money supply are best left to work themselves out.

Other economists (who may or may not think the first group overoptimistic with respect to the magnitude of the remaining fluctuations) believe that it is possible to improve the stability of the economy further.

One traditional alternative to a strategy of stable money-supply growth, the stable-interest-rate strategy, is superior only with respect to autonomous shocks in the demand for money and much inferior to a stable money-supply growth rate in the face of other autonomous shocks. So this alternative does not have much to offer as a stabilization strategy.

More attractive strategies are slight variations in the growth rate of the money supply around a stable trend or variations in the growth rate of government spending (or both) in accordance with current conditions. These strategies can work only if current conditions provide enough information that these policy shocks can on average offset the remaining autonomous shocks. The long period over which monetary policy has effects and the long period required to change the growth rate of government spending raise substantial problems for macroeconomists' predictive abilities. Most macroeconomists have sufficient confidence in their current predictive abilities to believe that this hurdle is surmountable and improved stabilization is possible. Whether this is in fact true and whether the benefits of further active stabilization policy beyond maintaining a constant growth rate of the money supply are worth the costs remain very much unsettled issues.

15.3 MACROECONOMIC POLICY AND REAL STEADY-STATE VARIABLES

Influencing the Investment-Income Ratio by Fiscal Policy

There are three basic variables which determine the growth path of real income: the investment-income ratio, the growth rate of labor, and the aggregate production function. Any policy influencing the steady-state growth path of real income must operate through one or more of these variables.

Governments interested in promoting economic development have often chosen to increase the ratio of investment to income, $i_t/y_t = \sigma$, through the use of fiscal policy. The simplest way to increase the investment-income ratio is to increase the real government surplus.[13] Rewriting [2.6] in real terms,

$$i_t = s_t + (t_t - g_t) - x_t \qquad [15.14]$$

Real investment equals real saving plus the real budget surplus less real capital outflows x_t. The idea is that saving finances new security issues by firms, government, and foreigners. If the government borrows less or even redeems some of its outstanding securities, more saving will be available to finance investment by firms.

It was seen in Sec. 8.3 that increases in the government surplus will reduce saving somewhat. This reduction is generally less than the increase in the surplus, however, so that investment is increased.

In Chap. 6, it was shown that a higher investment-income ratio implies a higher steady-state level—but not growth rate—of real income at each instant. Fiscal policy can therefore be used to permanently increase the level of real income and temporarily—during the adjustment period—increase the growth rate of real income.

The use of government surpluses to raise real income is not without costs, however. If the government increases the investment-income ratio through fiscal policy, the immediate result is less private and government spending for goods and services yielding current satisfaction—on this broad definition, less consumption. So long as this policy is not carried too far,[14] consumption will, after some future date, always be higher than it would otherwise have

---

[13] Remember that the real government surplus is the difference between real government taxes and spending, $t_t - g_t$. A decrease in the government deficit is an increase in the government surplus.
[14] See the discussion and references on this possibility at pages 197–198.

been. So there is a potential tradeoff of increased future consumption for a period of decreased consumption. Alternatively, increased present consumption can be obtained, but only at the cost of lower future consumption—as in the case of debt financing of wars—by reducing the government surplus or increasing the government deficit.

The direction and the degree of such a tradeoff are matters of individual value judgment. A government budget balanced except for capital investments is sometimes used as a benchmark. Larger government surpluses imply less current and more future consumption than would be desired by individual savers. Smaller government surpluses imply more current and less future consumption than would be desired by individual savers. Thus a larger or smaller surplus would be justified on the basis of a belief that individuals undervalue or overvalue their future consumption and that of their heirs.

On this analysis, the use of taxation to finance what are in effect capital investments by the government is nearly equivalent to an equal government surplus where all capital is privately owned.[15] The incentives on private and bureaucratic investors are somewhat different so that the investment projects may differ in efficiency, but otherwise the two approaches are equivalent.

Microeconomic Policies and Steady-State Real Equilibrium

Most policies substantially affecting steady-state real equilibrium are not at all macroeconomic policies. It may even be stretching the term to call the policies dealing with population or environmental quality microeconomic policies. An analysis of microeconomic policy is beyond the scope of a macroeconomics book, but a brief discussion of some macroeconomic implications is in order.

A great many discussions of the macroeconomic implications of various microeconomic policies are seriously flawed by a thorough confusion of growth rates and levels. Policies which do not affect the growth rate of labor can only change the steady-state level but not the growth rate of real income. In the period of adjustment immediately following such a policy change, the growth rate of real income will be higher or lower than the steady-state rate in order to effect the transition to a higher or lower growth path. This is only temporary, however, and thereafter the growth rate is unchanged.

A frequent proposal is to increase real income by reducing government grants of monopoly to businesses and unions. Such a policy would shift upward the aggregate production function in the sense that more real output would be obtained from given quantities of labor and capital. This happens because

---

[15] The government's failure to keep full accounts of government assets may obscure the meaning here. Suppose instead the government issued bonds equivalent to its capital stock and levied taxes sufficient to cover current expenses, depreciation, and interest. Net government investment would then be covered by new borrowing. Alternatively, the government could lease capital goods from private owners—as is done for example with many post offices—and balance the budget including rental payments (that is, depreciation and interest) with all borrowing done by private firms.

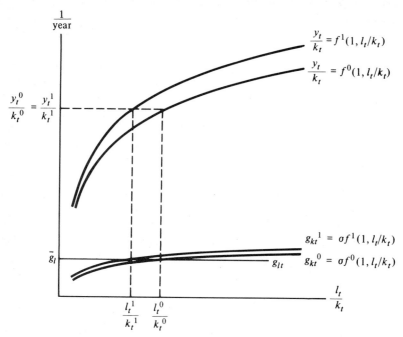

FIGURE 15.1 Effects of alternative aggregate production functions on steady-state equilibrium. The production function $y_t/k_t = f^1(1, l_t/k_t)$ exceeds the alternative $y_t/k_t = f^0(1, l_t/k_t)$ for every positive value of the labor-capital ratio. The growth rate of income is fixed at $\bar{g}_l$, but the labor-capital ratio is less in state 1 than it is in state 0. The income-capital ratio is the same in each case at $\bar{g}_l/\sigma$. Real income in state 1 exceeds real income in state 0 because there is more capital and the same amount of labor in state 1 and because given amounts of capital and labor produce more output in state 1 than in state 0.

labor and capital will be put to more valued uses. The effect on the growth path of real income is found in Fig. 15.1. The steady-state growth rate of real income is unchanged at the growth rate of labor $\bar{g}_l$. The level of real income at each instant of time is increased, however, because more output is produced by given amounts of capital and labor and because the amount of capital is in fact increased at each instant. A complete analysis of the removal of monopoly powers would require microeconomic theory as some groups win and others lose. The point here is that removal of monopoly power is a source of a once-and-for-all increase in real income and not of *continuing* increased growth of real income.

Many popular writers have seen a conflict between improvement of environmental quality and the continuation of economic growth. This dichotomy, too, is mistaken. What is proposed is that pollution of the environment as a result of the productive process be limited. This is done by preventing firms and individuals from using those productive processes which cause pollution. Other, less productive processes will be substituted. Thus the aggregate production function shifts down as less real output is produced from any quantity of capital and labor. This is just the reverse of the previous instance. It is seen from Fig. 15.1 that the steady-state growth rate of real income is unchanged, but the steady-state level of real income at each instant of time is lower because less is produced from given amounts of capital and labor and less capital will exist. This reduction of market goods and services may be more or less than balanced by the improvement in environmental quality, but that is another question. The growth rate of real income is slowed only temporarily during the period of adjustment.

The macroeconomic implications of alternative growth paths of population, participation, and average quality of the labor force have been analyzed in detail in the text and problems of Chap. 6. That analysis will not be repeated here. It is important to observe that changes in the steady-state growth rate of real income are only obtained through changes in the factors underlying the growth rate of labor. Other changes affect the level but not the growth rate of real income.

Are There Limits to Real Growth?

At least since 1798 when Thomas R. Malthus published his pamphlet *An Essay on the Principle of Population*, there have been recurrent prophecies of the imminent cessation of economic growth. The basic idea is always the same. Some particular type of resource is assumed to be absolutely necessary for economic production. This resource is available only in fixed, or nearly fixed, supply. Hence, it is argued, soon all of this resource will be used or used up and output must stop growing or fall, respectively. Predictions of cessation within 5 years enjoy more notoriety but provide a less steady source of income to the predicter than a less immediate date.

The reason that the prophets of doom always prove wrong is that the "absolute necessity" never really is. Increasing demand raises the price of the increasingly scarce resource and thus encourages its conservation and the discovery of substitutes. This has happened in every case. Doom is implied only if man is unable to adjust and adapt to changing conditions. It might happen, one supposes, but the force of history runs against the possibility.

15.4 MACROECONOMIC POLICY AND NOMINAL STEADY-STATE VARIABLES
Controlling the Steady-State Rate of Inflation

Recently, much public concern has been focused on the rate of inflation. This concern is natural in the face of accelerating inflation in the decade beginning with 1965. It is perhaps surprising to reflect that controlling the steady-state rate of inflation is a relatively easy task for macroeconomic policy. It takes no great sophistication or technical expertise to compute the trend growth rate of real demand for money. Add the desired steady-state rate of inflation to that number and the answer is the required trend growth rate of the nominal money supply.

It is remarkably easy to control the rate of inflation as long as the Federal Reserve System carries out its duties to maintain the required trend growth rate of the nominal money supply. During the 1960s the Fed instead chased unmaintainable goals of low unemployment and interest rates with accelerating money supply growth. And so the attainable good was lost for the unattainable better.

There are three issues connected with the steady-state rate of inflation: the implications of alternative rates; the costs and benefits of moving from one rate to another; and the costs and benefits of variable steady-state inflation rates.

The Implications of Alternative Steady-State Inflation Rates

Macroeconomics provides no well-established body of empirical evidence on the real implications of alternative steady-state rates of inflation. The hardest part of any scientific research is asking the right questions. At least until recently, the questions examined in research on inflation have not been well constructed.

The layman always finds it hard to understand why macroeconomists should have trouble explaining the effects of inflation when everyone knows it is bad. The problem is that what "everyone" knows is wrong with inflation either does not withstand examination or has to do with the effects of changing the rate of inflation from that which is anticipated. The implications of alternative fully anticipated steady-state rates of inflation require more careful thought.

The first observation is that the levels of prices and nominal incomes are irrelevant to human satisfaction so long as a rise or fall in prices is reflected in a proportionate rise or fall in incomes. There is no reason to be any more or less happy with an income of $10,000 per annum than with $100,000 per annum if prices are ten times higher in the latter than in the former case. It is of no importance whether we reckon our accounts in dollars or dimes so long as the real work done and goods received are the same.

Therefore, there is no obvious reason why one should feel any better or worse if one's income increases at 8 percent per annum with a 6 percent rate of inflation than if the figures were 2 and 0 percent, respectively. In each case, the actual growth in command over real goods and services is the same 2 percent per annum. There seems to be an illusory feeling by some people that in the first case the 8 percent increase in income is "rightfully theirs" and that inflation robs them of their hard-earned gains. But this is a false reason for opposing high inflation since the average growth rate of real per capita income in the United States is determined by real factors at a bit under 2 percent per annum. The rate of inflation merely provides a base to which must be added the real income gains—or losses—to obtain dollar gains.

Nor are problems of unfairly hurting retired people and other net creditors receiving fixed money income applicable. Nominal interest rates adjust to eliminate any advantage to debtors or creditors. Arbitrary transfers of wealth occur only when the steady-state rate of inflation in unexpectedly changed, as discussed further below.

The choice among steady-state inflation rates must be based on comparison of the associated real implications. Unless different steady-state inflation rates imply some different real magnitudes there is no reason to select one inflation rate over another.

Three sorts of real implications appear important: costs involved in economizing on money balances, costs involved in alternative means of financing government, and effects on the investment-income ratio.[16]

Government money creation substitutes for other methods of financing government expenditures. Higher growth rates of nominal base money cause higher rates of inflation but also, up to some point, yield higher revenues to the government. This revenue from money creation is sometimes imprecisely referred to as the inflationary tax on base money. The real expenditures financed by the tax equal the rate of change in nominal base money divided by the price level:

$$\frac{\Delta B_t}{P_t} = \frac{\Delta B_t}{B_t}\frac{B_t}{P_t} = g_{Bt}\, b_t \qquad\qquad [15.15]$$

Hence the real revenue from money creation can be thought of as the growth rate of nominal base money times real base money. From the taxation viewpoint, the tax rate is g_{Bt} and the tax base is b_t. So long as the tax base does not shrink too rapidly, increases in the tax rate g_{Bt} and therefore the rate of inflation increase government revenue. This higher revenue can be used to reduce other taxes. These other taxes will have involved costs from administration, avoidance, and distortion[17] which are avoided at higher revenues from money creation.

Against these costs must be balanced the costs from administration, avoidance, and distortion due to the new tax. These are primarily related

---

[16] If the rate of inflation is substantially greater or less than zero, the costs of changing prices, adjusting accounts for the effects of inflation, and similar calculations would appear to be sufficient to noticeably reduce the level of real income.

[17] For example, the income tax alters the value to the individual of work and leisure so that he works less than he would in the absence of the tax.

to misallocation of resources in an attempt to economize on holdings of base money. Partially, this is accomplished by more extensive use of bank deposits for transactions in which currency would otherwise be cheaper than checks. Bank deposits only use base money for fractional reserves. Indeed the Fed in effect pays at least partial interest on bank reserves through such activities as free check-clearing services, subsidized lending facilities, and the like. There may also be a reduction in the total demand for money as resources are used to match expenditures and receipts more closely so that average money balances are reduced.

Consequently, the elimination of overt taxes tends to shift the production function upward while the increase in the inflationary tax tends to shift the production function downward. There is no clear evidence about the nature of the net effect. Unless the demand for money is substantially interest elastic, the amounts involved are likely to be rather small in any case. For example, base money in 1974 averaged about $110 billion and grew at about 7 percent per annum. The total revenue from money creation was therefore about $8 billion. If the difference in the costs associated with the alternative types of taxes were as great as 10 percent of total revenues, the waste difference would only be $0.8 billion. This amount—which is surely a high estimate—amounts to less than three-quarters of a tenth of a percent (0.075 percent) of total income. While the sums involved are well worth looking into, they are not substantial enough to have any detectable effect on aggregate real income in the range experienced in the United States.

Some authors have placed great emphasis on possible effects on the investment-income ratio. It is argued that so long as the growth rate of real money balances is positive, lower steady-state values of fluidity imply higher investment-income ratios. The idea is that consumers perceive growth in real base money as both income and saving. Hence lower levels of fluidity for a given money multiplier imply that less perceived saving will take place in the form of increased real base money balances. Although this idea has spawned many elegant papers, the practical interest is slight. For the United States, the entire sum involved is about 0.03 percent of income or 0.4 percent of total investment.[18] Further, any such effects are easily offset by a slight alteration in the growth rate of the real national debt.

Choice of a steady-state rate of inflation is simultaneously the choice of the steady-state level of nominal interest rates and the steady-state growth rate

---

[18] These computations are based on 1973 data and the trend growth rate of real base money from 1953 through 1973 of 0.433 percent per annum. The reduction in saving due to growth in base money is

$$(1 - \sigma^*)\bar{g}_B b_t \simeq (0.9)(0.00433/\text{year}) \times (R\$94.55 \text{ billion}) = R\$0.368 \text{ billion per annum}$$

where 1973 is the base year. Investment for 1973 was R\$92.1 billion per annum, hence R\$0.368 billion/R\$92.1 billion = 0.00400. Net national product was R\$1,179.1 billion per annum, consequently R\$0.368 billion/R\$1,179.1 billion = 0.00031.

of the average foreign-exchange rate. There is no particular advantage to low or high interest rates where the differences reflect only differences in the inflation rate. Nor is it obvious why anyone would care whether the growth rate of the average exchange rate is positive, zero, or negative where the growth rate merely reflects the difference between American rate of inflation and the average rate of inflation for the rest of the world. Such changes in the exchange rate do not affect the prices of foreign goods relative to American goods either within or outside of the United States; so there is no effect on real exports and imports.

In sum, there is little hard evidence to suggest that any one constant rate of inflation is better than another. Calculations made for the United States suggest that for moderate rates of inflation, say between 0 and 10 percent per annum, the gain or loss from choice of any particular steady-state rate of inflation is not likely to be as great as one tenth of a percent (0.001 percent) of total income. The question of whether a little inflation is a good or bad thing remains open. For example, the calculation costs associated with any nonzero inflation rate have not been measured as yet, and could turn out to be large at much lower absolute rates of inflation than so far supposed. The analysis of Chap. 14 should be recalled, since it was seen there that no *constant* rate of inflation can affect the natural rate of unemployment so that no benefits can be expected there. There is no clear reason to choose any particular moderate inflation rate because of its steady-state implications.

This analysis applies only to an open inflation not encumbered with government price controls, usury laws, or other artificial constraints on the adjustment of prices. Attempts at suppression, whether conscious or through failure to alter nominal amounts in laws, can lead to substantial inefficiencies. Price controls enforced by the occupation troops in post-World War II Germany led to the effective abandonment of monetary exchange. The German "economic miracle" resulted from the unauthorized removal of these controls by the West German government. Restoration of money as a usable means of exchange and of prices as a guide to the allocation of resources to their most valuable use led to an increase of output of 50 percent in the last half of 1948 alone.[19] If a government enforces price controls, then lower rates of inflation are the only way to avoid economic disaster. In the early 1970s, many Western countries tried price and wage controls with disastrous political results for the parties which installed or advocated controls in subsequent elections. A little experience rapidly dampens voter enthusiasm for such approaches.

---

[19] Further discussion of this fascinating episode of literal mass starvation due to price controls is found in Jack Hirshleifer, *Disaster and Recovery: A Historical Survey*, No. RM-3079-PR, Santa Monica, Cal.: The Rand Corp., 1963; Horst Mendershausen, Prices, Money and the Distribution of Goods in Postwar Germany, *American Economic Review*, **39**: 646–672, June 1949; and Gustav Stolper, Karl Häuser, and Knut Borchardt, *The German Economy: 1870 to the Present*, London: Weidenfeld and Nicolson, 1967.

The Costs and Benefits of Unanticipated Changes in the Inflation Rate

The period of adjustment to changes in the steady-state rate of inflation has substantial costs and benefits.

Consider what happens if the trend growth rate of base money is increased by say 3 percentage points. First there is a boom as aggregate demand is increased. Whether it counts as a cost or benefit to trick people into taking jobs or selling products at wages and prices which would be otherwise unacceptable is a difficult question. But since people are indeed fooled into thinking they are better off than they really are, there is clearly a *political* benefit to those who engineer the increased base money growth just as there would be a political cost to those who dared to engineer decreased base money growth.

The other substantive implication is that as prices rise more rapidly than anticipated in previously agreed interest rates, creditors lose and debtors win. Interest rates rise as anticipations adjust so that this advantage is eliminated. But until the adjustment is completed, loans are made at what turn out to be unfavorable terms for the lender. In the case of a decreased growth rate of base money, the tables would be turned in favor of the lender. Whether the debtors or creditors predominate in numbers, the arbitrary transfers of wealth involved in unanticipated inflations appear politically costly. So politicians do not explicitly endorse increased inflation,[20] but merely carry out policies which eventually lead to it.

The Costs and Benefits of Variable Steady-State Inflation Rates

The great difficulty with a fiat monetary standard such as now exists in the United States is the potential variability in the inflation rate. A political decision can select any growth rate of base money, but political decisions can be changed. The temptations for increasing the growth rate of base money because of an impending election are great. If there is an increase, by how much? The political costs of returning money supply growth to the previous growth path (and causing a recession) may well be sufficient to guarantee that it is never done.

Making a long-term contract becomes very risky. Therefore, these valuable contracts must either be forgone or more expensive alternatives used to allow adjustment of money sums to reflect the actual rate of inflation. As these arrangements become common, it becomes harder for the government to cause either a boom or recession by altering the growth rate of the money supply. But consider the price: Money loses its usefulness as a standard of value for

---

[20] There have been political parties which openly advocated unanticipated inflations, but they have not been successful. The Greenback Party was founded in 1874. Its inflationist views were absorbed into the losing Democratic Party platform of 1896.

transactions to be settled in the future and a more expensive substitute must be found.

Consider how the United States adopted a fiat standard with the trend rate of inflation left to the discretion of the Federal Reserve System. In 1913 the United States was on a gold standard so that the price level was simply the price of gold in terms of all other goods and services. The relative price of gold would change from time to time with discoveries of new ore deposits or mining techniques, but advances in the production of other goods kept pace on average. So there was no persistent upward or downward trend to the price level.

The fractional reserve banking system led to recurrent panics and temporary drops in the money supply. The Fed was established to prevent the panics by issuing Federal Reserve Notes and maintaining the money supply. So long as the Fed was constrained to redeem their notes for a fixed amount of gold, the value of the dollar remained tied to the value of gold in terms of goods. If the Fed increased the money supply too rapidly, demands for redemption would reduce its gold holdings and the Fed would cut back its rate of issue. If it were to choose too slow a growth rate of the money supply, gold holdings would grow until the Fed increased the rate of issue in base money.

In 1933, the definition of a dollar was changed by law from 1/20.67 of a fine ounce of gold to 1/35 of an ounce. This altered definition implied a 70 percent increase in the equilibrium price level. The Fed, it will be recalled, had ceased to play by the rules and did not adjust the money supply accordingly. Instead the American gold stock grew steadily. Not until the middle of the Korean War was the American price level 70 percent higher than it had been during the 1920s.

By that time, the Fed had largely forgotten the rules of the gold standard. As inflation was continued at a reduced rate during the remainder of the 1950s, gold began to flow out of the United States. Concern over the balance of payments became severe during the early 1960s, and it appeared that the Fed would have to stop money-supply growth and thus engineer a recession to correct matters. In 1965, Congress repealed the law requiring the Fed to hold gold to the extent of 25 percent of deposits at the Fed and let the Fed know that the remaining requirement of gold against Federal Reserve Notes would be repealed when it became binding. This in effect removed all guidance from the gold standard to the determination of the price level. By 1968, the Fed ceased providing gold on demand even to foreign central banks, though it was not made official until 1971.

So the Fed is now free to decide the trend growth rate of the money supply on any criterion it chooses, including political pressure from the President and Congress. Predicting the price level 20 years from now is a political guessing game, not the subject of economic analysis.

The question naturally arises whether this system of monetary control is politically stable. Why should the political attractiveness of a little faster money creation be less at 20 percent per annum inflation than at 5 percent per annum? The author of this book can see no reason.

There does not appear any way to establish a stable, predictable growth rate of the money supply under a system of completely discretionary policymaking by the Fed. There appear to be two viable means of establishing a fixed-trend money-supply growth rate: a true commodity standard and a legally fixed growth path of the nominal money supply.

A commodity standard requires production and storage of a significant amount of some product—say gold—in order to provide at least a substantial fraction of the growth of real money balances. It is difficult to establish a central bank with powers sufficient to deal with a banking panic that cannot abuse those powers so that the commodity standard becomes ineffective. There are alternatives such as federal deposit insurance which can be used so that central bank powers need not be so great. But it must be acknowledged that commodity standards have not been generally retained in the face of the substantial costs that are involved.

An alternative that is increasingly popular with the Congress is setting by law or constitutional amendment a growth path of the nominal money supply. Such a legal rule would make the fiat monetary standard as predictable and stable as a commodity standard without the costs of production and storage or the danger of irresponsible central bank actions.

The Fed would be required to maintain the quantity of money within a certain percentage of the stated growth path at all times. This would assure that the average growth rate of the nominal money supply over any substantial period of time must be very close to the growth rate used in establishing the stated growth path. The percentage of variation permitted would establish a margin for error and, if desired, a margin for short-run discretionary varia-tions in money supply growth for reasons of stabilization policy. A similar proposal to limit the annual growth rate of the money supply to a certain range provides a less predictable standard since the Fed might choose to always be at the high or low end of the permitted range. The differences from the central growth rate would then cumulate over time.

If America is to choose a steady-state rate of inflation, a framework must be provided by which that choice may be expressed and enforced. If no choice is made, there is no reason to expect that the ills of continuing unanticipated increases in the growth rate of the money supply will be avoided. The political temptation is too great to reduce the unemployment rate now and worry about the increased inflation rate when it happens after the election. Any rate of inflation is consistent with either a commodity or fiat standard.[21] If no standard is explicitly adopted which limits the ability of the Fed to

---

[21] The definition of the monetary unit can be steadily changed under a commodity standard.

print money at will, the most likely prospect is continued accelerating inflation.

A difficult question is what steady-state rate of inflation to choose. Some would urge a gradual reduction in the growth rate of the money supply to one consistent with zero inflation. Others argue that the advantages of zero inflation over 6 or 8 percent are small at best and that the temporary increase in unemployment and arbitrary shift in wealth from debtors to creditors which are necessary to get to 0 percent outweigh any such gain. The research necessary to more accurately judge the magnitudes involved remains to be done.

That is how it is with macroeconomics. Answering one hard question leads to the posing of others. The work to be done grows at a positive rate.

☐ SUMMARY

The role of macroeconomics in policy decision-making and evaluation is to disclose the possible combinations of macroeconomic variables and how those alternatives can be achieved. Macroeconomic goals can be placed in three groups: stabilization of the economy, the real steady-state equilibrium, and the nominal steady-state equilibrium. The variance of the growth rate of nominal income is a useful measure of the stability of the economy. If an active stabilization policy is to be possible, it is necessary that policy can be conducted so that the effects of policy actions are negatively correlated with the effects of autonomous shocks. Policy actions must not be so large even then that they cause more instability than the autonomous shocks which they offset. These criteria are easily met by a monetary policy which offsets the effects on the growth rate of the nominal money supply of autonomous shocks in the money multiplier. A lively debate continues over whether monetary policy can in fact improve the stability of the economy further by variations in the growth rate of the nominal money supply in light of current conditions. Using the level of nominal interest rates as a guide to monetary policy is generally destabilizing to the economy. The feasibility of stabilization through variation in the growth rate of real government spending is also debated. The main question is the length of time between policy decision and the effect of policy action which may make unattainable the necessary condition of a negative correlation between effects of policy and autonomous shocks. A subsidiary issue is the size and costs of variations in spending required to obtain a given effect on nominal income. Changes in taxes can be made more quickly and cheaply, but there is considerable though not conclusive empirical evidence that changes in taxes have no effect on nominal income. The steady-state level of real income can be increased through increases in the government surplus which raise the investment-income ratio σ.

The adjustment to the higher investment-income ratio involves a period of reduced consumption levels, however. A nearly equivalent policy is the use of taxes to finance direct government investment. Policies which leave the growth rate of labor unchanged will affect the growth rate of real income only during a temporary period of adjustment. They can affect the steady-state level of real income permanently, however. Maintaining a selected steady-state rate of inflation is technically simple but the political temptations to do otherwise are great. The empirical evidence does not suggest that it makes a great deal of difference to the real economy what steady-state rate of inflation is chosen within broad limits. The major costs of inflation are associated with the adjustment to changes in the steady-state rate of inflation, not its level. Real effects of alternative steady-state inflation rates operate through economizing on money balances, alternative means of financing government, and the investment-income ratio. Attempts to suppress inflation by enforced price and wage controls and similar restrictions lead to reduced real income through abandonment of monetary exchange and misallocation of resources. American monetary arrangements leave the determination of the rate of inflation to the discretion of the Federal Reserve System. Political pressures for increased growth rates of the money supply prior to elections are likely to lead to accelerating inflation unless an explicit constraint on Fed decisions is imposed. Such a constraint might take the form of a return to a commodity standard or a legal rule establishing a prescribed growth path of the nominal money supply.

☐ **QUESTIONS AND EXERCISES**

1 What is the role of macroeconomic theory in the formulation of macroeconomic policy? Why can macroeconomics not tell whether a temporary increase in unemployment should be traded off for a permanent decrease in the inflation rate? Why is a knowledge of macroeconomics nevertheless valuable in formulating both the question and its answer?

2 Why is the variance of the growth rate of nominal income a combined measure of instability in both real and nominal variables?

3 Can you think of any reasons why deviations of the money multiplier from trend might be associated with deviations of fluidity from trend even if monetary policy maintains a constant growth rate of the nominal money supply.

4 How can it be that active variation in the growth rate of the nominal money supply in light of current conditions may lead to less economic stability?

5 Why is it necessary that someone who advocates stabilization by active fiscal policy believe that fiscal policy can affect nominal income? Why do some people who believe that fiscal policy affects nominal income believe that fiscal policy cannot be used for stabilization? Is there any inconsistency in these views?

6 Why does an increased real government suplus imply an increased ratio of investment to income?

7 In Fig. 15.1, why does $\dfrac{y^0}{k^0} = \dfrac{y^1}{k^1} = \dfrac{\bar{g}_t}{\sigma}$?

8 Why do macroeconomists not find much to choose among alternative constant rates of inflation? Can you think of any reasons why an anticipated inflation is bad in and of itself?

*9 Why do attempts to suppress inflation through wage and price controls convert a relatively harmless situation into a major disaster?

*10 Suppose that a law is enacted requiring the Fed to maintain the money supply within 1 percent of a specified growth path which has a growth rate of 4 percent per annum.

   (a) This specified growth path can be completely described by specifying M_{1976} in the equation

$$M_t = M_{1976}\, e^{0.04(t - 1976)}.$$

   Explain.

   (b) What is the highest legally possible average growth rate of the nominal money supply over a period of 6 months? Over a year? Over five years?

   (c) What is the lowest legally possible average growth rate of the nominal money supply over a period of 6 months? Over a year? Over five years?

☐ **REFERENCES FOR FURTHER READING**

Burns, Arthur F., and Paul A. Samuelson: *Full Employment, Guideposts and Economic Stability,* Washington: American Enterprise Institute for Public Policy Research, 1967.

Francis, Darryl R.: The Role of Monetary Policy in Dealing With Inflation and High Interest Rates, *Federal Reserve Bank of St. Louis Review,* **56**(8): 2–9, Aug. 1974.

Friedman, Milton: The Role of Monetary Policy, *American Economic Review,* **58**: 1–17, Mar. 1968.

———: Contemporary Monetary Problems, *Economic Notes,* **2**: 5–18, 1973, no. 2.

———: *A Program for Monetary Stability,* New York: Fordham, 1959.

Gramlich, Edward M.: The Usefulness of Monetary and Fiscal Policy as Discretionary Stabilization Tools, *Journal of Money, Credit, and Banking,* **3**: 506–532, May 1971.

Simons, Henry C.: Rules Versus Authorities in Monetary Policy, *Journal of Political Economy,* **44**: 1–30, Feb. 1936.

Tobin, James: *The New Economics One Decade Older,* Princeton: Princeton University Press, 1974.

Wriston, Walter B.: The Whale Oil, Chicken and Energy Syndrome, Address to The Economic Club of Detroit, New York: First National City Bank, 1974.

Answers to Selected Exercises

1.1 Both the human mind and electronic computer have limited capacities. Limitation of the scope of analysis to the main effects is necessary to obtain understandable answers.

2.3 Profits are the residual between the NNP value added of the firm and payments to other income recipients and of taxes net of transfers. The inclusion of profits in income assures that the NNP value added of each firm will equal its payments to income recipients and of net taxes; thus output and income are exactly equal.

2.6 (a) The GNP value added = sales − raw materials = $2,500,000 − $750,000 = $1,750,000. Note that accountants use the terms "net income" and "profits" interchangably.

(b) The NNP value added = sales − raw materials − depreciation = $2,500,000 − $750,000 − $300,000 = $1,450,000. Note that NNP value added also equals wages + interest + taxes + profits = $1,100,000 + $150,000 + $120,000 + $80,000 = $1,450,000.

2.11 Firms are the site of production, but the income from production is paid to the owners of the factors of production and in taxes. Firms can make expenditures for final goods and services (invest) only if and to the extent that their owners increase their security holdings.

3.2 (a) $y_1 = Y_1/P_1 = 1000.00/1.000 = 1000.00$. $y_2 = Y_2/P_2 = 1102.50/1.050 = 1050.00$. $P_3 = Y_3/y_3 = 1212.75/1050.00 = 1.155$. $y_4 = Y_4/P_4 = 1210.00/1.100 = 1100.00$.

(b) Year 3. Year 4. Year 3.

(c) Billions of base-year dollars. Year t dollars per base-year dollar. (Year 1 appears to be the base year.)

3.6 Yes; because the person with $10,000 per year could hold $2000 in currency and checking deposits while the $100,000-per-year person holds only $1500 in these forms. The point is that one's money is neither one's flow of income nor one's total wealth, but rather one's holdings of the particular assets which are money.

4.1 (a) Investment.

(b) Nominal income is measured in units of dollars per year ($/year); so its rate of change is in units of dollars per year per year—($/year)/year. This is also called dollars per year squared—$/year^2.

4.3 Increasing. Decreasing. Increasing. The elasticities are found by taking logarithms of $a_t = b_t d_t/c_t$. So $\log a_t = \log b_t - \log c_t + \log d_t$. Therefore $\eta_{a,b} = 1$; $\eta_{a,c} = -1$; and $\eta_{a,d} = 1$.

4.7 (a) $r^1 = (\$1000.00 - \$892.86)/\$892.86 = \$107.14/\$892.86 = 0.12 = 12$ percent.

(b) After-tax payment $= (1 - \frac{1}{3})(\$107.14) = (\frac{2}{3})(\$107.14) = \$71.43$. After-tax nominal interest rate $= \$71.43/\$892.86 = 0.08 = 8$ percent.

(c) Real loan $= \$892.86/(\$2/R\$) = R\$446.43$. Anticipated real after-tax interest receipt $= (\$71.43 + \$892.86)/(\$2.08/R\$) - R\$446.43 = \$964.29/(\$2.08/R\$) - R\$446.43 = R\$463.60 - R\$446.43 = R\$17.17$. So, the anticipated annually-compounded, real after-tax interest rate $= R\$17.17/R\$446.43 = 0.0385 = 3.85$ percent. (Note that the real after-tax interest receipt was computed by deflating the total nominal after-tax receipt of \$964.29 and subtracting the real loan. Why not just deflate the nominal after-tax interest receipt?)

(d) $r = (r^{r*} + g_P)/(1 - \tau^r)$

$0.12 = (r^{r*} + 0.04)/(\frac{2}{3})$

$0.08 = r^{r*} + 0.04$

$r^{r*} = 0.04 = 4$ percent

Annual instead of continuous compounding and tax payments were used in part (c).

5.5 The first step is to determine the relative positions of the LE curves in states 1 and 2. This is done in panel (a) of Fig. A.1. Consider any given value of the real rental rate of capital, say ρ_0, and draw the corresponding labor supply curves in states 1 and 2. Note that by assumption the participation function $\pi(\ldots)$, the average quality q_0, and the capital stock k_0 are identical in the two cases. Also n_1 is less than n_2. Hence, for any real wage w, the quantity of labor supplied will be less in state 1 than in state 2 because (a) the participation rate will be lower due to the higher value of $\rho_0 k_0/n_1$, and (b) the population base n_1 is also lower. The conclusion is this: For any given ρ, the equilibrium quantity of labor is less in the state with the lower population, other things being equal. Or, the LE curve in state 1 lies everywhere to the left of the LE curve in state 2 as drawn in panel (b). The KE curve is unaffected by the size of the population, so it is seen that in equilibrium $l_2 > l_1$ and $\rho_2 > \rho_1$. Since the equilibrium quantity of labor is smaller in state 1 and $k_1 = k_2 = k_0$ by assumption, it is shown in panel (c) that $w_2 < w_1$. Similarly, panel (d) shows that $y_2 > y_1$. Since the average quality of labor is the same in the two cases, the question about l/n refers to the participation rate. Since the effect of real wage rates on the participation rate is ambiguous—as is whether $\rho_1 k_0/n_1$ exceeds $\rho_2 k_0/n_2$—no general statement can be made.

5.9 The goods and services one must give up to obtain a dollar or can obtain in exchange for a dollar are $\$1/P$. The interest rate paid by banks on deposits is the return per annum on holding money as deposits.

5.12 $Y_1^e = P_1^e y_1^e = (1.25)(800) = 1000$. $\phi_1^e = M_1^e/Y_1^e = 200/1000 = 0.2$. All real variables including real income and fluidity would be unaffected by differences in the nominal quantity of money; so $y_2^e = 800$ and $\phi_2^e = 0.2$. $Y_2^e = M_2^e/\phi_2^e = 300/0.2 = 1500$. $P_2^e = Y_2^e/y_2^e = 1500/800 = 1.875$. $M_2^s/M_1^s = 300/200 = 1.5$. $P_2^e/P_1^e = 1.875/1.25 = 1.5$. $y_2^e/y_1^e = 800/800 = 1$. $Y_2^e/Y_1^e = 1500/1000 = 1.5$. $\phi_2^e/\phi_1^e = 0.2/0.2 = 1$. (Can you generalize about the ratios of the nominal variables? Of the real variables?)

6.1 Most European countries during the dark ages; isolated tribal communities. There could be real economic growth with zero population growth if there is growth in the average quality of the labor force or in the participation rate. (Note that

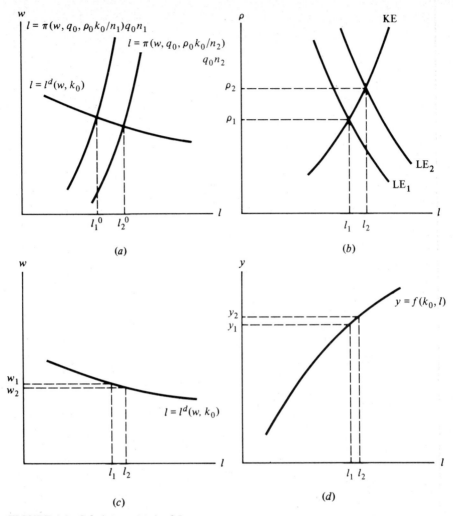

FIGURE A.1   Solution to exercise 5.5.

the model of this chapter is useful only where the growth rate of labor and the saving-income ratio are both positive.)

6.3 It is shown in Fig. A.2 (refer to Fig. 6.3) that the equilibrium labor-capital ratio is less in country 0 with the lower growth rate of labor. Since $y_t/l_t = f(k_t/l_t, 1)$ is an increasing function of k_t/l_t—see the derivation of [6.7] for the reason— country 0 will have the higher income per unit of labor. Cannot say for per capita income: The higher growth rate of labor in country 1 may be due to higher growth rates of the participation rate and average quality in country 1 so that the ratio of labor force to population is sufficiently higher in country 1 to offset the lower ratio of income to labor.

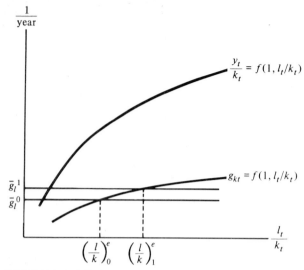

FIGURE A.2   Solution to exercise 6.3.

6.8 Yes. The comparative dynamics problem allows for the change in equilibrium real money demanded over a year's time (here 2 percent) while the comparative statics problem applies to an instant of time for which the equilibrium quantity of real money demanded is fixed.

7.1 (a) Because people do not immediately change their spending patterns when receipts of money are higher than anticipated.
(b) In equilibrium actual fluidity equals desired fluidity, and $\bar{g}_M$ does not affect $\bar{g}_\phi$.
(c) If the demand for money is affected by the level of nominal interest rates, there would be a parallel shift in the growth path of fluidity.

7.6 Just as it is expensive to adjust retail prices in response to every fluctuation in quantity demanded, so it is expensive to change prices in response to every random fluctuation in costs. Hence some retail prices are adjusted only when unanticipated wholesale price changes prove to be persistent.

7.8 (a) People will invest more resources in finding out what the world is really like. Thus there will be little lag in adjustment of aggregate demand to changes in monetary growth or in adjustment of prices to changes in aggregate demand. And so, there will be a much smaller temporary impact on fluidity and real income and a much quicker impact on the growth path of prices.
(b) The resources used to find out what is going on and to make frequent adjustments in an unstable environment would be used to produce more real income in a stable economy.

8.2 $1000 billion $+ 0.8(\$110$ billion $- \$100$ billion$) = \$1008$ billion. $10 billion/$100 billion $= 0.1 = 10$ percent. $8 billion/$1000 billion $= 0.008 = 0.8$ percent.

8.6 Desired spending increases by only part of the tax decrease at the original levels of real income and interest rates compared to the whole amount of an increase in government spending. Further, a tax decrease may increase money demand at the original levels of income and interest rates and so tend to reduce spending.

8.9 (a) Government borrowing reduces the amount of savings that can go to investment and thus reduces future real income. An unchanging debt does not reduce saving in this way.

(b) Steady-state real income is unaffected. The increased consumption (private plus government) during the war must be paid for by lower levels of consumption during the adjustment period after the war as the capital stock is rebuilt. Higher interest payments after the war will distribute more income towards those (and their heirs) who most reduced their private consumption during the war. This is generally thought to reduce equality of income distribution as the wealthy are assumed to cut back their consumption disproportionately during the war.

9.3 The units are

$$\frac{(£/\$)(\$/R\$)}{(£/R£)} = \frac{R£}{R\$}$$

where R£ is base-year pounds (pounds may be an index of all foreign moneys). This measures the amount of base-year pounds which can be obtained per base-year dollar at time t. Suppose, for example, that $E_t = £0.4/\$$, $P_t = \$2/R\$$, and $P_t^F = £3/R£$. Then at time t, \$2 could buy R\$1 of goods and services domestically or it could be changed for $(\$2)(£0.4/\$) = 0.80$ and used to buy $£0.80/(£3/R£) = R£0.267$ of goods and services abroad. An increase in the ratio makes foreign goods cheaper to Americans and American goods more expensive to foreigners.

9.6 No, because the excess of purchases over sales will be made up by excesses of sales over purchases to other countries. No, for essentially the same reason.

9.13 Yes, because exchange rates and nominal interest rates will adjust to the extent that the small country chooses a rate of inflation different from that of other countries.

10.1 This is quite backward. Income falls to adjust (nominal) money demand downward because of previous decreases in nominal money supply. Nominal interest rates are low when the expected rate of inflation is low or negative and are not a good indicator of the impact of monetary policy. Desired fluidity moves contra-cyclically because money demand changes proportionately less than transitory fluctuations in real income and because of procyclical movements in nominal interest rates.

10.5 The idea is that the Fed relies on the liquidity effect to reduce interest rates, but this is canceled out over time by the income and financial effects, and the expectations effect eventually raises nominal interest rates above their initial level. Thus the initial increase in the growth rate of the money supply will soon prove insufficient to maintain "low" interest rates, and further increases will be required. (Can central banks perpetually use the liquidity effect to offset the other effects? Does the fact that high nominal interest rates are highly correlated with high trend growth rates of the money supply across countries and over time suggest an answer? If the Fed tried to follow such a policy, would it be likely that the expected rate of inflation would continue to be formed with such long lags as have been historically observed? *Hint:* Does the probability which one puts on a head occurring change when a double-headed coin is substituted for a fair coin?)

11.1 R\$3000 + (R\$100/year)(1 year) = R\$3100. R\$3000 + (R\$100/year)($\frac{1}{2}$ year) = R\$3050. R\$3000 + (R\$100/year)($\frac{1}{4}$ year) = R\$3025. Since the flow of investment is small (typically 3 to 4 percent) relative to the capital stock, over a short period of time the percentage change in the capital stock is trivial.

11.3 (a) R\$500 billion/year $+ 0.3y +$ R\$500 billion/year $= y$
$$y - 0.3y = \text{R\$1000 billion/year}$$
$$(1 - 0.3)y = \text{R\$1000 billion/year}$$
$$y = \frac{\text{R\$1000 billion/year}}{0.7}$$
$$y = \text{R\$1428.57 billion/year}$$

(b) $y = (\text{R\$1100 billion/year})/0.7 = \text{R\$1571.43 billion/year}$.

(c) The change in $i + g + x = \text{R\$100}$ billion/year. The simple multiplier is $1/(1 - \text{MPC}) = 1/0.7 = 1.42857$. The change in income as computed in parts (a) and (b) is R\$1571.43 billion/year $-$ R\$1428.57 billion/year $=$ R\$142.86 billion/year. The multiplier times the change in $x + i + g$ is $(1.42857)(\text{R\$100 billion/year}) =$ R\$142.86 billion/year. It is called the *simple* multiplier because it is based on the simplifying assumption that $x + i + g$ equals a given number.

11.7 Short-period fluctuations in real income do not reflect proportionate changes in wealth or expected future income. So money holdings, a component of wealth, would generally not vary proportionately either. Persistent or permanent changes in income would change both wealth and the expected transactions proportionately and therefore money demand as well.

12.1 (a) Generally no, because there would be only five equations with which to determine six unknowns: y, r, ax, m^d, m^s, and M^s.

(b) No, because this adds one equation for a total of six but adds a seventh unknown, P. Yes, because repeated substitution can be used to reduce number of equations by 5 (from 6 to 1), and the number of unknowns by the same amount (from 7 to 2). This functional relationship would be called the aggregate demand curve.

12.4 (a) A decline in investor optimism shifts the aggregate expenditure curve down and so shifts the IS curve down and to the left. It is seen in panel (a) of Fig. A.3 that the decline in investor confidence leads to a decline in real income from y_0 to y_1 and in the interest rate from r_0 to r_1.

(b) In panel (b), it is assumed that the Fed increases the money supply so that the LM curve shifts sufficiently to the right that the new LM and IS curves (LM$_1$ and IS$_1$) intersect at the same level of income $y_2 = y_0$ as initially (LM$_0$ and IS$_0$). This reduces the interest rate further to r_2. If fiscal policy were instead used to maintain the original income, the LM curve would be fixed at LM$_0$ so that the interest rate would be the same as before the decline in investor optimism.

12.10 A rate of change in a stock—here base money—does not alter the stock at any instant of time. Unlike investment, the growth rate of base money can be very high when growth is accomplished by reducing government debt. Thus substantial changes in money can in fact occur in short periods.

13.3 A tax reduction in this case shifts the LM curve to the left and the IS curve to the right. The interest rate would certainly rise, but whether real income rises, falls, or is unchanged depends on the relative size of the shifts in the IS and LM curves. Figure A.4 shows the case in which the two shifts just cancel out in their effect on real income. Since consumption rises and government spending and real income

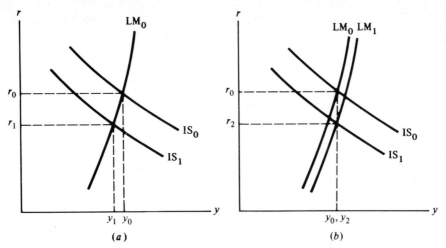

FIGURE A.3   Solution to exercise 12.4.

are constant, investment must fall. This is implied because the tax reduction increases private income and thus consumer expenditures while the increase in interest rates reduces investment for a given level of total income.

13.6   A real balance effect assures that falling prices will restore full-employment equilibrium. Since price level changes have important effects, the speed with which the price level adjusts is important.

14.1 $ur_t = (0.25/\text{year})[(10.4 \text{ weeks})(1 \text{ year}/52 \text{ weeks})] = (0.25 \text{ year})(0.2 \text{ year}) = 0.05 = 5$ percent.

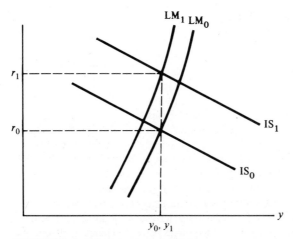

FIGURE A.4   Solution to exercise 13.3.

Probability

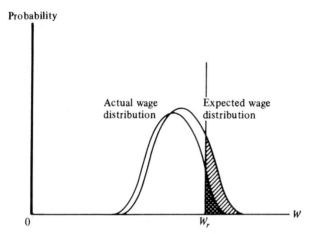

FIGURE A.5 Solution to exercise 14.5.

14.5 An increase in labor demand that is less rapid than expected implies that the actual wage distribution would move to the left of the expected wage distribution. This implies that the actual probability of getting an acceptable job offer per visit (indicated by the heavily shaded area of Fig. A.5) will be less than normal (the whole shaded area). This increases the average number of visits to firms and hence the average duration of search.

15.9 Enforced wage and price controls prevent the use of money and prices as a means of coordinating and allocating inputs and outputs. There are no substitutes nearly as efficient. Hence the economy either becomes a command economy in which the government allocates inputs and outputs or a barter economy with reduced specialization of production. Both—particularly the latter—imply a considerable reduction in real income.

15.10 (a) This is the equation of constant growth (refer to [4.27]) at 4 percent per annum from the beginning of 1976.

(b) From 1 percent below the standard to 1 percent above the standard is the maximum permitted variation relative to the standard over any period of time. Over 6 months ($\frac{1}{2}$ year), a 4 percent per annum growth rate implies a 2 percent growth in the standard plus up to 2 percent variation relative to standard. The maximum legal growth rate over 6 months would thus be (2 percent + 2 percent)/($\frac{1}{2}$ year) = 4 percent/($\frac{1}{2}$ year) = 8 percent per annum. For a year, this is [(4 percent/year)(1 year) + 2 percent]/(1 year) = 6 percent per annum. Over 5 years: [(4 percent/year)(5 years) + 2 percent]/(5 years) = 4.4 percent per annum.

(c) The same principle applies here. The lowest legal percentage change over any period is the change in the standard less 2 percent. Hence, over 6 months, [(4 percent/year)($\frac{1}{2}$ year) − 2 percent]/($\frac{1}{2}$ year) = (2 percent − 2 percent)/($\frac{1}{2}$ year) = 0 percent per annum. For 1 year, [(4 percent/year)(1 year) − 2 percent]/(1 year) = 2 percent per annum. For 5 years, [(4 percent/year)(5 years) − 2 percent]/(5 years) = 3.6 percent per annum.

Index

Accord, Treasury-Federal Reserve, 249
Adjustments, dynamic, 3
Age-eligible population, 35, 89 − 90
Aggregate demand curve, 161 − 165, 265
Aggregate expenditure function, 277 − 278, 294 − 298
Aggregate production function, 83 − 85, 114
  shifts in, 206
Aggregate supply curve, 161 − 164
  horizontal, in Keynesian model, 265 − 266
Aggregates, 2 − 3, 7 − 49
  growth rates of, 1963 − 1974, tables, 253, 257
Andersen, Leonall C., 188, 209, 324
Annual search ratio, 330, 337 − 339
  table, 340
Anticipations (*see* Expectations)
Arbitrageurs, 220
Average duration of search, 330, 333 − 334, 336 − 337
  table, 340
Average propensity to consume (APC), 269
Average quality of labor, 89 − 90, 117 − 118

Balance of payments, 223 − 224
  sterilization of, 224, 229 − 230
Balance of trade (*see* Exports, net)
Balanced budget shocks (*see* Fiscal policy; Shocks, fiscal)
Bank deposits (*see* Deposits, bank)
Bank of United States, 240
Banking Holiday of 1933, 242 − 243
Banking panics, 203 − 205
  during Great Depression, 239 − 244
Barro, Robert J., 44
Barter, 101, 210
Base money, 40
  (*See also* Money creation)
Base-year dollar, 30 − 31, 83
Baumol, William J., 279
Bonds, 73 − 74, 80, 279 − 281, 286
  (*See also* Interest rates; Securities)
Borchardt, Knut, 371
Bretton Woods Agreement, 221

Brown, E. Cary, 188
Brumberg, Richard, 306
Brunner, Karl, 254, 308, 324
Burger, Albert E., 49
Burns, Arthur F., 377
Business fluctuations, 44 − 47
  growth fluctuations, 46 − 47
  reference cycles, NBER, 44 − 46
    figure, 46
    1947 − 1962, table, 250

Cambridge equation, 104
  dynamic version, 122
  1974 values, 258 − 259
Cambridge *k* (*see* Fluidity)
Capital, 84, 85
  demand for, 87 − 88
  human, 76 − 77, 84 − 85
  market equilibrium (KE) curve, 93 − 95
  supply of, 90 − 91
Capital consumption allowance, 21
Capital flows, international, 212 − 213
  (*See also* Capital outflows, net)
Capital outflows, net: defined, 212 − 213
  determinants of, 215 − 217
  (*See also* Exchange rates)
Capital stock, 7 − 9, 84
  desired level, 273 − 274
  growth rate of, 113 − 115
Cash-deposit ratio, 41 − 42, 203 − 204, 240, 244
Central banks, exchange rate operations, 224, 229 − 232
  (*See also* Federal Reserve System)
Chicago School, 4
Circular flows of economic activity, 7 − 15
Commercial banks (*see* Deposits, bank; Money creation, by banks; Reserves)
Comparative dynamics, 3
  problem in, 129 − 135
Comparative statics, 3
Consols, 73
Constant price level, Keynesian, 265, 318 − 320
Constant returns to scale, 114

Consumer expenditures, 193 – 196
  consumer durables, rate of change of,
    145, 147, 193 – 196
  consumer expenditure function, 195
    as a source of shocks, 202, 206
  consumption, pure, 193 – 194
  consumption function: Keynesian,
    268 – 272, 306 – 310
    measured versus permanent income in,
      270, 306 – 309
    real money balances, 270, 308 – 310,
      317 – 321
    real balance effect, 145, 147, 308 – 310,
      318 – 321
Consumption (*see* Consumer expenditures)
Contractions (*see* Business fluctuations)
Controls, price and wage, 45, 246, 248,
  256 – 258, 349, 371
Convertibility deposits, restricted, 242, 243
Cooper, J. Phillip, 353
Corporations, 8 – 9
Correlation coefficient, 354
Corrigan, E. Gerald, 188
Cost-push inflation, 159 – 160, 348 – 349
Currency, 38
Cycles, business (*see* Business fluctuations)

Darby, Michael R., 44, 78, 106, 110, 167,
  173, 193, 209, 246, 254, 307, 308, 314
David, Paul A., 99
Deficit (*see* Government deficit)
Deflation:
  falling prices, 125
  of nominal variables, 34 – 35
Demand-pull inflation (*see* Inflation)
Deposits, bank: demand, 38 – 39
  interest on, 43 – 44, 128, 184 – 185,
    314
    implications for demand for money,
      104 – 107
  time, 38 – 39
Depreciation (*see* Capital consumption al-
  lowance)
Depression, Great, 4, 238 – 245
Depressions (*see* Business fluctuations)
Dernburg, Thomas F., 304
Diamond, Peter A., 198
Diminishing returns, law of, 85, 87,
  114 – 115
Disaggregation, valued by Keynesians, 322
Discount rate, 238 – 239
Discounting:
  by Fed, 42, 238 – 240
  of future amounts, 73

Discouraged-encouraged workers, 339
Disequilibrium, 137
Disposable personal income, 306
Distribution of income, 118
Double counting in national income ac-
  counts, 14, 16 – 17, 21, 24
Dynamic adjustments, 3
  (*See also* Shocks)
Dynamic Cambridge equation, 122
Dynamics, comparative, 3
  problem in, 129 – 135

Economic activity, flows of, 7 – 15
Economic Stabilization Program (ESP),
  256 – 258, 349
  misreported data, corrections, table,
    257
Eisner, Robert, 311
Elasticity, 53 – 55
Employment, 35, 158
  (*See also* Unemployment; Unemploy-
    ment rate)
Employment Act of 1946, 352
Endogenous variables, 113
Entrepreneurs, 8
Environmental protection and growth,
  366 – 367
Equilibrium, 82, 137
Exchange rates:
  central rate, 222
  expected growth rate of, 215 – 217,
    233
  fixed, 221 – 224
  floating, 217 – 221
    defined, 221
  implications for monetary policy,
    231 – 233, 370 – 371
  lower rate, 223
  pegged, 221, 224 – 225
  upper rate, 223
  (*See also* Capital outflows, net; Exports,
    net; Foreign exchange markets)
Exogenous variables, 113
Expansions (*see* Business fluctuations)
Expectations:
  exchange rate, growth rate of, 215 – 217,
    233
  of future taxes, 195 – 196
  inflation, rate of (*see* Inflation, expected
    rate of)
  money supply, growth rate of, 143 – 145
  nominal wage, 157 – 159, 161 – 162,
    331 – 333, 336 – 337
    (*See also* Search)

Expectations:
  price level, 159, 161–162
  state of long-term, 295, 311–313
  (*See also* Investment, shifts in demand;
      Term structure of interest rates)
Expectations effect, 166–168
Exports:
  gross, 13–14
  net: defined, 14
    determinants of, 213–215
    in Keynesian model, 276

Factor services, 7–8
  (*See also* Capital; Factors of production;
      Labor)
Factors of production, 7–8
  (*See also* Capital stock; Factor services;
      Labor force)
Federal Deposit Insurance Corporation
    (FDIC), 244
Federal Reserve System (Fed):
  establishment, 4
  during the Great Depression, 4,
      238–240, 242–243
  operations of, 39–42
Final goods and services, 7–8
  GNP, 16
  NNP, 21
Financial effect, 166–168
Fine-tuning, 360–361
Firings, 329–330
Firms, 7–9
Fiscal policy:
  controversy over effects, 5, 187–190
  defined, 178
  feasible magnitudes, 188, 190, 197
  lags, 188, 362
  monetary policy contemporaneous with,
      201, 255–256, 301–302, 304
  return to desired levels, 190, 192, 197,
      201
  stabilization, feasibility for, 361–363
  (*See also* Shocks, fiscal)
Fischer, Stanley, 353
Fisher, Irving, 6, 311, 341
Flow variables, 50–51
Fluidity, 104–106
  desired, 104–106, 122, 127–129
  and money-demand elasticities,
      105–106
  variations in: Keynesian model, 299–301
    monetary shocks, 143–150
    nonmonetary shocks, 175, 181–183,
      185–186

Fluidity:
  variations in: transitory income, as source
      of, 147, 169–170
  (*See also* Money, demand for)
Forced saving, 198, 364–365
Foreign exchange markets, 210–221
  defined, 211
  (*See also* Exchange rates)
Francis, Darryl R., 350, 377
Friedman, Milton, 4–6, 99, 104, 111, 161,
    173–174, 188, 209, 235, 237,
    241–243, 255, 262, 306, 308, 325,
    353, 377
Full employment, 82
Full-employment real income, 248
Functions, 52–54
  homogeneous, of first degree, 114
  implicit, 287
  movement along versus shifts in,
      201–202, 317

GNP deflator, 32–33
  tables, 253, 257
GNP value added, 16
Goals, macroeconomic, 352–353
Gold, 1933 increase in dollar price, 244
Gordon, Robert J., 325
Government borrowing, 13, 139–140,
    176
  (*See also* Government deficit)
Government budget identity, 139–140,
    175–176
Government debt, 179, 180, 198
  table, 199
Government deficit, 13, 176
  burden of, 197–199, 364–365
Government spending:
  direct substitute for private spending,
      179
  in Keynesian model, 275–276
  relative to income, 176–178
    table, 177
  (*See also* Fiscal policy; Shocks, fiscal)
Gramlich, Edward M., 377
Great Depression, 4, 238–245
Gross national product (GNP), 17–21
  figures, 23, 46
  tables, 20, 253, 257
Growth:
  equation of constant, 65
  limits to, 367
Growth equilibrium (*see* Steady-state equi-
    librium)
Growth path, defined, 121

Growth rate:
  defined, 64
  of a product, 65–67
Growth rates of major macroeconomic variables, 1963–1974
  tables, 253, 257

Haberler, Gottfried, 209, 308
Häuser, Karl, 371
Hayek, Friedrich A. von, 6
Heller, H. Robert, 210, 236
Heller, Walter W., 262
Hicks, John R., 263, 285, 304
High-powered money, 40
  (*See also* Money creation)
Hirshleifer, Jack, 371
Holmes, James M., 196, 315
Human capital, 76–77, 84–85
Hyperinflation, 128–129, 136

Illegal income, 19
Implicit deflator for GNP, 32–33
Imports, 13
  (*See also* Exports, net)
Imputations, 18–19
Income, concepts of: nominal, 30
  permanent, 76–78
  private, 13, 19
  real, 30, 83
  real per capita, 117–118
  total, 23
  transitory, 77
Income effect, 166–168
Inflation:
  anticipated, 368–371
  defined, 124–125
  effects: on fluidity, 127–129, 169–172
    on real money balances, 127–129,
      169–172
  expected rate of: effects on interest rates,
      74–75, 126–127, 166–169
    role in investment demand, 273, 295,
      311–313
  rate of, 122–125
  special theories of, 125–126, 348–349
  steady-state rate: choice of, 367–368
    implications of, 368–371
  suppressed inflation, 371
  unanticipated changes in rate of: effects
    on debts, 168, 372
    unemployment effects, 372
Inflationary tax, 369–370
Information, costly (*see* Search)
Inputs (*see* Capital; Factor services; Labor)

Interest rates, 67–75
  continuously compounded, 67
  effects: of expected rate of inflation,
      74–75, 126–127, 166–169
    of fiscal policy, 179–187
    of monetary policy, 166–169
  nominal, 74–75
  pegged, 249–250, 252, 358–360
  periodic compounding, 68–72
  real, 74–75, 118
  real after-tax, 74–75
  term structure of, 185–186
Inventories, 159, 266, 320–321
Investment, 11, 96–100, 273–275,
      311–313
  fixed, 266
  interest elasticity of, 311–313
    short-run versus long-run, 185–186
  inventory, 266
  investment-income ratio, 197–198,
      364–365, 370
  in Keynesian model, 273–275, 311–313
  shifts in demand, 202, 205–206, 273, 295,
      311–313
IS curve:
  debate on slope of, and shifts in,
      315–317
  derivation of, 287–289
  shifts in, 294–298, 301–302
IS-LM model (*see* Keynesian model)

Jevons, W. Stanley, 161
Johnson, Harry G., 128, 136
Jordan, Jerry L., 49, 188, 209
Jorgensen, Dale W., 311

KE curve, 93–95
Kendrick, John W., 28
Keran, Michael W., 188
Kessel, Reuben A., 186
Keynes, John Maynard, 4–6, 194, 263,
      269, 273, 279, 281, 289, 295, 304, 306,
      308, 316, 318, 320
Keynesian model:
  aggregate expenditure function,
      277–278, 294–298
  comparison with dynamic model: consumption function, 306–310
    importance of dynamics, 321–322
    investment demand, 311–313
    money demand, 314–315
    real balance effect, 308–310,
      318–321

Keynesian model:
  comparison with dynamic model:
    search and inventory behavior,
      320 – 321
    shifts in IS and LM curves, 317
    slopes of IS and LM curves, 315 – 317
  constant price level, 265, 318 – 320
  consumption function, 268 – 272,
      306 – 310
  equilibrium in, 293 – 294
  government spending, 275 – 276
  investment demand, 273 – 275, 311 – 313
  IS curve: derivation of, 287 – 289
    shifts in, 294 – 298, 301 – 302
  LM curve: derivation of, 289 – 293
    shifts in, 298 – 302
  money demand, 278 – 282, 314 – 315
  money supply, 282
  net exports, 276 – 277
  quantity adjustment mechanism, 265 – 268
  short period assumption, 264 – 265, 318,
      321 – 322
  taxes in, 270 – 272, 315
Keynesian-monetarist controversy, 3 – 5,
    187 – 188, 201, 259 – 260
  (*See also* Keynesian model, compari-
      son with dynamic model)
Kindahl, James K., 34
Klein, Benjamin, 44, 106
Klein, Lawrence R., 324
Kochin, Levis A., 361
Kravis, Irving B., 118
Kurihara, Kenneth K., 306

Labor, 84 – 85
  average quality of, 89 – 90
  demand for, 85 – 87
  growth rate of, 113, 117 – 118
  market equilibrium (LE) curve, 92 – 93, 95
  participation rate, 89 – 90, 117 – 118
  supply of, 88 – 90
Labor force, 7, 84
  civilian, 35
  total, 35
Lags:
  fiscal policy, 362
  fiscal shocks, 188
  monetary policy, 360, 362
  monetary shocks: interest rates,
      167 – 168
    nominal income, 150
    prices, 159, 161
    real income, 159, 161
Layoffs, 329 – 330, 337 – 339

LE curve, 92 – 93, 95
Leijonhufvud, Axel, 325
Liquidity effect, 166 – 168
Liquidity preference function, 289n.
  (*See also* Money, demand for)
Liquidity trap, 279 – 282, 292, 299, 301
LM curve:
  debate on slope of and shifts in, 315 – 317
  derivation of, 289 – 293
  with liquidity trap, 292, 299 – 300,
      318 – 321
  shifts in, 298 – 302
  vertical, 292 – 293
Logarithms, 54 – 56
Lucas, Robert E., Jr., 328, 350, 354

McCall, John J., 333
McDougall, Duncan M., 304
Machlup, Fritz, 236
Macroeconomic policy, 351 – 377
  (*See also* Fiscal policy; Monetary policy;
      Stabilization policy)
Malkiel, Burton G., 186
Malthus, Thomas R., 367
Marginal efficiency of investment (*see* In-
      vestment)
Marginal product, 85 – 88
Marginal propensity to consume (MPC),
      269, 306 – 308
Meiselman, David, 186, 188
Meltzer, Allan H., 128, 136, 254, 308
Mendershausen, Horst, 371
Methodology, 2 – 3
Microeconomic policy, 365 – 367
Minimum wages, 157, 245, 338
Mintz, Ilse, 46, 49
Mitchell, Wesley C., 49
Modigliani, Franco, 209, 306
Monetarist-Keynesian controversy, 3 – 5,
      187 – 188, 201, 259 – 260
  (*See also* Keynesian model, comparison
      with dynamic model)
Monetarist revolution, 4 – 5
Monetary base, 40
  (*See also* Money creation)
Monetary policy:
  under alternative exchange rate systems,
      231 – 233
  constant growth rate, 358, 374 – 375
  debate over strategies, 360 – 361
  fiscal policy contemporaneous with, 201,
      255 – 256, 301 – 302, 304
  ineptness during Great Depression, why,
      242

Monetary policy:
lags, 150, 159, 161, 167 – 168, 360, 362
pegged interest rates, 249 – 250, 252,
358 – 360
rules versus authorities, 361, 372 – 375
stop-go policy, 357
variable growth rate, 360
(*See also* Shocks, monetary)
Monetary standards:
commodity, 39 – 40
fiat, 39 – 40
discretionary growth, 372 – 375
fixed growth, 374 – 375
(*See also* Exchange rates)
Money:
broad money supply (M_2), 39
defined, 37 – 38
demand for, 103 – 107
effects of money substitutes, 205, 248
income elasticity of, 104 – 105
interest elasticity of, 105 – 107, 110,
127 – 129, 169 – 172, 248 – 249,
279 – 282, 292 – 293, 314 – 315
interest on money, short-term, and
long-term bonds, 104 – 106, 110,
111, 128 – 129, 184 – 185, 278 – 279,
314
in Keynesian model, 278 – 282,
314 – 315
shifts in, 205
as shock absorber, 144, 185, 320
total versus private income in, 196*n.*,
315
transactions, role of, 104 – 105, 122,
147
transitory income, small effect of, 147,
169 – 170
wealth, 104 – 105, 147
interest on, 43 – 44, 104 – 107, 128,
184 – 185, 314
narrow money supply (M_1), 39
price of, 34 – 35, 101
quantity theory of, 3 – 5
supply of, 102 – 103
in Keynesian model, 282
supply process, 39 – 42
Money creation:
by banks, 40 – 41
by government, 13, 41, 42
as a tax, 369 – 370
Money multiplier, 41, 203 – 205
(*See also* Shocks, monetary)
Money substitutes, 205, 248
Monopoly power:
effects on inflation, 126
effects on real income, 126*n.*, 365 – 366

Moore, Geoffrey H., 37, 49, 335, 350
Multiplier:
money, 41, 203 – 205
(*See also* Shocks, monetary)
spending, 147*n.*, 283

National Bureau of Economic Research
(NBER), 44 – 47
(*See also* Business fluctuations)
National income accounts, 7 – 28
National Industrial Recovery Act (NIRA),
126*n.*, 245
Natural unemployment rate, 334 – 335
Neoclassical growth model, 112 – 121
(*See also* Steady-state equilibrium)
Net national product (NNP), 21 – 25
figure, 23
table, 22
Neutrality of money, 127 – 129, 169 – 172
New entrants, 329 – 330
New searchers, rate of, 330
Nixon, Richard M., 256
NNP value added, 21, 23
Nonhuman capital, 85
(*See also* Capital; Capital stock)

Oil embargo of 1973 – 1974, 257 – 258
Open market operations (*see* Federal Re-
serve System)
Output, 7 – 8, 14

Participation rate, labor, 89 – 90, 117 – 118
Patinkin, Don, 308
Peak, NBER reference cycle, 45
Pegged interest rates, 249 – 250, 252,
358 – 360
Peltzman, Sam, 314
Permanent income, 76 – 78
(*See also* Consumer expenditures)
Perpetuity, 73
Phelps, Edmund S., 198, 328, 350
Phillips, A. W., 341, 342
Phillips curve, 341 – 342
(*See also* Quasi-Phillips curve)
Pigou, Arthur C., 308
Pigou effect, 145, 147, 308 – 310, 317 – 321
Poole, William, 353
Population, age-eligible, 35, 89 – 90
Population growth, 113, 117 – 118
Portmanteau variable, 104, 106, 122
(*See also* Money substitutes; Transac-
tions, role in money demand)
Postwar macroeconomic history, 247 – 259

Present value, 71, 73 – 74
Price indices, 29 – 35
  consumer price index (CPI), 33
  GNP deflator, 32 – 33
    growth rates, 1963 – 1974, tables, 253,
    257
  wholesale price index, 33 – 34
Price level, 29 – 31
Private income, 13, 19
Probability, 331 – 333
  of acceptable offer, 333 – 334
Production function (*see* Aggregate produc-
  tion function)
Profits, 8

Quantity adjustment mechanism, 265 – 268
Quantity theory of money, 3 – 5
Quasi-Phillips curve:
  long-run curve, 347 – 348
  tradeoff analysis, 342 – 346
Quits, 329 – 330

Rate of change, 61 – 64
Real balance effect, 145, 147, 308 – 310,
  317 – 321
Real income, 30, 83
Recession of 1937 – 1938, 246
Recessions (*see* Business fluctuations)
Reference cycle (*see* Business fluctuations)
Reserve-deposit ratio, 41 – 42, 203 – 204,
  240, 244
Reserves:
  fractional reserve system, 40
  required ratios, 42, 246
  required versus excess, 246
Rosen, Sam, 28
Rules versus authorities, 361, 372 – 375

Samuelson, Paul A., 342, 377
Santomero, Anthony M., 44
Saving, 25 – 26, 96 – 100
  saving-income ratio, 119 – 121, 195,
  197 – 198, 364 – 365, 370
  (*See also* Consumer expenditures)
Scadding, John J., 99
Schmidt, Peter, 188, 209
Schwartz, Anna J., 4 – 6, 173, 188, 237,
  241 – 243, 255, 262, 308
Search, 155 – 159, 328 – 335
  annual search ratio, 330, 337 – 339,
  table, 340
  average duration of, 330, 333 – 334,
  336 – 337

Search:
  average duration of: table, 340
  probability of acceptable offer, 333 – 334
  rate of new searchers, 330
  reservation wage, 333 – 334
  sequential search, 333 – 334
  wage distribution, 331 – 333
    actual versus expected distribution,
    336 – 337
Secular growth, 112
  (*See also* Steady-state equilibrium)
Secular stagnation thesis, 308
Securities:
  corporate, 8 – 10
  foreign, 14
Securities issues:
  corporate, 11
  foreign, 14
Separations, 329 – 330, 337 – 339
Shocks:
  autonomous, 355 – 356
  fiscal: balanced budget shocks, 178, 198,
    200 – 201
  defined, 175 – 178
  equivalence of Keynesian and mone-
    tarist comparative statics, 182 – 183
  government spending, 178 – 192
    comparative statics approach,
    179 – 183
    dynamic adjustments approach,
    183 – 192
    empirical results, 188 – 190
  lags, 188, 362
  taxation, 192 – 197
  (*See also* Fiscal policy)
  international: under floating exchange
    rates, 225 – 229
  under pegged exchange rates,
    229 – 230
  macroeconomic: defined, 137
    relative importance of different kinds,
    259 – 260
  monetary, 139 – 174
    banking panics, 203 – 205
      during Great Depression, 239 – 244
    monetary policy: defined, 139 – 140
      effects on interest rates, 166 – 169
      effects on nominal sector, 140 – 151,
      166 – 172
      effects on real sector, 151 – 166,
      169 – 172
      lags, 150, 159, 161, 167 – 168, 360,
      362
      money multiplier changes, 203
      restrictive, 151 – 152, 164 – 166,
      169, 171

Shocks:
  monetary: monetary policy: stimulative,
      140–164, 166–172
    (*See also* Monetary policy)
  nonmonetary: changes in behavioral func-
      tions, 201–203, 205–207
    investment demand, 205–206,
        311–313
    money demand, 205
  defined, 175
  fiscal (*see* fiscal *above*)
  international (*see* international *above*)
  policy, 355–356
Short period assumption, 264–265, 318,
    321–322
Simons, Henry C., 377
Sims, Christopher A., 188
Slope:
  as a growth rate, 65
  as a rate of change, 64–65
  rules concerning, 65
    figure, 66
Smith, Warren L., 209, 304
Smyth, David J., 196, 315
Solow, Robert M., 136, 342
Speculation on exchange rates, 230
Speculative motive, 279–281, 314
Sprinkel, Beryl W., 262
Stabilization policy, 353–364
  fiscal approaches, 361–363
  monetary approaches, 357–361
  necessary condition for, 356–357
  review of issues, 363–364
  sufficient condition for, 357*n.*
  (*See also* Fiscal policy; Monetary policy)
Stagflation, 159–160, 348–349
Standard of living, 117–118
Statics, comparative, 3
Stationary state, 112
Steady state, 112
Steady-state equilibrium, 112–136
  convergence to, after shock, 137, 143,
      159
  interaction of nominal and real sectors,
      127–129
  nominal sector, 121–127
  real sector, 112–121
Stein, Herbert, 262
Stein, Jerome L., 325
Sterilization, 224, 229–230
Sticky wages, 155–159
Stigler, George J., 34, 328
Stock market crash of October 1929, 239
Stock variables, 50
Stolper, Gustav, 371

Stop-go policy, 357
Suspension of cash payments, 242, 243

Taxes, 11–13
  in Keynesian model, 270–272, 315
  money creation as, 369–370
  (*See also* Fiscal policy; Shocks, fiscal)
Technological change, 114
Teigen, Ronald L., 209
Term structure of interest rates, 185–186
Thompson, Earl A., 198
Thornton, Henry, 6
Tobin, James, 279, 281, 377
Toribio, Juan T., 256
Trade deficit, 212
  (*See also* Exports, net)
Trade surplus, 212
  (*See also* Exports, net)
Tradeoff analysis, 342–346
Transactions, role in money demand,
    104–105, 122, 147
Transfer payments, 11–12
Transitory income, 77
  and cyclical fluctuations in desired fluid-
      ity, 147, 169–170
  (*See also* Consumer expenditures)
Transmission mechanism, 145, 147,
    182–183
  (*See also* Keynesian model, comparison
      with dynamic model)
Treasury-Federal Reserve Accord, 249
Trough, NBER reference cycle, 45

Underemployment equilibrium, 318–321
Unemployment, 36, 328–350
  cyclical unemployment, 328
  frictional unemployment, 328
  measurement, of persons, 36
  of resources, defined, 328
  search, 155–159, 328–340
  structural unemployment, 328*n.*
Unemployment compensation, 329*n.*
Unemployment rate:
  cyclical fluctuations in, 339–340
  cyclical unemployment rate, 336
  determinants of, 334
  effects of war on, 339
  measurement of, 36–37
  natural unemployment rate, 334–335
  Phillips curve, 341–342
  quasi-Phillips curve, 342–348
Unified monetary system, 221–224

Unions:
  cost-push inflation, 348 – 349
  effects on real income, 256, 365 – 366
  wage floor, 338

Value added:
  to GNP, 16
  to NNP, 21, 23
Variance, 353 – 354
Velocity of money (*see* Fluidity)

Wage:
  distribution, 331 – 333, 336 – 337
  minimum, 157, 245, 338
  nominal wage, 157 – 159, 161 – 162
    extended meaning in search model, 331

Wage:
  real wage, 87, 89 – 90, 118
  reservation wage, 333 – 334
Wage-price spiral, 126, 348 – 349
Walras' law, 286
Waud, Roger N., 188, 209
Wealth, 75 – 76
  in demand for money, 104 – 105, 147
  permanent income as substitute, 76 – 77
World War II, 246 – 247
Wriston, Walter B., 377

Yeager, Leland B., 236
Yield on money (*see* Deposits, bank, interest on)
Yields (*see* Interest rates)